Judge Edward Molkenbuhr, A. L. Cline, at first court appearance

Richard Rust, J. W. E., Mrs. Ehrlich and Edmond O'Brien

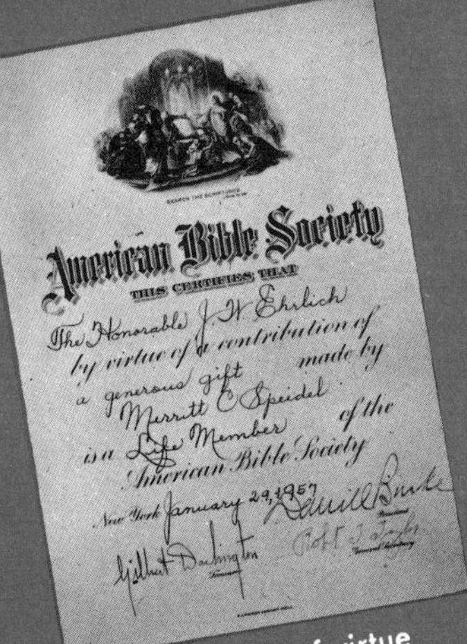

American Bible Society

This certifies that

The Honorable J. W. Ehrlich
by virtue of a contribution of
a generous gift made by
Merritt C. Speidel
is a Life Member of the
American Bible Society

New York January 29, 1957

The reward of virtue

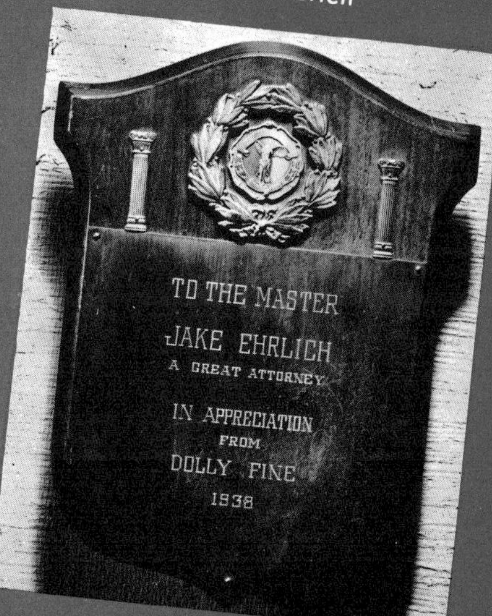

Dolly Fine's tribute

With Pantages at trial

Jean Collins as she was acquitted

A Life in My Hands

By the Same Author

EHRLICH'S BLACKSTONE

HOWL OF THE CENSOR

EHRLICH'S CRIMINAL LAW

CRIMINAL EVIDENCE

THE EDUCATED LAWYER

WHAT IS WRONG WITH THE JURY SYSTEM

THE LOST ART OF CROSS-EXAMINATION

TRIAL OF THE CONTESTED DIVORCE CASE

THE HOLY BIBLE AND THE LAW

A REASONABLE DOUBT

J. W. EHRLICH

A Life in My Hands

An Autobiography

G. P. PUTNAM'S SONS
NEW YORK

 Published simultaneously in the Dominion of Canada by Longmans Canada Limited, Toronto.

Library of Congress Catalog
Card Number: 65-10851

Printed in the United States of America

Dedication

THIS AUTOBIOGRAPHY is not merely the record of a string of occurrences, it is an attempt to seize and again enjoy them in their living moments.

Unlike the Apostle Luke's condemnation of lawyers in his eleventh chapter, I *have* carried man's burdens and have wept with him when God weighted him down with trials and tribulations.

Since it is a custom from time immemorial to dedicate a book to someone near and dear to the author, I am encompassed by the publisher's directive to make it short and to the point, naming those who are to be the recipients of this questionable honor, and stop there and then.

To whom may I honestly dedicate this history of a man? Is is to be dedicated only to those who have helped me up the ladder? Is it to forget and bury those who hindered me? Is it to be dedicated to those who spoke out of both sides of their mouths, and in their double way pleasing me and pleasing my enemies? No. None of these and all of these are entitled to this dedication; all of them must be given credit for my successes and my failures, my victories and my heartaches, my loves and my hates, my happiness and my despair, my moments of glory and my hours of depression, my strength and my weakness, my all and my nothing. To all of these I dedicate *A Life in My Hands.*

J. W. EHRLICH

San Francisco, 1964

Foreword

TO SAY that one *knows* Jake Ehrlich is not possible. This already semilegendary figure, well woven into the colorful historical tapestry of San Francisco, possesses more facets than the Telstar plus a relentless capacity for continuously advancing the stature of each dimension of his many-sided personality. All that one may really know of one's own J. W. Ehrlich are the aspects offered by time and propinquity. The others are heard of, read about or sensed.

My personal Ehrlich is an excellent friend, a superlative legal advocate, an erudite author, a rare social companion, a raconteur, and perhaps the greatest San Franciscologist of his time; a man who really and deeply understands that intricate and exotic metropolis. In the words of one of his fellow townsmen, regarding the man and the city, "He plays it like a violin."

On the obverse rim of this multicolored sphere is an excellent enemy, a wild and intractable legal adversary, a skilled manipulator of human beings and a source of frequently unorthodox, sometimes impious, gestures and convictions. Jake Ehrlich has always liked a fight. His hackles rise at any scent of the bogus or the phony. Above all, he is not a dull man or a person whom even the most obtuse might be inclined to discount, disregard or forget.

He is other things, too, most of them mutually incongruous: a devout and loyal family man and a veteran participant in big-city night life; a recognized classical and biblical scholar and equally knowledgeable among—for example—the green-baize-table set of Reno and Las Vegas. He has vigorously fought for such varied causes as free milk for California school children and —when much younger—prize-ring purses that would feed his own children. He is a banker as a founder and officer of the San Francisco National Bank and he has been both political kingmaker and kingbreaker.

All of this is just a part of the Ehrlich whom I know. All men are complex; the one whom many San Franciscans call the Master is one of the most complicated. Even the most carefully drawn introduction would fail to present the fine shadings, small colorful accents and subtleties that complete the portrait.

I leave that chore to this self-portrait which I introduce with pleasure and with affection for both artist and subject. One may be sure that Ehrlich will tell the truth. This tough, understanding, acrid-tongued—yet innately kind—man is a person for whom Diogenes would have had to hang up his lantern. Jake Ehrlich's sense of humor is too great not to be aware of the absurdity of pompous evasion or bogus rationalization. He loves the daily drama of his life too well to skip or rearrange facts. His ocular grasp of the world and himself is definitely 20|20.

GEORGE KILLION

A Life in My Hands

1: *Early Morning*

5 A.M.

At 5 A.M. I was awake and ready for the day.

I have always risen early. This has nothing to do with the early bird and his mooted success with worms. Worms interest me but meagerly and I've always suspected that a drafty nest or a quarrelsome mate had more to do with the early bird's being early.

I rise early because I'm convinced that minds function best before they undergo the near stultification of too much breakfast, too many early telephone calls and the usual exchange of platitudes that pass for elevator small talk. I incline to the theory that more days have been ruined by the misquoting of morning-paper columnists than by insomnia or wifely complaints.

I also rise early because it gives me a chance to read all of the newspapers thoroughly. I believe that the only effective conditions under which this can be accomplished are while still alone, a steaming cup of coffee in hand, and before the invitingly crisp newssheets have been turned to debris by my darling wife Marjorie.

Most of all, I rise early for a few wonderful moments with my other sweetheart, a lady known as San Francisco. From the wide windows of my apartment on Nob Hill, the town that has given me everything I really value—the sweet, wild, gracious, unpredictable city—lies spread out below me like a theatrical diorama.

At these high moments, San Francisco's profiled hills, tumbling valleys and fog-washed streets constitute an abstraction in shades of gray—the tones changing with the racing minutes.

There is no sound except perhaps a little fog music from the horns on Alcatraz or from the end of Pier 41 at the foot of Powell Street. Sometimes there is little to see at this hour—just shrouded buildings and a few unsurrendering blobs of neon blur.

But fog or predawn murk give me no trouble with what is spread below there; I recognize it all. That dark bulk on the fringe of historic Portsmouth Square where the Vigilantes mock-tried and sure-lynched their victims during the Gold Rush days is the Hall of Justice where I defended the life of brutalized little Jean Collins; and poor lost Laverne Borelli, who deserved the mercy I won for her; and Mass Murderer Alfred Leonard Cline, who did not. These and scores of others had stood beside me in that grim building and prayed that I was as good a lawyer as I was supposed to be. And so had I.

The small, one-story building to the south of the Hall—that was the spider web of the corrupt McDonough brothers. I helped turn their throne room into the dusty little cigar store that it is today. The shadowy mass behind them on Merchant Street is, or was, the Morgue, and well do I remember the first time my feet took me up those clammy marble stairs to a well-perforated gentleman named Henry Yee waiting to receive me on his slab. Behind it was the Central Police Station, the first port of call in many an itinerary that would wind up before a judge and twelve good men and true.

Just below my window is Chinatown, a narrow slot of darkness at this hour. There I'd listened to Louis Quan tell how Henry Yee had seduced his wife Choy Lin, for which he had to be killed and for which I later defended him. At the Kearny-Broadway quadrant I can just make out the outlines of Vanessi's Restaurant. It was to a booth in this old San Francisco establishment that I took Gene Krupa after his release on bail, so that we might discuss the delicate chore of extricating him from the unrighteous claws of justice. Gene, a famous bandleader of the Dorsey era of jazz, had become involved with the vegetation of a flowering plant known as *cannabis sativa*—a species of hemp from which they do *not* make rope.

As dawn spreads over the Berkeley hills and the fog thins

away on the bay and the first scurrying vehicles appear on the mist-wet streets, other familiar landmarks bring still other familiar memories of this lovely cosmopolite who flirted with me when I was young and impressionable, hooked her arm through mine and offered me her heady charms when I could little afford such indulgences, and then left me to dream of the future with her full assurance that the best was yet to come and that she'd stick with me to the end—if I lived up to her standards. I did and she did.

I value early rising because I feel smarter at such an hour, I enjoy a rendezvous with the city I love before she has a chance to put on her makeup and—if it must be admitted—I don't sleep very well.

As I said, I was awake today at 5 A.M. and ready for whatever would happen. The end of this day is some 400 pages ahead.

I have often thought how unlike the region of my beginnings this hand-picked home town of mine really is. I am a native of Maryland.

I was born—far from salt fog and cable cars and forty-five degree streets—on the lush flatlands of the Potomac, at the turn of the century in 1900. To my mind, this has in a fashion served to qualify me as a citizen of both centuries, with some capacity for looking backward into one or forward into the other with equal understanding and empathy for both utterly different eras.

Certainly my family home belonged in the first; in the century of Lee and Henry Clay and stovepipe hats and crinolines. It was a white-columned mansion from whose balconnaded second-floor windows one could glimpse the green expanses of Virginia across the lovely river that—an hour's flow below—coiled through official Washington.

We were in Montgomery County, near the county seat at Rockville, but actually quite far from any other civilization and culture than that created by my father and grandfather within the social microcosm of their own plantation. As I remember it, this was considerable. We were practically self-sufficient: we produced hay, corn, potatoes and an infinite variety of fruit and vegetables, as well as breeding hogs and other livestock—plus of course blooded horses and the ingredients for very fine sipping whisky.

We were self-sufficient in other respects as well. The house boasted a library that might well have been unequaled, for its time, in private homes anywhere. It was in bookcases that stretched two stories high, and was reached by a stately arrangement of mahogany catwalks and ladders. It lacked little in content. There were of course Shakespeare, Milton, Homer, Bulwer-Lytton, Fenimore Cooper and all of the 19th-century standards, but there were also writers who in those somewhat provincial times might have been regarded as contentious inclusions: wild-minded newcomers like Tolstoy and Dostoevski, Mark Twain and Victor Hugo. Even downright Johnny-come-latelies such as Bernard Shaw, Jack London and Oscar Wilde were there, for if my ultraliterate grandfather was occasionally remiss in keeping open the lines of communication with his government in nearby Washington (and with good cause, to his thinking), he was far more current in his contacts with the publishers and booksellers of New York and London.

In addition, we were well provided with periodicals. We received the Washington *Post,* the Baltimore *Sun* and *The New York Times* in the daily mail. For monthly publications there were *The Atlantic Monthly, Harper's* the *Literary Digest,* the *Pictorial Review* and—for the younger generation— *St. Nicholas* magazine. Personally I abandoned the latter at about the age of nine; I was far more fascinated by Captain Dreyfus and why he had taken such a reaming from the French military than by learning how to build a lean-to with only a pocketknife and a spirit of enterprise.

But the main intellectual stimulus in the Ehrlich establishment was good talk—substantial, nourshing conversation—and its high priest was our grandfather Samuel Quincy Ehrlich. Samuel Quincy conversed with the children—and particularly with me, as the eldest—as if we were people instead of lovable little nitwits, and the results were formidable. We began to think and move like people when other children were still worrying about the Easter bunny.

Grandfather not only talked to us; he read to us from the classics, from the old and new testaments of the Bible, from the *Farmer's Almanac,* from the Constitution, from anything but the flaccid little puerilities which deal with wolves who eat grandmothers and orphans who go to parties in mice-propelled pumpkins. Humpty Dumpty has never done anything for American childhood except postpone the contact of its bright, burgeoning minds with truer, more interesting and more useful information.

Which was what Grandfather gave us with his regular evening readings. This may sound dated but I'm convinced that if more fathers read to their young today there'd be fewer fathers talking to themselves on the way out of the visiting room at the Juvenile Hall. Anyway, this is principally the way in which I began to know the Bible and Shakespeare before I was ten.

Grandfather Ehrlich was a character; of that there is no doubt. A highly intellectual, expensively cultured Southern gentleman, he had been a cavalry commander under General Stonewall Jackson and continued to maintain a sort of a cold-war relationship with the rest of the Union long after his colleagues had packed in at Appomattox. To the last he insisted that he "damned near captured Washington, D.C." and could have done it if someone hadn't pulled the seat out from under him. How he missed being hemp hauled along with Mrs. Eugenia Surrat and the Booth group in hysteria-ridden postwar Washington was my major boyhood mystery, but I loved him inordinately and respected him even more abundantly.

My feeling for my father was less passionate. He was a cold, arbitrary, dictatorial sort of man, and worst of all, he had none of the humor which has been standard equipment for most of us Ehrlichs. I was never really able to make his acquaintance. We remained intimate strangers throughout our relationship.

My mother was a beautiful woman and remains a beautiful memory. She was a small brunette with great, lovely dark eyes. When dressed for a special occasion—and there were many at that house, often with twenty or more around the dining room table—she was superb.

There were six children. I—Jacob—am the eldest; then came Samuel, Jack, Myron and Alvin, and our sister Sarah. We were and are extremely individualistic: the same in the basic, family endowed characteristics; radically different in our personal approaches to life. Not one of us has turned out even partially similar. Each of us has excelled in some quite different fashion. And yet, like the variously shaped segments of a jigsaw puzzle, we all fit neatly together when occasional unity is required.

It was a good life, but it had its place in my personal chronology and is gone and well gone. I can vividly recall the mood and tempo, time texture and smallest detail of the period: the fireflies flickering over the evening fields; the grunting and snorting and whinneying sounds from the stock pens; the never quite disappearing aroma of horse sweat that scented these acres where the stallion was king and a good mare a treasured wealth; the sudden spurts of fascinated fear at sight of the white belly and whiter gullet of the cottonmouthed moccasin as it emerged from the Potomac to sun on the beach; the perfumes of old-fashioned cooking smells that drifted from the wide kitchens at the back of the house. It is wonderful to remember but safe in the past. I wouldn't know what to do with a moccasin or stallion, here on Powell Street, or for that matter with a big plate of hot, delicious, indigestible johnnycake.

I played the big brother role to the hilt and enjoyed it as I've always enjoyed running the show. Such advanced self-confidence also involves obligations and penalties. You have to produce, and it's unattractive to fail. There was the case of the wolf.

My brothers and sister and I were walking through a wood near the plantation one day when Sarah, a little ahead of us on the path, screamed. I quickly joined her and was told that she had seen a wolf, that it had slunk into the undergrowth just over there at the left. *A wolf!* Yes, a large wolf with big white teeth and a hungry look. The agonized eyes of Sarah and my brothers were upon me. I was clearly expected to perform like the hero I'd always claimed to be. I picked up a heavy stick and told them to go back along the trail. They obeyed, and with perspiration cascading down my back, I turned to face the white-fanged beast. I knew what wolves could do to fully grown men. What they could do to a small boy with a stick could make me the laughing stock of the local wolf pack. But I had no choice.

"Wolf!" I quavered, "where are you?"

A large and friendly looking shepherd dog came out of the bushes, wagging his bushy tail and eyeing me happily.

On another occasion, however, elder-brother leadership brought me more realistically to grips with life and its inequities. My brothers and I went to the local two-room schoolhouse, and the teacher was a tyrranical young man named Crockett whom we called Davy Crockett. Later-day experts undoubtedly would have diagnosed him as a sadist: he spent almost as much time in whipping as he did in teaching. He had equipped his desk with a kind of holster fastened next to the inkwell. Into this socket he could thrust his daily whip, withdrawing it quickly and efficiently and without loss of time or motion.

I say daily whip because Davy cut himself a new switch each day as he came through the woods on the way to school—a new one whether he needed it or not. He liked the feel of a nice new whip each morning. He chose his switches expertly and with considerable pleasure.

On this occasion Davy Crockett made other choices with the same pleasure but less expertise: he erred in the choice of the whipees. He chose to draw on poor Samuel, hitting him on the head. When I challenged the propriety of this assault, he drew again and whacked me. I was thirteen and stood 5′ 7″. He was 5′ 7″ and perhaps twenty-five years of age. I figured that my odds were as right as my cause, and I whipped him, adding salt to his wounds by confiscating his switch. It was then that I learned the occasional superiority of direct action over negotiation. Davy Crockett—from that time forward—respected Samuel and me completely and never struck us again, though he kept his taste for whacking the bottoms of others.

Soon after that I again found direct action an asset. The brothers Ehrlich had gone to a party at a nearby plantation. I had driven us in a buggy drawn by a fast, smooth pacer in a brand-new bridle and set of reins that were my father's delight. We tied up in the hitching area where more than a score of such rigs were finally placed. Then we joined our hostess for lemonade and cookies and parlor games. I have played a few parlor games in the subsequent years, but I have consumed few cookies and practically no lemonade at all in the interim. You have to put up with a lot when you're young.

When my brothers and I left to go home, we found that my father's new bridle and reins had been removed from our pacer. A beaten-up replacement had been substituted. We examined all of the other rigs. One was missing a set of reins. Here there was merely a rope, the other end being tethered to the hitching post. We said nothing and went home.

Later that evening I paid a neighborly visit to the stable of our underprivileged friend who had had only a rope tether for his nag. I found my father's reins and quickly canceled out the nine points of the law that possession is said to connote. Then I called on this neighbor and—with a jab and pair of right hooks—quickly negated any further equity for which he might have argued. Curiously enough, the gentleman demanded the return of his own reins. I explained that these items had been formally seized to cover costs, carrying charges and exemplary damages. He wasn't satisfied but he was silenced. I suppose this was the first out-of-court settlement I ever made.

The only variation to life on the plantation was an occasional trip with my grandfather on Circuit Day to the county seat at nearby Rockville. I enjoyed such visits to the outside world despite the fact that in 1912 and 1913 the town of Rockville, Maryland, wasn't exactly a busy place, except from the viewpoint of small boys and stray dogs. Nevertheless, on Circuit Day—the opening of the tenure of the Circuit Court—it was busier than usual, and for me there were the wonderful lawyers in their wonderful tall hats. I had never been impressed by the superiority of men over women until I saw great numbers of males wearing tall hats with infinite ease and grace. It was there in Rockville that I first decided to become a lawyer when I discovered that, as a group, they wore more tall hats per capita than any other type of citizen. Tall hats and frock coats or cutaways.

I regard it as a distinct loss to the profession that tall hat wearing has died out. I can think of nothing I'd relish more than stalking into a San Francisco courtroom, doffing my tall hat onto the counsel table, tossing my black suede gloves (and snuffbox) into the crown, and letting them have it before they got their mouths closed.

In Rockville in 1913, it was fascinating. Through my grandfather I met our family lawyer, Mr. Peter, but mainly I met his hat—his towering hat in which he kept his handkerchief, his cigars and occasionally a brief or two. He was an impressive man, and the other day at my Montgomery Street office when another Mr. Peter announced himself as also a lawyer and also from Rockville, Maryland, I was pleasantly stricken by memory and nostalgia. My visitor turned out to be the original Mr. Peter's nephew, a convert to San Franciscoism and in legal practice in the adjacent building. But—alas—no tall hat. *Sic transit gloria caputi!*

As impressive as it was to me, I knew that Rockville wasn't *all.* My reading and my grandfather's conversation had introduced me to the big cities of the Eastern Seaboard and Europe, and my grandmother—who had her own funds of information and who liked a gory, morbid story—had told me about another city on the Pacific Coast: a metropolis that interested me more than any of them. First, the ground of this town had been tossed into the air, then there was something about fireballs and suffocating winds, finally the waters of the ocean had engulfed the people. But these intrepid souls had eventually mastered their disasters and rebuilt their city. It was better than ever. It's name was San Francisco.

Babylon, Ninevah and Tyre, added up to no more fantastically exciting place than this incomparable phoenix of cities, and I regarded its natives as the greatest comeback champs in history. It was my dream to visit San Francisco, to mingle with its indomitable residents, to help them fight off fireballs and suffocating winds if necessary. Not that I *really* expected to actually visit San Francisco. It was as unattainable as the moon. Farther, because I could see the moon at night.

I grew up overnight, the result of a major disagreement between my father and me. One day I was a sixteen-year-old boy with a home and no responsibilities; the next I was a homeless sixteen-year-old adult with the immediate responsibility —among others equally blunt and practical—of becoming my own complete source of support.

I can't recall what occasioned the dispute. All that is certain is that it led to my father's declaration that I should bear witness to the fact that he, in his boundless bounty, provided the roof that stretched over my head, the groceries that expanded my belly, the clothing that saved me from nakedness. A routine disclosure, obviously. Fathers have been issuing such manifestos since shortly after the first umbilical cord was cut; I've issued a few myself. But this particular pronouncement came at what appears to have been the high—or low—point in our deteriorating relationship.

I told my father that I had no plan of life that included being indebted to the one who reminded me of the obligation. I told him that he could figure on a reduction of household expense to the extent of one head. I told him that if he were not my father I'd tell him to jump in the Potomac. Then I packed a few things and left the house without further explanations or further goodbye's to anyone, not even to my mother or grandfather. I knew they would understand just as surely as I knew that my father never would. He gave no sign of taking notice of my departure. It was nearly forty years between that day and the occasion of our remeeting.

The Army recruiting sergeant who interviewed me the next day in Baltimore didn't raise an eyebrow when I swore to being legally of age to be mustered into the First Maryland. Why should he? My voice had changed and there wasn't too much down on my jaw. Besides, enlistments were slack and his quota was unfilled.

I received my recruit training at Fort Myers, Virginia, and it was probably my plantation-learned horsemanship that pulled me through. Some weeks later I found myself at a cavalry post on the Mexican border, a somewhat self-consciously swash-buckling trooper, and I itched to get my hands on Pancho Villa, the picturesque bandit from Chihuahua and Sonora who was helling it up on both sides of the international line. But before allowing me a crack at Villa, fate had matched me with another adversary, a tough sergeant named Boyd.

The scene of my encounter with Sergeant Boyd, was a four-man tent on the coldest hillside in New Mexico. The time was a dismal 4 A.M.

I lay, partially awake and vibrating on my cot, clad in both my summer and winter uniforms, two suits of underwear and the major part of the Sunday edition of the El Paso *Herald-Post*. I was also wearing my shoes, an overcoat and two blankets. Sergeant Boyd came in, bearing a kerosene lantern and an order for Trooper Ehrlich. The order: Get the hell out of the tent and chop some wood. Remembering my successes with the wolf, Davy Crockett, the reins thief and my father, I decided to take a stand. I climbed out of the sack, stood fatly to attention —swaddled in all that clothing—and issued my ultimatum:

"Sergeant, I joined the cavalry to fight, not to chop wood, and what's more, you can't make me chop wood."

The sergeant responded in a quiet, rasping tone that seemed to lower the temperature in the already frigid tent by another 20 degrees.

"Ehrlich," he said, "I can't make you chop wood but I can make you wish to God you *had* chopped wood."

It was then that I learned another invaluable lesson in human dynamics. When an irresistible force meets up with an even more irresistible force, there is only one thing to do. Chop wood.

Boyd and I became good friends and it was he who taught me how to box. Years later, here in San Francisco, we ran into each other. I was a fairly prominent part of the community by then but I could still sense and respond to the mystique of quiet, self-sufficient authority that is really the only tool of the old Army noncom.

I was never able to get my sixteen-year-old hands on Villa, fortunately, but we did finally cross the border from Bisbee, Arizona, and we did sweep into Parral, Mexico, where Pancho was supposedly holed up. It was a great victory, according to the dispatches, but all I remember our finding in Parral were three less than ambulatory prostitutes, a flock of chickens, and some goats that even Villa's chefs had vetoed.

The important thing to me was that I was a man now; a man no matter what my birth certificate might have indicated if I'd had one. My food was self-provided, my clothing was self-earned, and the roof—all right, the tent—over my head was my own. Or Uncle Sam's.

I was a man. All I had to do was to acquire a little success. And money. And glory. A background to match my ego; that's all.

2: *Early Morning*

5:30 A.M.

THE SAN FRANCISCO *Examiner* and the San Francisco *Chronicle,* with black coffee to temper their excesses of taste—bad and good—have been my breakfast for many years. The men who publish and write these newspapers have been my warm friends and/or gentle enemies on a yarning, chatting and lunching basis ever since the days when I was able to pick up a café tab without personal trauma. I enjoy seeing the city, the state and the world through their sometimes bloodshot eyes. They may not always be right or wise—these foot-soldiers, subalterns and generals of the fourth estate in San Francisco—but they're rarely unwitty or dull. I feel that we even enjoy a superior grade of typos in our local newspapers.

On this particular morning I found that the *Chronicle* was headlining the bad coffee to be found in local restaurants, to the relative exclusion of Khrushchev's attitude on the Wall, the mighty risks of John Birchism, and practically everything out of Washington, D.C. Reverse chauvinism of this kind is one of the reasons why I am fond of a socially conscious publication; another is the completeness of its coverage of the more sententious aspects of my career. The San Francisco *Examiner*, which is the flagship of the Hearst fleet, is published by my friend Charles Gould. The *Examiner* may not report Ehrlich in precisely the same unique style that typifies its competitor, but it is sure to come up with novel and interesting data on the subject and his feuds with fate. Both papers have printed details I'd prefer were lost on the way to the linotype machine. However, between the efforts of these two fine newspapers, both sides of the story get told.

This morning the Ehrlich saga was varied and abundant. Both papers had me addressing a televised meeting of city fathers and financial district moguls that evening, though the *Chronicle* seemed to take me apart and was unsure of my role in the upcoming session. I was attorney for the building proprietor's group, and we were attempting to make changes in an archaic zoning code.

I also found myself on the society page of the *Examiner*, complete with photograph. The article was rather clever, having been written by me at the *Examiner*'s request on the subject of "Women and Divorce," but the accompanying picture had unquestionably been taken by a new employee with a damaged Brownie; it made the striking and unusual lines in my face appear to be mere wrinkles, and my hair looked just gray instead of the distinguished silver that it clearly is.

I also found myself in the main news section of both papers in connection with a criminal matter being handled by my office, and decided that if I were production manager of either periodical I would order the phrase, "Ehrlich, whose immaculate white linen and snowy cascade of handkerchief at left breast constitute a personal trademark" set up in permanent type as both an efficiency and economy measure.

Nor was this all. I was in Columnist Caen's column. I found that I was attending a luncheon at the St. Francis that I'd clean forgotten about. And the television editor informed his public that I was shortly to tele-debate Vincent Hallinan; the subject: "Is There a Hell?" I had the affirmative side of the controversy. This was the first I'd heard of it but I felt no qualms. I *know* there's a Hell. I've been there.

So this was my breakfast fare this morning: news of my town, of my friends and of me, over three cups of black and with the gray dawn view of the town spread out before me as I digested it. If I seem a little interested in myself, let me say quite freely that I am.

Any individual who is shy about discussion of himself is usually a sham, ill or an egotistical invert. He wants his virtues and excellencies to be thrust upon him. To disclaim pride of self is probably the basest of subterfuges, and ludicrous as well. Let the egotist take all possible pleasure in himself, for the world certainly won't let him get away with an iota more than he has due him.

Yes, I am an egotist; a mellow, philosophical, self-amused egotist, for I firmly believe that this is the only proper attitude for those examples of the human race who manage to get through the three score and ten without winding up in jail, the bughouse, or the water beneath Golden Gate Bridge. If they can travel further into the realm of human success and come up with a friend or a buck or an attainment or two in the bargain, they are geniuses. To all such miracle workers I take off my hat. We are fully entitled to perform like egotists.

With this maligned quality of egotism—which is actually only a serene and beneficent reflection of inner contentment—go other wrongly ostracized characteristics: uncompromise, arrogance and a reasonable degree of aggressiveness. Uncompromise is the countercoinage of defeat; arrogance is the only way to gracefully deal with outrageous fortune; and a just and measured aggressiveness is the reason why more men pay large sums of money to soldiers, policemen and lawyers.

And now as I finish my coffee and put down my newspapers and once more look down at the city I am about to again invade, a pungent but bittersweet thought assails me, as it does each morning when I leave my Nob Hill citadel for my tower-topped office with its view of seven counties. I think of a soot-drenched, belly empty, dimeless twenty-year-old named Ehrlich who dropped from the side door of a Nickel Plate boxcar in the Oakland freight yard—so many years ago—and said softly to himself through cracked, wind-chapped lips as he stared across the bay at the lights of the Golden Gate town:

"You don't know me, San Francisco... not yet? But you will."

It was so recently past the days of World War I that I was still wearing an olive-drab jacket. What else was warmer! I reconnoitered that grimy freightyard and tried to figure out how I was going to get across the bay. I was flat broke.

In those days ferryboats provided the only means of transportation between the continental rail end in Oakland and the transbay peninsula upon which San Francisco is situated. The train's passengers were accommodated in the upper-deck lounges and promenades of those comfortable old flat-bottomed, side-wheel-propelled tubs, but their luggage and trunks, plus the parcel post and mail and certain express goods carried by the railroads, were loaded onto a fleet of four-wheeled hand trucks and then onto the main decks of the boats by a small army of deckhands, freight handlers and roustabouts. Each of these would seize the tongue of one of the trucks and pull and wrestle his vehicle aboard as soon as the ferry slip's apron was lowered onto the vessel. I quickly found myself a tongue and a truck.

And this is how I arrived in San Francisco, black as sin, empty as a drum, broke as a bankrupt, pulling a large green van loaded with luggage and completely pleased with life and myself. I had at last made it to the city of my (and my grandmother's) wildest dreams. I abandoned the cart as soon as it lost momentum from the downward run into the Ferry Building, and quickly made for the nearest men's room. When I emerged with a half pound or so of Union Pacific roadbed removed from my face, hands and torso, I was ready to greet my new home town. I wasn't exactly fashionable but I was neat.

I walked out onto Market Street. This is San Francisco's wide main thoroughfare which begins at the Ferry Tower, plows the town in two in a generally westward path toward the Pacific Ocean but never quite reaches those cool, blue depths, cleverly preferring to bury its head midway between a pair of senuously rounded hillocks that often have been compared to a woman's breasts. At one end of Market Street, the Ferry Tower; at the other end, Twin Peaks.

It was late afternoon. I started to walk up Market Street.

It must be remembered that barely a dozen years had elapsed since the disaster that virtually destroyed this city in 1906 and which formed the basis for my grandmother's exciting chimera about fireballs and tidal waves. A great amount of reconstruction had been accomplished in the central area, completely devastated by the earthquake and fire, but there were still a large number of boarded-up cavities along the façade of new buildings, and there were far too many quickly constructed, quick-buck, one-story frame structures for any effect of real metropolitan elegance. In many cleared sites the bricks of ruined buildings had been grouped into rather dreary stacks; in others steel girders, all that remained of newer "fireproof" construction, still stretched dankly over puddled, weed-sprouting basements from which the debris had never been cleared completely. It was a sight that might have disillusioned a more superficial soul; it merely increased my fascination. I strode on up Market Street, ignoring the protests from my empty belly.

I admired the people about me. The men seemed more robust, more male, more capable of absolutely anything—good or bad—than any I'd seen, and I liked the curious, uninhibited feeling of democracy that seemed to exist between them. Teamsters and draymen addressed sulphurous warnings and bawdy wit to their so-called social betters and even to the police, as well as to their peers in the traffic interchanges that enlivened life on Market Street. Men didn't hurry single-mindedly along the pavements as they did in the East and the Middle-West, their eyes vacant and self-centered, their minds on their profits or problems. San Francisco men conversed with gusto. They guffawed explosively or made extravagant exclamations of scorn, disbelief or agreement. They cursed with inoffensive robustness, and they hailed newsboys, cabs and friends a block distant with strident whistle blasts achieved through two fingers hooked in the mouth. And they didn't feel called upon to eye me, in my motley, half-military garb.

I admired San Francisco women even more greatly. As I watched them on that initial trek up Market Street I remember how interestingly different I found them. They were *dressed;* that was the first thing. Not one of them looked as though she'd said, "I'm only going to the store at the corner for stays for my corset so it doesn't matter how I look." Not one had said, "I'm no longer young, so the condition of my hair and makeup really doesn't count." None had said, "I'll wear my old shoes downtown today; comfort is more important than appearance."

I remember them as if it were yesterday, and have admired them unfailingly through the years; these super-feminine women of San Francisco who that night helped to entice me into permanent citizenship: the careful, chic apparel, the smart hats, the rarely ungloved hands, the little white collars or jabots or dickeys at the neck, the corsages of violets, the fine look of conscious worth. And I especially remember that they *did* feel called up to eye me—a little—despite my unappealing appearance.

I completed my tour of Market Street, up past the gracious old Palace Hotel where I was to dine so often in the decades ahead, to linger a moment at Lotta Crabtree's Fountain in the shadow of the DeYoung Building where my offices would be, to Powell Street and a first look at a cable car, and then—drawn by some intuitive urge from my future—down Montgomery Street and into the financial district, my present milieu.

This area was relatively bleak and sparsely formed at that time, and there was nothing special about the darkness at what is now 333 Montgomery Street to suggest that someday this location might relate to me. There was no way that I could have foreseen that the triple triad address might one day describe a television version of my life story that would reach every home in America. As a matter of fact, I couldn't have foreseen a thing called radio, much less another called television. I hurried away from the obscurity of Montgomery Street and back to the bulb-brightened brilliance of Market Street which now—as twilight developed into night—was gayer than any white way in Manhattan.

As I stood there at its foot again, under the Ferry Building, I recall precisely how I felt. I was cold and hungry and broke, and my reasonable immediate dollars-and-cents prospects were few; I should have been miserable but I was confident and content. For the first time since I left the plantation, I no longer felt rootless, homeless. San Francisco, was no alien place, as so many other cities had been during the last weary months. I didn't know why, but I knew with quiet, calm assurance that along those unknown streets were friends to be, warm and stimulating experiences to come, opportunities, riches, successes to enjoy, a life to be lived. Not immediately, not tonight, but soon; maybe even tomorrow it would all begin. Those things I knew about my new home town, about my new life, the way you know about all good and right things in life. I was *home,* perhaps for the first time in my paltry twenty years of living. The beginnings were over. *Now* the living would start.

I had shipped my suitcase on ahead prepaid, so I walked to the Wells Fargo Express office on Mission Street and collected it. While there I talked with the team dispatcher. What were the chances for a job? They were pretty good if I could handle a team of horses. Handle a team of horses . . . why, I was the greatest horse-wrangler since Ben Hur! The man looked at me a little warily. "Who does Hur drive for?" he seemed about to ask and I'd have had an answer. Then he made up his mind, asked my name, jotted it down and told me to report to the stables at 5 A.M. I could have kissed him if he'd wiped the tobacco juice from the corners of his mouth. I was not only a San Franciscan; I was an *employed* San Franciscan. When I walked away from the Wells Fargo Building, I was walking in march-time to an invisible band led by me.

Just off Market Street, on Sacramento, was a hostelry favored by seafaring men, stevedores, Alaska fishermen and ladies who catered to this salty type of clientele. It's still there and I never pass it without experiencing a warm feeling in my heart. Because a warm feeling in my heart and a cold feeling in my pocket were all that distinguished me that first night in San Francisco when I showed up, dropping my suitcase heavily on the floor in front of the clerk's desk to demonstrate that it was well loaded, and asked for a room. I was given one and now I had an address as well as a job. Refreshments having been somewhat overlooked, I hastily crawled into bed. There was always the chance that I might dream about a steak dinner.

That was how I came to San Francisco; how I chose the city and why it was chosen. As lifetimes go it seems a long time ago and it was. Woodrow Wilson was still President of the United States; John Fitzgerald Kennedy was a four-year-old moppet playing in the sand at Hyannis. Button shoes were being worn and so were corsets and camisoles and derby hats. Prohibition was too new for people to fully understand why they hated it, and the words *desegregation, nuclear fission, tommy-gun, smog* and *gangster* were uncoined. Hitler and Dillinger, Marilyn Monroe and Babe Ruth and Gandhi, and many other well-known people who are now long dead, had not been heard of. A good meal could still be eaten for fifty cents, and a suit of clothes at less than twenty dollars wasn't hard to find. It was a long time ago.

As I lay on my hard bed at the City Hotel that night and reviewed the miles and months that I'd piled up since that cavalry post on the Mexican border I wasn't sure that the interim proceedings fell under the heading of progress or finding myself or merely racing my motor.

The expedition against Senor Villa had developed from a tango to a waltz and finally to a slow *paso doble,* with the Mexican sitting out the numbers that bored him. All the United States actually got out of the incident was a sort of military dress rehearsal for an unpleasantness to be known as the World War, and later as World War I. Because my enlistment was still recent when the sinking of the Lusitania became too much for Mr. Wilson to bear in the spring of 1917, I participated in this crusade to end international injustice, and soon found myself —in a quick sequence of moves—transported to Fort Myers, Virginia, to Hoboken, New Jersey, and to Bordeaux, France.

My somewhat premature military seniority, plus Sergeant Boyd's abrasive but effective success with my training and education, apparently produced a product that attracted attention in the right circles. I was recommended for Officers' Training School and I became a lieutenant. Intellectual conscience requires that I report that faint inner doubts as to the holiness of our crusade began to infect me shortly after I became involved. The rift in my faith first occurred at a military assembly attended, not only by Pershing and Petain, but by our ecclesiastical brass as well: the Catholic, Protestant and Jewish chaplains of high rank and undoubted influence. These divines called upon us humbler warriors to bow our heads while they addressed the Deity in our behalf and in behalf of our armies, our flags and our countries. With piously quavering voices and eyes devoutly upraised, they implored God to grant victory. To our side, of course.

I remember that it occurred to me while I stood there, my eyes properly fixed on my well-polished shoes, that it was about six two and even that somewhere on the other side of the battle line another group of men was assembled. It would also include generals, high-ranking priests, ministers and rabbis, and foot soldiers staring at their well-polished shoes. What's the use of a ceremony like this unless there are plenty of people present to help out with the bulk praying?

In my mind's eye I could see this other group addressing the same God, making the same appeal—in German of course—and that was when the logic of the situation first began to sag a little for me. They would have reached me more solidly if they had invoked my loyalty on a practical basis: in terms of this-is-our-team-and-we-have-to-win rather than God-is-with-us-because-we're-so good. Confronted on that afternoon with those two assemblies, each asking Him to stick with them, I had a feeling that the Almighty might possibly have some fleeting, private thoughts about the misuse of prayer. So I shrugged and passed on to more important things.

The war was over in November of 1918, and shortly I was back in the civilian world which I had left as a boy and which I had never known as a man. My army earnings, savings and winnings gave me the opportunity to have another whack at education, and that was just about all that I had—a whack. I tried brief returns to various halls of higher learning, but I soon found that the figure on education's price tag required more of a subsidy than I'd earned or saved or won, so I had to postpone formal self-improvement and move in an other direction for the moment.

The direction that I found most profitable (in a tough, traumatic sort of a way) involved pugilistic encounters with my fellow men, although some of those hardly fell within that category. During the next few years and in some of the gamiest, most odorous human cesspools conceivable, I fought and beat or was beaten by the most motley cavalcade of subanthropoids, near cretins and quasi delinquents that I have ever met before or since. There were occasional athletes and sportsmen among them—tough Irish kids from Boston's Jamaica Plain and Charlestown, gutsy little Jewish and Italian battlers from New York's East Side and Chicago's West Side—but most of the rule-breaking, foul-skilled operators that I faced under the lights of scummy, third-rate "clubs" in the drabber districts of Boston, Buffalo, Philadelphia, Chicago, Cleveland, St. Louis, Kansas City and Charlestown were predatory animals, and the only way to fight them was to become—for the moment—another predatory animal.

In most of the clubs the winner's purse was no more than $50; the loser was lucky if he could get carfare out of town. There were times when the winner's take was less; times when the winner had to put up a later and second battle in order to actually get paid. The men who ran these clubs were extremely handy with technicalities that might relieve them of their obligation to pay off.

In New York State, because of the provisions of the Walker Act, a fighter might not be paid in cash. If he won his match he was awarded a "prize" ; hence he was a "prize-fighter." The prize was usually a watch which never actually left the premises of the fight club: a "commissioner" would technically "purchase" the prop watch from him for a fixed sum—$25, $50 or $100. In this way the law was winked at and the fine art of manly defense permitted to become the medium for making club owners rich and fighters poor. This was long before honest and understanding men operated fight arenas. It was long before men such as Benny Ford who protected every kid who fought for him. He is also my friend today.

It was a rough life and a precarious one, but little by little it brought me closer to San Francisco, and at last I arrived there and found myself started on my new life. I had been drifting ever since I left the Army. I intended to drift no longer.

For a man reared with fine horse flesh, who loved to ride and was good at it, it may seem strange that during the last forty years there have been few horses in my life. It may seem strange to others, that is—not to me. When I went to work for the Wells Fargo Express Company as the driver of one of their teams, I found that driving and delivering were merely minor facets of the job. There was more. It was the more that was ultimately to convince me that the best way to know and love horses is in a purely equestrian capacity; it was that more that resolved me to dedicate my life to nonintimacy with horses in other than this capacity.

I quickly found that Wells Fargo not only wanted a driver

for its four dollars daily; it also wanted a companion, valet, dietician, chambermaid and masseur. At times it required even more clinical services. Anyone who labors under any misapprehensions about a five-day week should do some research on working conditions in the early twenties.

The intake and out-take of my horse became my most important responsibility, and the constant need to take out what had been taken in was—I believe—the most important factor in my subsequent disinclination to mingle freely with horses on any level. I found it constantly demoralizing to realize that all that I raked today I would certainly shovel tomorrow.

However, I was sure of one very important and satisfying thing. I was no longer moving in circles. I was moving upward. The buildings to which I delivered my shipments contained not merely the addresses of these goods but the offices of people—the kind of people who would know me well in the years to come, or know *of* me. I was sure of that long before any popularization of the philosophy of positive thinking; I was solidly convinced of man's need to believe in his own destiny with a faith second only to his faith in his spiritual source. Let him turn his faith in himself into a deep and unassailable credo and he'll neither disgrace nor betray it, nor will he permit it to be unfulfilled. I had complete faith in Jake Ehrlich, the boxer-teamster; ergo, nothing that Jake Ehrlich the lawyer has ever accomplished has surprised me very much.

But Freddie Hahn surprised me.

Freddie was one of those nearly faceless persons from out of the past whom one is unreasonably pleased to meet again for having shared some not-too-well-remembered portion of that past. I'd bunked with Freddie somewhere in the cavalry, and when I ran into him one day on Kearny Street we shook hands and clapped each other on the shoulders as if we'd climbed Everest together. It turned out that he, too, was new to San Francisco and without an address or a job.

We had dinner at the old States Restaurant on Market Street, recalled "old times," and worked ourselves into a comradely spirit of euphoria that resulted in a rather peculiar pact.

Hahn was looking for a place to live. We decided that he would double up with me at my hotel, that we would deposit our earnings in a joint fund to be deposited in the safe there, and that we would use that fund and our combined efforts for our mutual advancement: We proceeded to carry out this plan at once.

It worked out fine in a unilateral sort of way. I was able to get him a job, he became my roommate, and the first two-man credit union was started.

Several weeks later, after a particularly corrosive day with the Wells Fargo livestock, I decided to substitute a steak dinner for my regular fare. My regular fare was a definite nondelicacy known as tripe stew, which retailed at the Greek's around the corner from the Wells Fargo stables on Brannan Street for fifteen cents a bowl, with crackers and bicarbonate of soda free. Tonight, however, I was hungry and I wanted steak and French fries and a bowl of minestrone and a big wedge of apple pie, all of which could be obtained in those days for seventy-five cents at the Bay City Grill of fond memory to San Francisco old-timers: the food, the price and the place.

I made a one-dollar levy on the fund in the safe at the Hotel. The desk clerk eyed me sadly. There was *no* fund. White faced and stricken, I hustled up to the room we shared. There was no *Hahn,* there were no Hahn vestments, no Hahn effects, no smallest souvenir of my evanescent colleague. I was now as empty of pocket as of stomach.

Disconsolate, I wandered out of the hotel and onto Market Street with some idea of finding Freddie and adjusting matters. I soon gave that up, however, for I realized that no one as rich as he was now would fritter away his time in a region as depressed as this. Besides, I was ravenously hungry.

For some reason I decided to take my hunger, my anger, and my desolation into the Terminal Hotel. The Terminal—today just a vacuum between two other buildings—was then the Waldorf Astoria of waterfront dumps, and it possessed a kitchen.

I addressed myself to a man who turned out to be its proprietor: a large, formidable Czechoslovak who didn't appear at all surprised at my request—dishwashing for dinner eating. He led me to a formidable stack of dishes. Without even pausing to remove my jacket, I went to work. I soon discovered that I was not alone; two of us were bathing the chinaware, the heavy and encrusted pots and pans. My assistant turned out to be my patron, the dour proprietor. Amazed that anyone who didn't actually *have* to do so would get involved in such drudgery, I asked him why he was working, too.

"I dunno," he said. "I figure that anyone who wants to eat this bad needs some help."

And he did as much of the work as I did. Later we became good friends, and in the years to come I was to represent him in legal actions. I tried to do so without cost to him, but he was always a man with a sound sense of equity and would never have it so.

"You washed the dishes, didn't you?" he'd ask belligerently. "Okay, I pay my tab, too."

Years later I also ran into Freddie Hahn, as one usually does all of the defaulters in one's life. Our second reunion took place at Murphy's Spa—a newspapermen's hangout and speakeasy next door to the old *Bulletin* at the Market-Grant intersection. I was now a successful young lawyer and as popular with my fellow men as only a case-winning, drink-buying young attorney can be. Freddie, a little more worn and beaten than his years added up to, was mopping the floor late one night.

"Hello, Freddie!" I said, dismissing all thoughts of anger and resentment.

"Hello, Mr. Ehrlich!" he replied, with a small, tired, resigned smile. I joined my friends.

Those beginning days became busier and busier. To my Wells Fargo job I added another: I became a freight clerk nights at the Western Pacific Railway office on Mission Street. And I went to law school in the evenings. Before long I was making the traditional squirrel on the treadmill look like a loafer.

A typical twenty-four hour stint for me then, as I look back upon it, makes even me shudder, and my life today is no sinecure. I was up at 4:30 for a day of express deliveries. My meals were strictly hand to mouth, when and where I found the time. I considered myself lucky if I could get a bath and a change of clothes between the Wells Fargo job and the evening classes. Afterward, well into the night with the white collar job and the clerical drudgery at the Western Pacific. The only variation was provided by the evenings when, after classes, I caught a streetcar out to the "Bucket of Blood," or National Hall, in the Mission District, and fought four rounders for purses that came in handy toward the purchase of expensive law books, even if the bruises and black eyes didn't and were hard to explain to my employers and professors. I got little sleep, but I don't think that any lawyer ever did quite as much traveling as he studied: most of it was accomplished on trolley cars or on the high, swaying seats of Wells Fargo drays. One of the critics of my book on Blackstone * described himself as much "moved" as he read it; I can assure him that I had been "moved" frequently as I first studied the Blackstone Commentaries.

In these unmonotonous ways I spent my first two years in San Francisco and wove my way into the warp and woof of my chosen home, earning the right to place myself ahead and above certain others I would meet whose substance and place in the community had been acquired in easier and less personally assessed ways.

And then I met a girl named Marjorie.

* (*"Ehrlich's Blackstone,"* Nourse; Capricorn Books, 1964.)

3: *Early Morning*

7:00 A.M.

THIS IS election day in San Francisco—this day I've chosen as the prototype around which to hang the story of my life. I had forgotten it until a few moments ago when the morning's first telephone call brought me the voice of my old friend Leo Friedman, who is running for judge and who will make it if my friendship and efforts count for anything.

"What are my chances, Master?" he asked.

"Well, Judge . . ." I replied, and told him.

I've been called Master by my fellow townsmen for a long time now. The title was invented in friendly satire by San Francisco newspapermen to whom the use of flamboyant nicknames is a gesture of affection, respect and elevation to inner membership, but the gentle irony involved in no way detracts from certain connotations of truth for the word. That which I haven't been able to master I've been able to handle with a pretty plausible explanation. What more can a world with a sense of humor expect of a man with a sense of proportion?

The election of Leo Friedman was more than just another election to me. He opposed an incumbent judge, whose path had crossed mine on numerous occasions of late and rarely harmoniously or—to my thinking—with equitable consideration of my personal or professional interests.

My credo of friendship and non-friendship is a very basic thing. I don't believe in semifriendship nor do I believe that one should dilute or adulterate intelligently conceived attitudes of bitterness and resentment against those at whose hands one has suffered. Too often when one turns the other cheek or permits time to mellow anger, one suffers again at the very same hands.

But I've also found that reasonable reprisal tends to have a salutory, chastening and deterrent effect. And the least that friendship should evoke is equal, remembering friendship. I never fail a friend. I never forget an enemy.

Leo Friedman and his opponent in the current election fell neatly within the terms of the foregoing personal syllogism. Leo had been around for a long time and was the most qualified, all-around lawyer I knew. While I was a brash trooper on the Mexican border he was already a qualified practitioner. Later, as a member of the district attorney's staff, he had functioned as the prosecutor of Roscoe "Fatty" Arbuckle during that famed trial in the twenties. During the years that followed he had become one of San Francisco's leading criminal lawyers: the defender of David Lamson, Donald Panetoni, Sheriff Emig and many others whose troubles were deep and serious. Most pertinent of all, as far as I was concerned, he had always been an excellent friend of J. W. Ehrlich. The other candidate and I, as I have already indicated, had enjoyed a somewhat different relationship.

So I had placed more than a little of my resources at the disposal of Leo who—nevertheless—was rated by the political writers as having only an outside chance to win. In San Francisco, incumbent judges usually remain incumbent judges. I had undertaken only two such attempted reversals of precedent before. The stories of the fate of both of these targets of mine will appear later.

Now my breakfast was over and I was ready for the day. On the way out of the apartment I quietly opened her bedroom door and looked in on my wife. She was still asleep.

She was just past twenty and as femininely attractive as only a white uniform can make a woman when I first met her, this Marjorie who became my lifelong wife in a world and society where multiple marriage is a commonplace. I've never known a finer woman. I've never known one who knew more about love and loyalty.

Along about my sixth month in San Francisco I had obtained

another little extra job, and it was this that brought us together. On weekends I joined the staff at the Marine Hospital, a facility of the U.S. Public Health Service, and my function was to conduct a sort of inventory of the medical supplies and other properties in the pharmacy. Part of my wages were luncheon and dinner in the officers' dining room of the hospital. My appetite has always been small, and the dietitian soon became professionally aroused at how little damage I did to the trays of food that were sent out to me.

She decided to interview this apparent nonenthusiast for her carefully planned menus. If I couldn't work up an appetite for the diet I could certainly do so for the dietitian. Marjorie Mercer was a pretty little Quaker girl from Frank Lloyd Wright's hometown, Spring Green, Wisconsin. And I was hooked.

Marjorie was a little less sold. It wasn't easy to convince her that I was the great man whom she heard about almost continuously (from me) during the weeks that followed. At first she suffered from the misapprehension that I was merely a very busy, very glib young man with very large plans.

We dated, of course, but no woman was ever dated or courted so meagerly in respect to activities involving cost. All that I earned was going into the project of making me into a high-toned lawyer and making me *look* like a high-toned lawyer. I hadn't forgotten those tall hats back in Rockville, Maryland. They weren't being worn or flourished by lawyers any more but I'd gotten the message. A lawyer had to have something adorning to wear and something impressive to flourish or he might just as well be a meter reader or a washroom attendant, for all the effect he'd have on people. Effect! Hell, I wanted to have impact!

If I couldn't wear tall hats and frock coats, I *could* wear a tall peak of pristine linen in my handkerchief pocket; I could wear clothes that would attest that I was no boxcar bum (any longer); and I *could* convince people that I was prosperous. This sartorial feat didn't leave me much money for other and more practical purposes however, and my courtship of Marjorie was on a kind of piggy-bank basis—one of the reasons why I tried to make up for my defections as a spender with abundant conversation about my glorious prospects.

We went to numerous cake-and-lemonade orgies which were by courtesy of Marjorie or her girl friends at the hospital. We attended movies at the hospital, courtesy of the U.S. Public Health Service. We organized picnics on the shores of the little lake close to the hospital, and we went for long walks along the green cliffs above the ruggedly beautiful Golden Gate. Eventually my arguments (or perhaps my remarkable examples of thrift) mesmerized Marjorie, and one day I was able to ferryboat her across the bay to neighboring San Rafael for our wedding.

My total capital, after paying for two boat fares and one marriage license plus the fee of the justice of the peace, consisted of three cart-wheel dollars, a fifty-cent piece, and two dimes. For the honeymoon there was a salt-water voyage—the return trip across the bay—and the wedding banquet was a bag of hot roasted peanuts shared on the promenade deck of the old and long-gone Northwestern Pacific ferryboat *Ukiah* as we watched the sun drop into the Pacific through the Golden Gate and the beam of yellow from Mile Rock begin its nightly sweeping of the harbor. As soon as we landed in San Francisco we both reported to our respective jobs.

During the last near half century I've seen scores of nuptial pageants performed at Grace Cathedral, St. Mary's and the Babylonian synagogue on Arguello Boulevard that have avalanched into the divorce courts before the wedding gift silver rated a first polishing, but that simple little five-minute interview with a small-town J.P. has produced an extremely durable product. There's probably some sort of great truth implicit in all this, but if so it escapes me, except that I often wonder if it wouldn't be wise for us to regard a marriage as valid and effective in the same way that a final decree of divorce is granted in most states of the Union—a year after the preliminary or interlocutory decree is granted. Or longer.

I'll not soon forget the gentleman who married us. He was

an old-fashioned lawyer named Herbert de la Montanya, a member of a pioneer California family. He had no conventional marriage certificates at hand, so he merely recorded the facts of the occasion on the reverse side of his professional card and presented this vest-pocket-sized document to Marjorie.

Years later when Judge de la Montanya was rounding out his judicial career in San Rafael and I was fulfilling my destiny somewhat farther afield, I found myself asked to represent a wealthy San Francisco stockbroker who had been mixing gasoline with alcohol in the old gentleman's bailiwick; a serious offense at the moment in that region. I also found that the long arm of coincidence would place me and my client in his courtroom within a few days of precisely twenty-five years of my initial appearance in his chambers. I was able to juggle a postponement so that we might go before him on the precise anniversary of that occasion.

The day that my client's case was called, Marjorie and I had been house hunting in Marin County and she was in the courtroom with me when my now very much worried broker friend appeared before the judge.

As we assembled before the bench I was able to comment casually on the interesting coincidence that my last appearance before this court had been exactly a quarter of a century away, to the day and hour. Judge de la Montanya was astounded and said so.

"You must be mistaken, Mr. Ehrlich. Surely I would remember it if you had ever appeared before me. I have followed your career with great interest. I am sure that you have never been in my court, sir."

"Your Honor is mistaken. As a matter of fact, I believe that a transcript of the proceedings and of your pronouncement in the matter is available."

"Sweetheart, do you have your wedding certificate with you?"

I turned to Marjorie.

She handed me the little professional card with the inscription on the back, and he nearly came apart at the seams. He was utterly delighted.

"This is *indeed* cause for a celebration," he said, and it was and we did, immediately after the recess that followed the levying of an unprecedented $100 fine against my delighted client.

And so as to life and love and matrimony, Marjorie and I endured and survived and eventually accomplished and prospered as the path became a road and the road a smooth and pleasant boulevard. But that was all still ahead—as were Jake Jr. and Dora Jane, our children, and their children. Directly ahead on the path that stretched through the mad twenties and the complicated, eventful thirties there were enough near derailments and potential tailspins and psychological beartraps to have totally unstrung me had I been able to foresee them. Thank God, all that I had in this category was my mystic, fanatic egocentricity. I wasn't too sure about Mr. Harding or Mr. Coolidge or Mr. Hoover or even Mr. Roosevelt. All I was sure about was Mr. Ehrlich. I believed in him. I was damned sure that *he* wouldn't let me down.

4: *Early Morning*

7:30 A.M.

ONE OF THE few advantages of going to Hell is that it's all downhill. The same thing applies to living on San Francisco's Nob Hill: going to one's office in the morning is just a matter of pleasantly applying the laws of gravity.

The descent this morning was as astringently refreshing as ever. The pavements were still fog-damp and somehow completely cleansed of yesterday's grime, as if the mere coming and passing of night possessed some strange detergent power. Chinatown lies halfway down the slope of my hill, and as usual, it was up and about earlier than the regions that surround it.

I like Chinatown and the Chinese, and once I had a branch office there. I can see it now as I clamber down Clay Street. Its second story windows haven't changed much, except that on them it now says JICK BOW HEE, IMPORTS beneath a set of Chinese ideograms and a pair of placards which attest that Mr. Jick has contributed to the FREE CHINA FUND and the MISS CHINATOWN BEAUTY CONTEST. I can't see through the dust on the window but I know just how that office looks, every odorous inch of it.

There was room for one desk and two chairs. The chairs were for one attorney and one client; if the clients were multiple, the situation was strictly SRO and not too much of that. In one corner was a safe that I had accepted in an unguarded moment as part of a fee, and in the safe there were rarely more than a couple of fresh shirts and a fifth of bootlegged Haig & Haig. The function of this mass of steel was not to safeguard wealth but to impress customers. For impressing Chinese in those days, a massive safe was second only to a cash register. I had only the safe. Even in that brass-tacks period, I felt that the holier-than-thou Bar Association might frown upon my use of a cash register.

For those whose hair tends to rise at such brash props to a young lawyer's attempts toward success, let me confess further. There was a time when a broad stripe was painted across the middle of my desk. It was there for the benefit of financially backward clients. I was only a few short years away from a cavalry saddle, and I was still in full use of a trooper's brash reasoning. I was forever aware of the impending threat of rent day and not averse to using this direct method for dramatizing the need for my would-be litigant to "get it on the line."

As time went by, it no longer became necessary for me to put such an admonition into blunt, traumatic words. At some point close to the termination of my client's sad story I would merely fixedly stare at the painted line that banded my desk. All but the most obtuse quickly got the idea. Even during the years when subtler amenities began to prevail, the memory and the moral apparently lingered on. It was as though an unseen but durably phantom line were still painted across the mahogany.

People seemed to forget to decorate it less often than they did with other lawyers whose early needs had not required cash-and-carry legal service to the degree that mine had.

But my Chinatown office served its purpose. It brought me cases with meat on them: colorful legal problems which I felt were up to my talents and taste; jobs of defense that were profitable both in terms of money and glory. I was substantially on the way up by then. I was known. "Get Jake!" was a sort of a theme song on the upper barred-window floors of the Hall of Justice, and it was music to my ears. If I wasn't keeping much beside my will and insurance policy in my safe deposit box, I was at least able to buy a round of drinks at a speakeasy without first balancing my billfold. But the move to Chinatown was an especially good one and I—who never pass up a hot tip from a gypsy, a fortune cookie or a tea-leaf reader—should have been sure of it when a strange old Chinese gentleman walked into that Clay Street outpost of mine the morning of the day I moved in.

He appeared to be as old as Confucius and as dignified. He was wearing the long, black Peking gown no longer seen on Chinese in this country, and on his head was the round, satin, button-topped hat associated with early Oriental emigrants. A braided queue would have completed the picture but there was none. There was a long wisp of beard, however; a beard that spoke only of China. With all the aplomb of a Manchu mandarin, my visitor sat down in my spare chair and solemnly nodded at me.

"You Jake Ah-lick."

It wasn't a question. I smiled and offered him my hand and a cigarette. He lighted the latter, holding it perpendicularly pinched between his thumb and forefinger, the way the elder Chinese do—to slow the burning and make the cigarette last. We waited together in silence for quite awhile, smiling mildly at each other and contemplating eternity. Then he spoke again.

"You Jake Ah-lick, law-yah. You mama, she die. You got foh blothah, one sistah. You see, I know."

I nodded in acknowledgement of his knowing. He puffed a little longer on his cigarette and then went on.

"Jake Ah-lick, you wise man for come here, Chinatown. Soon, you catch velly big case. Much face for you, much money. You be Num-bah One law-yah, Chinatown. I tell you true. Laytah, you be Num-bah One law-yah Sam-san-chee-say-oo. I tell you true."

Sam-san-chee-say-oo is the Chinatown variant for San Francisco, which is completely unpronounceable for older Chinese. I nodded gravely. He nodded back, removed the glowing coal from the end of his cigarette, fastidiously placed the dead butt dead center of a fairly scrofulous handkerchief, folded the handkerchief many times around it and stood up. Apparently the audience was at an end. I stood up, too. He went to the door and then turned toward me once more.

"Remember!" he admonished me. "You be Num-bah One. I tell you true."

Several moments passed before I summoned the presence of mind to look out onto Clay Street to see whether he departed in a ricksha, a palanquin or a puff of smoke. There was no sign of him. I never saw him again.

But he was a harbinger; a fully licensed one as far as I was concerned. Not long after that I caught my "velly big case."

I was at my downtown office when the call came. Quickly, I hustled up to the Clay Street branch. The people who wanted to see me were Chinese, and I felt that they'd talk more freely in their own bailiwick. Orientals seem constitutionally unable to communicate with Occidentals except in reluctantly released layers of information, and often it takes an interminably long time to get past the first few superficial levels of frankness.

The facts, as the police had them at this point, were robust and explicit. They concerned a quiet, moon-faced little insurance broker named Louis Quan.

Quan had a loyal wife and a close friend, and the tense of the verb is correct in both cases because the wife was apparently no longer loyal and the friend was certainly no longer alive. Choy Lin, the wife, was—as they say in Chinatown—*chaw-quay haw-ku;* in other words, a desirable woman. She was rounded where Chinese women usually aren't and she was slim and lithe in areas where white women aren't. Quan liked her a lot; so did his friend and protégé Henry Yee.

If a little rain must fall in every life, Henry Yee was Louis Quan's cloudburst. As a boy, Quan had known Yee in Canton before coming to the United States himself, getting an education, earning a place in the Chinatown business world and plucking the peach-tree blossom who was to gladden his heart, bear his children, and damn near send him to the gallows.

When Yee finally arrived in America, he needed the fare down from Seattle. Quan provided it. Then Yee needed room rent. Quan came through. Yee then wanted to go to work at the New Shanghai Café, where the pay was good and there were even foreign-devil customers, which meant tips. Quan pulled a few strings and Yee was soon dealing out chow mein and getting the wrinkles out of his own belly. But there was a certain amount of work connected with this job, and Henry felt that work was an inartistic activity. He resigned. Quan let him sleep in the basement of his small insurance office, and helped him in other ways.

Then Henry Yee acquired a taste for Quan's delectable wife, and Louis decided it was time to turn stingy. He told Yee to stay away from the family apartment on Stockton Street, two blocks away from his office. Once when he came home late he found the door locked against him. When Henry Yee opened it a little later and let him in, Louis Quan was pretty annoyed. This was going too far.

Meanwhile Henry had at last found employment suitable to his temperament and esthetic sensibilities. He had been given a job at Radio Station KSAN. Generally speaking, he was a singer; a singer of love songs. More specifically, he was a singer of love songs to Choy Lin, to whom he openly dedicated these anthems for all Chinatown to hear and gossip about. Louis thought this was going more than too far.

But his one-time beneficiary really went the full distance in terms of too-farness when the importunate Mr. Yee once more tried to pick up a midnight snack of forbidden delights in Mrs. Quan's boudoir. This, the cuckolded husband's relatives told me as they grouped about my desk, was the end. Louis wrote finis to the romance with a Smith & Wesson .38.

From the standpoint of early information, it looked as though poor Quan didn't have a chance. There appeared to be a certain degree of premeditation; there was no element of self-defense. Worst of all, in the eyes of the press-oriented grand jury ultimately asked to select the precise flavor of murder that Quan had apparently committed, he had immediately asked to be represented by "Jake Ah-lick." That meant only one thing to them: Louis Quan was a smart cookie who knew just what to do before, during and after a homicide.

I recall how often this attitude was reflected, even by august members of the judiciary who are theoretically above anticipation of fact. In one case I was arguing for reduced bail for a client. The judge wished to know the grounds for my plea.

"Because he's innocent, Your Honor," I said, "and this is very high bail for a man who's innocent."

The magistrate looked puzzled.

"Innocent!" he said. "Then what are *you* doing here?"

It turned out that he *was* innocent.

When I went down to the grim old building on Portsmouth Square to see Louis, I found that I had three fine, fat, fouled-up things going against me. The beautiful wife Choy Lin was demurely devoid of any mitigating information. My fatalistic client had adopted the district attorney's opinion of his own character and motives and virtually accepted a trip to Death Row at San Quentin as a *fait accompli.* And he had furnished the state with an extremely competent confession.

"I went home for talk to my wife," it alleged. "I hear knock at door. I open door. I see Henry Yee and I think may be-so he do something to me. I pull gun out. I try knock his head with gun. Bullet come out. Bullet go through head. I leave. That's all."

Yes, that was all; for a few flat, cold moments I was sure of it as I read it and contemplated the smug smirks of the master minds in Homicide as they examined me for signs of the malaise that they were not going to find. Instead, I nodded as though I'd pulled the winning sweepstake ticket out of the hat.

"It's a cinch," I told myself, half aloud.

There were hoots from the assembled sleuths.

"He's cold meat, Jake; *that's* your cinch!" said one of the inspectors. I demonstrated polite amazement.

"You must have some other case in mind, Mr. Sherlock Holmes. This is the clearest instance of justifiable homicide since David put Goliath away."

"How'd this David make out with the jury?" asked the inspector with instant professional interest. I looked him over carefully but he was on the level.

"Jury!" I replied, "he wasn't even booked. They had smart cops in those days. What I can't figure out about this little argument in Chinatown last night is how Henry Yee wound up with only *two* slugs in his cheating carcass."

Inspector Harry Husted, the first officer, quickly answered that one.

"*Three,* Master. There were three bullets in the bugger."

Ah, that was fine! Louis, a precise, pragmatic man, had told me he'd squeezed four slugs from the gun at his unofficial brother-in-law. I believed him.

"Three? Louis thinks there were four and *he* was there."

"He's stringing you, Jake. There were three in the stiff and none anywhere else in the apartment. I know. We frisked that place right down to the termites. Three did the job and only three were fired."

All of it good to know. In those days the defense had no "discovery" laws to enable it to know what the prosecution hoarded in the way of evidence; I might have had to wait until the trial to find out the facts in the case. I could see that the police were sold on a trey-volley and figured me for my stubborn faith in something else. If I could only locate the missing fourth bullet, I could make the state's information look more than a little sloppy.

Two, three, four or forty, I still had a tough job. The Japanese had just bombed Pearl Harbor, and to most Caucasian jurymen any Oriental was an Oriental and not entitled to much compassion, in trouble or out. To make things even harder, Henry Yee was getting more sympathy from the Chinese than was my client, on the basis—apparently—that all the world loves a lover, even an illicit one. There was also the fact that he was a radio singer, if this title can correctly be given to one who emits the strange sounds which pass for vocal endeavor in Chinatown.

Henry Yee's self-composed lyrics were something to give pause to even the most romantically inclined. I had the little anthem he sang to Choy Lin translated:

> Always I am dreaming of you,
>   I hope you will pardon me for what I have said,
> It will not hurt if I die because of love,
>   I am sick because of love;
> If you should keep me in suspense,
>   My date of death will not be far away;
> Oh my dear Choy Lin, where is the God of Love,
>   I am like a lone goose . . .

The lone goose, incidentally, was getting a lot of mileage on poor Louis Quan's bedroom mattress at precisely the period that he was droning out these heartbreaking lyrics over KSAN, it turned out later. Poor Louis was a sort of chronic convention delegate.

It was a tough one. To hang the crepe higher and blacker on my (and Quan's) chances, the prosecutor was talking nothing but the death penalty. My adversary, in this and many other similar contests, was John J. McMahon, more commonly known as Ropes McMahon because of his whimsical single-mindedness concerning capital punishment.

I figured that if I won this one the feat would fall under the general heading of a miracle, and not a cut-rate miracle. I called all of Quan's relatives and friends and the ancients of his tong together at my Clay Street office. Although I was the great and utterly nonpareil Ah-Lick, I told them I had a case of Murder One to defend, sans witnesses, sans evidence, sans even a small iota of fight in the heart of my client. I could win but I needed a certain specific stimulus in order to counteract the other deficits: I needed one hell of a lot of money. The relatives, the elders and the hard-eyed businessmen stared at me impassively and then one of them spoke.

"How much, Mister Ah-lick?"

"Fifty thousand dollars."

"Foh pay-off?"

"Yes."

"For pay who?"

"For pay *me*. Every damn cent of it."

I got the fifty thousand. And I wondered how much longer my Clay Street office would continue to be a safe and pleasant place in which to while away an idle hour or so and commune with an elderly soothsayer who had spoken of luck. But—now that I looked back on it—he hadn't mentioned longevity.

The $50,000 did a lot for my morale. All I needed now was something to take to court besides my massive faith in Mistah Ah-lick. All I needed was something the state didn't have in the way of evidence.

Or a witness.

About four o'clock one morning I climbed the dark, fetid stairs at 1104 Stockton Street that led to the Quan flat. At each landing a guttering, red-shaded gaslight defied city, county and rational laws to the extent of turning Stygian darkness into a shadowy murk, but offered no help in reading the scatter of names printed there in English and Chinese ideographs.

The cool morning air wasn't allowed to reach this labyrinth, and the inside aroma—composed largely of scents suggestive of wood rot, bean curd and soy sauce, unaired bedding, urine, *ylang-ylang* and at least one sharp infusion of opium—had me impossibly attempting to breathe neither in nor out. At the Quan landing I was met by a large, obese, unfrightened rat who turned and waddled sluggishly down the hall, only after looking me over without undue haste, as if to make sure I didn't have anything he really wanted.

I stood motionless for a second or more on the threshold of No. 202, where the Quans had lived and Yee had died. Choy

Lin and her children had moved in with relatives, and Louis Quan was of course tossing miserably on one of the steel-strapped wall bunks at the nearby Hall of Justice. The flat should have been left exclusively to me, the rats and Henry's ghost. Still, I waited for a moment and listened. There were only the usual furtive and anonymous night sounds, the absurdly sinister creakings, the nameless scurryings, the midslumber expostulations of babies and old men; and from the harbor the ubiquitous loving of the foghorns while from over on Columbus Avenue a police squad car sirened a careening course toward some unlucky prowler. Closer at hand, silence. I keyed my way into the flat.

Somehow and even at 4 A.M. the setting suggested neither murder nor clandestine romance; much less did it seem a background for domestic bliss and child rearing. Under the beam of my flashlight (I was distinctly uninterested in stimulating any attention or talk in Chinatown or the police department about my explorations), I found myself looking at the dreariest living quarters this side of the city pound. Choy Lin may have excelled at amour but as a homemaker she was something less than a freshman.

The three rooms were reasonably clean but quite barren of any "woman's touch," unless the small shrine holding the household gods fell into that category. Aside from this and a number of anemic poinsettia plants in pots, plus a gaudy calendar lithograph of a simpering Chinese female in the act of ogling a swan, there was nothing. The bedrooms were neat, bare and without access to sunlight during the day, their windows being almost flush against the bricks of the building next door. The kitchen windows offered an unexhilarating vista of another pair of kitchen windows across the air well.

With so little to examine it didn't take long to check out the premises. I explored it all, even nosing through the food containers and the strange assembly of herbal remedies and Chinaside cosmetics that cluttered the cell of a bathroom. I found nothing. Once I thought I was having company when there was the sound of movement in the black corridor outside, and then I realized that it was only my fat, verminous friend with the long tail, or one of his colleagues.

I turned my attention to the precise spot at which Louis Quan had claimed to have stood when he transferred Yee to the nether world. I held my flashlight just as he might have held his revolver, and let its beam follow all of the possible trajectories that a bullet might have taken. Perhaps nighttime and complete darkness is the best way in which to investigate the physical evidence of a murder case, because I suddenly found my white shaft of light peering and fingering at a tiny hole at the juncture of baseboard and floor. In the ordinary light of daytime it might easily have been overlooked by even a careful policeman, as it actually had been. I examined it more closely and removed the lint and dust that partially concealed it. Not too deeply imbedded in the aperture was a piece of lead. I had my something. Tomorrow I would send around a ballistics expert to turn the little hunk of metal into evidence for Louis.

But although the first pale coloration of dawn was seeping down the air well into the melancholy little flat, I wasn't quite sure that I was through yet. I had the feeling that there was *something* else . . . some kind of something; just *what* I had no idea.

I stood in the center of the living room-kitchen and slowly played the beam of my flashlight about me, full perimeter. Again —almost as if the shaft of light had hunches of its own—it slowed and stopped on the little shrine in which all self-respecting, non-Christian Chinese keep their household gods. I walked over to the small stage that supported them. I examined the ivory statues of the Eight Immortals, the vases containing wax flowers, the braziers for the burning of incense, the little tray of . . . *wait a minute!* Why should seven of the ivory figurines be gray with dust and the eighth—the statue of Quan Yin, Goddess of Mercy —be quite clean, as if it had been handled regularly?

I removed Quan Yin from her teak pedestal and examined her carefully. Nothing. She wasn't hollow, and there were no places of concealment in the beautiful little statue. I was about to replace her when I decided to have a look at the teakwood base.

It was not solid, as it appeared to be from the front; its rear pediment could be removed, not easily but with a little physical persuasion. Inside was a packet of letters. They were held together by a multicolored silk handkerchief. The envelopes of each were addressed to Quan Choy Lin, and not at the Stockton Street house number. The return addressee was Henry Yee. The contents of the letters were inscribed in Chinese ideographs, but that was all right with me. I had found my something.

At the landing where I'd encountered the overweight rat I nearly collided with an underwear-clad gaffer carrying out a lard can definitely not filled with lard, his plumbing being either in disrepair or nonexistent.

"Good morning, father!" I said, for at that point it was, as far as I was concerned.

"Argh?" he replied, not at all convinced.

But he was wrong. It was a very good morning. After coffee and a look at the morning papers, I took myself and my kerchief-load of *billets-doux* down to the watch-repair shop of Pok Sam Low. Shortly before this I had restored Pok to general circulation in society following an unkind claim by the Narcotics Bureau that what he was smoking in his pipe of an evening was grown in poppy fields rather than in tobacco plantations. My watchmaker friend was grateful; had he gone to prison, he would have had great difficulty getting the kind of tobacco he really did smoke.

He took the jeweler's glass out of his eye and asked me what he could do. I gave him the letters. He read a little while, sniggered a bit, read some more. Then he spoke.

"This love stuff only for damfool."

"I didn't ask you to make like Confucius, Sam Low. I want some facts, some information."

He readdressed himself to the letters in much the way that a man takes on the comic section of a newspaper. Finally he put them down, shaking his head in amused disgust.

"Okay. It tell mostly how this fella Yee like make love to

Choy Lin. It tell how many time, where, when. He thank her. He like some more; alla time some more."

Yes, it was a fine morning. I packed up my evidence and started out of the tiny shop. Pok Sam Low called to me.

"One more thing, Mastah!"

He held his hands out in front of his abdomen, as if he were holding an imaginary watermelon.

"Choy Lin gonna have new baby. Fathah not Louis Quan. Fathah Henry Yee."

As I've said, miracles may be expensive but they're worth it. I not only had something that the state didn't have; I had something that Louis Quan didn't have. He was about to become a father without having lifted a finger.

We went to trial with Ropes McMahon thinking he had a prefabricated conviction and execution on his hand, and the press agreeing with him. The case was heard before Judge Edward Preston Murphy, a lifelong friend of mine. Even he thought that I was backing the wrong man this time; that my perfect record on murder acquittals was about to be fractured.

McMahon performed like the master executioner that he was, painting Quan as a vicious man who took the law into his own hands merely because another man liked his wife. The lone goose Yee he pictured as a harmless, lovesick boy who had admired from afar and been brutally slaughtered for his silliness. Choy Lin, who came to court in a dress of well-calculated drabness and with a hair style that substantially modified her spectacular good looks, was portrayed as a dear little innocent wife and mother. Ropes put on an excellent showing and concluded by asking for death in the gas chamber for Louis, the milquetoast turned murderer.

When the defense was finally permitted to put on its obviously indefensible case, I called Choy Lin. She settled herself in the witness chair in the demure, saddened but forgiving wife pose that had been so effective up to the moment and waited for Mistah Ah-lick. She'd heard he could be a difficult interrogator, but not in this case—not in *this* case, the district attorney and the police had smugly assured her.

I fed her a few easy, polite ones. She answered them easily, politely. We fenced courteously and her confidence increased. This was precisely the way they had told her it would be. Then I pulled the packet of letters from my pocket. Her eyes went to them and she gasped. Her face whitened, as if I had removed a small, portable cobra from a box and draped it around my neck.

"I may want to discuss these letters with you, Mrs. Quan . . . but first, let me ask you . . . just what were your *actual* relations with Henry Yee?"

From there on in it was like boiling water over a gas jet with the directions pasted on the side of the pan. It took a few leading questions, a little encouragement, a little cueing here and there, but when Choy Lin had finished testifying, her hearers no longer needed a program to identify the players. She told how often, how long, and when and why and where she had loved the lone goose. She told how patient her husband had been and how many warnings he had given her lover. She told how Henry had pushed her husband out of their flat when he wanted to make love to her. She told how Yee had threatened to kill her husband. And much of the time as she talked she gazed, as if mesmerized, at the packet of letters I held in my hands. Sometimes I tapped them reflectively against the railing of the jury box, sometimes I absently riffled the edges of the envelopes, and finally—toward the end—I tossed them casually on the counsel table. They had performed their function. When Choy Lin was allowed to end her testimony, I cordially conducted her to her seat. McMahon was glaring at me as if I'd spit on the national colors. I smiled cordially at him, too. I was feeling cordial toward everyone at that point.

I then put Louis on. I had him tell his entire pathetic tale of love for his wife, of practical friendship for the treacherous Yee. I scotched the claim that he had taken the law into his own hands by having him relate how he had gone to his tong, to Sergeant Jack Manion of the Chinatown detail of the police department, with requests for help against the slow, polite rape of his wife. I had him repeat their words of indifference. And then because it was the 23rd day of December and two days before Christmas, I had him finish with the story of his last Christmas with his family: the tale of how the children had come to him at his insurance office and pleaded to be fed. Their mother was away, pleasuring with the lone goose.

The jury brought in a verdict of Not Guilty.

But Louis didn't exactly escape punishment. Later on, the elders of his tong tried him for the crime of "taking a human life." They fined him $600.

These were the thoughts that came pungently back to me this morning as I descended Nob Hill and looked up through the early morning mists at the tiny second-floor office where a very much younger Jake Ah-lick had taken on some of the wonderful problems of another day and another world.

5: *Morning*

8 A.M.

JUST AS I am usually the last one to leave it at night, I am invariably the first to arrive in the morning at my office on the 16th floor of 333 Montgomery Street, two blocks from Chinatown, two blocks from the Stock Exchange, four blocks from the old Hall of Justice where I must have spent a substantial number of the man hours of my life, and not more than four blocks from some of the finest restaurants in the world.

This morning I found that I had been preceded, which was unusual. There was a lovely and unhappy woman waiting for me, the wife of one of my legal associates.

"Jake, I'm miserable and you've simply got to help me,"

she said, without other preamble. "I've had it. I want the fastest, surest divorce you can get me." And then there were tears. "He's got another woman."

She was married to one of the nation's leading trial lawyers, a man whose very instabilities were probably the prime reasons for his sometimes brilliant but often merely odd courtroom pyrotechnics. Trying to persuade her to the contrary or to stem the tide of her emotion would have been useless. I gently shepherded her into my office and sat her across from me. This was strictly the wrong time of day for this particular scene. At 8 A.M. I could hardly offer a highball and a few comforting words and suggest a good night's sleep before any radical decision.

"Darling," I said, "divorce is an action in social bankruptcy in which neither the bankrupt nor the creditor gets any real part of what he or she rates out of the deal. Actually it's a recourse that should only be regarded as a last resort by badly cheated or desperately unhappy persons, and I'm sure that you fall into neither category. Why don't you buy a couple of expensive new dresses at Magnin's, have lunch at Paoli's, then see how you feel about it tomorrow or next week? Maybe it won't exist by then."

She shook her head.

"I couldn't possibly forget this awful woman, Jake. She knows what she's doing. And so does he."

"My dear, all she knows—if your information is correct and there *is* such a woman—is that the great man has deigned to unburden himself of confidences to her. All he knows is that he has a new, adoring audience, for the moment. She'll be gone and he'll be back home before we can get the complaint drawn up, if you continue with this unhappy action."

"Meanwhile, what am I to do?"

"Is this the first time that he has enjoyed these . . . little interviews?"

"You know it isn't."

"All right, then you will do what you have done the other times. You will suffer, you will hate his guts, you will seriously consider divorcing him, you will remember that you love him and you will forgive him. That will be the end of the syndrome, full cycle, until the next time that fate brings together a ready tongue and a willing ear in the husband department of your family."

She eyed me with a look that was equal parts anger, frustration and dawning amusement. Then she smiled.

"You're a hell of a divorce lawyer, Master. According to protocol, you're supposed to be sympathizing with my complaints, promising to strip my husband of all he has, and quoting me five-figure fees."

I patted her hand.

"*Six*-figure fees, dear. He could stand it. But it has occurred to me that if you really wanted a divorce you'd have gone to some businesslike little practitioner who'd already have had you on the dotted line for a common-sense tab, and with no argument about the futility of divorce. It had also occurred to me that the real reason you came to me was that you thought you might Ehrlich your hubby out of his wits, panic him out of this other babe's arms and back into yours without actually having sued at all. Could I possibly be right?"

She smiled at me, patted her hair, started for the door and then looked back from the doorway.

"Of course you're not right, Jake. That would be . . . unethical."

We both laughed at this one and she was gone. But she would be back—often, perhaps. And eventually, when all of the frosting was gone from the cake that my colleague so strangely sought to eat and keep, I would get her divorce for her. But—to me—divorce and embalming are two processes that should never be undertaken prematurely.

Neatly centered on my desk, I found my agenda for the day. It read as follows:

8:30 A.M. Stewart Hopps matter; attorneys for receiver of U.S. Marine and Foreign Insurance Company

8:45	Mrs. Jean Carter
9:00	Mrs. Monica Smith
	Daughter of V. McN. (charged with Murder I)
9:30	President of S.F.Police Officers Assn.
10:00	James Mason
10:30	Court–Hon. Harry Neubarth–Dept. 8, People *vs.* V.McN.
12:00	Lunch–St. Francis–Colonial Room
2:00	Sally Stanford
2:30	Albert L. Johnson
3:00	George Jue
3:30	Stanton Delaplane
4:00	Representatives of Downtown Business Groups
4:30	Taping of Television Show
6:00	Lou Lurie (at his office)

This was a schedule to warm and soothe the mind: a fine, full, miscellaneous day of challenges that included claims upon my time and skill from the worlds of politics, business and finance; visitations with a leading moving picture actor, a former madam, the charming widow of a Supreme Court justice, a Chinese restaurateur, a man charged with murder, and the leaders of my largest single group of clients, the San Francisco Police Officers Association. What man between the Kremlin and the White House could contemplate a more invigorating program of activity? Mentally, I licked my chops.

By now, Libby my secretary, had arrived. In the television series on my career I am regularly shown being assisted by smart and beautiful secretaries. Elizabeth Hanson is both. I believe in beautiful women. If they can also manage to be cerebral, the combination falls under the heading of delightful phenomenon. I don't expect foreverness, too, knowing that eventually all women succumb to the delightful malady of love, its aftermath, marriage, and the inevitable by-product, children. In all these Lib has succeeded.

For nearly twenty years Libby Hanson has been well known to a generation of my friends and colleagues.

And by now, Ed Dullea has arrived.

Ed Dullea is my partner, doer of difficult deeds, first line of defense and friend. The son of Charles Dullea, one of San Francisco's toughest, straightest police chiefs, Ed is the kind of a man you're delighted to have with you at a fight, a frolic, a foot race or a Supreme Court hearing. Educated by the Romans at the University of San Francisco, he is a Jesuitical logician to much the same degree that I am an Old Testament technician. (Ed's two brothers, gentlemen of distinction, are Charles W. Dullea, Jr., S.J., President of the University of San Francisco, and John F. Dullea, S.J., Professor of Theology, Santa Clara University.) Together and with practically all of the leading faiths monopolized between us, we make it extremely difficult for any sort of one-dimensional label to be placed on our combined thinking.

It's 8:30 and Ed Dullea has arrived.

"Good morning, Master!"

There's a *certain* Hibernian quality to the reading he gives the final word in that greeting . . . I sometimes *wonder*. . . .

6: *Morning*

8:30 A.M.

Agenda: Stewart Hopps matter

The attorneys for the Rhode Island Insurance Company came right to the point. They wanted $10,749,701—ten million, seven hundred and forty-nine thousand, seven hundred and one dollars and no cents and no discount for cash. They wanted it from my client, Stewart E. Hopps, head of the U. S. Marine & Foreign Insurance Company of San Francisco, and they expected to get it shortly after our next reunion in the courtroom of Superior Court Judge Tom Keating of Marin County. The legal grounds for their case were quite good.

The Rhode Island Company, which took a dim view of Hopps' business acumen, and with some degree of reason, alleged that my client had improperly subtracted the above named amount from the assets of his firm, and their receiver—a lawyer named Windsor—wanted a $10,000,000 rebate, but immediately. I had examined the facts and the law pretty thoroughly. I had also discovered that Windsor had acquired some substantial confidential information on U.S. Marine & Foreign from Mr. Hopps' secretary. The situation looked bad. While the opposition smugly sat there in front of me I racked my brain for an out for my client. There appeared to be none. I ended the interview and small-talked my visitors to the door. Among these exchanges there was an inquiry concerning the whereabouts of Mr. Hopps himself. This led to an absent-minded comment from me that he was often a hard man to locate, and the casual rejoinder from one of the other lawyers that Mr. Windsor, too, had had the same trouble when *he* represented Mr. Hopps.

I was literally and figuratively humming when I returned to my desk. Sometimes a small, intuitive application of precisely aimed information is more effective than a large use of general legal lore. I buzzed Dullea.

"Ed," I said when he appeared in the doorway, "an attorney would have to be mighty careful to avoid even the appearance of conflict of interest in a lawsuit, no matter how strong his case might otherwise be—no matter if only a dollar's worth of equity were involved, right?

"Unquestionably."

"And for ten million dollars' worth—"

"—he'd have to be ten million times as careful."

"Okay, then. Get Stewart Hopps on the phone and tell him that we've just earned him ten million dollars." And I told him of my plan.

"Master!" he said when I was through—without the Hibernian inflection.

The simple little gimmick worked like a charm when we got to court. I tried to prove that Windsor had been attorney for Hopps in previous litigation and that he possessed confidential information as to his business affairs that strictly precluded his present role as counsel for those who would reach into his bank account and impoverish him. We were finally able to settle the matter for $70,000, which represented the actual costs involved. Hopps, unfortunately, continued his blast-offs into the stratosphere of high finance and eventually ran afoul of the Federal Government. But he was and is a multimillion-minded operator with real nuclear impetus to all of his financial plans and dreams.

I rarely encounter a money-laden litigation of this kind these days without being reminded of my first case, my first client, my first fee. The fee was $25, and even this modest sum was not paid without complication.

My client was an angry little woman with an enormous disillusionment about men and a microscopic amount of cash on hand. She wanted a divorce from a husband who supported her poorly and overenjoyed the company of other ladies.

I remember that her name was Audrey. Curiously, the Audreys of my experience have all been given to carrying on lawsuits and hard-nosed about female competition. In my reactions, these have come to be characteristics that go with the name.

When this Audrey visited me, I had just moved into my first private office, on the fourth floor of the Chronicle Building at the five-pronged intersection of Kearny, Geary, Third and east and west Market streets. The beautiful bronze fountain that actress Lotta Crabtree gave San Francisco fronts this building on a small traffic island where Tetrazzini used to sing to San Franciscans on New Year's Eve.

My office—really more of an oversized mop and broom closet—was tucked behind the building's elevator shaft. Often as the great counterweights for the old-fashioned elevator charged noisily up and down a seeming hairsbreadth from a client's back collar button, I felt that I was more *in* the elevator than next to it. And the mere interviewing of a client called for rearrangement of the furniture and acoustics, synchronization of the conversation to the movement of the elevators, and no additional guests.

As might be expected, my first client received a welcome far out of proportion to the magnitude of the case and the fee. I had even borrowed law books as desk props for the occasion, and my new diploma impressively reposed behind the best frame money could buy at the Woolworth store at Market and Fifth. With dignified but winning solicitude and just the right touch of hauteur, I explained to the embittered Audrey that I would maritally disenfranchise her erring husband in a comparative trice. Then the first rift appeared in the lute of our relationship. She had no money for even *my* cut-to-the-bone fee.

"Not any!" I echoed, aghast.

"Not any," she replied firmly. "That bastard hasn't given me a dime or spent a dime on me since the day he put these on my finger." She pointed to a glittering engagement ring and a companion wedding band.

I eyed them.

"When you come to think of it, my dear," I said, "the mere sight of those rings must bring you painful memories."

"They don't!" she said callously. "I just think of them as joolry."

"But in time they will, Audrey, they will! In time the sight of them will tend to make you hate yourself forever having turned your loveliness over to this unfeeling clod. And," I added more meaningfully, "their sale would just about defray the cost of this divorce."

Abe Attell's pawnshop across the street got the jewelry, I got my first fee, and Audrey got her divorce. Although there is still some lingering doubt about the latter.

Because of the meager nature of my compensation and because my client's husband operated his elevator close to where she lived, Audrey consented to serve the subpoena on him. He failed to put in an appearance in court and the divorce decree was granted by default. A number of years later I met Audrey in the company of a new husband and a gaggle of children acquired via this gentleman. When the introductions were over and I'd been thanked again for my valuable services, for want of anything else to say, I commented that I'd had a skilled process server in Audrey.

"Oh I never served the louse," she said. "I thought it over and I come to the conclusion that he just didn't deserve to be told."

A little startled, I explained the possibility of unpleasant complications. She blithely brushed my warnings aside.

"Don't worry, Mr. Ehrlich; I could ruin him if he ever tried to make trouble. He went and got married again and *he couldn't have known he was divorced from me!* Why, I could have him arrested for bigamy!"

Those were strange, wonderful, excitingly insecure, fearsomely competitive days. Cases were hard to come by during the first year, and I carefully cultivated the respect and friendship of those energetic talent scouts of the criminal courts, the police. To hear a squad-car siren go screaming by in pursuit of a bandit was to think, almost automatically: Bring him in, boys; bring him in to Jake!" Some people believe that clients derived from the friendly policemen who make the arrest results in fees that are decently split with the officers concerned. This doesn't happen, but the friendly policeman has helped me pay rent and buy groceries during the lean years. The happiest of telephone messages for me had been the "Hello, Jake, I just pinched a burglar," from my friends in the police department. This came over the phone at Garfield 824 twelve hours before they were coming to take my furniture away. I could have kissed both the cop and the burglar.

This morning, so many comfortable decades away from $25 fees it might be convenient and certainly more dignified to forget that the rungs at the bottom of the ladder were often scuffed and muddied because of their proximity to the soil. But my sense of humor—among other things—denies me that kind of expedient.

Besides, $25 possesses an interesting significance when considered immediately prior to the $25,000 I earned fifteen minutes ago by merely remembering that a lawyer doesn't completely sever his relationship with one client when he passes on to the next.

7: *Morning*

8:45 A.M.

Agenda: Mrs. Jean Carter

Mrs. Carter is one of the loveliest ladies of my acquaintance, and her arrival in my office this morning on a matter connected with the disposition of her late husband's estate brought memories of a man for whom the adjective unique constitutes emasculated understatement. He was my friend, my client, and possibly the only State Supreme Court Justice of our time who stood ready to implement his convictions with arms as well as words, according to the language and intent of not only the Constitution but the Bill of Rights.

"Have you gotten over missing him, Jean?" I asked when she was seated.

"Can you get over missing happiness, Jake?"

Jesse Washington Carter was probably the last of the great dissenters. Born in a small, rural northern California hamlet, he worked his way through law school and ultimately became district attorney of Redding, California, where, in the words of one of the natives, he was "rough on the innocent and hell on the guilty." But if he was a tough prosecutor in a tough community of lumberjacks and mountain people, he was also a tough fighter for the rights of the common man. When he became a member of the Supreme Court he developed into what one political writer described as "the dissentingest dissenter that ever dissented in California," but much of his unwillingness to conform to the majority must have made sense because of twenty cases that went to the United States Supreme Court bearing his dissenting opinion, all twenty of his judgments were upheld. He was a heller in the field of nonconformance.

It was nonconformance that brought me into his camp as his attorney. Jean and he had purchased a ranch home in the Sleepy Hollow section of Marin County, a deluxe exurbanite region where Republicans are commoner than brunettes in Ethiopia and in which a ranch home usually means a patch of cabbage behind the garage. This hard-nosed Democrat, who sought to accomplish some fairly honest ranching on his 45 acres, as a catharsis for briefs and law books, was at odds with his neighbors from the first. When he attempted to build a reservoir in his canyon, to hold some of the wet-month water over for the dry months, they called it a dam and invoked every agency of government short of the Atomic Energy Commission. It began to look as if they were going to drain his dam over and above his violent protests and by superior force. That was when he retained me.

I had been advised of the situation not only by him but by the front pages of every newspaper in the region. SUPREME COURT JUSTICE MOUNTS GUARD OVER DAM WITH RIFLE. JUSTICE CARTER THREATENS DEPUTY SHERIFFS WITH DEATH. That sort of thing. I hastened up to Sleepy Hollow, hoping to get there before the militia. If I couldn't persuade him to rely upon some crafty legal device that I hadn't yet conceived, I could at least join and reinforce him.

It was late afternoon when I arrived at the Rancho Carter. Gathered at the property line below the justice's acres was a clot of workmen. They were nervously determined, having been advised by the authorities and their superiors that they were on sound legal ground, but it was obvious that they were not *happily* determined. They were just as certain that they were on Justice Carter's ground, that Justice Carter was a pretty good shot, and that Justice Carter would undoubtedly shoot anything or anyone who tampered with Justice Carter's dam, reservoir, private lake or whatever the thing was. Their circumstances could not have been described as pleasant working conditions. They were approaching the actual disassembling of the dam in a gingerly manner.

I mopped my forehead and climbed up to where I could see a lone figure in a leather jacket, levis and a Western hat. He was seated on a fence, cradling a deer gun in his arm. It was clear that the Honorable Jesse Washington Carter was not there to enjoy the sunset.

We exchanged greetings, and he asked me whether I thought I could obtain an injunction against the skulduggery that was about to take place a few hundred feet or so down the wash. I told him that I was sure of it but that it would probably not be accomplished until later that evening or perhaps the following morning. He shook his head unhappily.

"That's too bad," he said. "In the meantime someone may get hurt."

I thought that one over. I could see the headlines.

"I take it that you might use that gun, Jesse."

He nodded.

"I will defend my property from trespass."

"I believe you. And there will be no trespass. I have another arrow for my bow. I will see you for supper."

I walked back down the gulley. The foreman and his crew eyed me despondently.

"He gonna shoot?" asked the foreman.

"As sure as God made little green apples. What is your regular quitting time, you and your gang?"

He brightened up a bit.

"We usually knock off about five."

"Exactly. And it's half-past four at the moment."

There was a brief silence. The foreman looked up at the lone figure seated on the fence.

"I don't like to be too hard on the men. I like to give them a few minutes to wash up, put away their tools, that sort of thing."

"And dust themselves off. Yes, sir! You're a damned good supervisor. Of course, all this would take up about a half an hour?"

"About that."

"So you can knock off right now."

It was refreshing to observe the energy and the pleasant good-will the men put into the business of gathering their tools, washing their hands in the stream, etcetera. The foreman hailed me once more as I started back up the hill.

"You think maybe things might be a little different in the morning?"

"I'm sure of it. I have still another arrow for my bow."

The reference to my archery seemed to puzzle him a bit but he turned and joined his crew. And in this possibly ignoble way did I prevent the Battle of Sleepy Hollow.

By morning I had transformed my other arrow into an injunction and thus safeguarded the judge's territorial inviolability as well as the bodily safety of one very anxious work crew. The injunction was very properly granted on the ground that the problem was state and not county business. The State of California wasn't interested in molesting its most unusual and unpredictable Supreme Court Justice, and the minor damage that had emanated from the little reservoir was promptly handled through insurance, without need for further action at the local level.

Much petty feudalizing, accomplished improperly with the aid of biased or self-interested local officials, might routinely be negated in this way if a determination of jurisdiction and authority were made at the outset. However, in this case there was a serious aftermath to the wretched back-fence acrimony involved. Shortly thereafter, Justice Carter died of a heart attack. His widow is convinced that the seizure was a direct development of the fight pressed upon him by his neighbors and their abetting friends in official circles. His son, my friend Oliver Carter, graces the Federal Court bench.

And now, just a few years later, this charming woman sat with me in my office, and when our business was concluded we compared pungent, robust memories of her late husband. As she arose to depart she asked me about two large bronze mementoes which always intrigue my visitors, as they are intended to do. Both of them call attention to my obvious worth as a lawyer and a human being. One is a parchment scroll presented to me by the American Bible Society, and the other is a bronze plaque engraved with praise of the Master over the name of Dolly Fine, one of San Francisco's most unforgettable madams. Their propinquity gives me infinite pleasure.

Mrs. Carter enjoyed this, too, and so I conducted her on a tour of other pleasantly gained and treasured memorabilia of San Francisco's and my past. The beautifully mounted bronze doorknob from the old Hall of Justice, the county seal on its front almost erased by the grasp of countless hands, the inscription below reading: TO MY FRIEND, JAKE EHRLICH, THIS KNOB FROM THE OLD HALL, WORN SMOOTH BY YOUR CLIENTS ON THEIR WAY OUT over the name of Assistant Deputy Chief of Police Al Arnaud, probably one of the greatest and most learned cops San Francisco has ever known. And the original lock, plus its key, to the old Spanish cell block at San Quentin, presented to me by that penitentiary's warden, Fred Dickson. Dickson is a personal friend and a good, practical humanitarian in a field too full of visionary "correctionologists," and he is now chairman of California's Adult Authority, the agency which decides when and how prisoners should be released on parole.

Directly across from my desk and on a mahogany foundation far firmer than many of those upon which it so often finds its base, is a rather large and almost lifelike figure of justice—a sexy bit of statuary. The mammary glands are Lollobrigidian, the legendary sword of justice is strategically placed to please the pure of heart, and the most substantial garment worn by the lady is the traditional blindfold. This was a gift from my previously mentioned landlord, Louis R. Lurie, whose tongue is so firmly and continually in his cheek that I sometimes wonder how he handles his meals. I keep the statuette in full view at all times, to remind myself that justice is at its best when hampered by an absolute minimum of obscuring garment.

Along with the usual cups and gavels and plaques (and even a trophy attesting to my sartorial preeminence that I find extremely useful as a hatrack, there is a twelve-foot bull-whip atop the piece of furniture which becomes a bar after 6 P.M. There are those who profess to believe that the bull-whip is used on clients who fail to produce a substantial retainer immediately, but this is of course absurd. Actually the whip was acquired a few years ago in a Tia Juana saloon. An undesirable citizen was amusing himself by flicking its knotted tip at the posteriors of the gathered celebrants, among whom some friends and I were numbered. I laid this character to rest and requisitioned the whip. Fistic decisions as conclusive as this come rarely these days—at least as far as my international record is concerned—so I treasure the trophy.

I found my attractive tourist still willing, so I took her farther afield in the exploration of my memory-filled offices. In the law library there are affectionately inscribed photographs of a myriad of other wonderful, colorful people whose lives have touched mine in professional or sentimental ways. My colleagues, Jerry Geisler, for instance, and Bill O'Dwyer of New York, Tom Loan, Mel Belli of Dallas fame, the unforgettable Dudley Field Malone and—of course—those two peerless defenders of the hapless downtrodden, Raymond Burr and Edmond O'Brien.

From the entertainment world there are Bing, Tyrone Power, Marie "the Body" McDonald, Marlene Dietrich, and poor Billie Holliday in the "Good morning, Judge" stance with me beside her, Gene Krupa in the same melancholy pose, and James Mason, Bill Dozier, Gary Copper . . . the list is long. From the world of sweat and resin there are Willie Ritchie, Bermondsey Billie Wells, Maxie Rosenbloom, Tom Sharkey, Joe Benjamin, and of course Jack Dempsey.

And there is also John C. Houlihan, one of my proteges, now Mayor of one of California's large cities, Oakland. And Morris

Weisberger, president of the Sailors Union of the Pacific. He can, and has, stopped the sailing of every ship on the Pacific Ocean—greater sea-faring power hath no man. And there is Russell L. Wolden, City and County Tax Assessor. I managed his father's campaign for the same office in 1926. Also there is Francis W. Mayer, Chief Assistant District Attorney of San Francisco County.

Other portraits we examined together were: the columnist, Cobina Wright; motion picture script writer Tony McCarthy; columnist for the Los Angeles *Herald-Examiner,* Bill Kennedy; Mike Connolly, syndicated columnist; Edward B. Dienstag, my chief assistant in the operation of the Saints and Sinners Milk Fund; Howard J. McGrath—now practicing law in Washington D.C., with Peyton Ford—was Governor of Rhode Island, United States Senator, and later Attorney General of the United States; Dorothy Manners; Harold Zellerbach of the Crown-Zellerbach financial empire; and the beautiful Nancy Cooke DeHerrera Jackson.

There are few newcomers in this gallery of men and women with whom I have shared mutual affection, admiration and respect; particularly few from the realm of contemporary politics. Here, as in boxing, where I find no real heavyweights to admire since Dempsey and Baer, the faces of the friends that peer down from my walls are of vintage excellence: San Francisco's wonderfully picaresque Jim Rolph, who ran the town when I was trying to get my feet on the first rungs of the ladder; Herbert Lehman, one of the relatively unsung political giants of his time; and Alfred E. Smith, the nation's last victim at the hands of the religious bigots. No portraits of latter-day political messiahs frown or simper or stare down from my walls. As with the precursors of Dempsey and Baer, none of them have made the grade.

But the gem of my collection is a short letter. It speaks simply and sincerely and with respect and admiration of something I did as a lawyer. It is signed by Chief Justice Earl Warren, whom I have known since he was a tough, working district attorney across San Francisco Bay, in Oakland. I showed it to

Justice Carter's widow and told her that in the real essentials Warren is the same sort of jurist that Jesse had been. She nodded with understanding.

"They were at opposite ends of the poles in some respects, Jake, but they thought alike where the rights of the individual were concerned. The Chief Justice is no mealy mouthed conformer, either."

"Conformer!" I said. "Hell, he might even have *helped* Jesse defend that reservoir."

8: *Morning*

9 A.M.

Agenda: Mrs. Monica Smith
Daughter of V. McN. (Murder One, charged)

The big chimes that sound from the clock of the Pacific National Bank had barely reached the ninth stroke when Mrs. Smith was ushered in and seated in my visitor's chair. She was tense, carefully controlled, working-class respectable, and somewhere between young and not so young any more. Or perhaps she had been young until the day before yesterday when her father had terminated the existence of a fellow cab driver at a Potrero district saloon.

The French have a useful phrase, *déjà vu,* meaning the feeling of having gone through a specific situation before, and this is what I felt as Mrs. Smith told her father's story in tight, disconnected, embarrassed little phrases, without real hope of help or realistic understanding of the true plight. I looked at a different face and heard a different name and a different story, but there was the same anxious searching of my expression for some indication of my thoughts, the same small evasions of ugly truth, the same red eyelids and cotton-dry mouth, the same bottom-of-the-heart fear that I and later the press and still later the court and the jury and the world might not understand that *this* very special murderer was quite different from all other murderers. All these seemed like never-changing factors in an often played scene.

Only that part of the familiar drama that concerns money offers the alternative of difference. If my prospective client is financially sound, rich, or able to obtain the funds with which to pay for a homicide that he has carelessly or self-indulgently committed, the sky is the limit as far as I am concerned when we get to the fee-fixing stage of the interview.

Once when a newspaperman asked me what I regarded as a fair and just fee for a defense against a charge of first-degree murder, I spelled out my answer. "E-V-E-R-Y-T-H-I-N-G," I told him, and I meant it then and now. There are few if any services within human experience so valuable to the recipient as those which snatch him from certain and violent death. There is no treasure even remotely as priceless as exemption from an otherwise enforced one-way trip to the little green octagon in which the State of California erases those sentenced to death under Murder One. In such cases, and when I think that the circumstances warrant it, I ask for and get every dollar, diamond, deed and dividend that the candidate for extinction possesses. And he or she is still getting a glittering bargain, for reasons that should be crystal clear within the telling of these next several major murder cases.

This is not to say that I accept none but the $50,000 and $100,000 fees with which the press is so fond of crediting me. I have defended judges and other attorneys and police officers without fee because I regard this as a responsibility to my own kind and to the personnel of the agencies with which I work. Men and women whose characters I have admired and with whose motivation I have sympathized I have represented without cost to them when their inability to get up the money would have put them in the hands of amateurs. And still others, worthy people who could pay but modest amounts but whose faith in me appealed to my heart or my egotism or both, I have surprised by accepting their small fees along with their sometimes heartbreaking faith in my ability.

In this category fell the case involving the man whose daughter sat across from me this morning, trying to hold back her tears and twisting a leaf of Kleenex into shreds. It was clear to me that her father was no more a premeditated murderer than was the Archbishop of San Francisco. I told Mrs. Smith that I had already come to this conclusion and planned to appear for her father at the Hall of Justice at 10:30 A.M. when his preliminary hearing was being held. Miraculously, she turned into a pretty young woman again right in front of my eyes, thanked me with refreshing brevity and fine Mission District dignity, and departed with head up and heels clicking with a proper feminine briskness.

The defense of persons accused of murder has always fascinated me. Unlike the other crimes on the calendar of antisocial behavior, it is an offense of which any human being alive might conceivably find himself or herself charged. There is no one who is immune from pulling the plug on his fellow man, given the right stimulus under the right circumstances at the right time and place.

Larceny requires a larcenous heart, of which I believe there are actually and relatively rather few. Trafficking in dope is alien to all but the ill, and rape is a crime (often a spurious one) that is obviously open to one half of the population at most and which clearly becomes less necessary with the advancing times. Bigamy is certainly limited to fools, and kidnaping to subconsciously motivated suicides. But murder is everyone's unplanned and uncontemplated crime of perhaps the next moment. Just let a condition of lowered resistance, plus a bad headache or a hangover or a lost job or a handy weapon, coincide with the wrong epithet from a neighbor or an interrupted clandestine rendezvous or a nagging wife or a lying husband, and you—Mr. Average Citizen—find yourself signing a statement down at Homicide and mumbling nonsense about how everything suddenly went black.

Murder is the most democratic of crimes. I have defended more than one hundred persons for this "most dreadful of offenses." Most of these accused killers were housewives, actresses, society women, insurance brokers, musicians and—in the parlance of the underworld—ordinary square Johns. Only one was a professional murderer. This gentleman, incidentally, was not convicted of any of the many murders he committed.

In the early days of my practice I found myself involved in a number of murder defenses that wound up rather curiously. One of these concerned a young Italian boy who will be Luigi B. Nameless, for the sake of the narrative, because he ultimately matured into a sound and respectable resident of the town's ultra-Italian North Beach area.

Luigi had been balling it up at a now famous and fashionable establishment called Mike's Pool Room, in the Broadway and Kearny quadrant. Mike's is of bistro status today and caters mostly to the smart set. In those days it was a dump. Although Prohibition was still in effect at the time, whisky was easier to get at Mike's than a punch on the nose, which could also be widely available there.

Luigi had been leaning heavily on the bottle. So had another customer, a pharmacist from nearby San Jose who was a proud veteran of World War I. Customer Number Two's name was Jackson, and Mr. Jackson was indulging in the not uncommon barside recreation of passing remarks at the expense of the military prowess of Italian troops involved in the late war. Considering the somewhat over-Latin flavor of the immediate community, this might have been regarded as indiscreet. Luigi, well snockered and ardently Italian, had taken the matter up with him.

Jackson threatened to defeat Luigi decisively in combat and was promptly thrown out of the establishment. Luigi upbraided the proprietor for not having accorded *him* this honor, and was himself thrown out into the night.

A short time later Jackson was found face down in a neighboring gutter. He was dead. The police questioned all hands at Mike's Pool Room, put two and two together, and found that it added up to Luigi B. Nameless. They arrested him, charged him with murder, and his family called me.

I made his acquaintance at the preliminary hearing and found him to be a surly, belligerent, tough-Tony type. He didn't know nothin' about nothin'! After being thrown out of Mike's he'd gone straight home and right to bed. "You do the rest, Counselluh! Earn yuh money!"

The prosecutor related the facts as he—or the police—knew them. I had nothng to say. Luigi was held to answer, which meant that he was bound over for consideration of his case by the grand jury and probable trial in superior court, the evidence having been deemed sufficient for such action.

"Hey, you! Hey, you . . . Jake Ehrlich!"

It was my client, hailing me from as far as his handcuffs would stretch from the sheriff's wrist. I gave him an icy stare. There's nothing in the rules that says you have to *like* a client.

"Whassa mattuh! You din' say nuttin!"

I said something.

"You button your lip and get back to that cell!"

He looked as if he'd just learned that Santa Claus was a police sergeant.

We went to trial before Superior Court Judge Robert McWilliams, whom I knew to be a good, solid lawyer and an unlikely man to accept anything less than the real legal McCoy from those before him. I waited until the jury was impaneled and then I addressed the Court.

"If Your Honor pleases, I would like to offer this transcript of the preliminary hearing before the district attorney makes his opening statement."

I laid a transcript upon the bench and received the cold, suspicious stare I'd anticipated.

"This comes too late, Mr. Ehrlich. It should have been presented before the defendant pleaded 'not guilty.' "

"I respectfully submit that justice is more important than

formality, Your Honor. This is a mere four pages. It will take only a minute. Sixty seconds."

He accepted it and I knew the cake was baked. He started shaking his head before he reached the end of Page One. The state did not have a case. It had a corpse and at least 5,000 Italians who might have taken exception to Jackson's propaganda line. But had I exposed the weakness of this pasted-together batch of circumstantial nonevidence at the preliminary hearing, the police and the district attorney's office might have gone to work on the job of putting together a better case and possibly produced one. Now, with the jury impaneled and a higher court hearing well underway, Luigi could never be tried again if Judge McWilliams would only toss out the ad-libbed botch of rumor and hearsay with which he was confronted; the element of double jeopardy completely precluded such a possibility.

The judge read the transcript to its last word, then tossed it back to me.

"It will not be necessary for you to make any motion, Mr. Ehrlich. The charge against the defendant is dismissed. The jury is discharged. Clerk, call the next case!"

My client accosted me in the corridor outside the courtroom. He was still truculent and wild-eyed.

"Hey, Counselluh! For all that money my family paid, don't I get no jury trial?"

Another case of about the same time and in the same district had a somewhat different and more satisfying pay-off.

This incident in applied violence took place at the establishment of Isadore Gomez, an illegal refreshment center of Pacific Street on the eastern slope of Nob Hill. In those earlier days in San Francisco, this thoroughfare was Pacific Street until it reached Van Ness Avenue; Pacific Avenue from thence westward. The eastward strip enjoyed the presence of pimps, prostitutes and barkeeps, while the western, or avenue, end housed only the residences of the rich and respectable. Thus when a certain rather pompous society woman of the period high-toned a department store sales clerk with an airy order to charge her merchandise to "my residence on Pacific," the latter pseudo-naively squelched her with the question: "Street or avenue, ma'am?"

The Casa Izzy Gomez was probably the most famous San Francisco speakeasy of its time. Large, crummy, amiable of atmosphere and completely without any of the furtive clandestinity of most of the town's Prohibition joints, it was patronized by every kind and type of local resident from bank presidents to bank robbers.

Gomez himself was an enormous Portuguese gentleman of infinite bootlegging and gambling skill, who took a dim view of sanitation, small dogs and customers who objected to jelly glasses as drinking vessels. I know that he was once bitten by a small dog, but I have no way of accounting for the other two bigotries. Never since the beginning of his time in San Francisco (and it was rumored that he had landed in a galleon with the original Spanish explorers) had anyone ever seen him unhatted. And never had he been known to forget the face of a customer, except in one instance that was extremely advantageous to me and to my client, whose name will not appear in this account, and not because he developed into such an exemplary citizen but because he didn't. I have no desire to add to his present burdens.

On this occasion there had been a rather serious conflict in one of the shadowy corners at Izzy's, and an immediate evacuation of all those present down a narrow stairway leading from the second floor to Pacific Street. Thoughtlessly, the suddenly galvanized refugees had left behind them and under a table the limp body of one of their erstwhile friends.

When the police arrived, they searched the area thoroughly, looking past, over and around the liquid merchandise as they did so, and came up with an overcoat. The label sewn in its pocket gave the name and address of the man who was to become my client, and the cops were able to come up with fair-to-middling proof of ill will between him and the gentleman on the floor. They pinched him, and he called me before his name was dry on the blotter.

I wasn't able to do much about the coat, but fortunately I was able to chat with Izzy promptly and pleasantly. I explained the risk and inconvenience that lay ahead for the defendant in case someone was able to place him at the scene that night. Things indeed might go badly for him.

"In that case I didn't ever see him," said Izzy, squashing a cockroach with a sidewise motion of one of his size twelves.

"In fact, you have a phenomenal memory for faces and you would certainly have recognized him had he been there, yet he's a perfect stranger to you. Is that right?"

"You mean this guy I never ever seen? Right. He's a perfect stranger. But what the hell you gonna do about that benny with the moniker in it?"

I told him I'd think of something and started down the stairs. Creasing his belly over the top bannister, he called to me.

"About that guy I never ever seen, Master . . . I don't know how it happen that he's got a four-seventy-five drink tab against him on the books. . . ."

I settled the bill.

As to the coat. Bail was granted at the preliminary hearing, and then a certain amount of informality prevailed following adjournment and the departure of the judge. As we arose to leave the courtroom I noticed that the mooted overcoat lay carelessly tossed across one of the counsel tables, labeled only with a police property clerk's tag and as yet not admitted as evidence for the prosecution. It was a bitterly cold day. My client casually and in the most natural manner possible climbed into the state's only real piece of evidence against him, thoughtfully tucked the property clerk's tag out of sight, and strolled through the courtroom door promptly. After all, the recovery of a man's own property is no larceny.

Between Izzy's inability to recall the guy he'd "never ever seen" and the curious enigma of the mislaid overcoat, the state's case tended to dwindle and wither and undergo postponements. A dismissal was finally granted, but then it was spring and my client and I attended the final hearing. He was coatless, the weather being fine. He rarely wears an overcoat these days and never, *ever,* is his name found in the pocket.

When Izzy Gomez passed on a few years later and was honored with a mass funeral that a movie star would have envied, I attended. I had a forked purpose, as the Indians put it. I not only came to pay my final respects to a colorful San Franciscan; I also wanted to verify the rumor that he was to be coffined with his hat on his head. No one will ever really know whether this actually happened, because Izzy was interred with his hole card covered, as it were, but the graveside odds were six-two-and-even in favor of Gomez ascending or descending toward the hereafter with his hat firmly jammed on his head.

Requiescat in pace, cum Stetsonis!

9: *Morning*

9:30 A.M.

Agenda: President of S.F. Police Officers Assn.

Ray White, the elected head of the policemen's association, showed up five minutes early with a casual, "Howdy, Jake!" a friendly peek into Dullea's office and a dour shake of his head as he settled into a chair and lit a cigar. The cops were having their headaches these days.

I enjoy my legal representation of the police organization. I like and admire most of the officers with whom or against whom I've worked throughout the years. I regard the department as a most vigorous and vital organ of government, and I find it interesting and challenging to be involved in its official life. As clients, the cops are a wonderful catharsis for the smug conservatism of some of my stuffier clients, intriguing contrast to some of the lawbreakers whose interests I handle, and entertaining company when the liquor and the stories flow.

The police were unhappy this morning and with cause. San Francisco, in common with most American cities, has been suffering the kind of growing pains that fall within the category of civil rights strife. Picketing, sit-ins, shop-ins and mass demonstrations of various kinds have been occurring in every possible public and commercial establishment and as an added feature to every parade, celebration, and ceremonial arrival of distinguished visitors.

Personally I have excellent reason to support and defend the rights of minorities and was doing so when many of today's sidewalk liberals and do-gooders thought the Fourteenth Amendment was a rule governing Rose Bowl selections. Without fee I've handled cases involving civil rights deprival, and without support from multi-initialed organizations I've lighted roaring fires under reactionary persons and agencies whose indifference or callousness nourished those deprivals. But in common with many minority-belonging, minority-minded and minority-understanding citizens who fought for these ideals when the issues were clear and equitable, I am beginning to look at the ineffectual, hate-breeding demonstrations that are taking place around me with doubt, resentment and a genuine sympathy for the intelligent minority members who must now be desperately searching for some new and less violently assisted minority to join.

In the first place, despite the fact that it had no acquaintance with more than a relatively microscopic group of Negroes prior to the nineteen forties and no consequent skill at dealing with them, San Francisco has been fair and generous to its exploding population of outlanders. Secondly, the Negroes have been and are being fitted into the economy, into the schools and into housing, as speedily as good intent and constant effort can accomplish this herculean feat. Third, informed information indicates that a substantial percentage of the troublemaking and property-destroying demonstrations that fester in our streets have been stimulated and carried out by white persons; adolescents who would be quickly transported to Juvenile Hall were they to perform the same nuisances without the protection of "a cause"; neurotics who now have a channel for unhealthy energies; young hoodlums whose natural inclination to boot policemen in the groin may now be safely exercised in the name of saving mankind. A dubious advantage lies in the fact that less hubcaps are being stolen on demonstration nights.

This sounds like bitterness. To any such charge I plead guilty and call the first witness for the defense; the average San Francisco police officer, who must have prototypes all over the country. He now qualifies as a member of an underprivileged minority; an underdog with a cause for which it is currently unliberal and unpopular and even un-American to offer a defense. But minorities and underdogs have always appealed to me, and I undertake the representation gleefully, feeling that my long-held status as a defender of the have-nots is being usurped by today's imposters of liberalism—the bogus civil-righters.

It was this odorous and nearly unsolvable mess that had brought the head of the San Francisco Police Officers Association into my office that morning, and I invited him to get it off his chest.

"Last night's riot at the Sheraton-Palace was just about the end, Jake," he said. "The hotel requested protection, and an injunction against entering the premises was obtained. We were there in force, not because we wanted to be but because we were sent. The hotel refused to permit arrests, however, and the mob quickly took over. Naturally we were their prime targets as soon as they found out that we were only present to model our uniforms and smile prettily when insulted. I saw scores of violations of city ordinances and had to look the other way. Because they weren't disturbing the peace at all, these clowns; they were ushering in a new era of equality for man."

"The same thing happened to the cops in Munich about thirty years ago," I told him. "The louts who threw beer glasses at the policemen along the Karlsplatz weren't breaking the law. They were just ushering in a new era of National Socialism, and it was regarded as un-German to interfere with the bastards. Tell me the rest of it."

"Well, the men are pretty fed up with the uselessness of their presence at such brawls if police work is not their reason for being there. They feel that it cancels out the authority and dignity of the badge. As experienced working cops, they figure that smiling at trouble now will only lead to heavier trouble next time. Heavier trouble means injured cops and tougher arrests when people finally get fed up and request a little paddy-wagon action. So we want the association to act for us. We'd like someone to either let us work as cops and enforce the law or put our spare uniforms on clothing dummies for these demonstrations, order us out of the region of the picket parade for the duration, and let us catch a burglar or two in the meantime in the name of the civil rights of the average citizen."

There was only one thing to do in the face of such an appeal. I called recently elected Mayor John F. Shelley, I called Police Chief Thomas Cahill, and I called the editors of the San Francisco *News-Call,* the San Francisco *Chronicle* and the San Francisco *Examiner.* In the name of 1,800 right and irate police officers, I told them that the letter of the law must be upheld according to an oath of office which the mayor and the chief of police shared with these officers, that a lawbreaking crusader for the rights of man was no different from a lawbreaking burglar, banker or bishop, and that each should be arrested and jailed as soon as observed in commission of his crime; that the penalty to the community for by-passing such responsibilities might easily be the destruction of the morale of its police department—something to really think about.

The response was immediate and dynamic. Coldly impersonal arrests were made at subsequent demonstrations. The presiding judge of the municipal courts issued a statement to the press that a lawbreaking picket arrested meant a lawbreaking picket prosecuted; that career lawbreaking pickets would be released only upon posting a bond of $500; that no lawbreaking picket would again be released on his own recognizance. The chief of police announced the training and creation of an elite police corps for the control of out-of-hand demonstrations. And the newspapers took a considerably less indulgent news and editorial tone in dealing with the strange army of invaders who'd been defying the police, arrogantly taking over private property, and perverting the Constitutional safeguards to the uses of blackmail. I felt good about human responses in San Francisco again. It could let broadmindedness become folly and stretch patience into self-imposition, but it's a town that has no taste for being made a fool of in the name of moral reform and good works. Even the famed Vigilantes were eventually chased out of town.

My espousal of the cause of policemen in trouble is no new thing with me. It goes back to November of 1935 when a big, beefy, almost bald German-American named Henry Ludolph walked into my office. He stood over my desk and noisily cracked his enormous knuckles. He was the picture of misery.

"He's trying to get me," he said.

"Who?" I asked, not a little jarred by the bone-cracking gambit. *"Who's* trying to get you?"

"That man, Atherton," said Ludolph.

Now I *was* interested. I knew about Edwin N. Atherton. He was the head of a private investigating firm which had just contracted with the city to probe its vice status—for $100,000. I offered my caller a chair.

Henry Ludolph was a lieutenant at the Harbor Police Station and a former heavyweight boxer. The Harbor station is located in the center of San Francisco's maritime district, where physical prowess is of far greater use to a policeman than forensic skill or criminological lore, and Lieutenant Ludolph had a well-earned reputation for being able to coax the most recalcitrant seaman or longshoreman to abandon hostilities and return to propriety with a minimum of exertion. He also possessed a reputation for being extremely conservative. Where the spending of money was concerned, Ludolph suffered from chronic constipation. His frugality, plus various investments and windfalls, had enabled him to amass a fortune of $50,000. If the word fortune brings a smile in connection with this figure, remember that I speak of the early thirties when $50,000 (according to Department of

Commerce statistics) was the average citizen's average income for about 22 years, 10 months and 18 days. Had Ludolph's investments not been sound and his windfalls substantial, he might have had to forego such minor necessities as food and clothing in the amassing of this obvious eagle's nest egg. It is enough to say that Ludolph was—as cops went in 1933—a fat cat. The salary of a San Francisco police lieutenant then was $250 a month. I asked my visitor for a breakdown of his phenomenal substance.

"I started out with a pretty good stake," he said. "On July four, nineteen-oh-eight, when I'm a young cop, I get a chance to bet on Battling Nelson against Joe Gans. The odds is two and a half to one and I take the Swede for two hundred and fifty dollars. I won. I got a stake."

This had been a quarter of a century before, and I didn't ask any questions about how a greenhorn harness bull could have put his hands on $250 for a pugilistic wager, but the odds were good considering that Nelson chilled Gans in the seventeenth round and should have done it earlier according to the experts.

"From then on I guess I was just lucky," continued the big lieutenant, punctuating his word with knuckle cracks. "Lucky but careful. I bet on the horses when I get sure things. I make little investments where I can't lose. And I don't throw my money around like some of these knuckleheads around me. And I'm a family man; I never blew no money on the hotsy-totsies."

I knew for sure that no one had ever accused Ludolph of being a good-time Charley. I asked him about the little presents and the sealed envelopes that so often seem to come a policeman's way. He went off like a Roman candle.

"I'm as clean as a whistle or I wouldn't come to you," he shouted at me, apparently overlooking the fact that most people who came to me were popularly supposed to do so for quite a different reason. "There are nothing but fifty-cent bookmakers on the waterfront. What would I do with petty larceny pikers like them! I tell you I never took a nickel of graft in my life."

It wasn't the nickels I was thinking about, and both of us knew that there's plenty to be done with, for and from fifty-cent bookmakers, providing they book enough fifty-cent bets, but the man's indignation was impressive and I was already picturing him on the witness stand. He'd play better than Barrymore. The faint sauerkraut tinge to his accent wouldn't do him any harm, either. I asked what Atherton claimed to actually have on him, aside from the fact of his great riches.

"He claims I been collecting. For me, for the mayor's last campaign, for the organization; all that kind of crud," he replied dolefully. "He wants I should put the finger on *everyone;* on the other guys in the business; on the guys he claims are gambling; on the McDonough Brothers, even."

So this was the prelude to the first skirmish in the great civic war that was to transform San Francisco. It was the first gestative spasm of the borning San Francisco that would gleefully clip its own umbilical cord at the climax of the natal struggle, disowning its allegorical mother—unbridled license; and its father—organized graft. And to a very great extent the birth would be midwifed by a neither ultramoral nor reform-minded lawyer named Ehrlich.

Psychologically, the key to the state of mind of most cops regarding extracurricular fringe benefits is contained in a phrase that Ludolph had just used to me and which most policemen used in referring to the job of being employed by the San Francisco Police Department. They never described it as being "on the force," as they do in New York City, or "in the department" or "in the cops" or any of the other commonplaces pertaining elsewhere. Their term for being a policeman was being "in the business," meaning only and exclusively "in the business of being a San Francisco policeman," with all of the commercial and other special connotations that go with that phrase. It was as subconscious a usage as it was significant; Freudian, the experts might label it.

There was no question that graft on a large and well-organized scale existed, flourished and excluded all competition or free enterprise. The only question and wonder is how the occasional honest officer—and there was a large minority of these—managed to survive in this barrel of bad apples.

The reasons why the grafters flourished so long and so openly were peculiarly San Franciscan. Always a robust-minded town, San Francisco had convinced itself that vice was a necessary evil. There were many, as a matter of fact, who weren't nearly as convinced that it was as evil as they were that it was necessary. All were aware, however, that the police were not exactly overpaid, but most assumed that they were able to pick up enough extra money here and there to subsidize the deficit between what they received and what it took to support them and their families. Naturally the sophisticated assumed that this deficit was being rightly and appropriately defrayed by those for whom the cops did favors. No harm done, less taxes to pay by the solid citizen, and no injury to the city's moral values if one can manage to mentally look the other way and think about it as little as possible.

The direct beneficiaries of this civic sophistry were two brothers named McDonough, Tom and Pete. The McDonoughs were nominally bail bond brokers, but like icebergs, they kept most of their size, weight and substance well submerged. Tammany never ran New York City as completely as the McDonoughs ran the right to break the law in San Francisco and to peddle licenses, franchises, subcontracts and short- or long-term privilege.

From their scrubby little office at Clay and Kearny streets, close enough to the Hall of Justice for the chief to wince if Pete McDonough raised his voice in anger, these Argus-eyed, squid-handed brothers supervised the many-splendored night life of San Francisco. They kept an eye on the nightly take of every hustling girl on Eddy Street, knew to the dollar how much Russian Mike or Bones Remmer or Eddie Sahati folded into their pockets after a night's play, and had the drawings on any burglary, con-game or safeblowing that happened *before* it happened—or it *didn't* happen.

The McDonoughs had lawyers and courtroom fixes—in all price categories—for sale. They created judges and uncreated them. They got city and county ordinances passed, defeated, amended and shelved. They bankrolled madams and assigned territories to bootleggers. They provided protection for pimps, dice hustlers, bookmakers, pickpockets, after-hours operators, lamsters and every stripe of fast-money specialist. They eliminated competition for their clients and acted as clearing house, chancellery and postoffice for the underworld. They performed special and vital functions at election time and they served as fiduciary agents for statesmen too high up to stoop to face-to-face collections. And . . . oh yes, they provided bail bonds.

I had always regarded the McDonoughs as lice and leeches on the body politic. My reasons were not entirely pious. To a much lesser and more scrupulous degree, certain branches of great political machines have been performing similar services of privilege distribution and unofficial licensing for many, many years, but I have been unable to feel moral outrage about their wheelings and dealings, because of the *quid pro quo* nature of these well-known and commonly accepted machinations. Patronage and favors for the politically loyal are deep in the American tradition whether they be right, wrong or in accordance with the purest civic ideals. The McDonoughs, however, didn't merely wheel and deal, they sold and extorted, threatened, reprised, ruined and destroyed.

Often they had approached me with offers, cases, clients or glittering propositions. Often these pitches came at a time when I could well have used them, especially during the earlier years of my practice, but I had turned them all down. I had no qualms of conscience about trying to make a deuce in the hole appear to be an ace in my legal practice of the time (or now, if necessary), but I drew the line at playing in the kind of a game where my deuce might miraculously become an ace, with a little help from the McDonoughs.

The other new character in the cast of this real-life drama was Ludolph's apparent Nemesis, Investigator Atherton.

In order to best understand how Atherton joined the cast or ever arrived in San Francisco (he was a denizen of Los Angeles), it becomes necessary for me to introduce Princess Kamokila, who had been a client of mine.

Ordinarily one is privileged to run into a lady like Princess Kamokila not more than once in a lifetime. Ordinarily this is enough.

The Princess was strictly hundred-proof royalty; half of her at least, and it would have been difficult to decide which half, as all of her was equally attractive. Her mother had been Princess Kuaihelana of Hawaii's royal ruling house, and her father was James Campbell, a ten-millionaire sugar and pineapple king.

If the Princess, who called herself Mrs. Alice Campbell in her less regal moments, was comely and charming, she was also a little strange and naive in respect to non-Polynesian ways. Her life in San Francisco was complicated, unpredictable and insensate in a daffy, feminine sort of way.

She was a great admirer of vocal music, especially her own, so she decided to open a night club featuring herself and her singing. Prohibition was on its way out and the Princess expected to cash in on this new development, although the procedures for conversion from speakeasy drinking to more open public entertainment had not been accomplished and no one was sure what was legal and what was not.

Her establishment was called the Club Kamokila, and she had located it in what had been the basement Sunday School of a defunct Methodist church on downtown Bush Street, a thoroughfare known as Lysol Alley. The number of young ladies who lived there made their livings—as the idiom of the time had it—"the best way they knew how." The Club Kamokila's former churchly atmosphere had been well disguised with palm fronds, coconuts and art studies of grass-skirted ladies, as well as pictures of Diamond Head and Waikiki, and the lights had been turned down and nearly out. There were abundant soft music and hard drinks, and many of the young ladies from the nearby apartments no longer had to risk pneumonia and police attention on the damp Powell Street pavements.

The Princess came to see me early in her career as a dispenser of Hawaiian hospitality.

"Jake, I want to run a lively place," she said, with all the sophistication of a ten-year-old who announces that she intends to make mud pies, "and I expect to pay my way. Who are the people who usually get paid?"

I told her about the McDonough brothers but I also told her she'd be foolish to pay off simply because others did. I advised her to meet only her legitimate bills and to stay away from matters where cash-and-carry "juice" was required. If they attempted to squeeze her I'd take them on. I welcomed a chance to get a handhold on the McDonoughs, and twist.

Although the Princess quickly fulfilled her plan to "run a lively place," it wasn't the city machine that got to her first. It was ASCAP, the organization which collects royalties for the commercial rendition of the music written by its composer members. They claimed she'd been singing a number entitled "You're Gonna Lose Your Gal" without fee payment, and they made it clear that she was going to lose her club if it continued. We settled that one.

The next night the police came. Making as noisy and disturbing an event of it as possible, they arrested her manager and a bartender for violation of the Wright Act— California's own version of the Volstead Act and a law now negated by repeal. When the matter came to court I had it dismissed. I did a little personal research on the situation at the same time and found that not one other drinking establishment in San Francisco had been so harassed. "They" were working Alice in Blunderland over. And me, by indirection.

Then there were complaints from the neighbors. People who had made no outcry at having their Sunday morning slumbers violated by "Nearer My God to Thee" found nightly versions of "The Cockeyed Mayor of Kaunakakai" on the steel guitar more than they could bear. Softer instruments were found.

Then the police came again. It turned out that my lovely *wahine* client had neglected to get a dance hall license. She applied for one. They were back with other complaints and finally wound up by stationing what promised to be a permanent uniformed detail at the doorway of the club. To my mind, the fine Hibernian hand of the McDonoughs was now clearly involved, and I went to bat and got the police guard removed. The captain in command at Central Station, who was indeed a very great and good friend of the McDonoughs, burst into the pages of the San Francisco *Examiner* with a statement.

"The Kamokila Club is a dive and one of the worst in San Francisco. This woman is not fooling anyone with this society bull. I'm going to close the place every night." His official report to the chief said about the same thing, adding only some surmisals as to the activities of unescorted lady guests at the club. However, on the basis of the public statement, I filled a $20,000 slander suit, actually a modest foray against the captain's financial resources and one that was based on his known income.

The Princess exploded a small test-size nuclear bomb that shook us all up. With her own lovely hula hands, she made certain cash dispositions and then put in a call to the Hall of Justice. She got Chief William J. Quinn on the phone. She had a perfectly reasonable question. She asked it with her usual naïveté.

"Is a hundred and fifty dollars the right amount to pay six policemen for protection?" she murmured sweetly into the phone, after identifying herself.

After they'd calmed Quinn down, he provided action. He called the captain at Central Station, whose sensitivities had been so offended at the Kamokila Club. He called District Attorney Matt Brady. He called Mayor Angelo Rossi. He called for an immediate investigation—the standard, drearily familiar immediate investigation that is always demanded when the fat falls into the fire.

I phoned the Princess and requested an audience, and she came down to my office. She just couldn't for the life of her understand why she shouldn't have paid the cops and checked on the payment afterward, just to make sure she hadn't been overcharged.

"Yes, and you could have demanded a receipt and a money-back guarantee, too," I said. "What I want to know is where you got the idea and when you stopped taking advice from me?"

She waggled her head mysteriously.

"Well, there was this fellow who knew this automobile salesman who had this friend in the mayor's office. He said I should pay. And after all, it's only money. And he also said that unless I got rid of you I might have problems for a long, long time. He said you were . . . what was it he called you . . . a 'hard-nosed bastard,' and that you wouldn't play ball with the right people."

"You can tell him he's right," I said. "When I play ball, it'll be with the Giants and I'll pitch. And when *you* start playing ball with the right people, Princess, you can turn in your grass skirt and head for the showers as far as I'm concerned. No more ad-libbing or it'll have to be with a new lawyer."

She promised to behave, and we got ready for the next moves from the opposition: those from the Hall of Justice, from Central Station, from the mayor's office, but particularly those from the seamy little office at Kearny and Clay. We weren't kept waiting long. All in one day King Kalakaua's grand-daughter received a subpoena to appear before the Grand Jury, notice that the police commission was temporarily tabling action on the important dance permit, and a telephoned threat against the life of her young daughter, Pineapples McFarland. The Princess acquired a pistol and a bodyguard and restricted young Pineapples to the upper floors of the Fairmont Hotel, where she lived. I concentrated on observing the McDonoughs and found that they were in a remarkably disturbed frame of mind for a set of veteran professionals and that they had taken an extraordinarily dedicated attitude toward the task of ejecting me from the picture. I liked that and planned to make it a contest.

The Grand Jury meeting was largely a standoff. The Princess admitted that she'd made a pay-off but couldn't for the life of her remember whom she'd actually paid off; like Chinese coolies, policemen all looked alike to her. The policemen who might logically have been the ones to have been paid, according to Chief Quinn's still furious cerebrations on the matter, were subpoenaed and questioned under oath but refused to answer the questions and were fired. The friend of the friend of the friend who had advised disbursements from his lofty perch in the mayor's office denied such counsel but admitted that he had suggested "getting rid of Ehrlich." Nothing of interest or of value really happened at the Grand Jury meeting except that an investigation of the Grand Jury itself was initiated.

The upcoming meeting of the police commission was more diverting. It occurred on an evening when Marjorie and I were scheduled to attend a formal party at the Palace Hotel. I was in white tie and tails and saw no reason to hide them because of a brief appearance before a covey of officials who might be critical of such attire. I descended from my car and crossed the sidewalk into the Hall of Justice between the ranks of a hastily drummed-up guard of honor composed of half-schnockered cops and newspapermen who had tumbled wildly out of Cookie Picetti's Star Bar next door upon the announcement of my arrival. An impromptu and spontaneous cheer was wrung from this raucous crew and a speech was demanded, but I pressed relentlessly onward.

The San Francisco *Examiner* described the event with real journalistic fervor: "He rolled up in a black car a half a block long, dressed like a ringmaster for a circus, attended by a South Seas giant and hula dancers."

I don't remember the giant but there *were* some young ladies in the party, borrowed from the Club Kamokila for the evening. Together with my claque and an augmentation from Mr. Picetti's clientele, I entered the room where the board was meeting. Before the president could reach for his gavel I got the floor, and politely acknowledging the presence of all the members, the chief, the deputation from the Star saloon and my entourage, I launched into my statement.

"Careful study of the Constitution convinces me that its provisions and protections extend to people who operate and work in night clubs as well as to runaway Negro slaves, citizens deprived of due process by illegal arrest and seizure, and policemen who invoke the Fifth Amendment when asked delicate questions. Guests of the Kamokila Club have been deprived of the right to the pursuit of happiness, as guaranteed in the Constitution, if their choice of happiness takes the form of disporting themselves to the beat of music—in other words, dancing. All other San Francisco night clubs have dancing and we are going to have dancing, too... beginning tonight. The police have made a circus of Princess Kamokila's attempt to start an honest business in San Francisco, and it is going to have to stop. This is to advise you that the police are going to have to break down the doors of the club if they want to get in from now on."

I departed, leaving behind me a wake of frustration, anti-Ehrlichism and near apoplexy.

There was dancing on that and subsequent nights. The police and even the McDonoughs were temporarily unsure of themselves and did nothing. But the general public was also unsure. It was apparently unsettling to seek pleasure in an establishment in which so many things had happened and could happen again. Business suffered. The Club Kamokila finally closed, a delayed-action victim of the conditions that prevailed. But the unpredictable lady from Honolulu couldn't merely leave town. She called a press conference.

San Francisco was one with Sodom and Gomorrah and up to here in corruption, she said, and it reeked of bought illegalities, official venality and under-the-table deals. This was fine, as unspecifically far as it went, in terms of my personal plans and policy. I was still trying to get a bead on the McDonoughs, but I felt it would lead absolutely nowhere because the fuzzy-minded little lady had no precise information to offer. Where it did lead was to another Grand Jury subpoena.

Now the Princess became coy again and didn't want to attend the party that she had invoked ("They're just trying to entrap me, Jake"), but I convinced her that she should put in an appearance, explaining in some detail the penalties for contempt. She answered the subpoena and murmured a mass of shapeless, faceless generalities that added up to zero. The jury had nothing upon which to base a true bill, although they obviously were convinced that all this smoke meant a little fire. They let her go.

When the press got to her in the corridor, she made a suggestion that wound up on Page One and that ultimately had more effect on the Grand Jury than anything she'd said inside.

"San Francisco is on trial," she declared. "When the community is not courageous it must expect vice and crime. When one has to pay for respectability it does not seem fair. Let all good and patriotic citizens band together, raise a hundred thousand dollars, hire a private investigator and clean up the city."

The little *chanteuse* from Honolulu had just done the most effective singing of her career. The Grand Jury thought it over and finally demanded and got $100,000 with which to hire a private investigator. With this substantial sum they obtained Edwin Atherton, a man who knew precisely what to do with $100,000 and a city that was wide open for a practiced peeper.

The Princess didn't stick around for the fireworks. She suddenly conceived the idea of marrying her voice coach, a gentleman named Blickfelt, and took off for her native Hawaii. When I was last there, visiting in Maui, I heard strange rumblings at night from the big island to the south of us. I was told that they came from the live volcano of Kilauea, but I'm not convinced that this is true. When last heard of, Princess Blickfelt was in that general area.

Investigator Atherton was a man to whom the end justified the means. He cared little where the chips fell—even the human ones—which is how I became involved and why I became as watchful and thoughtful of Atherton as I was of the McDonoughs before the final card was played.

Like a tiger on the prowl, Atherton's spoor and tracks were well in evidence long before he first hove in sight. His technique and subtleties were of the kind developed and esteemed in secret police expertise, and this was indeed only reasonable: he was a former member of the Federal Bureau of Investigation. He didn't interrogate; he insinuated himself into the confidences of those he interviewed, by gentlemanly and even cordial devices. Each gambler or madam or information-laden citizen who afterward came to me professionally, perplexed and troubled about what they might have said that they shouldn't have, told practically the same story. He respected them because they each had the reputation of being the straightest straight shooter in the town. He had no intention of hurting them in any way or bringing about their prosecution or even any cessation in their respective businesses; all he wanted was the higher-ups. I found myself wary of Mr. Atherton and his works very early in his investigation.

It developed that my wariness was justified. He was on the right side in the upcoming purge of San Francisco ills, but he rapidly began to demonstrate that he had no compassion for the little people, the handmaidens and foot soldiers of the System. This substantially affected his rating as a human being in my book, as I regarded many of the proletariat of the vice cosmos as just as much victimized as the public itself. I stubbornly cling to the belief that policemen and lawyers and judges and graft investigators have a vital responsibility to operate first as compassionate human beings and then—if doing so doesn't negate that—in their more professional functions, but in accordance with law and not convenience.

My other reason for taking a dim view of the Atherton investigation was its tendency to find, publicize, prosecute and destroy *a few* of the alleged malefactors, and with the help of easily confected press publicity, to convey to the public the idea that these few were all of the city's underworld and that a great public benefit had thus been wrought. Most reform-labeled civic probes follow the same pattern.

Atherton, a "commercial policeman" who headed a business firm with services to sell for dollars, somehow soon became confused in the minds of the press and public with dedicated, objective, no-ax-to-grind law-enforcement officers. The fallacy of prepaying a peeper-for-profit $100,000 to dig up $100,000 worth of bad news was soon forgotten as Atherton began to submit his reports, his token information, his dreary lists of names and addresses. In time it was almost forgotten that his fearless inquiry was costing the city a lot of money. When he tried to get even more money, he failed to do so, largely—I'm sure—as the result of my efforts to prevent the further bite.

Opening his headquarters in the Keystone Apartments on the west side of Nob Hill, he and his investigators gathered their information by wheedling, flattering, promising, threatening and the oldest and shabbiest police trick of all—turning one man against another by convincing Man Number One that Man Number Two has already talked.

In rather short order Atherton submitted a seventy-page report to the Grand Jury. In it—but only as a conclusion unsupported by evidence—he said that corruption in respect to vice grossed about $1,000,000 yearly in San Francisco. Guessers from the city's sidewalks with about an equal amount of authority to their opinions thought that the figure was nearer $4,000,000, at a minimum, and were sure that gambling alone provided better than $1,500,000, with prostitution coming up with $1,000,000 more and abortion contributing close to $100,000 annually in the surest, most discreet and regular payoff of all. Atherton's report mentioned $400,000 from prostitution but was unable to speak very precisely about the income from abortion.

One hundred and thirty-five houses of prostitution were listed. There would come a day, not far in the future, when I would state in open court that I could stand on the front steps of the Hall of Justice with a handful of buckshot and hit a different bordello with each piece of shot. There were at least 300 operating seraglios in San Francisco at the time. Atherton was able to list about a third of them.

The police, however, were his principal targets—about a hundred of them were mentioned specifically—but the report somehow managed to indirectly smear everyone with a badge, the vast majority of good cops along with the relatively few bad ones. And the McDonoughs were disemboweled without mercy of course. This was the one really useful and substantial product of the investigation. A reporter friend of mine from the *Examiner* stopped me as I was leaving the Hall of Justice after a court appearance and asked if I'd read the portion of the report that dealt with the famed brothers. I hadn't and he gave me the text.

I particularly remember these lines: "McDonough Brothers is willing to interest itself in almost any matter to defeat or circumscribe the law. It has officials and employees in key positions to take care of any contingency. No one can conduct prostitution or gambling in San Francisco without the direct or indirect approval of the McDonoughs."

"What do you think of that?" he asked.

"I think Tom and Pete should learn a good trade."

He grinned.

"What's your opinion of the report itself, Master? I mean all of it."

"It's kind of like a book on taxation that makes no mention of the Treasury Department."

"How do you mean?"

"Well, it carefully describes the process of collection from the earliest stages all the way up to the McDonough brothers. In a book about taxation you wouldn't expect the reader to accept the idea that all monies collected got no further than the Department of Internal Revenue, would you?"

"You mean . . . ?"

"I don't mean anything except that Atherton just quit short of real information. Let's have a drink."

Later I walked on down Kearny Street, passing "the fountainhead of corruption"—which is what the *Examiner* had taken to calling the McDonough office in its columns—on the way back to my office. There weren't many people there and absolutely no policemen. Pete wasn't in sight but Tom McDonough was standing in the always open corner doorway, his thumbs hooked into the pockets of the vest that girded his paunch, the usual Optimo clenched between his teeth, his face an imperturbable dead pan. He didn't look like a person who could be made to say uncle simply because he was being clobbered for having outlived his times, or like an operator who had stopped being interested in "almost any matter to defeat or circumvent the law." He didn't even look like a man who might be interested in picking up a good trade.

"Hi, Master!" he said.

"Morning, Tom," I replied. And despite my conviction that the McDonough brothers had to go, surely and forever, I somehow and irrationally—I suppose—felt a stronger feeling of admiration and warmth for this man who quite honestly and openly *was* what he *was* than for the purchased righteousness and facile manipulativeness of the man who would destroy him. Rascals, no matter how much their morals molder, are rarely a bore.

Dutch Ludolph I *had* to help because he was one of the unfortunate caught in the cruel and man-killing middle between the machinations of McDonough and the counter machinations of Atherton. I was especially convinced that I should defend Ludolph when I heard the Dutchman's full story. Atherton apparently wasn't willing to settle for a squealing Ludolph (if there was anyone to squeal on), or a repentent Ludolph (if there was anything for the lieutenant to repent). Atherton wanted a broken, destroyed and thoroughly stigmatized victim despite the fact that the worst officially charged against Ludolph, if proven, could only have shown that he loved to bet on the horses. I arranged an interview with the investigator, with the Dutchman to be present and the meeting to take place in my home.

Atherton, a big, handsome, Jack Armstrong type with the frank, open smile of a casket salesman, opened the session with a request that my policeman confess to something at once, on paper, and with names and addresses abundantly included. If there were enough names, he might consider granting immunity.

My ice-cold "Just a minute, shamus!" brought him to a grinding halt. "My client is here to demonstrate reasonableness and decent intent," I said. "He is not guilty and he has no names with which to bribe you. And if he *were* guilty of some undeliberate misdeed—and he is *not*—his statement to you would be limited to that fact. If he were to know of any names that concern you—and he doesn't—he would quickly become my ex-client were he to give them to you. We are together here tonight for the purpose of convincing you that you've listened to malarkey and caught a dachshund in your bear trap. I advise you to drop your charges and forget about the matter, in which case we will do the same and no hard feelings."

Atherton's spuriously cordial smile became a cold grimace. "So you won't play ball, eh!"

It has always fascinated me that investigators harbor a deep resentment for interrogatees with no taste for ballplaying. In this connection the authorities seem to prefer players who pitch to those who catch, bunt or bat the questions out of the ball park. They cynically or callously ignore the fact that when they wheedle or threaten a citizen into "playing ball" they usually turn the poor man into a despised informer. When a client of mine is solicited to "play ball with us" by some pseudosuave modern Javert, I am frequently prompted to borrow from his own dialectic and explain that I'm regretfully forced to keep my man on the bench this season because of insufficient spring training. I now dropped this one on Atherton in behalf of Ludolph, and added a charley horse for good measure.

Atherton was not amused. He quickly took another tack; it seemed there was a penalty for being unwilling to become a ballplayer. He promised immediate prosecution of the Dutchman for "taking bribes." I cordially invited him to proceed with this prosecution, and did so with no fear of harm to my client. I no longer had any real respect for the probe jockey's capability for scoring, even in a situation heavily weighted in his favor. At gathering general information, near information, rumors, whispered asides and irresponsible scandal, he was an ace; at rounding up documented fact that could be turned into legally admissible evidence, he was still an ace, but with a broad A.

I was not surprised when I learned of the version of this meeting that Atherton gave the Grand Jury. He told them that the police lieutenant had pleaded for a break, suggesting that he might trade information for immunity. The investigator claimed to have spurned this offer. Now I was *really* determined that the first courtroom test of his charges would be beaten.

This touched upon the professional honor of the assistant district attorney, who had become Atherton's Grand Inquisitor —a man named Leslie Gillen. The battle was joined.

Gillen was a determined but grimly humorless and somewhat inflexible man who had studied law while covering the City Hall beat for the San Francisco *Chronicle,* and his allegiance was more closely bound up with himself than with his boss, District Attorney Matthew Brady. It was said that Brady was very friendly with the McDonoughs, a contention that was significantly supported by a $2,500 IOU bearing his name and admittedly made out to Tom McDonough. Certainly Brady was not delighted at the prospect of having to carry out the prosecutions of the detractor of his benefactor.

One thing upon which both Gillen and Brady were in complete agreement—and this must have been a relief to them —was J. W. Ehrlich. The district attorney regarded me as a threat to both his personal dignity and his political longevity. He was right in both particulars, as I regarded him as something less than the greatest public servant San Francisco had ever had. Gillen gave the impression of being somewhat above and beyond the kind of practice in which I specialized at the time. Some years later and after being dropped from the public payroll, he undertook precisely the same kind of practice. His legal skill and his sense of humor had improved in the interim and he did fairly well. At that time, however, he belligerently declared that I was a sinister and malign influence and that he was determined to do something about it.

The first manifestation of this determination occurred one morning shortly after Ludolph's indictment by the Grand Jury for accepting bribes. I had cleaned up my mail and leaned back in my swivel chair to gather my thoughts and figure out the strategies of the day. My gaze swept the ceiling and—in a matter of seconds—changed from casual to intent. I found myself staring at some smudge marks on the electrolier which hung there. They weren't ordinary smudge marks. They suggested the fingers of an alien presence in the room; someone had been horsing around with that lamp. Using my chair as a ladder, I climbed on my desk and peeped into the electrolier. Damned if I hadn't been bugged! A small microphone nestled cozily between the bulbs, and its wire was spliced neatly into the support that led down from the ceiling. I was delighted. I checked the room's wiring and discovered that a new and different colored section of two-ply line junctured off toward the elevator shaft and up to the next floor, where it meandered into an office that had been vacant until recently and that still carried no name on the door.

Surely Atherton, Brady and Gillen weren't going to do things by halves and cheat me of all my prerogatives as a subject of surveillance. I examined my telephone. Ah there it was: the wonderful little pair of extra wires that would have betrayed all my confidential conversations. I felt whole, complete, uncheated and cared for.

For the next several weeks I enjoyed myself utterly. For the benefit of those on the other end of my tapped telephone, I called up total strangers—interesting ones, of course, like the Swedish Consul General and the chiropodist at the St. Francis Hotel's Turkish bath and Archbishop Hanna and a man who sold marijuana cigarettes at the Southern Pacific Depot—and gave them cryptic messages, hanging up immediately in the style esteemed by James Bond.

On other occasions I told my baffled telephone correspondents that "a package would be delivered at Sutter and Jones," or at "Twenty-first and Geary" or "in a mop closet on the third floor of the Main Postoffice." Morbid curiosity prompted me to check out some of these meaningless deliveries and I was made very happy indeed to learn that always present at the alleged delivery points were casual-looking loiterers who seemed to be discreetly watchful from under the turned-down brims of hats or over the tops of carefully read newspapers. On still another occasion and when in a particularly paranoid mood, my message referred to "a pay-off" to be made at Tony's. Considering the number of establishments in San Francisco whose proprietors are named Tony, my unseen sleuths must have had a frantic day.

When time permitted, I also made good use of the little bug in the electrolier. Calling in one of my associates, I developed fits of chattiness, passing on to him juicy morsels of real and concocted gossip that usually concerned the more intimate aspects of the lives of Atherton, Gillen and Brady. I went into intimate details about the curious and bona fide biological habits and eccentricities of one of Gillen's confreres, as supplied me by the town's leading madam. I related unexpurgated and almost forgotten incidents from Matt Brady's early life. I speculated as to what unusual things Mr. Atherton had to do for his kicks in a town which he'd virtually closed to more routine pastimes. It was both pleasant and satisfying to speculate on the mental attitudes of the gentlemen in the empty office upstairs who were put to the trouble and embarrassment of transcribing all this.

And then one day I became bored with the whole ridiculous business, and anticipating the arrival of a client with whom I really did wish to talk intimately, I rushed out of the office and up the stairs to the room above me. The door was open, carelessly enough. Two flabbergasted gentlemen with earphones over their heads, one of them with a half-eaten ham sandwich transfixed an inch from his mouth, stared at me as if I were the Archangel Michael, flaming sword and all.

I wasted no time on amenities. Taking advantage of their shock, I gathered up all the electric equipment in sight, wires and all, and flung it out the window. It hung there for the next several hours, like something the building had coughed up, reaching downward for three floors. I never did find out what happened to the two gentlemen whose function was listening. The tapped telephone received equally summary treatment. I had no complaints from any of the sponsors of these perversions of Bell's handy invention, and when Mr. Gillen and Mr. Atherton were later questioned about them by the press—at my instigation—both gentlemen blandly disclaimed any knowledge of them.

I decided that if Edwin Atherton had been frittering away any of his $100,000 on such electronic devices, he should be discouraged. I brought suit against him in Superior Court, demanding that he be dismissed from employment at once on the ground that he was not a legal resident of San Francisco, and further demanding that he immediately return the $25,000 he'd already been paid. Later I amended this suit. The amendment specified that he would only have to return $24,000, as whatever he had done could only be worth about $1,000. I was sure I'd thrown at least a $1,000 worth of equipment out onto Market Street.

Now that I had undertaken the defense of the first victimized innocent bystander in the war between Atherton and the McDonoughs, I found myself inundated with bids for professional counsel and/or representation from others who found themselves in the squeeze of the situation. Some were as blameless as he; others had been playing with fire. In the former category were four of the nine policemen who had been suspended from duty as a direct result of the Report. (The newspapers had taken to referring to the Atherton thesis in this manner.) I immediately accepted the policemen as clients. For awhile my offices resembled the squad room at Central Station. Those in attendance who weren't clients apparently felt they might be candidates for that status.

Among those who came to see me with a little more on their minds at the moment were two ladies of the town whose fame had placed their names high on Atherton's lists. One of these was Sally Stanford, whose autobiography gives a lively and uninhibited account of her interchanges with Atherton, as well as of her own version of that particular interview with me. She relates the minutes of our conference more robustly and interestingly than I could.

> Jake is strictly a swinger in the field of Blackstone [wrote Sally]. He is the legal profession's master of manipulation, unpredictable footwork and polite intrigue. He is locally credited with having invented connivery and at plain and fancy

scheming he makes Machiavelli look like Simple Simon on an off day. Yet he is a scholar of international reputation, the author of a whole shelf full of books on law, and a gentleman of culture when culture is more to the point than a right hook or a verbal dynamiting. Just retaining him for the defense in a serious case usually means that you're two-thirds of the way toward a Not Guilty verdict.

On the other hand, nobody ever has accused him of modesty, tolerance, humility or personal rectitude, then or now. Jake has always burned his candle, not only at both ends, but he has somehow managed to light it in the middle, too. And as for . . . being reasonable, the Master's idea of a modest fee is and was all that you, your family, your in-laws and your Uncle Fred back in Michigan can raise. You are free to retain your dental fillings and such copper coins as are in your possession.

And yet, despite the high tariff, most people who have had him in a crisis seem to feel that the money was well spent.

The lady goes into my alleged skills and accomplishments at greater length and then relates the details of our first meeting.

Jake smiled and shook hands as cordially as if we'd never faced each other across a courtroom [she referred to an occasion in each of our salad days in San Francisco when she had undergone some harassment from the authorities and I had functioned very briefly as a special prosecutor for the county]. In those days he was slender and dark and saturnine and interested in expensive tailoring. I asked him the question that was on my mind. [Her question concerned Atherton's probable capability for preventing the McDonoughs from selling whatever they were selling in San Francisco.] Most lawyers make a little church of their hands and pressed-together fingertips as they ponder such questions. Jake doesn't make little churches with his fingers. He makes something far more rectangular that looks like little banks. He made one now.

"You are undoubtedly asking me this question because you are deeply interested in graft as a sociological problem, aren't you?" he asked.

"I'm what?"

". . . and not because you're even remotely thinking of engaging in prostitution, or bribing anyone, I presume. Because, as an officer of the court and a member of the bar, I couldn't consider discussing the matter with you otherwise. To do so might be construed by some idiotic eavesdropper as giving advice on how to circumvent the law."

"I'm a quick study."

"Why, naturally," I said. "Naturally! What else? As a matter of fact I'm gathering material for my doctorate thesis on 'The Beneficial Influence of Extracurricular Income on the Morale of Police Officers.' "

Jake inclined his head amiably as if pleased at such a marvelous opportunity to cut up academic touches with another scholar of similar interests.

"In that case I can speak freely about the subject at hand," he said. "You ask if the system of cooperative collection and disbursement allegedly invented and perpetuated by the McDonough brothers for the insurance of uninterrupted and unembarrassed operation of prostitution and gambling will continue long. Or, in short, will the fix remain fixed. The answer is no. The McDonoughs are through and so are a number of people in their and the city's joint employment. Their regime may not end today or even tomorrow, or perhaps even the next day or week. But its days are numbered and you can write that into your thesis in indelible ink, Miss Stanford."

"And if this should occur I take it that all previously protected publicans and sinners would be strictly on their own?" I asked. "And perhaps need a good lawyer to handle their headaches if and when the wheel comes off?"

Again he smiled with pleasure at my quick intelligence. I reached for my checkbook. Jake Ehrlich thus became my lawyer and the relationship extended through a whole series of hassles. One of the few really sound reasons why he isn't my attorney even now [in 1964] is that he finally priced himself out of my legal budget when he reached the top of the legal heap. But we've always been close friends and I'm very fond of him even though it depresses me about him and the pressures of life in general to see a man immerse himself so deeply in the useful and dramatic role that he plays [Edmond O'Brien enacted it on television as Sam Benedict] that he finds himself with little time for other things of perhaps greater human importance.

But guts was one thing never lacking in his dapper, belligerent little frame and he not only advised and protected me well (for a hell of a fee) but he was soon up to his own well-tailored bottom of the crazy maelstrom that was the first offshoot of the Kamokila fiasco.

This was Sally's view of me and the situation at the moment and I couldn't have phrased it any better myself, particularly in respect to my splendid courage and sound footwork.

For the sake of giving dimension to the episode on the electrification of my offices, I shall crib a little more from Miss Stanford and present her version of the incident. It has pleasantly gaudier aspects than those of my necessarily subjective account:

Shortly afterward I dropped in on my high-priced attorney and was a little shook as I entered his office to see him put his finger to his lips in the well-known shushing gesture and then point to the electric light fixture over his desk. Smiling happily up at the ceiling, he started to speak to me and to the fixture in a tone that was obviously somewhat gaffed.

"I'm glad you dropped in, Miss Stanford, and I feel sure that I know your purpose in coming here. Stop me if I'm wrong. You wanted me to add your name to the long list of citizens who are anxious to testify to the fine character and complete honesty of my client, Lieutenant Henry Ludolph." And he gave me a wink you could have seen on Van Ness Avenue, twenty blocks away.

"That was precisely my purpose," I said. Like I indicated before, I'm quick study. "And because I know of Ludolph's modest circumstances, in that he has never taken as much as a pretzel from anyone, so help me God, I would also like to contribute to his defense fund," said I, not doing so.

"Thank you, Miss Stanford. That will not be necessary," said Jake, knowing damn well that I had no intention of doing so.

"But I'm wondering if in the course of your peregrinations around the night-life areas of our city you have ever heard any tales or rumors about the private life and personal habits of Mr. Les Gillen of the district attorney's office. I have heard that the poor fellow is hooked on some . . . well, some pretty strange recreational idiosyncrasies."

"Strange, indeed!" I said. I didn't know Gillen from Wee Willie Winkie at the time. "I have heard that the unfortunate man is addicted to bedroom capers that would make the people in the Krafft-Ebing case histories look like a passel of Eagle Scouts." And I quoted mythical examples of odd-ball sexual delight until Jake nearly fell off of his chair.

And that is Sally's contribution to this series of baroque episodes from my life and times. Her reasons for concern about Atherton were better founded than were Ludolph's, for her Garden of Eden was still in full bloom as was that of Dolly Fine, my other visitor and new client.

Dolly was also an unusual woman. She was beautiful, intelligent, articulate, and I would add smart, except that her cleverness was tempered by a tendency toward quick and extreme decisions that sometimes brought her quick and extreme penalties. Shrewdness is vitally important to a madam. Dolly lacked it in large gobs.

But she was charming and I liked her. Despite the fact that it is not conventionally considered proper to speak well of ladies in the love business, I have found among them women with concepts of kindness and honesty that would look well in the moral wardrobes of many "nicer" women. Such a woman was Dolly. She was to become sensational headline material as the Lady in Red (journalistic successor to the phrase, fountainhead of corruption), but neither she nor I could have known that such bizarre prominence lay directly ahead on the morning she dropped in to ask if I actually thought a smart, sophisticated, fun-loving town like San Francisco could really be closed down by this real-life Dick Tracy from Los Angeles. I had to call it as I saw it.

"Yes," I replied. "Actually as hell."

Unfortunately for Dolly, I didn't say positively, too.

Two weeks before Christmas, in 1930, I took poor, bewildered Henry Ludolph to trial before Superior Court Judge Silvain Lazarus, one of the kindest, most philosophical jurists San Francisco has ever known. (His son Leland is now a municipal court judge and is carrying on in the same tradition of decency and liberal, empathetic interpretation of the law—rare elements in a world of uncompromising didacticism or ax-grinding obeisance to special interest.)

Ludolph, who knew of many prominent men who might more reasonably be occupying his uncomfortable spot on that foggy, gray morning in December, was being charged with picking up four bribes totaling $175 from a pair of bookies known as the Beber brothers. The chief witness to this alleged transaction was named Louis Bucchiere. Mr. Bucchiere had three separate means of livelihood, and it would have taken much research to determine which of them was the vocation and which the avocations. He was a now-and-then vegetable peddler and sometime janitor at the Chronicle Building; he was an undercover agent or stool pigeon for Mr. Atherton; and he was a bootlegger and convicted shakedown artist for himself. He was other things as well, as I was able to convey to the jury before the trial was over.

His story was as sincere, honest and straightforward a piece of testimony as two sincere, honest and straightforward operators like Gillen and Atherton could compose. He was a friend of the Bebers, but not of course to the extent of aiding or abetting them in their illegal enterprises; just a sort of a social, stand-around-and-watch-and-listen type friend. He had heard Ludolph tell the Bebers they couldn't make book in his precinct unless they first did business with him. He had watched Ludolph accept money. Gillen questioned his star witness very thoroughly and smoothly, and Bucchiere answered thoroughly and smoothly. They made a splendid duet at this two-part harmony bit and one might have thought that a performance as fine as this simply must have had ample rehearsal—if one didn't know better. But Bucchiere's excellent grasp of English phrasing when Gillen asked him why the bookmakers had been so willing to make payments to a uniformed police officer was impressive.

"The Bebers wished to eliminate unfair competition with the help of the police," he said, getting the answer off with a certain tacit quality of accomplishment. Gillen finished his examination shortly, and I advanced upon him hungrily.

"Bucchiere, did I hear you right? Did you just say, and I quote: 'The Bebers wished to eliminate unfair competition with the assistance of the police'?

"Thatsa right," he replied.

I gave him and the jury my thunderstruck look.

"Thatsa right?" I mimicked.

"Thatsa right," came back to me righteously from the witness.

"Louis, why don't you admit that you're a broken-English type who never got out of the fourth grade back in Italy and that 'eliminating unfair competition' isn't the sort of language that would naturally come out of your mouth in a thousand years and that Mr. Gillen gave you the expression to use in court today?"

"Thatsa right!" he said, and then looked at his boss, whose hoarse, furious objections were now tumbling in, but too late. I began to discuss the witness' past with him. With one bad answer already dropped into the jury's lap and Gillen's wild stare torridly playing upon him, the district attorney's stooge would have answered no to a direct question about whether or not he was wearing pants. But I did manage to get him to admit—after several equivocations—that he *was* an alien who'd never bothered to take out citizenship, that he *had* been a bootlegger, that he *had* been a bookmaker, that he *had* been convicted and *had* been sent up for impersonating a Federal officer; that because of this and other things he was at all times subject to deportation and therefore that it would be very unsmart for him to testify in any manner except that which the district attorney found pleasing. After a little more of this I let him go and Gillen unsuccessfully tried to rehabilitate his witness.

His only others were some solid citizens who testified they'd seen Ludolph in the Beber brothers' handbook and that he had not been there for the purpose of making arrests. I was ready for them.

William Ferriter was my first defense witness. Bill had been the attorney who represented Bucchiere when he was charged with the shakedown impersonation of a government man. He quickly characterized his erstwhile client as "a thing that crawls." I asked him if he would believe the man under oath.

"No. He is a professional perjurer."

I now put Ludolph on the stand and shook Mr. Gillen up considerably by asking the cop if he'd visited the handbook on nonpolice business as claimed and getting a prompt, frank, affirmative answer from my client.

"What were you there for?"

He clasped his hands firmly and looked at the jury with almost truculent frankness. I hoped he wouldn't crack his knuckles but he did.

"I was there to pick up some money." *Craaaack!*

"I see. And was this money owed you?"

"It was."

The jurors were almost on the edge of their seats. They hadn't expected *this* kind of honesty from the defense. I asked the big policeman what the money was for.

"Well, I had a bet on a long shot. The horse won. I came in to get my winnings."

"And as the winner you expected to be paid, *not* because you were a police officer and not so the place could continue to operate, but because you were a legitimate winner on a horse race, like any other citizen here?"

"That's right!"

I didn't ask the horse's name, the date or any of the other details. I gambled that Gillen would figure that Ludolph's story was spurious and would already be trembling to expose it. I gambled right. As soon as I stepped away from the witness, the prosecutor was on him like a panther. His approach was openly cynical, scornful and purring with the purpose of a cat who can feel the mouse between its teeth.

"You wouldn't be able to give any precise details about this alleged horse race, would you?"

Ludolph was bright-eyed and confident.

"I sure can, sir. It was a horse named Hidden Sight and it came from behind to win in the eighth race at Narragansett and paid sixteen to one odds. I remember the thing pretty good because I was on the streetcar going home from work when I got the good news, the first I'd had in a long, long time. Just before we come to the Twin Peaks Tunnel, this guy sits down in front of me with a late copy of the *Call-Bulletin* and I see the results in the stop-press box on Page One. I remember it was printed in red ink in the lower left-hand column of the paper. And I remember, too, taking a pencil stub and figuring out my winnings as soon as we'd come out of the tunnel and the light was better. I had ten dollars on his nose to win."

Being naturally tenderhearted in those days I didn't want to look at Gillen. Instead I looked at the jurors. You could clearly see what *they* were doing. They were riding that swaying streetcar through the Twin Peaks Tunnel, mentally reaching for their pencil stubs as they read that race result final, figuratively nodding their heads in acceptance of obvious fact as they worked out $10 at 16 to 1 and came up with $160 of the $175 the state claimed that Ludolph collected.

The rest was easy.

Gillen, somewhat unstrung now, attempted to make much of Ludolph's gambling bent and to question him rather senselessly about his motives in raiding and/or not raiding Beber's place in the past, but it was too late for this sort of prosecutional line. I unabashedly told the jury that what we were pillorying in this expensive trial was nothing more or less than a good, honest policeman who was also a horse-player. American folklore has no fonder figure than the dyed-in-the-wool horse-player, so it wasn't at all hard to tuck Ludolph tidily into the hearts of each juror as a man they could understand and like. And then I quickly recalled their attention to a man whom they couldn't like, Louis Bucchiere.

"And who did our district attorney and his companion in malfeasance, Edwin Atherton from Los Angeles, choose to help them attempt to bring this fine police officer to the ground?" I asked, or something very much like it. "How deep into the muck, mire and filth of the gutters of the lower underworld did they dig for this verminous perjurer, this snaky little rat who would sell a man's life for half a cent!"

The snaky little rat, still seated in the courtroom, turned uneasily to find who it was that was receiving the outraged attention of twelve pair of eyes from the jury box, discovered it was he, and tried to lodge himself further into his clothing, turtlewise. I continued. I asked my listeners to try to imagine how deep in the slime they'd had to dig to come up with a Bucchiere; a battener on the bodies and souls of his betters. The battener turned a deep coronary scarlet. One got the idea he was perhaps giving up undercover work. Then I went back to the evil cabal which I saw existing between our weak and foolish district attorney and the immigrant from Los Angeles. Under certain circumstances the very name Los Angeles has sinister and malign significance to San Franciscans. This was one of them. And a Los Angeleno clutching 100,000 good San Francisco dollars was a thought to invoke fury and anguish. Particularly when all that it had purchased to date was the attempted sacrifice of a beloved San Francisco police lieutenant whose weakness was playing the horses.

The jury deliberated for only two hours and forty minutes, which was reasonable considering that they went out at dinnertime. They of course brought in a verdict of Not Guilty.

So Atherton's first intended victim was acquitted and so were all the other policemen charged with graft when their individual trial turns came. None of them played ball so none of them struck out. The investigation continued for awhile and then, having collected the full payment promised him, Atherton went south to an anticlimactic decrease of publicity.

I was personally satisfied with what had occurred, as I had

been able to prevent numerous little people from suffering for offenses for which other unmentioned and unmentionable persons were responsible. And yet almost as an indirect and delayed action benefit of the investigation, the McDonoughs and the System were through. Simply by having attention called to them, they perished as active corrupters in much the same way that germs die when the sunlight reaches them.

Ludolph retired from the department shortly afterward and still survives, a hale and hearty San Francisco oldster. I'm sure that he still plays the horses and I hope that he finds a 16-to-1 winner occasionally. Gillen and Matt Brady are long deceased. Sally Stanford owns one of the finest and most popular restaurants in the west, and Dolly Fine is now the unknown and anonymous wife (as far as her past is concerned) of a prominent businessman. Her hobby is civic betterment.

As for Atherton, he passed brilliantly into relative oblivion. When he died in Southern California several years ago, his brief two-paragraph obituary referred to his activities in behalf of amateur sports. Nothing was mentioned of his San Francisco activities, two decades before, in respect to professional sports.

10: *Morning*

10 A.M.

Agenda: James Mason

Mr. Mason arrived on the very moment of his appointment. Most actors I know resemble their public selves not at all when they are at more private pursuits. John Wayne, for instance, looks more like a retired railroad brakeman than a cinema star; and Edmond O'Brien, who has regularly played Jake Ehrlich on television, looks far less like a lawyer or actor, in private life, than a suburban commuter with three children and crab-grass problems.

James Mason is the exception. There is something undeniably histrionic about the way he opens a door, straightens his tie, or puts the part back in his hair. He has lived with verve and flair for so long that it is clearly impossible for him to omit them in speech and conduct.

Today Mason had come to San Francisco about a divorce from his lovely wife Pamela. We discussed the financial aspects I'd been able to arrange, and then he asked me why I had ended the television series based on my life which Metro Goldwyn Mayer had made and released over the NBC network. This was the show called *Sam Benedict,* starring Academy Award-winning Edmond O'Brien. I had personally written many of these segments, all of which were filmed in San Francisco on the actual locales of the episodes. I told Mason that I had canceled the show regretfully after a disagreement with the National Broadcasting Company. In doing this I don't often see E. Jack Neuman who was the show's executive producer nor did I hear often from Frederick C. Houghton who drew the first contract for me at M.G.M.; two great and good friends.

"They shoved me into a seven-thirty P.M. time-slot and I just couldn't do the robust, socially realistic kind of stories that I preferred to do and then see them broadcast at an hour when children are watching television. For instance, I had a tremendous script idea involving artificial insemination. There were other of a similar nature. Hell, you can't expose this sort of material—which has a perfectly valid right to be seen at a later hour—to kids who nowadays make their own selections of TV programs.

"I couldn't get NBC to give me a later time-slot than 7:30 P.M. so I killed the series. I am preparing another series. This time I'll control all of its ramifications. I'm not only interested in getting my ideas and the fruit of my experience across to the public in this form; I like show business and show people. I've been dealing with them all my life."

As I chatted with the actor I was reminded, of my first contact with the entertainment world. It had occurred more than thirty years before. I was a very young lawyer and very impressed with myself when Alexander Pantages telegraphed me to come to Los Angeles and help get him out of a jam.

Pantages was one of the biggest names in show business at that time. This was the era of rugged individualism and tycoon entrepreneurs in the entertainment world, and men like Keith, Proctor, Shubert, Loew and Pantages controlled the business far more completely than is possible in these days of countermonopolistic legislation and greatly expanded tax strictures. They were powerful; they were rich. Worst of all for my prospects for doing anything for Pantages, they were suspect in the public mind. Seduction or rape were activities that the average person (*ergo* the average juror) regarded as component parts of the living pattern of such personalities. Pantages was charged with rape.

There was no doubt about it; Alex was a rough cob. Born in Athens, he had come to the United States before the turn of the century, made his stake the hard way by operating nickelodeons, burlesque houses and even penny arcades and shooting galleries. He'd added to his pile during the Klondike gold strike in Alaska and then returned to California where he owned cabarets on the old Barbary Coast in San Francisco. He opened theatres, sixty in all before he was through, and they extended from the Canadian border to Mexico. To be booked regularly for Pan-time was the hope of all the big variety stars from the East. Pantages' only real competitor in the West was the Orpheum Circuit, which was later to become a part of the hydraheaded RKO (Radio-Keith-Orpheum) entertainment monolith. By 1925 he was worth $25,000,000.

One fateful afternoon in 1929 a seventeen-year-old dancer named Eunice Pringle dropped in at the Los Angeles Pantages

Theatre to see Alex about a booking. She had never met him, and crashing his office was not the orthodox way in which to get auditioned; most such interviews were—then as now—prearranged by theatrical agents.

Eunice had an agent. He was a reputedly Machiavellian schemer and rumor had it that his dancer's apparently naive drop-in on Pantages had been no mere happenstance. At any rate, she had bought a ticket at the theatre and then ascended to the Pantages office on the mezzanine. The rest had been chaos, whether you believed Pantages or the girl.

Eunice—described by the Hearst paper the *Herald-Examiner* in Los Angeles as, "mature for seventeen and the sweetest seventeen since Clara Bow," and by even the more sedate Los Angeles *Times* as, "a full-blown beauty"—sobbed out her story to the police within the hour. Pantages had flung her into a mop closet, stifled her screams, "wrenched" her underwear from her body (women wore a combination garment called a chemise in those days—an item that was impossible to remove without some cooperation from the wearer), and then violated her.

Pantages claimed that she had violated herself, or rather that she had violated her garments, pulling and tearing at them until they gave the appearance of having been removed with a cargo hook. He further claimed that, in the Biblical sense, he knew the lady not, adding that suspecting him of rape was ridiculous because sex was a more than plentiful Hollywood commodity.

However, when the case came to trial, Pantages, with his fractured English and generally goatish manner, made a poor witness, and limpid-eyed, dulcet-voiced Eunice proved an excellent one. She was an all-time hit with the jury and the press. Such red-blooded Americans as were not outraged because she'd allegedly been deflowered by an allegedly rascally Greek were equally outraged because the defloration had not been accomplished by a red-blooded American.

There are more mental rapists around than anyone imagines. Their common characteristics are to convict when they serve as jurors in morals cases, to vote for stiffer penalties for their more overt prototypes, and to find the rope when lynch mobs form.

Pantages was prosecuted by Buron Fitts, an extremely successful district attorney of the period. And he was defended by a battery of lawyers among whom was Jerry Geisler, one of the ablest of American criminal defenders and a friend who became one of my most respected intimates. Despite this fine legal representation, the theatre man was convicted.

It was then that I received a telegram.

One of the best pals of my younger days had been Rodney Pantages, the tough old tycoon's son and the head of his northern California organization. Rodney played piano and I enjoyed sawing away on the violin. Occasionally we would get together for some light musicmaking at his apartment above the box office of the San Francisco Pantages Theatre on Market Street. (I have always found relief from pressure in playing the violin. Hence the line that one reporter used during a crisis of my fight against District Attorney Matt Brady: EHRLICH FIDDLES WHILE BRADY BURNS.)

Rodney Pantages gave certain counsel to his father following the latter's conviction; the result was that I was summoned to Los Angeles. Geisler had brilliantly carried the appeal all the way to the Supreme Court, which granted a new trial in a forty-page ruling that would create vital precedents for the adjudication of rape cases in California. For instance, the trial judge had flatly opposed any effort on Geisler's part to inquire into the character of the alleged rapee, holding that the nature and degree of her chastity, if any, had no bearing on the situation. Thus they went the all-men-are-innocent-until-proven-guilty credo one better by mandating that all women are virgins and that any effort to prove otherwise is forbidden. The Supreme Court's decision, which commented that, "The testimony of the prosecutrix was so improbable as to challenge the credulity," reversed the lower court's somewhat sentimental thinking and ruled that any relevant testimony or evidence to the effect that an allegedly damaged party in a rape matter might have been predamaged—and often predamaged or predamaged with her own consent and eager connivance—was admissible. We still had the press attitude toward Eunice to contend with, but with upper court help of this kind we were off and running again.

Geisler and I opened our defense with a move which seemed a bit ridiculous at the moment—precisely the effect we sought. We re-enacted the rape. Geisler, a bit on the portly side, played Pantages like a punch-drunk Barrymore. I was and am on the svelte side, which qualified me for the only remaining role in the cast. We performed the scene with realistic finesse right up to the climax.

We had a serious purpose in mind, actually. Rape is an ugly word and an uglier deed, but as an actual act performed under the circumstances described and within the confines of a mop closet, it becomes a grotesque and somewhat inconceivable buffoonery. I believe that we made our point of physical logic. In addition we were able to relieve the alleged deed of some of its overtones of sinister bestiality. A rapacious tycoon behind a locked door in a silken bower is one thing; an alleged conquest among the brooms and mops in a janitor's closet is something else.

Now we needed a clincher: something that would blight the look of shocked innocence in Eunice's eyes, blot out the tremulous sound of remembered horror in her voice, and prove that she had—in the idiom—been around.

The chore of turning up such vital information had fallen to me. In the days prior to the trial I checked out every possible lead to Eunice Pringle's past. I succeeded not at all. And then one night at the Vernon Country Club I had the good fortune to run into a former client of mine, a used-car magnate whose hoardings referred to him as Honest Olaf. I had defended him on swindling charges in San Francisco. We'd won a sort of a draw, with Olaf disgorging and the state not prosecuting.

"I see you're in that Pringle case," said Olaf. He shook his head. "That dame; she's sure built. And that sweet-little-old-me tone in her voice, *man!* I sold her a car and almost gave her the keys without the down payment. Almost but not quite."

The small-world factor again.

"*You* sold her a car! What was her address then?"

"Crise, it was almost a year ago, Jake. But we can take a hike over to my lot and look at the paper, if you like."

I liked.

Olaf's records showed an address in Hollywood which I hadn't known of, but more interesting was Eunice's credit-reference listing of the agent whom I'd suspected of having masterminded her Pantages visit. I will call him Mr. Svengali.

I taxied back to Hollywood and to the address given on the credit application. It was one of those sad small stucco nightmares peculiar to Los Angeles and generally described as a bungalow court; the kind of place which seems to have tremendous appeal to subjects of ninety-day marriages, immigration from Iowa, and successful suicide projects.

The manager was a workworn old lady with holes cut in the sides of her shoes to permit the protrusion of bunions. On her faded dress was a small gold-washed emblem that proclaimed membership in the GOSPEL TRUTH ASSEMBLY. On the wall of the tiny cubicle that was both her living room and office was a violently tinted chromo of the Sea of Galilee, and to its right was a framed manifesto to the effect that: HE IS THE SILENT HOST/IN THIS/CHRISTIAN HOME. On a battered but neat stand by the more comfortable chair was an obviously often consulted Bible.

I introduced myself and asked the manager whether her tenant list had ever included a Miss Eunice Pringle. She shook her head. No Miss Pringles, ever. This was a puzzler. Then I had a hunch. I asked if she'd ever had a Mr. and Mrs. Svengali.

She nodded. "They were in Number Forty-five. Been gone now for five months."

I figuratively winked at myself. I sat down in the big chair close to the Bible.

"Were they married?"

"*Of course* they were married," she retorted indignantly. "We don't *have* unmarried people at Moonbeam Glen."

I shook my head sadly.

"The reason I ask is that I'm afraid you were deceived by this couple. I'm here in behalf of another man whom they're attempting to deceive. You've read about the Pantages case, haven't you?"

Her mouth tightened into a tiny crease and her eyes attempted the same feat. She nodded remotely and it was clear that she had heard all about Pantages.

"As a righteous woman who would want to see justice done, I know you'll help me in this matter."

The narrow lines became narrower.

"I wouldn't help that rich despoiler of women if my life depended on it. They had men like that in Babylon before the Fall. The *beast!*"

She edged toward the door. I laid my hand on the worn old Bible.

"This is a wonderful book, full of wonderful truths. I believe that it is in Psalms, the one hundred and first chapter, the fifth verse, that: 'Whoso privily slandereth his neighbor; him I will cut off.' Or her, I suppose."

Some of the straightness left the lines of her mouth.

I continued: "And then there is the quotation that goes: 'Let none of you imagine evil against your brother in your heart and love no false oath, for these are things I hate.' " I thumbed through the book and there was silence between us. " 'Imagine evil' is the divine wording, as I remember it."

She sat down on the other chair. Her tone was faltering now.

"I don't want to help Mr. Pantages. He is an adulterer. A *rich* adulterer!"

"Rich!" I said. " 'Take heed and beware of covetousness, for a man's life consisteth not in the abundance of the things he possesses.' You know, of course, that the Lord often made many men wealthy in worldly goods . . . Abraham, Lot, Job and others. None of us prospers unless the Lord wills it."

She looked directly at me for the first time.

"You are religious, young man?"

I could safely answer this one truthfully, if imprecisely.

"The Bible is an old, old friend of mine. I know it well. It has helped me out of some difficult spots in my life. It has been my good fortune to have read the Old Testament in both the original Hebrew and Aramaic. I love all that I have read."

And then I told her some of what I knew about the Bible, a book that has fascinated me since my boyhood. I quoted verses that referred to bad citizenship ("Put not thine hand with the wicked to be an unrighteous witness"); verses that dealt with sneaky bungalow-court lechers ("For the land is full of adulterers and the land mourneth"); and verses that talk turkey about the duties of a witness ("Let them bring them forth, and shew us what will happen; let them shew the former things, what they may be, that we may consider them and know the latter end of them; or declare us things for to come").

The manager of the Moonbeam Glen bungalow court stepped onto the witness stand with firm conviction and an obviously devout sense of mission. Her eyes and mouth narrowed as she glanced across the courtroom and discovered the erstwhile tenant of Bungalow forty-five. For Mr. Pantages she had a wintry smile of Christian charity. Then she dug in and testified the state's case right out of the window and far into the sultry, smoggy distances of the City of the Angels.

The really good need only to be shown what's really good. They'll do the rest themselves.

I was next requisitioned by the demigods of Hollywood in the defense of a portion of the female anatomy known as the mammary glands; specifically the mammary glands of Miss Jane Russell, an erstwhile actress, sex symbol and protégée of Howard Hughes. At that time Mr. Hughes made motion pictures, was the head of the Hughes Tool Company, and produced aircraft.

His major cinema triumph was a documentary Western dealing with the life of Billy the Kid, but it also featured numerous bosom shots of Billy the Kid's fiancée, played by Miss Russell. The title of the film was *The Outlaw*. The entire seventh reel was devoted to panoramic coverage of the exterior aspects of Miss Russell's lungs. When the picture was unveiled in San Francisco at its world première, the local police promptly pinched the management of the United Artists Theatre for violation of Section 471 of the Penal Code, which is highly sensitive to films that are, "offensive to decency and the moral senses." And a block away from the offending theatre was the President Burlesque which—unmolested by the police—offered comedy sequences involving physical romance with a goat.

Howard Hughes retained me to make sure that *The Outlaw* got a square shake in the courts, and he backed me up with ace publicist Russell Birdwell, who was to see that the square shake or the foul judicial miscarriage—whichever developed—would get the widest possible coverage in the national press. I was determined that the widest possible coverage was something that would *not* happen to any courtroom fiasco of mine. I was determined to win. So I ordered large photographic blow-ups of Leonardo da Vinci's "Madonna and Child" plus mammouth reproductions of other classical masterpieces in which king-sized busts were featured.

The case was heard by a jury before the Honorable Twain Michelsen, the presiding judge of the municipal courts at the time. Twain was a book judge. He was afraid of no one and not easily influenced by pressure groups. And it was Twain and not the jury upon whom I was counting for a clean bill of health for my client. Where public morals are concerned, I haven't too much faith in the broadmindedness of juries. The average one tends too greatly toward the striking of hypocritical postures when it comes to guarding the morals of others. My strategy was based upon a unilateral appeal to the man on the bench, with the jurors more or less along for the ride and to legalize the proceedings.

The prosecution professed to be severely shocked at being confronted by ladies' chests, or rather by Miss Russell's chest. It suggested that the jury and also the City and County of San Francisco should be similarly shocked. That was its entire case.

I showed the jury and the court the da Vinci picture and asked them if they were at all titillated by what they saw; asked them if they lusted because they were suddenly plunged into awareness of the fact that a woman's upper body is different in front than it is in the back. They tittered. Then I took the court and jury to the projection room of a movie distributor on nearby Golden Gate Avenue and showed them the film itself. At three in the afternoon and after a lot of courtroom palaver, the effect was anticlimactic—even a little soporific.

When we were back before the bench again I gave them my argument. After cleaning up the usual precedents in which the rulings had been as broadminded as the subjects were often boring, I suggested that the police—if they'd been offended by the sight of Miss Russell's tissue—should attend an opera opening, where 95 percent of the women present would be pinchable on the same grounds.

"In order to arrive at a guilty verdict," I told them, "you must have been sensually, sensuously and even sexually excited by seeing this picture. You must have been placed in grave jeopardy of becoming a bad man or a bad woman by reason of having seen it, instead of the good, moral, upright men and woman you now are."

The good, moral, upright men and women nodded solemnly at each other and I knew I'd earned my fee. But I took no chances. I asked Judge Michelsen for a directed verdict of acquittal. He took my motion under advisement.

The next morning Judge Michelsen was ready with his instruction to the jury. With no reference to my motion he got quickly to the point.

"There are some fanatical persons who would object to seeing Miss Russell in a low-necked dress, but we must consider that the plot of this show was laid in the desert, which is hardly the setting for woolens, high necks and long sleeves. I must embrace the principle that life is sordid and obscene only for those who find it so."

He glanced at me from over his bifocals with a faint glint of amusement and continued: "I must therefore find that the charge of the police does not correctly fall within the scope of Section 471 of the Penal Code . . . and direct the jury to bring in a verdict of Not Guilty."

I don't know what his successes were in other directions but I do know that *The Outlaw* succeeded for Howard Hughes to the tune of nearly $12,000,000. As he had done me many services in the moving picture world, I was glad to be of assistance to him in San Francisco.

Some months later I was able to serve show business again in a similar case, but there was a pleasant difference. The charge was still too much flesh and not enough clothing, but this time the flesh was real instead of celluloid. This time the fractured statute was Section 311 of the Penal Code and the fracturer was Miss Sally Rand of fan and fanny fame. Section 311 implies, "indecent exposure, corrupting the morals of an audience, and conducting an obscene show." This in a city which a few years later was to look the other way when young girls modeled topless bathing suits on the Marina Green in full daylight.

However, in 1946 the naive citizenry still enjoyed such small and near naughty thrills as Miss Rand provided when she slowly undulated up a meagerly lighted runway to the melancholy rhythms of "Clair de Lune" with only a six-foot fan with which to hide her quasi nakedness. Until November of 1946, that is.

At that time and at the Club Savoy on O'Farrell Street, six apparently mature policemen stomped in during Miss Rand's act, professed themselves as heartily shocked and arrested her. She called me immediately. I had often represented her in the past and was happy to take up the cudgels against the blank brains who felt that San Francisco—the alleged Paris of the Western Hemisphere—was being menaced by a woman with a nice nether profile, a white fan, and a gift for making talcum powder look like clothes.

Sally wasn't exactly a newcomer to nudism. A veteran of vaudeville and moving pictures as well as of the chorus lines of Broadway, she had moved into the headlines in 1933 with an attraction at the Chicago World's Fair entitled "The City of Paris." This near extravaganza consisted largely of Sally and some associate females wearing orifice patches. A few years later she starred at the San Francisco World's Fair in an attraction entitled "Sally Rand's Nude Ranch." This—again—consisted largely of Sally and other females wearing holsters and badges over their principal points of interest. Running out of world fairs, she had then undressed profitably in Los Angeles and Las Vegas for short periods of time and finally journeyed to San Francisco for a rendezvous with destiny and six easily shocked cops.

We went to bat the next morning in the courtroom of Judge Daniel R. Shoemaker, a relatively sophisticated jurist and no man to blanch at an eyeful of the female form. My blond and beautiful client arrived, superbly poised, severely tailored, and carrying an enormous bouquet of roses that was the gift of the San Francisco Chapter of the League of Decency. At least that was the name I wrote on the card.

The prosecution put Captain Joseph Walsh of Central Station on the witness stand. In shuddering tones, Captain Walsh explained that his six policemen had been exposed to more temptation than they could easily bear. He related their agony at having to watch Miss Rand reduce a full costume, garment by garment, to a mere patch over the lower torso. He pointed out that their manly need to turn their heads aside had so impeded the performance of their duties that they were unable to capture the patch for evidence, as had been their order and intent. But they knew it was a patch, a small one, a flesh-colored one, triangular in shape, with ten beads sewn at each corner.

When the stricken police captain was finally led from the stand, I offered some remarks. I said that it was strange that in crime-busy San Francisco (a Mafia murder was shaking North Beach to its wine-scented foundations) six police officers were required for the incarcerating of a 110-pound, limpid-eyed blonde, unarmed except for a triangular three-inch patch surmounted with thirty beads. I remarked that this little girl, who had never been known to do or say anything obscene in her life, was performing a rhythmic composition that was respected in the highest artistic circles and elsewhere. I referred to the nude masterpieces of Praxiteles, Michelangelo and Rodin. I commented sadly upon the shame of such an arrest in a cosmopolitan city like San Francisco . . . and in midflight I noticed that Judge Shoemaker was paying more attention to the lower portions of Miss Rand than he was to my appeal. Suddenly he roused himself and matter-of-factly pointed out that he'd been quite unable to pass upon the defendant's alleged lewdness until he had actually and personally seen it in action—an entirely logical statement.

"May I suggest, Your Honor," I quickly suggested, "that we adjourn until tomorrow morning, at which time my client will perform her specialty for you? Thus instead of secondhand accounts and narrow-minded criticisms, we'll be dealing with the naked truth."

Judge Shoemaker thought this a very good idea. Meanwhile I pointed out that the lady should be exempted from further constabulary harassment, and he thought that a good idea, too. He provided her with a court order that would release her at once should she again be nabbed for moving rhythmically to music with only a patch as protection.

That night the Savoy was loaded with customers and policemen eager to be corrupted. The latter watched with bright-eyed intensity as Sally mounted her dimly lit runway. At a point which they apparently regarded as the height of her frenzy of lewdness, they ascended the stage and ordered the lights turned on and the fans cast aside. Miss Rand stood revealed in a suit of long flannel underwear. Where the triangular patch once forbade greater inspection of the premises there was a small placard. It read: CENSORED. S.F.P.D.

They arrested Sally anyway. This was understandable. There was no other way for them to get offstage without looking like damn fools. Thanks to our court order she was released in time to make her midnight show.

The next morning Judge Shoemaker, Assistant District Attorney Frank Brown, numerous court and Hall of Justice attachés, every newspaperman in San Francisco who could make it and I were guests at the command performance at the Savoy. Sally did her dance in her regular way, with her usual fans, her talcum negligee and her pen-wiper-sized patch. She wowed her audience. Afterward she served Bloody Marys and patch-sized sandwiches. A good time was had by all.

Back in the courtroom, Judge Shoemaker disposed of the charges.

"Anyone who could find something lewd about the dance as she puts it on," he said with reminiscent thoughtfulness, "has to have a perverted idea of morals."

He found her Not Guilty on all counts.

Shortly thereafter I went south to Hollywood again and again found myself in a courtroom with my old friend and colleague of the Pantages case, Jerry Geisler. The problem at hand was an intricate one.

Joan Bennett needs no identification in this era of super-publicizing of movie stars, and her husband Walter Wanger is almost as well known. The third party to the triangle was a representative of the Music Corporation of America named Jennings Lang. Mr. Lang was not only Miss Bennett's specific agent for motion picture commitments; he was also her dear and true friend. He was much younger than Mr. Wanger.

At this time Wanger was at what now appears to have been the nadir of his career. He was close to broke and owed a vast sum of money. He was not exactly the most sought-after talent in the profession and was currently employed at a cut-rate studio in the low-rent district of Hollywood. Worst of all, he thought his still beautiful wife was gladdening her life with extramarital activities.

He thought this so frequently and intensely that he hired a private detective. On December 13, 1951, Wanger took a pistol and stationed himself in the parking lot opposite the Music Corporation of America. When his wife and Mr. Lang parked there shortly after matinee time, he fired two shots at Lang. Mr. Lang went to Midway Hospital, Mr. Wanger went to jail, and Miss Bennett went into hysterics.

The journals of the nation whirled into orbit. Wanger quickly became top copy material. It was suddenly remembered that he was a former president of the Academy of Motion Picture

Arts and Sciences, a college regent (Antioch) and a director of the American Red Cross, as well as a great producer and the man who had made the first outdoor technicolor sound picture —*The Trail of the Lonesome Pine*. The publicity was large and the potential blow to the motion picture industry the most serious since Roscoe Arbuckle and Virginia Rappe had gone into a St. Francis Hotel bathroom in San Francisco, with only Arbuckle surviving the experience.

Less than twenty-four hours after the parking lot episode Lang's friends called me. They wanted me to represent him. It was hard for me to understand how a defense lawyer could possibly be of urgent use to a clearly qualified plaintiff in an assault case, but I was to learn.

My client in the Wanger-Lang shooting case was actually the motion picture industry as a whole. Unless the duration of the legalistics involved and per se the longevity of the publicity could be foreshortened to the utmost, the picture industry stood to suffer a black eye from which it might never recover. They wanted a speedy end to the mess. They would get it. I, too, saw no profit or benefit in permitting another banal version of the oldest disaffection in human history to become a Roman holiday for prurient scandal addicts across the nation.

When I arrived in Los Angeles, I found that the moving picture industry's fear of nationwide reaction was bigger than even its certainty that it could handle the lashback. Miss Bennett had retained Grant Cooper, a prominent attorney, apparently under the vague misapprehension that she was to be prosecuted in some way. Geisler was defending Wanger. The district attorney, a brilliant and ornate lawyer named S. Ernest Roll, was himself handling the prosecution. He was somewhat miffed at the moment because no one, but *no* one, was making any statements on advice from their counsels (including me).

The Los Angeles press was already beating its drums for what it expected to be the most noisome scandal of the decade. The *Daily News* unreticently promised that, "The whole matter would wind up in one of Hollywood's most sensational trials now that Lang has retained Jake Ehrlich." The *Mirror* opined that, "The entrance of Jake Ehrlich indicates it will become a joust of legal giants."

The joust never took place. After a careful discussion with all concerned as to what was best for everyone (including a multi-billion-dollar industry), we permitted our clients to make conservative, low-key, sensation-screened statements to the press. Shortly afterward, with the press in attendance, Wanger was wholesomely reunited with his wife and two children. Somewhat later he appeared before Superior Judge Harry J. Borde without preamble or excitement. Geisler, with the agreement of Mr. Roll, had submitted the case to the court on the basis of the information given to the Grand Jury. This meant that there would be no lurid testimony, no photographs, no sensational disclosures. Wanger was found guilty of assault with a deadly weapon as quietly as an indiscreet motorist is convicted of driving at seventy-five miles an hour. He was sentenced to serve 4 months in the county jail and had started doing his time before the nation's scandal fans had finished drooling over earlier details. Jennings Lang briefly disappeared into the world of therapies and then quickly re-emerged, not better than ever but perhaps wiser. And I returned to San Francisco, a little wealthier and deeply aware of at least one major difference between our two communities—a Franciscan might be willing to lose his head over a beautiful woman, but that's all.

James Mason agreed with me that the lawyerly duties required by his fellow stars are apt to be more exotic and unpredictable than those demanded by merely murdersome citizens in San Francisco, and we repaired to Joe Paoli's, sixteen floors below on Montgomery Street, to drink to the wholesome conventionality of his current claim to my services. And subsequently, I settled the James Mason case with his wife, Pamela, for about a million dollars, mostly in real estate which had been under her control for many years. Thus was avoided the possibility of a hot, headline ridden divorce case; and the result was complete satisfaction to both parties. Mason's satisfaction is best reflected in his own words: "The amount of the settlement was only a flea bite."

I've had other clients from the world of the theatre whose cases and problems I am unable to treat so lightly. There were Bandleader Gene Krupa and a wonderful Negro singer named Billie Holliday. They were victims, each in different ways, of involvement with the nightmare trade in narcotics.

In the year in which this is written, Krupa is more or less a name from yesterday, so transient is the fame of popular musicians. In 1943, however, he was a top-flight attraction, billed as the King of Drums, and he earned $100,000 a year.

On the 18th of January of that year at the conclusion of his last performance at San Francisco's Golden Gate Theatre, he was grabbed by narcotics agents as he left the stage and taken to his dressing room for a strip-frisk and questions. Someone had put the finger on him as a marijuana smoker.

I would like to make some informed comments about marijuana, which is legally categorized with morphine, cocaine and heroin as a habit-forming drug. Morphine is a drug. Cocaine is a drug. Heroin is a double drug, there being no other word with which to emphasize its built-in, inescapable, pervasive evil. But marijuana is no more habit forming than spinach or tutti-frutti or cornflakes. Even its well-publicized malign effects are questionable as universal characteristics, as not *all* persons react perversely to its stimulus and there are those—many of them—who don't react to it at all. Marijuana is popularly labeled an addicting drug because it is *officially* labeled an addicting drug and the official label was allocated to the nuisance weed as a convenience to law enforcement. The smoking of marijuana is not a quasi stimulatory pastime to be recommended, but neither —for many persons—is the use of benzedrine, barbiturates or even hard liquor. Yet the possession and ingestion of these specifics are not regarded as felonies, supposing prison sentences, extralegal harassment by the police, and ostracism as dope fiends by an uninformed society.

Gene Krupa was suspected of smoking marijuana cigarettes.

As he was being searched and bullied and humiliated in his dressing room at the Golden Gate Theatre a young man watched the ugly proceedings from the corridor outside. His name was

John Pateakos. He was an instrument jockey; a porter and handyman who had joined the band at this humble level only a week before. A Krupa-worshiping band buff more than an average employee, he was flabbergasted. Worse, he was frightened, for he knew that while there was no marijuana in the dressing room, a certain amount of the weed was stashed in Krupa's suite at the St. Francis Hotel. Anxious to protect his idol from trouble, he slipped out of the theatre and headed for the hotel five blocks away.

He wasn't alone. An agent had watched his departure, and when John let himself out of the suite, minutes later and marijuana in hand, he was snatched by members of the narcotic squad. It didn't take them long to persuade an already frightened boy to "cooperate."

In this case, I was in at the pinch. Gene, who had never been in this kind of mess and who was actually a quiet, decent boy, was pretty well shaken up by the raid at the theatre. When he called me, I contacted the police and found they intended to take him into custody at the end of his second show that night, probably in his dressing room. I planned to be there.

Although both federal agents and city and state narcotic cops were present the night before (when the initial raid and the trapping of Pateakos took place) and on the occasion of Krupa's arrest, the musician was booked as a county offender, the charge being "contributing to the delinquency of a minor," a misdemeanor. But the uproar from the press was instantaneous and rabid and I knew there was more to come. I bailed Gene out and we waited. Forty-eight hours later District Attorney Matt Brady, my antagonist and adversary through the years, issued a noisy statement to the press about the monstrous infamy of my client, and then had him rearrested and rebooked. This time Krupa was charged with "using a minor to transport narcotics," a felony. A felony conviction would mean San Quentin and the virtual end of Krupa's career. In New York City, for instance, musicians and entertainers with felony convictions may not be granted a "café license." Thus they find themselves black-listed in the capital city of the entertainment world.

As far as I was concerned, the picture was clear. Matt Brady was up for re-election. His accomplishments had been few, his failures many. He badly needed a master stroke of prosecutory achievement. The conversion of Gene Krupa into a monster and the crucifixion of that monster was to be his master stroke.

Well, it wasn't.

I'd had a head-to-head talk with Gene and he convinced me that he was innocent.

"I wouldn't con you, Master," he'd said. "I don't know a damn thing about this caper. The first time I pick up on the fact it's marijuana that's got them bugged is when the fuzz lay the story on me after they drop the net on Johnny [Pateakos]. They tell me he picked up the muggles in my suite, and I come all unzipped. That's a scene I don't dig, Jake; tea, goof balls, bennies —all that funny kind of quick energy. I don't need it! I got *me;* that's plenty. If the kid had muggles, I sure don't know where he got it."

I believed him. I've been listening to liars for a long time. I can tell a lie from an honest yarn without help from scopolamine, a lie detector or the third degree. All that was needed to doubly confirm my faith in Krupa's story was Pateakos' story and we got that a few days later at the preliminary examination in juvenile court.

Pateakos didn't invent anything. He didn't have to; his story was already invented for him.

"Why did you go to the St. Francis Hotel, John?" asked the prosecutor.

John was as nervous as a rabbit at a convention of cobras. He kept moistening his lips and uneasily eyeing Krupa. When he spoke it was in the general direction of the ceiling fixture.

"Mr. Krupa asked me to go to his room and get an envelope from his coat pocket. I asked him, 'Is it in the camel-hair jacket?' He said, 'No.' So then I left. I ran part of the way."

Narcotic Agent Joseph V. Giubbini, the sharp-eyed sleuth

who'd noticed Pateakos take off from the theatre, had already described the mechanics of the boy's arrest.

"After we'd talked to Mr. Krupa for about fifteen minutes, he asked us if he might wash, as he was perspiring quite a bit, and he left the room. I followed. Krupa was walking with Pateakos. I separated them. I then asked Krupa where he lived and where the key to his room was. He stated that he lived at the St. Francis Hotel and that the key was at the desk.

"I became suspicious and telephoned to the St. Francis, identified myself, and then asked them to give the key to the room to no one but Mr. Krupa. I then left Mr. Krupa with Agent Polcuch and went to the St. Francis alone. I went up in the elevator. As I stepped off on the floor on which Mr. Krupa's room was located John Pateakos was waiting to get onto the elevator. I stopped him and took him with me to the band manager's room where I searched him and took from his trousers pocket one envelope containing two marijuana cigarettes, one half of a smoked marijuana cigarette, and another envelope containing thirty-seven such cigarettes.

"I questioned Mr. Pateakos and the band manager, who was in the room, and a moment later Agent Polcuch came in with Mr. Krupa. I then took Mr. Krupa into his room, where I talked with him for a few minutes. Then Agent Polcuch came in. We conducted a search of Mr. Krupa's room and in the writing-desk drawer I found fragments of marijuana . . . approximately one tenth of a regular marijuana cigarette . . ."

Marijuana cigarettes are usually about one third to a half of the bulk of an ordinary cigarette in size. Agent Giubbini had found one tenth of one third of a half of an alleged marijuana cigarette. He went on.

"We questioned Mr. Krupa for awhile and after about twenty-five minutes we took Mr. Pateakos to our office, where we allowed him to sit down and think it over. He finally stated that—"

I objected and the objection was sustained by Judge Tom Foley, who was hearing the matter. The boy was released, his statement being regarded as sufficient basis for prosecution of both the misdemeanor and felony charges. Krupa was continued on bail. He immediately left for the East to fill an engagement in Boston. Trial on the misdemeanor was set for the 18th of May, some ninety days later.

In the meanwhile I discussed the matter with Tom Foley. I pointed out the obvious damage that the continuing publicity was doing to Krupa's professional career, as well as the human and social inequity of the penalties he was already paying—guilty or innocent—prior to any judicial determination of guilt or innocence. He agreed with me. I was also convinced that we were in agreement on another point: if Krupa would come back to San Francisco and plead guilty to the misdemeanor, he would be fined $500 and no further penalty, no prosecution on the felony rap.

I wasn't happy at the prospect of having Krupa expediently admit guilt for an offense of which I was convinced he was innocent, but I felt that it was the lesser of two evils; that a misdemeanor conviction with no imprisonment was better than fighting a felony prosecution in the courts and newspapers with the District Attorney using the situation for campaign material—his *only* campaign material of the moment—during the pre-election months ahead. I also had an emergency plan in regard to the plea. But I was especially encouraged by what I regarded as my understanding with Judge Foley. I had forgotten that he was a close political colleague of sixty-eight-year-old Matt Brady, who hated me, who had been district attorney for twenty-four years and who wanted to make it twenty-eight, and who was an extremely uninhibited man in respect to getting what he wanted in life and politics.

I called Krupa in Providence and told him what the score was and what I'd decided to do.

"You call 'em, I'll play 'em, champ," he said. "I'm with you."

Meanwhile we'd heard that John Pateakos was in Los Angeles and was sounding off about being out of pocket because of the trouble (that he had caused) in San Francisco. He felt that Gene Krupa should have continued his salary during the period when he was in jail; in fact, he required a good deal more than just his salary as an instrument jockey. I agreed with him. I felt that when a mere porter and errand boy becomes a singer and—in a sense—a composer, his earnings should match his singing accomplishments. I also felt that he was dunning the wrong creditor and that those who had inspired his vocalisms should pick up the tab for the performance.

But Pateakos was now telling the press that he intended to take Krupa before the State Labor Commissioner, and foreseeing further hideous headlines, I sent Roy Sharff, one of my associates, to visit the young man in the Southland and settle his strange and somewhat incredible bill.

On the 18th of May, Krupa and I stood before Judge Foley. In my pocket were five $100 bills for the payment of the fine that Judge Foley and I had discussed. Foley levied the fine and then doubled-crossed me when he went on to sentence Krupa to ninety days in the county jail. At the end of the ninety days, less the usual five days from each month for good behavior, Krupa would be tried on the felony charge.

Brady immediately assigned Assistant Dictrict Attorney Les Gillen to the prosecution of Krupa on the felony. Gillen was in fine fettle and for two reasons: because the defendant had already pleaded guilty in the misdemeanor conviction, he felt logically certain of a fast and fancy conviction on the felony; it was his first chance at me since the Ludolph case, in which I'd struck him out, and the Atherton Investigation, which I'd turned into a pillow fight. He apparently figured he'd send Krupa to "Q," elect his boss, gather some handsome headlines for himself and eviscerate me professionally—and all with a cowed kid's lie, a tenth of a third of an alleged marijuana cigarette and a few well-chosen words about "the monstrous perfidy of depraved, drug-crazed jazz-musicians."

We went to trial before Judge Foley on June 28th. The courtroom was packed. There was not only the usual morbid spectator trade; we were also playing to jazz fans and hipsters, dead-serious protagonists and antagonists of the drug problem, an unusually large slice of the press, and more than a few average citizens who just wanted to find out whether Ehrlich had at last bitten off more than he could chew.

The prosecution was a little embarrassed at the outset: its star witness was—according to its best conclusion of the moment—on the lam. Not even the Federal Bureau of Investigation had been able to turn him up, its interest having been inspired by the nonresponse of Pateakos to a draft-board summons. It was all very distressing. I knew precisely where he was but felt no obligation to mind Brady's business for him. As far as the Army was concerned, I figured we could win the war without Pateakos.

When the prosecution had finished apologizing for the nonappearance of its wandering witness, I moved for a dismissal on the grounds that when Krupa pleaded guilty to the offense of contributing to the delinquency of a minor, a misdemeanor, the District Attorney was precluded from prosecuting him again for the same act as a felony since the possession of the marijuana by Pateakos involved in both of the counts was the same and only possession, and the District Attorney may not cut this one possession into two offenses, and further, that the misdemeanor was included and was part of the felony and the felony thus contained the misdemeanor. This was and is known as the doctrine of included offenses, which incidentally made new law in the State of California.

Now, and for the first time, Gillen and Brady, et al had themselves a peep at my hole card; now they understood why I had not actually goofed when I let Krupa plead guilty on the misdemeanor. When the actual moment of truth came, Krupa would have to be acquitted. Gillen screamed his objection and Tom Foley sustained it. I—however—was no longer deeply concerned. If the jury convicted my client, I was sure that the upper courts would reverse.

Krupa made an excellent witness, answering all questions honestly, intelligently and without evasion. Gillen attempted to establish the fact that virtually all dance and jazz musicians depended upon drugs for the production of good music, and made something of an ass of himself with his attempts to question Krupa and to address the jury in what he regarded as hipster idiom. Nevertheless, the musician was convicted by these fine people and was sentenced by Judge Foley to a term of one to six years. I immediately filed notice of appeal, and execution of sentence was stayed pending action of the Appellate Court. Then I crossed the Bridge of Sighs that connected the old Hall of Justice to County Jail Number One and visited Gene in his cell.

He had changed from the neat blue suit he'd worn in court and was seated cross-legged on his bunk, drumming away on the bars with his practice sticks to the tune of "Melancholy Baby," droned out by the jailhouse radio. He flashed me that never-failing smile that I always remember when I think of Krupa. He had a question for me while I was trying to think of a tactful opening gambit.

"Hi, champ! Where do we play next?"

I laughed with him.

"New York, maybe . . . Chicago, who knows! Certainly not San Quentin."

"I'll write my agent tonight."

We smiled at each other and I knew why he needed no artificial stimulants to help him put on a good show.

"Are you really that confident in me, Gene? After today's bad news?"

"Like I said, Jake, I'm with you. You give the downbeat, I'll play the notes."

The stormy weather wasn't over.

On July 10, 1943, the Associated Press carried a story that the FBI had grabbed John Pateakos in Los Angeles. Pateakos stated that he had been laying low because he'd been paid to do so. Payment had been made by a representative of Attorney J. W. Ehrlich. The amount of the payment was $650. Pateakos was now in the custody of District Attorney Matt Brady of San Francisco.

I was in New York on business at the time the story broke and was promptly interviewed by representatives of the news wire services. Had I subsidized Krupa's former horn jockey? Had I corrupted him with $650? I told them that if and when I took up applied corruption as a form of occupational diversification I'd do so with class and start with a more substantial figure than $650.

My statement was put on the wire, and in San Francisco, Matt Brady began to mumble vague threats to the local press about what he might do to me and to Roy Sharff. I decided it was time to put a few cards on the table, and climbed aboard the next plane.

When I appeared in the District Attorney's office the next morning, I tried civility and reason for openers. I gently and good-humoredly offered him the full and complete story of our dealings with Pateakos, which were palpably innocent enough. Rudely and hostilely, he refused to accept it. He was going to have Gillen take Sharff to the Grand Jury, to "take him apart," to bring about his indictment and conviction. I continued with the quiet approach.

"You'll have to try to indict me, too, Matt."

"We'll do that. Mr. Gillen tells me this is a flagrant case of law violation."

"Brady, you are an old dunce and Gillen is a deputy dunce," I said. "As for Gillen and his malarkey about flagrancy, you know damned well that he's sore because I trimmed him in the Ludolph case and made a bum of him in the Atherton back-stabbing contest. You, also, being a bush-league, church-social and barroom politician, have your own reasons for envy, resentment and spite. And even fear, I guess, to judge from the lengths to which you're going in order to avoid being unfrocked at the elections this fall. And so now you're thinking of taking me and my associate to the Grand Jury, you old reprobate!"

He was standing at his desk now, his face scarlet, his speech an inarticulate sputter. I thought I might as well spill the few remaining beans, as long as I'd gone this far.

"Matt, you're through!" I was feeling like an ancient prophet of doom and wishing I had a few additional inches against Brady's imposing height with which to pronounce the remainder of the Ehrlich Curse—or a thunderbolt to hurl as a climactic prelude to exit. "You might as well clean out your desk and have your name taken off the door, because I'm going to see you're beaten so badly in November that you never look at a ballot box again without throwing up. I'm going to lick you good, Matt!"

He had just begun to find his voice when I walked out and it waxed noisy in the district attorney's office. The gist of the noise was that Ehrlich was damned sure going to appear before the Grand Jury.

And Ehrlich damned sure did.

John Pateakos was there also, huddled between an escort of bruisers from Brady's office and trying his best to evade the flash-gun marksmanship and shouted questions of reporters. With the District Attorney as his duenna, he appeared before the Grand Jury for almost an hour, apparently being in good voice. When his testimony was over and he'd been smuggled away to whatever fastness had been prepared for him, Brady came to the anteroom with a small statement for the press.

Pateakos had been corrupted, he told them in his best press-wheedling tones. He said that Pateakos had asked for $800 but had settled for $650. He said, very ominously, that "two prominent attorneys" might be involved. He wouldn't mention the names, and then left the room, ignoring or avoiding my glare.

Sharff was next. When Gillen asked him to tell the jurors whether he had contacted and paid Pateakos, he blithely answered in the affirmative. What for? For an alleged indebtedness owed by our client, Gene Krupa. Proof? Sharff had it. He offered as evidence two handwritten documents, both the work of Pateakos.

The first of these read: "Received from J. W. Ehrlich the sum of $500 in full settlement and payment of all my claims against Gene Krupa and Frank Vienere. It is understood that this amount is calculated upon the basis of wages unpaid, clothes lost for me, and traveling expenses in accordance with my understanding when joining the Gene Krupa band, and reimbursement for moneys laid out, together with all possible claims and demands."

The second read: *"To Whom It May Concern:* This is my free and voluntary statement that the settlement I have this day made with Gene Krupa and Frank Vienere was made purely upon the basis of my legal claims against them. There was no understanding as part of such settlement that I was to do anything with reference to the case of Gene Krupa in San Francisco, nor that I was to change my testimony in any way. Likewise, no promises were asked of me before settlement was made, and no requests made of me as to my future acts or conduct."

This was the information that had been available to the District Attorney at the time of my return from New York, but which he preferred to ignore and consequently go to the Grand Jury half cocked. The Frank Vienere mentioned in the statement was Krupa's manager. The amount paid Pateakos was $150 less than he claimed.

I was the next witness called. I was asked why I had failed to inform Brady of the whereabouts of his witness. I explained that the District Attorney was a man who didn't exactly welcome my assistance, and that I, too, regarded it as no part of *my* duty to assist *him* in the performance of *his* duties. In that area we enjoyed a solid meeting of minds.

Lacking other means of harassing me now that the payment to Pateakos had been pretty well deflated as a sinister act, Gillen attempted to stigmatize me with innuendo-tinted questions and trap-door inquiries, but this was playing ball with my ball and bat and he got nowhere. When my interrogation was over, I asked permission to offer a relevant document: an affidavit from the woman with whom Pateakos had stayed while in Los Angeles. Contrary to what Brady claimed for his witness, Pateakos had never left the city of Los Angeles during the entire period of his elopement, according to her sworn statement.

In the end, Brady's promise was broken for him by the grand jurors. They refused to indict either Sharff or me. On the other hand, my promise to Brady was carefully kept. I turned my law practice over to my associates for a time slot that was to stretch to election eve, and I went to work on Brady. I made speeches, I buttonholed friends and strangers alike, I wrote articles and spent money—all in the cause of Pat Brown, Brady's opponent in the race for District Attorney and now Governor of California. I was able to persuade my friend Lou Lurie to switch his support from Brady to Brown; a changeover that lost Matt a myriad of billboards with which Millionaire Lurie had regularly supplied him during other elections. I was also able to convince Publisher Paul Smith of the San Francisco *Chronicle* that Matt had been pointed, nose first, in the public trough far too long. Matt lost the *Chronicle;* one of the leading papers in San Francisco. He also lost his job. The Ehrlich Curse had worked again.

And—best of best endings—I was able to keep my promise to Krupa. John Pateakos, with a little harmless inspirational guidance, recanted. I took him into juvenile court before Judge Theresa Meikle on February 15, 1944, and under oath the boy admitted that he'd lied when he said the marijuana belonged to Krupa. Under pain of prosecution for perjury, he further admitted that the narcotic agents had persuaded him to testify otherwise because, as John frankly put it, "They said it would go easier with me if I did." And it did, which proves that even finkery has its golden moments.

This rather tardy conversion to right thinking helped materially, but what really freed Gene was my claim of included offenses which Brady and Gillen scorned and Judge Foley refused to sustain. "When the State accepts a plea of guilty for the offense which carries the lighter sentence, it is without right thereafter to prosecute for the offense which carries the heavier penalty," said the Appellate Court in the decision that negated a serious injustice but failed to prevent a painful human experience from lousing up the youth of a fine man who didn't deserve it.

On May 29, 1944, the District Court of Appeal of the State of California took 22 printed pages to decide that I was right and reversed the conviction. Foley, Gillen and Brady, Incorporated, again looked like what they always were—The Unholy Three.

Most of these people have gone their various ways and exist no more insofar as I'm concerned. Foley and Gillen and Brady have died, Giubbini is running a drugstore in suburban San Mateo, and Johnny Pateakos disappeared into some limbo of his own. Looking backward at the chaos of the moment—courtroom battles, headlines, a manhunt, revenge exacted, a district attorney defrocked and another man catapulted not only into the latter's job but ultimately into the governorship and eventually who knows where else—I sometimes wonder about the cosmic, long-view meaningfulness of anything and everything. Probably the greatest degree of perception into our destinies lies in the aphorism that, "Sufficient to the day is the deed thereof." But one thing I'm damned good and sure of—a hell of a lot of things happened because of one tenth of one third of a cigaretteful of the flowering hemp Webster defines as "a wild tobacco."

The second case had overtones and aftereffects and an epilogue that were somewhat more somber.

Billie Holiday was one of America's great blues singers. She's singing no more because of two things, in my opinion: because of dope; because of our unintentionally vicious and certainly unknowledgeable treatment of those who are addicted to it.

I feel strongly on the subject of America's criminalization of its addicts, of its refusal to implement on a functional level according to what it knows to be true on a scientific level. There is hardly a physician, psychiatrist or professional authority today who fails to recognize that narcotic addiction is an illness instead of a crime; that it is a problem to be solved with treatment rather than with punishment and incarceration; and even more importantly true, that it's a problem deepened by the application of penalty.

Once we beat and tortured and imprisoned our mentally ill, turned them into pariahs to a degree that even though we've reformed our methods and beliefs, stigma still attaches to the status of the insane in the minds of the unlettered and the unfeeling. But we found out how wrong we were. We took our poor, deranged fellow humans out of the hands of police and jailers and we turned them over to doctors and nurses.

But we have not yet reached the point of enlightenment where we can stir ourselves from the tradition and taboo of the moment about another type of invalid, the addict. We warily eye these agonized and entrapped humans as the wise men of Salem eyed their witches, and we set our police on them, we shoot them down when in their panic they seek to escape, we throw those whom we do capture into felons' cells for long terms of incarceration. When for some strange reason their illness—though largely untreated—doesn't cure itself, we submit them to the same process all over again, referring to them as "incorrigible recidivists."

The ironic thing is that although narcotics have been used by limited numbers and representations of people since the beginning of time, only recently and under the sponsorship of the United States Government have their uses been popularized. The invention of the hypodermic needle and the advent of the American Civil War were virtually simultaneous. The military doctors of both sides of this struggle used morphine, via the new device, to kill the pain, but they apparently didn't realize how addictive it was. In the so-called peace that followed there were 500,000 morphine addicts in the country, unlisted casualties of the hostilities just ended. There were no laws against the peddling of narcotic drugs in drugstores and none were enacted until 1916 when the Harrison Act made it difficult for an addict to obtain drugs, placed a premium value on the commodity, and in effect made criminals out of invalids.

World Wars I and II helped amplify the evil. Drugs were again used to narcotize pain, but doctors had learned their dangers as well as their benefits, and more care was taken to prevent addictions. Still, there were many war-incurred addictions.

Now there are probably better than 500,000 addicts in the

country. The Treasury Department's Bureau of Narcotics, plus a myriad of local law-enforcement agencies in the city, the county and the state (all competing in a rather ludicrous fashion), are entrusted with the delicate problem of dealing with these unfortunate victims of our times. They understand little of the nature and scope and profundity of the subject. They believe that they might eventually "dry up" addiction in the United States (and by that they mean reduce it to a minimum of about 60,000 addicts) by alert policework, endless intercourse with informers and relentless prosecution. To me, this method and philosophy suggest Hitler's handling of those whom his administration regarded as "undesirables." He gassed them.

I don't believe that the problem will ever be solved in the United States until narcotic addiction is completely removed from the category of crime and placed in the hands of professional therapists.

I said that Billie Holiday ultimately became a victim of dope and of society's method of dealing with addicts. When I knew her and defended her, she was also the victim of a sometimes equally destructive force called love.

Billie, whom her fans called Lady Day, was about at her peak as a jazz and blues singer when I met her.

She had been arrested for possession of opium in a San Francisco hotel while appearing at a local night club known as Café Society Uptown. The arrest had been made under circumstances which did no credit to due process or respect for the Constitution. Chicanery and the most obvious connivery were employed in trapping her. The picture wasn't a pretty one, but like many pictures I've seen its effect was augmented by a frame; it was the frame that interested me, and Lady Day had been elaborately framed.

She wasn't exactly a sharp show-business sophisticate, this Amazonian Baltimore blues singer with a voice as full and creamy as a thick milk shake and a beat that was better than the drummer's. In matters of men and money she was still fourteen and foolish. She bought furs and diamonds as though her multithousand-dollar fees might vanish unless she spent them fast, and she bought men in the same manner. The men were a more dubious investment; the diamonds at least stayed bought.

Her most expensive and questionable investment in the man market was a quiet, complicated, track-covering gentleman named John Levy, whose name was ethnically misleading. John may have been a wheeler, but as far as Billie was concerned he was rarely a dealer, except in the commodities of hooks, jabs and straight rights. He was her manager. Managers usually take 10 percent of their principal's principal. This manager took about 90 percent and occasionally let his star have the remainder. If she was good.

Billie had always been the dependent type. Once she had depended on heroin, and this had finally brought her to the Federal Reformatory at Alderson where it had taken ten months to rehabilitate her. When she returned to the night club circuit something more than a year before her San Francisco engagement, she felt that she was through with dope. At Alderson, no real attempt had been made to get at the reason for her use of narcotics, so there was no real reason to believe that dope was through with her. However, I was able to determine to my own satisfaction that Billie was clean of the habit when she came to San Francisco. I know a junky when I see one. Billie suffered from a different addiction then.

The details of the arrest were interesting and significant to any objective student of narcotic policing.

Billie and John Levy had been lounging out the day in pajamas in their hotel suite when the telephone rang. The singer took the call. It was for Levy. He took the telephone and exchanged a few monosyllables with the person on the other end of the line. Later he asserted that someone unknown to him had asked for a business appointment and that he had agreed to it.

When he put down the telephone, Levy handed Lady Day a small package and told her to flush its contents down the john. She was doing that when there was a sharp rap on the door of the suite. Without hesitation, Levy opened the door—a significant phase of this interlude. Levy, who ostensibly had some personal reason for wanting the package to pass from immediate existence, nevertheless took the promptest action to permit its apprehension by the gaggle of intruders composed of my old friend and adversary Colonel George White, one of his minions from the Bureau of Narcotics and two San Francisco police inspectors.

The next few seconds in the now well-populated suite were like a photo finish of a dead-heat rat race. Miss Holiday and White arrived at the john at about the same time, with Billie flushing and the agent groping. The lady had thoughtfully ricocheted something that was later described as "a bottle of opium" against the side of the commode in the course of carrying out her man's orders, and all that the colonel and his men were able to grab from the churning waters were a few fragments of glass. This, however, proved sufficient for the arrest. One of the fragments contained a brown substance which turned out to be opium when analyzed. Billie and Levy were taken to the Hall of Justice, and this is where I entered the case.

It was then that two other interesting developments took place.

The first was that Colonel White was clearly drawing a bead on Billie, and on Billie only, in his complaint, although Levy was booked, too. Completely disregarding the girl's simply and obviously unimprovised story of what had taken place in the room prior to his entrance—or refusing to believe that the two might at least be equally guilty—White was obviously trying to send Billie and only Billie to prison. Item two: Levy had somehow been exempted from bribery charges despite the fact that the Colonel freely stated that the manager tried to bribe him to let Lady Day go and to "forget the incident." "I declined his offer to do that," stated the Colonel in describing the incident, apparently momentarily forgetting that such an "offer" has felonious aspects. The mere fact that Colonel White would blithely put himself on record as having merely "declined" the offer was ample proof to raucously cynical pressroom commentators that Mr. Levy and Mr. White enjoyed a mutually assistive relationship in the enterprise at hand (i.e., Billie's dumping), and that the offer of cash ransom and its pious turndown were but well-played refutations of what might be a too obviously engineered consignment of the singer to the penitentiary. After all, Mr. Levy would want to move freely about Harlem in the years to come, and there were many loyal and often uninhibited admirers of Lady Day in Harlem and elsewhere in the manager's tomorrows.

I was faced with the accomplishment of a two-fold purpose. I was being asked to defend a client against an apparently ironclad case for the prosecution but—far more difficult—I was also required to unframe an apparently airtight frame-up. It was the latter challenge that hooked me.

Finkery, in all of its many manifestations and aspects, repels and angers me more than any other phase of human misconduct. Trouble, strife, head-on hostility and relentless contest are basic substances of human relationships. Where they are concerned I say let the best man, the best argument, the best fight (and the best lawyer) win. But the sellout, the frame-up, the planned and clandestine dumping, treachery from the trusted —these are outside all rules, noxious to the nose, mind and heart, and beneath the contempt of any but the mentally and morally mediocre.

I decided to unframe the frame-up, to obtain Miss Holiday's acquittal, and to clearly document Mr. Levy's status and function in the case.

One of my greatest difficulties was the fact that my client was still in love with her manager. Not that she didn't entertain even darker suspicions of his character and aims than I did; she merely took the position that no matter what he did to and against her she still loved him. This proved highly unhelpful to me. It was like trying to shoot down a quarry with a shotgun loaded with twelve-gauge marshmallows.

Meanwhile I had obtained Lady Day's freedom on bail and

she had gone back to work at Café Society Uptown. This was one case in which publicity provided benefits. The café was packed nightly, which delighted its operator, Joseph Tenner, a bulbous former police character with a propensity for opening and closing resorts that often figured in seamy headlines. I dropped in to hear my client sing and to take a reading on the psychological temperature of the situation, as well as to hear what Mr. Tenner and others had to say of the relationship between Billie and John Levy. I found the singing delightful and the gossip, gathered from various sources, even more worth my time and loss of sleep.

Levy, according to night-life scuttlebutt, had come to the end of the line as far as Billie was concerned; he had been looking around for his nearest exit for quite some time. He had enough of her money and now owned a Manhattan spot in Harlem called the Club Ebony. He had another girl. He wanted out. But he couldn't just dump a woman as popular as Lady Day, whose generosity to him was well known everywhere. He had his own public image to think about. He had to do something more subtle and conclusive, something that would leave him looking loyal and faithful and appealingly noble

I was interested in the transcript of the Grand Jury proceedings on Billie's arrest when it was made available. I noted that Colonel White, always super-resourceful, had not been content with the official analysis of the brown substance as opium; he had supplemented this evidence with a tremendously ingenious and creative analysis of the remainder of the broken pipe as "an improvised opium pipe." He reiterated the story of Levy's magnanimous attempt to bribe "this poor girl" loose from the rap, and he made it quite clear that he had never before had any social, official, commercial or other contacts with Levy. "I knew him by description and reputation but not by sight," was the way he put it. The most interesting result of the Grand Jury's cogitation, however, was the fact that it had decided to honor someone's recommendation and not embarrass Mr. Levy further. He was not to be prosecuted.

In most cases of narcotic prosecution, all parties—near, over, under, about or close to the captured drug—are relentlessly prosecuted. Levy had been spared this indignity. People are ordinarily spared this indignity only because they have in some way endeared themselves to the authorities. The present case might of course prove to be the rare exception to that rule but I thought not. I was convinced that I knew the shell under which the little pea lay.

I asked Billie to come in for a conference next morning. Although I couldn't decide whether the puffiness of one of her eyes, shaded by dark glasses, was a black eye or not, I suspected it was and asked the melancholy girl about it.

"Yeah, he beat me," she said, starting to cry. "Soon's the Grand Jury set him free, he came to the hotel room, beat me bad, took my eighteen-thousand-dollar fur coat, split out for New York. He's gone for good now and I ain't got nothing. I'm scared, Mr. Jake; I'm scared all over."

I was hoping for the impossible I guess.

"All right, Billie, are you mad enough and hurt enough and scared enough to tell me the truth about him—to help me show people how he put you in this jackpot?"

She snuffled into her handkerchief before replying.

"I can't do that, Mr. Jake. I love him."

I was back with my twelve-gauge marshmallows. There are times when love should be grounds for mental commitment.

We went to trial before Judge Wollenberg, to whom I've referred before. The prosecutor was Al Weinberger, the man I'd battled so vigorously in the Borelli murder case. It was clear that Al figured he had an easy one this time. The defendant had a narcotics record. The evidence was chemically authenticated. The principal witness for the prosecution, Colonel White, was a cool and knowledgeable expert, resourceful under cross-examination, famed and popular as a dope fighter. Al had already cut a notch in his briefcase for this one. Even White, a man not prone to count chickens that were still in their shells, was wearing the tight little smile of a man who had already heard the jury's verdict and liked it.

Prosecutor Weinberger's statement to the jury was a flawless indictment; it put Billie squarely in a prison cell. Colonel White then turned the key in the lock with a cool, businesslike piece of testimony that was straight from the manual. When I got to my feet for the defense, my client stood convicted. I knew that I was going to have to match procedures and ethics with the people who had dealt with John Levy. I was going to have to cut corners, throw curves and deal an occasional card from the bottom of the deck if this palpable frame-up were to be short-circuited.

I questioned White about the decency and dignity of a Federal official by-passing the need for a warrant in making a raid by taking a city policeman along. (City police, at that time, could break and enter a premise, warrantless, merely on their hunch that a felony is being committed.) Weinberger promptly objected, but the jury had heard the question and was deprived of hearing the answer which—had it been handled skillfully—would have made White's action look far better than it did.

I then asked him how long he'd known John Levy ("Since the arrest."), if he'd met him at any time previously ("Never!"), and if he and Levy had ever discussed how to carry out the raid ("No!"). By now the jurors were looking at Colonel White with new interest.

I asked him if he'd been instrumental in getting Levy freed. The question was killed by Weinberger's objection and Judge Wollenberg's sustainer, but it had been heard—well heard, thoughtfuly heard. I asked the narcotics ace to explain the curious anomaly of the double arrest and the single prosecution.

"Here is a man," I said, before he could answer or the question be stricken, "who swears upon his oath that John Levy and Billie Holiday committed a crime, to wit: that they possessed opium. Now we are in open court and his testimony is *not* that these two people at this place, on this date, possessed opium! He says, in effect, that John Levy did *not* possess opium, but Billie Holiday did!"

The question was stricken but it was heard.

I then asked Colonel White to identify a picture I'd had

blown up from a negative bought from the camera girl at Café Society Uptown. There was no question as to what it showed, and the jurors were obviously curious to see it, but Weinberger furiously interposed objections. This was a clear-cut mistake. The twelve citizens who were to pass upon this alleged crime were beginning to wonder if they were not being given *some* of the truth, carefully *chosen* truth, and only *as much of the truth* as someone regarded as good for them. I was determined that they should explore this suspicion even more thoroughly, no matter how indirectly the stimulus to do so might reach them.

I proceeded directly into the breach in credulity created by my line of questioning, and turned implication into broad accusation.

"Isn't it true, Mr. White," I asked, tapping the photograph that had been ruled out of testimony and now lay on the counsel table, "isn't it true that you sat with John Levy and listened to him tell you he wanted to get rid of Billie Holiday and planned with him as to how to catch her in the possession of—"

"Objection!"

"Sustained!"

The jury stared at White with more than a little interest now. He *seemed* to be such a fine, dignified-looking man, but . . .

I kept hitting.

"Isn't it a fact that when you walked into that apartment and headed for the bathroom you knew just where to go because you'd been told where to go to find the opium?"

Red-faced with anger now, the Colonel denied this outright charge of a rigged arrest. I suggested that he was fully aware that Levy was a known informer and a practicing stool pigeon. My words were stricken but—again—they didn't go unheard. Then I took up the matter of the bribe offer. I let the jury listen to the witness give a bald and unqualified No to a question as to whether he had charged or intended to charge and prosecute John Levy for, "attempting to bribe you, if such an attempt took place." The jury faces reflected respective attitudes toward such a seeming dereliction of duty, and I decided to let my old friend off the hook. His testimony, even in its court-throttled nonanswers to my questions, had served many important services. And like the hangman, he was only doing his duty as he saw it and according to the custom and mores of his bureau. He looked delighted to get off the stand.

Next I reversed the mood and direction of the proceedings and put my client on the stand. It isn't considered smart defense strategy to put a defendant in a narcotics case on the stand, and there's ample reason for this. If they are actively addicted, they make weak and often uncontrollable witnesses; by their appearance and mannerisms they convict themselves; they are inevitably dangerous to themselves under cross-examination. But I wasn't worried about Billie. Whatever this naive, guileless girl could say could only serve to indict the people and the times that had produced her.

Her story, drawn from her with all the gentleness I could muster, was not a glamorous one, not at all what the prosecution's portrayal of her might have led the jury to expect. Her large family had been migrant until the father had deserted it for a Dallas morgue when a hospital there had refused him care and treatment for pneumonia because he was a Negro. Her mother had taken the children to a sister's home in Baltimore, opened a small restaurant, and teetered back and forth between plain poverty and utter poverty. Billie had left school after the fifth grade. Her mother needed her in the restaurant.

Success came suddenly and accidentally. She had never become used to it, and always secretly and with desperate, gnawing fear expected to be plummeted back into the greasy pots and pans of dishwashing tubs. One day her inner unrest had been eased by some white powders her lover gave her. That led to prison.

"But I volunteered for the cure," wailed Billie from the stand, "and I got cured. And I *never* took no opium! And I ain't had no drugs since. I came home and society took me back. Thank God for allowing me this second chance."

I asked her if she knew Mr. White, and she replied that she'd seen him often at Café Society Uptown.

"With . . . ?" and I didn't finish the question but merely pointed toward the disallowed photograph the jurors now knew so well.

"With John Levy. Always with John Levy."

I asked her if she ever fought with Levy.

"Fight!" She raised her eyes toward the ceiling and broke into a laugh that was half a sob. "We didn't do nothing else but, that cat and me. I keep asking him about where all my money go and he keep telling me to shut up. I keep asking him to give me some money and he keep beating me limp."

"What were your annual earnings?"

"About two hundred thousand."

I asked her if she and Levy planned to marry.

"Yes. We were sweethearts and I turned my whole life over to him. He took every penny I made. He bought everything, done everything. We were supposed to get married and we didn't and that was why we was arguing and he was so mad at me the day the police came."

I led her through the story of the raid. The big, childlike woman told it in a fashion that was impossible to disbelieve, giving it a quality that made White's version sound calculated and contrived, although it had actually been neither. Then I asked her where her fiancé was now. Weinberger made a furious attempt to interpose an objection but Billie spoke first.

"He's gone. He lef' me."

It was quite effective.

Now the prosecution cross-examined. And now Weinberger's cool, clipped expertise was somehow gone. He managed to hit the wrong notes right from the outset.

"Has Mr. Levy been acting as your business manager?"

Billie looked at the prosecutor as if his nose were painted green.

"Business manager! He's my *man!*"

The courtroom—but of most importance, the jury—exploded

with laughter. Not scornful laughter—kindly, understanding laughter. Weinberger struggled on toward his next *gaffe.*

"You handed the phone to him instead of taking the call yourself?"

"Of course! I *never* did anything without John telling me!"

"You mean to tell me that you intended to throw an object as large as this package into the—"

"Man, I didn't notice how large it was. If your wife asked you to throw something away would you notice how large it was? You'd just *throw!* I'd just do anything John told me . . ."

The great, welling, understanding laughter again. I knew that Billie had been unframed, that John Levy's machinations were completely undone long before the jury brought in its verdict of Not Guilty. Billy kissed my hands over and over, leaving them moist with her tears.

"I been so scare," she said, "I been so scare!"

The story doesn't have a happy ending unfortunately. Lady Day returned to her dependence on the wrong kind of men and stimulants and died of an overdose of narcotics at age thirty-two.

She is one of the principal reasons that I fail to admire our kindly, understanding treatment of narcotic addicts.

I have previously referred to the rarity of gratitude among people from whom this virtue might reasonably have been expected. Like many general statements, this one commits cruelty upon those who were the exceptions. It would be wrong to go on adding that the appreciation of those who have remembered is, like Portia's candle shining in the darkness, a far-reaching beacon.

One of the most unforgettable of these gestures was made by Caryl Chessman, the man whom the State of California murdered some years ago as punishment for a number of alleged crimes that certainly didn't include murder.

Chessman, it may be recalled, was the so-called "red-light bandit" who was sentenced to death by a somewhat intemperate Los Angeles jury and the then existing mob psychology after having been apprehended in connection with a number of lover's lane robberies. The capital penalty was applied to this unfortunate man under California's almost unique "Little Lindbergh law" which defines "kidnapping" in a singular way and which provides death as the only therapy for those whose conduct falls within this odd and arbitrary definition. Chessman, who may have robbed (even this claim was not clearly proven) but who did not kill, managed to qualify to a dozen of his peers as a "Little Lindbergh kidnaper" (though neither did he kidnap) and was sentenced to extermination in the green box at San Quentin.

At the time of his arrest he was apparently a young, socially underprivileged person who was having trouble keeping his balance in this hectic, uneven civilization of ours, but he was not a professional crook or vicious or even as much of a menace to the body politic as certain junketing senators on the loose in Central Europe.

During the six years that passed between his conviction and his sacrifice at the hands of the state, Chessman successfully developed his intellect. He wrote two books; he explored the law as well as he could from the confines of Death Row; and most significant of all, he made an unforgettable impression on the world in general. People and organizations and publications so far away from his grim haven that even its locale was merely a strange, technicolor vagueness became well read on the details of his case and ardent adherents to his cause.

I, too, became interested. My interest and eventual participation resulted from a television panel discussion; the subject was capital punishment in its relevancy to the Chessman case. Pat Brown, then the State Attorney General, spoke in favor of speedier execution of death sentences. I spoke against any and all kinds of death sentences, speedy or otherwise. My opposition to murder by fiat was based more upon my basic convictions than upon the Chessman case at the outset of the debate, but as I went on I found myself becoming more and more aroused by the many ways in which Chessman's rights had been circumvented by careless or corrupt or pathologically hostile officials. My indignation must have gotten through to the television audience, because immediately after the broadcast I was contacted by a number of people who urged me to do what I could for the unfortunate man in *Cell 2455, Death Row*—the title of Chessman's interesting book.

I decided to appear in support of Supreme Court Justice Carter's decision, which had granted Caryl a twenty-four-hour stay on the eve of execution. Building my argument about the legal technicalities of a faultily transcribed record of the trial by a drunken court reporter, I asked for a complete review of the case. I was also able to insert a number of other hitherto ignored truths into my argument, to call attention to the degree that the Los Angeles judge had by-passed due process, to point out that he had—in effect—turned a trial into a lynching by virtually ordering the jury to bring in a death verdict. The U.S. Supreme Court must have been impressed. It referred the case back to the district Federal court, which meant more time for the fight against the cyanide pellets. Chessman, unfortunately, was up to his ears in a stew prepared by too many cooks. His lawyers, advocates and counselors swarmed about him like well-meaning but many-minded gadflies. He wrote me as follows:

> DEAR MR. EHRLICH:
>
> I want you to know how sincerely I appreciate the critical legal assistance you have rendered in my behalf. When you stepped into the case, my reaction was one of agreeable surprise, tinged with awe. For to me, as to others, the name of J. W. Ehrlich is a formidable courtroom legend. Your presentation before the State Supreme Court in opposing the Attorney General's motion to vacate the stay of execution granted by Justice Carter emphatically revealed why.
>
> Thanks to your fine assistance, the case now—as you are well aware—approaches a climactic phase. Should you have any suggestions or advice as to its handling, I and those assisting me will be abidingly grateful for them. I fully realize that they could spell the difference between life and death.
>
> From my standpoint, the unfortunate thing is that I am financially unable to employ, full time, your legal generalship

in this forthcoming fight for life in the United States District Court. Unhappily, I simply haven't the funds to do so. Notwithstanding the considerable extravagant speculation about the amount of money my book has earned or will earn, the fact is that royalty payments are made only on a semi-annual basis, three months after the close of each period, and prior to your entry into the case, I had already committed myself to the very limit of my resources.

Again, in closing, my sincerest thanks.

Respectfully,
CARYL CHESSMAN

I was not interested in his royalties, but others were. After obtaining this substantial stint of fighting time for Chessman, I found myself elbowed aside by some of those whose interests in the case were differently motivated. The poor man was finally led to his death amid a crescendo of bickering, legal fancy dancing, pro-and-con rhetoric, righteous denunciations from the smug death dealers, and insensate breast beating and teeth grinding from the well-meaning but afunctional bleeding hearts.

Personally I have never forgotten the calm, dignified expression of appreciation that came to me from a man who was up to his neck in the quicksands of death. Here, illogically enough, was one of the most unforgettable exceptions to my cynical generality about ingratitude.

11: *Morning*

10:30 A.M.

Agenda: Preliminary Hearing, Municipal Court V. McN. (Charged with Murder One).

Ten minutes before my scheduled appearance in court at the Hall of Justice, I stepped into a taxi.

I am a taxi type. During the long years of moving in every possible transportational pattern on this hilly, narrow-streeted town, I've exhausted all of the commoner possibilities for getting from one place to the other. From my first automobile, an unnew and hard-to-come-by 1926 Buick sedan, to my last one, a Fleetwood Cadillac, I sensed that people are as much owned by their cars as they are owners of these unwieldy impediments. Now I prefer to be driven. And I prefer to be driven in cabs because cab drivers are usually the best and most quickly found sources of quick companionship, ready entertainment and sometimes valid information. In what other conceivable manner may one get a ride, a horse tip, an argument, a fairly good joke about Nixon, a probably fake rumor about the mayor and a blow-by-blow account of what passed between the cabby and his wife that morning at breakfast, and all for what it would cost to garage one's car, if one had a car.

On this particular morning, as so often happened, the hackie I found waiting for me down on Montgomery Street was an old friend. In fact, he was more; he was an erstwhile sporting colleague. More than forty years before, according to our hastily accomplished arithmetic, I had faced him in at least one four-round bout at National Hall. He was of the opinion that he'd gotten a draw but memory or vanity played him false: I had cooled him in the fourth. However, it was good to see him again and he claimed equal pleasure at the reunion.

His name was O'Brien and with his wife and two children he'd lived a few blocks away from me in the good, gray, respectable Richmond district during the years when I toiled behind the flanks of the Wells Fargo horses, studied law, and took up some of the economic slack by occasional forays into the ring.

Then as now, he hacked the streets of San Francisco, and occasionally we'd share a streetcar seat on our trips to and from our homes. Then one day—a world and almost a lifetime away—we'd just not seen each other again. He hadn't heard what had happened to me, and in some strange fashion he hadn't associated his fistic opponent and neighbor with Jake Ehrlich, the lawyer. He was astounded and impressed and nearly pulled into a mail truck ahead of us. I had heard nothing of *his* destiny, and I, too, was strongly affected when I was told what had happened to him.

The reason for my not having run into him during the period when we still lived in the Richmond district had to do with the fact that he'd gone a little broke and become a little careless about his first and only crime. He'd held up a man just a few blocks away from home and almost in front of the local police station. It was easy for the police to nab him. It was also easy for society to salt him away in San Quentin: he was a poor man and without friends. He might have regarded me as a friend had he thought of it, but he knew that I was a poor man, too, and never thought that I could be of much help. He served a long term; he never saw his wife and children again.

The story made me very thoughtful. We had been two men of the same age and period, each with a wife and two children, each with about the same degree—or lack of degree—of worldly prospects. Each of us had known poverty and need and desperation at about the same rungs of ladders that were good for about the same potential for carrying our respective weights; and each of the ladders had been headed upward. I don't deceive myself that I possessed some rare and shining character that forbade all possibility of human error, nor do I remember any significant suggestion of weakness or warp in the bright-faced, healthy-minded youngster whose boxing was for the same family feeding purpose as mine. Yet his path took him to a cell in San Quentin while mine led me elsewhere.

I don't believe that destiny is by any means a mysterious and inscrutable procedure, nor do I believe that most people are blind pawns of condition or circumstance, but I *do* believe that the borderline between success and failure, happiness and misery, and even right and wrong, is often microscopically hair-line.

O'Brien was still chattering about the old days when we pulled up at the new Hall of Justice on Bryant Street. He said that he'd never married again; that he lived alone in a small hotel in the tenderloin. He told me that my old flat was still standing (he'd let a fare off several doors away only last week) and commented sourly on the current crop of fighters in our mutual weight class.

"Either you or I could have handled any of them the worst day we ever had." He grinned as he pulled the flag down and wearily started to get out of his vehicle. I waved him back behind the wheel. Somehow I didn't want this tired, cheated ghost from out of the hopeful yesterdays to open a cab door for me today. I was pleased to discover that I could only find a twenty in my billfold, and I gave it to him, refusing change. He thought that twenty was too much for a tip.

"That's no tip, Obie. That's a lost bet. I bet myself that you'd have kicked off years ago. This is one I'm happy to lose."

If there'd been such a bet I'd have won it, I told myself as I watched the empty-eyed oldster in the battered leather jacket pull into the traffic stream and suddenly realized that he'd recognized me, and not the reverse. I'd have won it, because for all human purposes and happy uses, the young, vital O'Brien I knew had passed away long ago in a San Quentin cell where society had sent him to be rehabilitated. The actual death of the man's heart and soul probably occurred at about the time that he knew for sure there'd be no more letters from his wife and children. The body was later paroled and still drives a cab in San Francisco.

The scene in the courtroom was very familiar. The shift from the grim, brooding old Hall of Justice on Kearny Street to the bright new trial rooms at the new Hall had actually meant no changes in the atmosphere or the cast of characters. The tense psychological climate of nervous suspense was still there, as were the bored and impersonal clerks, the calm, familiar judicial face behind the bench, the sick and searching eyes of the long-addicted trial watchers, the staccato ticking of the electric clock on the wall, and the single and somehow incongruous contribution of color provided by the staffed American flag in the corner. It was all just as it has always been for Act One, Scene One, Trial of a Man for Murder.

Even the faces of the members of the press were about the same. Frank O'Mea, in his twenty-third year of being at the Hall for the *Examiner,* white-haired Baron Muller on hand for the *News-Call,* Charles Raudebaugh, Paul Avery and Berney Jarvis fronting for the *Chronicle,* and their usual retinue of bored, developer-dappled photographers; the Fourth Estate's constitutionally unimpressed outpost on the crime and justice front. I also saw, a few yards away, my friend and protégé, Harry S. Wainright, who is fast becoming the leading criminal trial lawyer in California.

The reporters caught me in the corridor outside the courtroom. Was I really going to undertake another criminal defense? The fact that he'd hired me meant that my client was guilty and desperate, didn't it? Did the guy's good-looking daughter have anything to do with my taking the case? What would be the defense? The questions were plastered on me in a way that bespoke sardonic humor, raffish regard, irreverent respect, reluctant admiration and a full awareness that double-edged banter and uninhibited repartee were media which I, too, understood and enjoyed.

I've always placed a high value on the coinage of my relationship with the working press. Unlike some lawyers who posture and pontificate before their interviewers or pretend to overlook or ignore them, I tell them as much truth as possible. I never, or rarely, lie to them, and I don't find fault with what's been written about me. After all, the newspaper writer only calls them as he sees them, and no one ever won an argument with an umpire, no matter how poor his eyesight may be.

Then there is always the risk of falling prey to the diabolical sense of humor of the people behind the typewriters. Once during an exchange of controversy with Paul Smith, former publisher of the *Chronicle,* I had closed my remarks with the trite old chestnut about, "not caring what was said about me just so long as my name was spelled right." It was a mistake. In the next morning's *Chronicle* story of the litigation at hand, my name appeared eighteen times, spelled eighteen different ways. I never used *that* particular banality again.

So now I gave them all that I could reasonably offer about the case. I presented my client as no sniveling lily white with a snappy alibi but as an ordinary guy in trouble because of an oversupply of booze and an undersupply of judgment and luck. I went along with the raucous jokes about his good-looking daughter, because daughters who are as well stacked as they are loyal to daddy are elements with which newspapermen can identify. And I posed for the usual corny pictures. Then I asked and got their advice on police aspects of the case, which they certainly understood better than I. Anyone who assumes that rapport with the working press isn't one of the more important and powerful dynamics in a criminal lawyer's system of defense is naive. When I pushed through the swinging doors of the courtroom, I was pretty sure that my client would at least have fair treatment in the upcoming editions, and perhaps more. I turned out to be right.

Inside, I met him for the first time and was permitted to have a brief but adequate interview with him, plus his daughter, in an adjacent holding room. He turned out to be an amiable, white-maned and obviously alcoholic old duffer upon whose face and body was the undeniable patina of a lifetime of toil. A jury would love him. His story was properly unpat but properly unshakable in the essentials. I knew that I would walk him out of this building and onto the street when all the legalistics were over. We returned to the courtroom. If his daughter had become pretty as the result of the earlier conference, she was beautiful now. Somehow the good feeling had gotten through to her, too. I told her to be sure and linger in the corridor for the photographers when the hearing was ended.

The formalities of the preliminary hearing, a legal amenity at which only the determination is made as to whether a felony has been committed, were over in minutes. The assistant district attorney, a young man who was now clearly aware that the push-over period in the case was ended, recited the basis of his complaint. When he had finished, I moved for a dismissal on the grounds of "an obvious case of self-defense," fully aware that the creation of the corpse in the coroner's green filing case downstairs couldn't possibly be this easily disposed of, and I was ready for the young prosecutor's indignant rejoinder with some tart remarks about "official revenge" and "legal lynching parties"; anything to give the young man a taste of the type of hostilities that were to come.

The motion was of course denied and I demanded bail. Again the lad had blood-pressure problems, but after some discussion the judge took the motion on submission, pending the decision of the Grand Jury as to what sort of a homicide indictment would be voted. My client was then bound over for appearance in Superior Court.

The young prosecutor casually sauntered over to the defense table; *too* casually. He put a great deal of care and effort into what was intended to shape into a superior, unconcerned, saturnine smile, but all that came to his lips was a nervous grimace. I remembered a lot of grimaces of my own from the almost forgotten first morning of my career as a lawyer and was touched.

"I've heard an awful lot about you, Mr. Ehrlich," he said, a little too gruffly for good effect, "and I know that you're pretty good. But you certainly don't expect to see this man of yours convicted of anything less than Murder One, I'm sure. Why, he went *back* to that bar and cold-bloodedly cut down his victim. If that isn't clear-cut premeditation I . . ."

Touched or not I had to let him have it. Staring at him sternly in the fashion that San Francisco newspapermen of half a century have described as "glaring from under massively beetled brows," I gave him my message.

"My client expects to be in Oregon for the opening of the duck season. I have promised him that he may do so. I never break a promise." And as a man who has no trouble recognizing an exit line when one develops, I left. Duck season! If that old rummy raised his rear from the seat of his cab until he got me paid it would certainly be over *my* dead body.

On my way out of the Hall I ran into another character out of San Francisco's and my past. He is one of those who must remain incognito here. He is in a legitimate business which requires that he enjoy the goodwill of both the police and the people whom they arrest; he is a nice fellow; I promised him that I would do so. For these sound reasons I will call him McCoy. Every bit of information he's ever given me has turned out to be the real McCoy.

Together we walked down the broad granite stairs of the Hall and into the saloon of the Boyd Puccinelli restaurant, which—for sentimental reasons—Boyd prefers people to refer to as Café El Trovatore. The policemen, attorneys, bail bondsmen and just-released underworldlings who patronize this splendidly rococo establishment (which separates its bar from its restaurant with a dazzling floor-length curtain of glittering beads) stubbornly persist in calling the place Pooch's. Because it was close enough to noon to make Scotch whisky feasible, we ordered two portions and I listened to McCoy. He was full of indignation about a political stratagem which he called "juiceless juice."

Juice, in the argot of the precinct workers of corruption, is the power to enfranchise the operation of an illegal enterprise: a handbook, a gambling game, a house of prostitution, an after-hours night club. A person who is able to peddle this privilege is known as a juiceman. Before the Atherton investigation, juice was a commonplace commodity in San Francisco, but in recent years its availability has diminished. McCoy claimed that there was a new wrinkle in the juice industry.

"You know how it's been in Frisco ever since that Los Angeles bastard blew the whistle," he said with deep disgust. "No action whatsoever, even though every other son of a bitch and his brother who ain't in the ministry or too old to care wants it bad. Every time a new candidate starts running for mayor the strongest thing he can get going for himself is a hot rumor he's going to open up the town; a story he don't deny too hard until he gets elected. After he's in the job he plays it cool and keeps things just like they was before, being afraid of the papers and squares like the district attorney. And everyone stops fixing up that back room and goes instead to Vegas or Contra Costa County or somewheres they can chippy a bit. Until the next election. And the next rumor. Politicians got to get all the votes they can, I guess, but it looks to me like a real scam."

I agreed that this was a fair summary of the situation and asked about the new development he'd mentioned.

"Well, when Shelley was running for mayor last year the rumble was stronger and louder than ever. Frisco wasn't going to become no Babylon, but there was going to be less rousting of two-buck bookies and hard-working whores; know what I mean? A little more fun around town for the tourists; a few more bucks for the locals. Dig?"

I made it clear that I dug. He shrugged in disgust.

"What happened? The same as always, nothing. Shelley was elected and came on just as noble and square as all the others. But this time there was a difference. A lot of people were so sure the town was going to open that when juicemen began to appear and sell juice . . . they *bought!* And they're *still* buying."

"Wait a minute, McCoy! What happens when the police knock them over; these purchasers of juiceless juice?"

He chortled at me.

"You ain't heard? There's a new kind of crime going on; a thing that's keeping the cops so busy they ain't got time to find out why so many cars is parked in front of the lodge hall or next to the saloon that was going broke last year. The new kind of crime is called . . . civil liberties. You put a seventeen-hundred-man police force to work picketing a thousand or so pickets and they ain't got much time to check out other things where the beefs ain't too loud."

I thought of the policemen who had been in to see me that morning with their complaints about diversion of duties. I thought of the applications for more funds with which to put more policemen in uniform. I thought of politicians and public servants and statesmen who couldn't see the forest for the trees.

McCoy went on with his story, unmindful of my abstractions. "Sure, a few places get knocked over now and then. But not enough to make any of these dopes who buy this juiceless juice understand they're being scammed. And a little salve handles *them.*"

Together, we gave this curious commerce a little thought. Honest corruption was one thing but *dishonest* corruption was an interesting new scab on the town's somewhat bedizened complexion.

"Funny thing!" mused McCoy. "This yahoo Atherton managed to louse up a lot of lives; to embarrass a whole gang of careless but not really guilty guys into early retirement; to hound at least one poor devil into suiciding not only himself but his whole damn family, too; to turn a loose, freewheeling town into a tight, nowheeling town. And yet the bastard never really got the guy he loaded his gun for. He never got McDonough. It took *you* to do that and without informers, tapped wires or cooked-up evidence. It was you who really broke their backs, Jake."

I ordered another pair of preluncheon tonics.

"Possibly, son. But not because I saw myself as a protector of civic virtue. I have a clear picture of the qualifications required for the throwing of first stones at sinners, and I've always been a little short of halos. I put the McDonoughs down for two good reasons. One, they were squeezing just as many little people as was Brother Atherton in their desperate scramble to escape the heat. Another, they took *me* on. I don't know which reason was more important to me. The big difference between me and

Atherton was that he wanted a witch burning. All *I* wanted was a knockout. Even a TKO was all right with me."

McCoy chortled.

"So you amputated their juice line. I don't know of no better way to have turned anyone off. It must have been an awful temptation to a young, ambitious lawyer with connections. All that demand and no more supply."

I laughed with him, remembering many things, many people and many pressures of the moment.

"It wasn't only my great moral sense that kept me straight, son. It was also that the times and the people had changed. It was no accident that a paid reformer like Atherton could come to a town like this and light a fire that would burn out so much that was once regarded as fireproof. You're right when you say that Atherton wasn't able to destroy the people he'd nominated as targets, but you and I know that he was able to embarrass the conditions that produced these people, and only because San Franciscans were already a little embarrassed about them. It was one thing to have a free-and-easy, lively, open town. It was quite another to find that some grafter had price-tagged your open-mindedness and its by-products and was running a brokerage on their commerce.

"You've always been a live-and-let-live guy, Jake," McCoy said curiously. "How did *you* feel about it?"

"Like any normal whisky-sipping San Franciscan. There wasn't much choice between a bad reformer and a bad grafter. I fought them separately and beat them individually. But then and now—and I'm thinking of your complaint about mayors who won't open up the town—there is and was the fact that winked-at graft is obsolete in San Francisco. Every mayor who's elected to office—no matter what shabby subterfuge is used to get him there and no matter how high his hypocrisy count may run—knows that San Franciscans may do a lot of loose and lusty talking about the good old days, but you'll find that they're infuriated when a policeman accepts a friendly hello from a former bookie; and that they write letters to the newspapers when the cleavage of Bimbo's chorus line goes a little closer to the umbilicus. Nobody really drinks champagne out of women's slippers any more, McCoy."

"Yeah, I guess you're right, Jake," he said sadly. "And all because of a guy from Los Angeles . . ."

"And a gal from Hawaii, and another gal named Dolly."

"Dolly Fine," he interjected with a slow, reminiscent smile. "I made a lot of dough with her."

Everybody made money with Dolly, including me.

As I have said, Dolly was one of those who came to me when the McDonough heat really began to get hot under her business career. She asked me for an evaluation of the situation, and I told her that there *was* no more situation; that vice was through in San Francisco. She then asked me what to do and I told her to fold her sheets and blankets and fade away. Apparently the advice she bought so expensively from me matched neither her wishful thinking nor her plans, for she stayed right with the situation and kept her bedding at its usual uses.

Even when she was called to testify before the Grand Jury she wasn't too perturbed, although I explained to her that the best she could get as the result of such an invitation was an unpleasant and unprofitable draw. And there were other possibilities of an even uglier nature if she should make the not uncommon feminine mistake of verbally fudging a bit while under oath.

Blithely, she appeared before the jurors, clad in a chic outfit and wearing a demure smile. There is no question but what Dolly was lovely and had splendid taste in clothes; there is also no question but what her calling was well known to one and all. Which made her coy disclaimers of knowledge about certain seamy things a little hard for the jurors to take.

When they asked her about the times when her "business became slack," she just didn't know what they meant and said it in just those words. Questioned about her "patrons," she was baffled at the meaning of this word in connection with her. She was equally disingenuous in respect to all other embarrassing questions. But she hadn't fooled anyone and when her responses and attitude were reported in the newspapers, the weight of official and public opinion began to stack against her.

I said she hadn't fooled anyone, but now that I think about it I have to admit that I am wrong. She fooled herself. As intelligent a woman as she was, she had accepted the courtroom defeats of Atherton and the rain check given her by the Grand Jury as proofs that the status was going to remain pretty quo in San Francisco, particularly if time gave her a little leeway.

Atherton turned in his final report in May of 1937, picked up his terminal paycheck plus a generous dollop of money to cover an underestimated budget for "information," and departed the city by the Golden Gate forever.

The investigator's final report was on the melancholy side. He admitted that he had accomplished little and blamed, among others, the mayor. ("In making the statement that this investigation was not supported by public officials, I have Mayor Rossi in mind.") He also felt that the Grand Jury (which hired him) had not been constant in its love for him. The investigation, in his hindsight estimate, had "a synthetic beginning" and was unwanted by any large proportion of the public. When the reporters saw him off to Los Angeles at the Southern Pacific Depot, they asked if he thought he'd done any good in San Francisco. Dolefully, he shook his head.

"It'll all wind up in a whitewash," he said, thus documenting himself as a regulation bad loser and managing to cast a vague aspersion upon the innocence of Ludolph and the others who were vindicated by due process, juror unanimity and Ehrlichian eloquence.

The press and some of the less prescient of the politicians took the attitude that $100,000 worth of nothing had been accomplished, and even the far-flung *Saturday Evening Post* said that from the perspective of the City of Brotherly Love it was quite clear that San Francisco "didn't want to be cleaned up."

One of the few really concerned persons who was convinced of all this chatter was my client Dolly. Despite a somewhat cloudy condition in the climate of San Francisco's night life, Dolly closed her moderately pretentious place at 555 Hyde Street

("It's Really Alive At Five-Fifty-Five," as some unknown cab driver poet put it) and took a five-year lease on a more elegant establishment at 1275 Bush Street, a few blocks west of the fated Kamokila Club. Blithely she invested $20,000 in furnishings, and before long was doing an earth-shaking business if a record of six "courtesy arrests" in the next six months is any criterion. Fines levied for all six pinches totaled $75.

But on April 24, 1938, her roof fell in. I was at the Beverley-Wilshire in Los Angeles at the time and had just retired when my telephone rang. It was Dolly's voice, but I could sense the presence of others at her end of the line from her first words onward.

"I'm in trouble, Jake. Deep trouble."

"You've just been arrested and it's for more than just the usual things?"

"Right. Will you represent me?"

Of course I would, I replied and gave her the age-old litany of the defense attorney. "Have nothing at all to say until you see me. Make bond, smile prettily but silently at the press, and then make yourself scarce to one and all. I'll see you as soon as I can."

The next morning I bought the San Francisco papers and digested them with my breakfast. They were practically afire. In a nutshell, Dolly was in the wringer all the way to her rib cage. She had been caught entertaining a brood of teen-age boys. The selling of sex to men is a misdemeanor, involving fines and county jail sentences at the very severest—and very little actual public opprobrium. Offering ladies to young boys is a very easy way to break into the penitentiary on a long-term lease in California—and the bitterness of the public reaction is apt to be maximal.

I felt that I knew Dolly pretty well. Although occasionally unsmart, she was never completely insensate; and if not exactly a pillar of society, she was actually a decent woman in the basic human essentials. It didn't add up for me that she would knowingly do business with young boys. It turned out I was right.

I made a few calls and found out how my client had been sandbagged by fate. In the first place, the "boys" were boys in the same sense that many a hairy-chested, gruff-voiced, dinner-coated youngster of today is still technically a minor although able and allowed to go out on the town for an evening of adult laughs and as much sex as he can get on an amateur basis.

No matter; they were still minors of from fifteen to seventeen years of age—all eight of them—and young enough for one of their mothers to have monitored her son's telephone conversation with a pal of his on the afternoon before Dolly's unscheduled professional demise.

"Man, we're going to really live tonight!" Prospective Sinner Number One jubilantly gloated to P.S. Number Two, and—unknowingly—to his own flap-eared mother. "After the prom, we're all going to Sally Stanford's place!"

The guardian angel in attendance on Sally Stanford, my other client in scarlet enterprise, was apparently working a double shift that night. Sally looked the boys over, guffawed heartily at their claims to attainment of early middle age, then threw them out into the cool, postmidnight shadows of Pine Street. Craftily shadowed by the police officers that the eavesdropping mother had set on their coltish trails, the lads dropped down the slope of Nob Hill and knocked on the hapless Dolly's door.

Here they were met by a Negro maid to whom any gentleman in a dinner coat with bona fide money in hand was a genuine customer in good standing. The maid explained that: "Miss Dolly is tied up and things is kinda busy but thass allright, genl'men, I'll just put you in the back room and you can sorta rest yourselves for awhile, y'understan'; sort of get yourselves set for a *large* evenin'."

She was so right. The evening turned out to be titanic.

Police Inspectors Bill Merrick and Frank Lucey burst in on the busy little establishment on Bush Street like hungry hounds at a barbecue; alarm bells sent alarmed customers trouserward; priestesses of the temple turned from dulcet overtures to raucous profanity; the African lady who had caused the whole hassle locked herself in a john and promptly lost the key; and, according to the San Francisco *Examiner,* "eight white-faced youngsters" were collected.

The *Examiner* went on to record the astounded appearance of "a tall blond woman in a scarlet evening gown" and her first public statement of the moment. It was tersely expressed, piously conceived.

"My God!" she said.

When shown the eight young men whose presence had so dynamically upset the revels, she looked—in the words of one policeman—"like she'd discovered mice in her wardrobe," and when she regained the power of speech she made a further disclosure.

"So help me!" she said, "I don't know how the bastards got in here. I never saw them in my life and I certainly didn't let them in."

As soon as the hinges were pried from the john door and the frenzied maid sanctuaried there was released, she and her employer enjoyed a lively exchange of information and opinions, but it was too late for recriminations. Merrick and Lucey took the names and addresses of the young men and sent them home to their families. The older and therefore lawful male sinners were poured into their garments and sent in other directions. Dolly was taken to the City Prison in the pie wagon, as were the maid and the girls. Miss Fine was booked as "the keeper" of a house of ill fame (a strange misnomer for such a gay establishment, to my mind), and the young ladies were charged with being present in such a place, no act of prostitution having been actually witnessed by the police. But no one was under any illusion that the worst was not still to come.

The headlines on Page One of each newspaper—once the full enormity of what nearly happened had been grasped by reeling editorial minds—gave some hint of what awaited Dolly if the viewers should ever get their hands on her. Headline writers swerved from news-telling to news-gaffing, then to editorializing, and on down to public incitation in their feverish 48-point blurbs.

DOLLY FINE TARGET OF SAN FRANCISCO PARENTS

MOTHERS UNITE TO FIGHT VICE

NOT FIRST TIME BOYS "ENTERTAINED," SAYS QUINN [The chief of police]

COURT GIVES WARNING OF HEAVY PENALTIES; WHO IS RESPONSIBLE?

These statements referred to a woman who at the moment was not only unconvicted of the crime alleged, but who was as yet even uncharged with the offense. More evil had escaped to torment the conscience of the town than even I had anticipated. I was determined as I listened to this sick, sad prelude to a witch burning that one unfortunate woman would not be made the scapegoat for the guilt complex of small insensate element of a community that apparently thought that it could wipe its civic slate clean with one single gesture of seeming righteousness.

I was suddenly filled with a consuming determination. I vowed that Dolly Fine was not going to be conscripted as a patsy for the simon-pures of the community, especially not for those who lived in glass houses. This included a great number who were already reaching for stones. As for me, I knew the location of a few good-sized brickbats myself. One such was particularly on my mind that morning as I climbed aboard the train at the Southern Pacific Depot in Los Angeles and headed back to San Francisco and what promised to be a real fight.

"What are they going to try to do to me?" was the first thing Dolly asked when I met her at the Cliff House at Pacific Ocean Beach immediately after my return. As a restaurant the famed Cliff House possesses only two merits, as far as I am concerned. It looks good on picture postcards and it draws the tourist hordes away from the more desirable eating places. Few San Franciscians ever go there. I had chosen it in the hope of minimizing the chance that my striking client would be recognized.

I replied to her tremulous question with the only honest

answer I could give. "They're going to try to stone you to death as their fellow knuckleheads did your predecessors in Old Testament days. Or something pretty similar, Dolly."

She digested this for a moment and was suddenly no longer tremulous. When the chips were down, Dolly could come up with courage enough. Her next question was asked in a firm, poised, almost objective voice.

"Are they going to get away with it, Jake?"

"Hell, no!"

"What makes you think not? There's so many of *them* . . . the cops and judges and the Christers and the newspapers and the lily whites . . . and God only knows what all . . . and in this corner, fighting at one hundred and ten pounds, only me."

"And *me*, Dolly; J. W. Ehrlich, Barrister at Law." I winked at her, and her somber mouth line curved into a smile. "You want to know why they can't get away with it? I'll tell you. Because they're fools, led by fools, frightened by fools, instructed by fools. Blind bigotry has no brain, girl; intolerance has no courage." I thought again of the supercharged headlines in the morning papers and of the fearful and hysterical promises of vengeance from the district attorney, and I felt a momentary tendency to regurgitate. "If this were merely a routine prosecution of a routine offense, Dolly, I'd be giving you a routine defense and my personal feelings would not be involved. But it's quite something else. So I'm going to pull out all the stops. Before I'm finished the people of this town may learn a little more about the various kinds of sin. One thing sure; they'll be able to tell the players apart without a program."

And suddenly we were laughing, the moment of doubt and hysteria was past, and Dolly was herself again.

"How much will it cost me to be saved from being stoned to death?"

"A lot, probably. However, part of my fee won't be paid in cash, Dolly."

She smiled her rather sweet and unmadamly smile.

"Don't tell me you plan to take it out in trade, Jake?"

"Not me, Miss Fine. I'm a man who believes that the best

things in life are free, or should be. What I have in mind is a solemn promise which you'll honor the way you honor your other just debts . . ."

"And the promise . . . ?"

". . . is that if I snatch you away from the lynching party Matt Brady and the vigilantes are lining up, you'll get the hell out of prostitution and stay out of it forever."

She looked me in the eyes very carefully, as if to seek out the gimmick—if gimmick there was—and then asked a question.

"Why?"

"Because I can't stand waste. If you were a blowsy slattern, I'd take a fee for your defense and let you return to whatever level of life you chose. But you're too intelligent and attractive a woman to be committing suicide on the installment plan in this fashion. Suicide is utter waste. I hate waste."

She nodded in understanding and we shook hands on our bargain.

"Now that I've talked myself out of a lifetime of fees," I said, uncomfortable in the new seriousness of the moment, "let's get down to business. Tell me the whole story. Everything!"

After I had all the details, it became baldly clear that keeping my promise would be an uphill hike. I dropped in on the district attorney, Matthew Brady, to find out whether his official bite was as bad as his press-reported bark, and discovered him in a foment of righteous rage. Neither extremes of diplomacy nor ironical references to his own past intimacies with the matters that now outraged him were helpful in bringing him back to earth.

Mr. Brady, who hadn't yet quite regained his breath following the Athertonian storm, was one of the flannelmouthed professional Hibernians portrayed so juicily in the movies by the late Barry Fitzgerald. White of mane and with back bowed by long and affectionate propinquity to the political feeding trough, he was rarely one to be caught out when the panic was on. From the first hour of Dolly's affair he had been wildly scrambling to every podium, rostrum and lectern within the city limits, in order to inform the voters that their youngsters "would be protected from loose women" in San Francisco. It was clear that he was still committed to this bombastic twaddle and thus impervious to reason. It was also clear that my defense of Dolly would have to be by frontal assault.

The newspapers continued to harangue their readers with incendiary copy of a nature to convince every mother in town that her moppet son might be giving up marble playing in favor of more robust pleasures, and that leering streetwalkers thronged the grade school playgrounds. Police Chief Quinn quickly got into the act with a stalwart statement to the effect that his officers had found it impossible to close Dolly Fine despite a record of thirty raids on her brothel. In the terminal raid he said that, "the police struck to protect the morals of boys of high school age," but didn't specify what prompted them to strike on the other twenty-nine occasions. The impressiveness of his clarion call was somewhat diminished when press inquiry revealed that the police had no file on Dolly—none at all. There wasn't even a good snapshot of her at the Hall, much less a clear set of fingerprints. Nor was it clearly explained why the police had never petitioned the courts to abate the Fine establishment—an entirely logical recourse open to officials of such dedication.

Simultaneously, an incredible assortment of relevant and irrelevant social phenomena broke out on all hands:

Item: The Reverend Dwight R. Copper, Pastor of Emanuel Baptist Church, announced "Drive the Sinners and Publicans Out!" as the title of his upcoming Sunday sermon and made the Monday papers with "a call to all good Christians to rise and act" that could have recruited a fair-sized lynch mob had it been issued from a soapbox instead of a pulpit.

Item: The PTA revealed its horror-stricken findings: Dolly's house was less than 100 yards from Redding Elementary School, which—as an institution of primary learning catering to children of six, seven, eight and nine years of age—would hardly seem to have offered Miss Fine much in the way of business prospects.

Item: The police department immediately ordered a "blockade by officers" of ten other "known bordellos," something of an irony in law enforcement and one which suggested the extension of this gentle policy to the picketing of burglars as they burgled or the issuance of traffic citations to holdup getaway cars. Stamp out crime by making it inconvenient or costly!

Item: One of the afternoon papers purchased the serialized memoirs of "A Girl of the Tenderloin" on the assumption that its readers might care to come to more intimate grips with the subject on everyone's minds and tongues at the moment. Three installments of this gripping real-life saga of a fallen woman were published before the influx of letters from readers who didn't want to come *that* intimately to grips with the subject brought this dismal documentary (ghosted by a police reporter) to an abrupt end.

Item: Three male members of the Grand Jury approached the district attorney and then the chief of police and finally the San Francisco *Examiner* with a truly selfless offer to undertake, "an undercover field investigation" of the town's bordellos, if subsidized. The offer was regretfully declined.

And so on, *ad maxima nauseam.*

If the din of journalistic recrimination reached to the high heavens after the raid, it must have become audible even in outer space five days later when Dolly disappeared from public view. Due in Judge Theresa Meikle's court on the misdemeanor charge of being a "keeper," my client became newspaperdom's best publicized absentee since Judge Crater, particularly as she had just been indicted eight times (one for each of the "youngsters") for violation of Section 702 of the Welfare and Institutions Code, which makes it a felony "to permit or encourage a juvenile to enter a brothel." Each account carried a penalty of 2 years in prison, plus a $5,000 fine. In extremis, Dolly might have been sentenced to a cumulative term of 16 years, with fines totaling $40,000. In the present mood of the witch burners, such an insensate stroke of revenge—or something numerically close to it—was by no means an impossibility. Even a volcano rarely stays red hot very long. My blond friend might be purchasing a cooling-off period rather expensively in terms of her bond forfeiture and other minor penalties, but then again, the price might be worth the advantages gained.

The newspapers continued to shrill the hue and cry. Dolly was reported in Nevada, in Mexico, in Hawaii and even—curiously enough—in Alaska, where she'd been born. The chief of detectives of Chicago got into the act with a really daffy yarn to the effect that she was in his overseasoned and undercivilized bailiwick, being comforted by "known members of gangland." Another report had her headed for France with a secret husband and a large-denomination nestegg. Still another one, apparently circulated by a catty nonfriend, related that she was, "in the East, getting a face-lifting and various other plastic surgeries." Dolly needed plastic surgery like Custer needed another Indian.

Meanwhile, quite certain that I had masterminded the whole disappearing act and was actually having secret daily parleys with my client, the newspapermen were sticking close to me. My disclaimers met with mockery, but as long as my utterances were enjoying such a bull market with the press I took full advantage of the situation to heap coals of fire upon the heads of the spuriously righteous.

I wanted to know why the chief of police and the district attorney and their own bosses had failed to erupt in sniveling recrimination at hundred-year-old ills until an octette of young delinquents described as "scions of socially prominent families" dipped themselves in the fleshpots. I stated that I could "stand on the front steps of the Hall of Justice with a handful of buckshot and with one throw hit fifty whorehouses"; that one such establishment (the Palm Hotel) was close enough from the office of the chief of police to permit the "inmates" to read his morning mail without binoculars; that there were at least 580 other similar facilities in San Francisco . . . so why pick on Dolly Fine for special crucifixion? They printed all of it.

I pointed out that Madam Fine hadn't bear-trapped Bush Street, that it was a mite unlikely that the delicately moraled octette had been in her place because—in the language of the code—they had been "encouraged" to go there. I suggested that it was improbable that they had visited the establishment for the purpose of choral singing or a prebedtime game of musical chairs. And I pointedly asked the district attorney to provide the press with some facts and figures (especially the figures) on his long and sentimental friendship with Pete McDonough, San Francisco's grand old man of vice, whose purchased friendship kept more red lights burning in our town than ever twinkled in Chicago, New Orleans or Galveston.

The papers printed these nuggets of knowledge and viewpoint, and I found that people were reading and thinking, but it was unfortunately true that the papers also printed some fantastic things of less sense and value to our case.

The afternoon *Call-Bulletin,* in its great wisdom, sent a young reporter on the town to sniff out the vice queen and, lo, this editorial alchemist unearthed (if not Dolly), "a slender, exotic, dark-haired dancer" who said she knew Dolly and where she dallied. The fugitive madam, claimed the dancer, was living in a dismal and fogbound suburb of San Francisco named Sharp Park where she wallowed in luxury ("silk and satin everywhere"), sated her senses with lurid literature (*Trapped By Love*), and when literature and luxury palled, "just listened to the ceaseless rumble of the surf." The story was good for three days, however; it is well understood that an afternoon paper must take (or make) its news where it finds it.

The morning *Chronicle* came up with a yarn with more meat on its bones. Three days after Dolly withdrew from circulation, the *Chronicle* revealed that one of its writers had been granted an interview by the Lady in Red on the day before she "fled." It had been a cozy tête-à-tête permitted with the rather inane understanding (under the circumstance) that nothing that passed between them would be published. Now, because Dolly had been unsporting enough to fly the coop, the *Chronicle* no longer felt bound by its representative's promise to respect such a confidence. It published all, with quotation enclosures, exclamation marks and an occasional asterisk.

"I've lived all my life by the code of the underworld," the *Chronicle* quoted my client as confiding, and at the moment

I happily could have drop-kicked Dolly into orbit. "I have three alternatives. I can squeal. I can run. I can kill myself. But whichever way I go, I'll go with class."

Fine! This little séance had apparently taken place during the grim hours before the Cliff House conference and despite my telephonic admonition to speak not at all to the press. The rest of it was equally bloodcurdling to the eyes of a defense attorney. The Lady in Red stated that she'd "always tried to run a decent house" and "keep her girls healthy" because "nothing is more pitiful in life than a prostitute who has risen from the streets, tasted luxury and liked it, and then found herself once again in the gutter." The story might have been remotely acceptable as a fund-raising pitch for a home for fallen women, otherwise it was merely excruciating. My intake of Scottish therapy that night was doubled.

In one day less than three months Miss Fine reappeared. According to a little-known statute, a bail bond may still be regained and the bailee exonerated under certain conditions provided that he or she puts in an appearance in less than ninety days. It was now one day less than the specified ninety days, and the heat of the press and the righteous rancor of officialdom had diminished considerably. I explained all of this to Larry Brady, Dolly's brother, and told him to re-explain it to his sister and then produce her at once.

Within an hour I was contacted with the when and where of my client's surrender. The how I'd pretty well worked out by myself. And because I believe that even a stubborn, self-serving district attorney is always entitled to one final chance to cleanse himself of an ill-advised commitment, I paid one more visit to Mr. Brady. Would he consider a rational degree of leniency for his victim if she were to become available for due process?

"Jake," he said, "go peddle your papers! I'm going to give that woman the works. The full works. And you, too, if you try any of your tricks."

I smiled into his big, red, hostile Hibernian face and felt like David casing Goliath's forehead for the precise point at which to loose the shot. For I *had* the shot and had carefully laid it away for this occasion before dropping off to sleep that night three months before in the hotel room in Los Angeles.

"Thank you, Matt!" I said. "You're made it easy for me."

Then I walked down to O'Connor Moffat's (a fine Irish-Catholic-owned store where I often traded) and bought a long, wine-colored veil and a pair of dark glasses.

At three o'clock of the next afternoon I took the ferryboat across the bay to Oakland. Close to the center of this sleepy but wholesome little city is a beautiful stretch of water known as Lake Merritt, named in honor of a man whom not one Oaklander in ten thousand can identify. Children wade there, sailors rent dories and swans hiss at both. Here also waited Dolly.

"Hello, Master!" she said. "What do you know?"

"I know that nothing is more pitiful in life than a prostitute who has risen from the streets, tasted luxury and . . ."

She giggled.

"Stop, for Pete's sake! I got carried away. And the son of a bitch had such a nice sympathetic manner and hair on the back of his hands. I've always been a sucker for a man with hair on the back of his hands."

"I'll raise some. Now let's get back to town and face the music. The tune is likely to be 'There'll Be A Hot Town In The Old Town Tonight,' with Matt Brady giving the downbeat with a blackjack, but we'll see if we can't provide him with some new lyrics. Let's go, Lady in Red!"

She smiled her cool, relaxed smile. A woman can become very relaxed in ninety days of early to bed and no customers (or policemen) at the front door.

"I'm not worried, Jake. I'm with you."

I'd be kidding myself if I pretended that the thrill of possessing the complete trust and confidence of a client ever really diminishes an iota. It's the same for me now as it was on that faraway day when I first stood before the bar of justice, shoulder to shoulder with a sad little mixed-up miscreant who believed that I would win his freedom merely because I said I would. And I did.

I put the dark glasses over Dolly's violet eyes and swathed her in the veil. She looked like the star of *La Dame Aux Camelias* and loved it. We headed for San Francisco.

The surrender at the Hall of Justice was a legal and journalistic tour de force, being timed to fall neatly within the time allowed for bail redemption and the hour before the deadlines of the first editions of both morning papers. Pandemonium broke loose in the second-floor pressroom, and there was considerable scurrying in the district attorney's office as well, but I had more or less cleared the tracks in the essential places and Dolly was rebailed (at double the previous bond) and released to freedom before anyone could think of any really important official questions to ask her.

The *Chronicle,* apparently unexpectant of any more off-record interviews, was singularly unbiased in its reportage of Dolly, noting that she had apparently never left the city after all. Thus Miss Fine shaped up as something less than an *actual* fugitive from justice. The *Examiner,* in describing her discreet and winsome (if wordless) manner, compared her to Snow White and apparently bridled any temptation to suggest that she might have been shacked up with a septette of dwarfs.

On September 7th we went to trial on the misdemeanor charges before the Municipal Court, Judge Alden Ames presiding, and a jury of 7 men and 5 women. The district attorney was represented by his assistant the knowledgeable Ben K. Lerer. The principal witness for the People was Inspector Bill Merrick, and the only major prosecution exhibit was the much mooted red evening gown that had colored so many headlines. This trial, however, was not our main concern; the key strategy was being saved for the felony trial where years instead of mere days might be involved when penalties were meted out. The misdemeanor jury, with no alternative, found Dolly guilty. The court sentenced her to a $300 fine and a 6 months' county jail sentence, suspended pending good conduct. According to the *Chronicle* reporter, who was strangely fascinated by the fiduciary aspects of this act of justice, Dolly settled this tab from society with a $100 bill, two $50's and five $20's, leaving visibly enough of the

Treasury Department's fine green stationery in her billfold, "to bail out a regiment of bookies."

We were scheduled to go to bat in Superior Court on the eight felony charges on October 6th. I arose even earlier than usual that day and at six o'clock I assembled in my office as tough, talented and undismayable a crew of process servers as money could buy. Their subpoenas, calling for five individual presences in court that morning at ten, were given them with instructions to serve the parties named within minutes of the hour of seven. I wanted to make sure that none of my witnesses had any opportunity to warn any of the others and thus inspire any evasion of service. Then I ordered coffee and sat by the telephone to await Mr. Brady's call. It came at five minutes after seven, a truly impressive tribute to the punctuality of the process servers.

Matt was unhappy. Unhappy but somewhat more respectful and courteous than I'd found him of late. It appears that he had been awakened by a number of "our best people"—parents of some of the boys who'd visited the Maison Fine. They had been subpoenaed to court, it seemed, and . . . "well, these just aren't the kind of people you haul into court over sordid messes of this kind. The photographers and reporters and all . . . you understand, Jake! Now if there could be a meeting in Judge Isadore Golden's chambers a little before court, we might come to a . . ."

I explained that I was busy peddling my papers, and placed the telephone receiver back on its hook. Within minutes I had a second call; this one was from Judge Golden.

"Jake," he said, "the district attorney tells me that you're bringing the parents of these boys into court. He's pretty upset about it. Can you give me some idea of what you plan to do with them?"

"Certainly, Judge. The district attorney is making use of the state welfare code—which I believe to have been enacted into law for completely different purposes—to prosecute my client for permitting or encouraging these boys to enter into dissolute lives. I know and he knows, and so does every other half-smart person in town, that no such thing took place and that none of these boys has become dissolute because of anything that happened to them that night. But if these obvious truths are to be cynically disregarded, I suggest that we examine all of the important allegations involved, commencing with the claim that the boys entered into dissolute lives as a direct result of having visited Miss Fine's place. And what better authority on their morals is there—before and after that night—than their own parents? Let's hear what these people have to say in open court, under oath, according to due process. If they will attest that their sons have become dissolute, then it appears that Miss Fine might be guilty of something, though of what I'm not sure. If they cannot or will not do so, then Miss Fine didn't lead them anywhere at all and is not guilty. Do you follow me?"

He chuckled.

"I follow you, Master . . . all the way through the district attorney's dilemma and back. Just the same, please come to my chambers a little before court and we'll have a few words together, the three of us."

"I'll come, Judge," I replied disgustedly but I wasn't in the least disgusted. Now I knew where the aces were; the deuces, too.

The resemblance between Dolly and Snow White was even more marked when she met me outside the Hall shortly before ten. She wore no makeup, her hair was in a bun, and she had on a dress for which I'd shopped the better part of the previous afternoon. She could have taught Scripture at Wellesley on her appearance alone.

We walked sedately to the courtroom and I was able to discover no trace there of the despoiled parents of the dissolute youths. I felt even better. The district attorney's dilemma was rather devastating, now that I considered it. Against my obvious defense, he knew he couldn't hope to win without the testimony of the parents. It was pretty clear that he wasn't going to be able to produce any parents and that he was in no position to force these particular parents to put in appearances, or that he had no wish to do so. On the other hand, he was in no position to betray the noisy threats he had so publicly made, especially with the press ready to turn on him if he reneged. The last thing he could do would be to let Dolly off with little or no penalty. He was in a hell of a spot and I was almost sorry for him—but only almost.

It transpired that Judge Golden was more sympathetic. When the three of us were seated around his desk, he pointed out that although a serious breach of the law was obviously involved it might be difficult and time consuming and even costly for the state to fully and adequately present its case . . .

"But it could ultimately do so," interrupted Brady, blackly but without any great assurance.

The judge allowed that this was true but wondered whether Mr. Ehrlich, in the interest of expediently handling the matter, might consider pleading his client guilty if she were to receive, "a nominal sentence; say, a year on each count, to run concurrently."

I removed some nonexistent lint from my coat.

Brady mumbled something dark and undoubtedly corrosive to himself and then offhandedly suggested that inasmuch as his office was heavily burdened at the moment he might stand still for a sentence of 9 months in the county jail and a $500 fine. His Honor thought that a 9-month sentence was very generous indeed, *very* generous. They eyed me owlishly. I intently examined the calendar on the wall.

"How about six months, Jake?"

I reacted as if someone had spilled hot soup on me.

"Six months! Thirty days and a twenty-five-dollar fine is more my idea of justice tempered with mercy."

If it had been dark in those chambers Brady would have glowed a dull red, like a horseshoe just removed from the blacksmith's coals. His reply was incomprehensible.

A half hour later Dolly and I, plus the district attorney, stood before Judge Golden. Had the *Examiner* man been present, he might have regarded Brady as the one bearing the closest momentary resemblance to Snow White—at least in respect to a new modulation of voice. In a tone that could hardly be heard beyond the bench, he followed my plea of guilty to one count of the indictment with the muttered statement that: "The People will drop the other seven counts with the feeling that justice has been accomplished." Dolly was then sentenced to serve 60 days in the county jail and fined $500.

Two days before Thanksgiving and 27 days subsequent to her appearance in court she was pardoned and immediately abandoned the city and her former profession forever.

Oh yes . . . the red dress! It or one very much like it showed up at the next police ball. It looked very well on its wearer, I'm told. Sin, it must be understood, is often only a question of the eyes of the beholder. As for me, I was satisfied that I'd cheated the morality ghouls of their prey and their victory. Still, I think I'd have given up my fee—or some of it—to have had the opportunity to put some of those overprotective parents on the stand and to ask them a few questions. Particularly the fathers, with Dolly's little black book in my hand as source material.

With Dolly closed and purchased juice discredited and subject to cancellation through volition of any one of the increasing number of straight cops in the department, the McDonoughs were practically dead in San Francisco. It became my function to preside at their obsequies.

In a sense, it was Pete McDonough's terminal desperation which prompted him to make the move that, for him, was unknowing hari-kari. Now that he could no longer batten on vice, it became important to him to depend on bail-bond business for his revenues.

Characteristically unable to participate in a business field without dominating it, he sought to pressure and steamroll the enactment of legislation that would fix certain qualifications for bondsmen. The principal qualification that he attempted to foist upon the business was one which specified that no person could be licensed unless he could post a cash bond of $250,000.

A quarter of a million dollars is a lot of money. No one who aspired to function as a bondsman at the moment possessed any such a amount except McDonough. Ergo, if the law passed, McDonough would be the only bondsman in business. He would control bail bonding in California.

Others and I decided that such a development would be a bad thing for the bond business, for people in trouble, for the law and law enforcement, and even—in terms of his immortal soul, perhaps—for McDonough himself. With the legislative issue on the subject now open for tinkering as the result of McDonough's self-serving gambit, we tinkered. We were able to change and modify the requirements, and then—with the state insurance department newly charged with the supervision and policing of bail-bond operation—to provide the business with but two licensing requirements. Candidate bondsmen need only post a bond of $5,000 with the state. This meant that any otherwise acceptable person in possession of this relatively nominal sum could enter the field. Qualification Two required that the candidate be of proven good moral reputation, of unblemished conduct, and free of any sort of a police record. This meant that the McDonoughs were automatically expelled from the only business left to them which provided an entree to crime and vice in terms of profit or prestige. They were finished.

For awhile they loitered forlornly on the scene and then, as though unable to exist without the perverse nourishment to be suckled from the shady, night-blooming way of life from which they'd been expelled, they quietly passed away. Their seat of power, the one-story corner office from which they reigned, is now a vacant hulk plastered with the exhortations of almost-forgotten political candidates, the announcements of soon-to-be-forgotten pugilists, and a very small card stating that the former tenants have moved elsewhere. But no juice.

12: *Morning*

11:30 A.M.

My thoughts turned once more to the many faceted past as I departed Pooch's and headed across Bryant Street toward my luncheon appointment at the St. Francis Hotel. It was a bright, crisp, blue day of the kind that San Franciscans persist in calling a typical San Francisco day despite the fact that the same thing occurs regularly in Portland, Oregon, and Portland, Maine, as well as in a thousand towns in between. I decided to walk the half mile or so to the hotel on Union Square.

Even here in the rough-hewn, strictly utilitarian industrial district of San Francisco's South of the Slot, the past intruded upon my present. Probably because of the taxi ride with O'Brien, I told myself, and wondered why it took a casual contact with an old friend to raise both foul and bittersweet memories; wondered if there is a natural human inclination to banish such ghosts to a mental attic until chance briefly hauls them forth; finally decided that if man is the sum total of his human experiences and lifelong personal contacts, he'd be a damned fool not to inventory and study these factors in his making more often than he apparently does. And so much for philosophy, I concluded as my abstractions nearly got me run down by a truck in front of the Federal Building at Seventh and Mission streets.

Here there were ghosts, too. Ghosts of the men and women I defended in the big, solemn, old-fashioned courtrooms Uncle Sam runs with so much dignity and perhaps a degree of pomposity in this serene old granite building among the tattoo parlors, wino joints and disinfectant-scented hotels. Here, I'd joined forces with a manhunting cop to accomplish the freedom of a man who was probably guilty of every conceivable crime except the one of which he stood illegally convicted. And here I became the first American lawyer to invoke the courts against a high Nazi official against whom even the Federal Bureau of Investigation hesitated to act. And here I filed one of the few effective actions ever taken to aid and protect Caryl Chessman in his ill-fated battle to escape the gas chamber. Even here, in this quiescent, nineteenth-century building, with its self-important ambience and snail-paced regimen, there were lively ghosts for me.

I crossed Market Street, and from the Jones Street intersection stared up at the grimy shaft of the Bureau of Internal Revenue, formerly the Empire Hotel, and from high on the thirteenth floor another memory beckoned to me—the memory of a woman who murdered in order to keep from being murdered.

Jean Collins, according to the cynical, was just another stupid dame who believed that there was only one man on earth worth loving. He was also the only man on earth who could have all of her earnings in exchange for all of his abuse. To her this was fair exchange. It was an opinion she held with fanatic conviction until the 9th of January, 1941. This was the day upon which she killed him. It was also the day when I became her attorney and perhaps her only friend on earth.

Tony Barcelona was the object of all this devotion. Barcelona wasn't precisely a *man.* I speak with knowledge because I met him both dead and alive.

I saw him for the first time less than two weeks before he left this world. I met him in a tenderloin saloon owned by one of my clients.

San Francisco's tenderloin district was a world apart in those days, especially between nightfall and dawn when those who prowled its neon-painted thoroughfares would have made Damon Runyon's harlequin characters look like Y.M.C.A. secretaries. Sixteen blocks square, in dimension only, it was the setting for a considerable amount of what the smart operators call action, and its principal collateral function was that of providing entertainment, creature comforts and sanctuary for its own. These citizens' interests were secular, their attitude chauvinistic; to them all foreigners were square Johns, and most activities other than their own were ostracized with the adjective legitimate. A legitimate caper meant an enterprise that was of merely modest financial return, pedestrian in tempo, and as dull as it was wholesome.

And yet they were not crooks per se, although they were frequently the companions and confidantes of crooks, and occasionally the left-handed abettors and not easily incriminable benefactors of those who actually crossed the line of law. But really heavy crime, as the police refer to it, was frowned upon by them because they lived with a sharp and realistic awareness that murder and major robbery and kidnaping and the other malefactions popular in eastern and southern underworlds might topple their happy little honky-tonk and eventually bring in the Federals and other undesirables. So they contented themselves with gambling and prostitution and what O. Henry called "the gentle grafts," and there was little violence among them that demanded the use of more than the fists or—*in extremis*—a blackjack.

If there is some suggestion of the sordid in this description of a departed culture, then consider that even the most robust of the cabarets, bars, nightclubs, draw-poker clubs (legal in California then), water holes, after-hours joints and breakfast clubs were operated with a toughly disciplined degree of festivity that would compare favorably with what goes on at some of the far tonier Bachelors', Spinsters' and Junior League Balls with which the house detectives of our best hotels have to cope regularly.

On the positive side, the establishments possessed color, a hectic sort of spontaneity, and a minimum of monotony. The proprieties were simple and basic. One paid cash and quickly for all service, refrained from fingering the anatomy of escorted ladies, and became sick in the street rather than in the Gent's. A lady was never hit with anything but the fist; a well-advanced drunk was held exempt from violence no matter how abusive he became (unless he attacked Motherhood or the Flag); and the police were never provided with the correct names or true directions of flight. Otherwise a patron might do anything he felt capable of accomplishing, and the self-assurance and advanced imagination of some tenderloinings I've observed was remarkable. On one of my professional visits to the Streets of Paris, on Mason Street, an inspired celebrant of race-track success loosed a bagful of live squabs upon his fellow guests and the amazed chorus line; another uninhibited type was arrested at the Tuxedo Club for assaulting a fellow drinker with a swan stolen from Golden Gate Park's Stowe Lake; still another unfettered soul assuaged his humiliation at having been refused further liquor at the Actors Club by calling every unemployed bass player on the union's list. Offered immediate employment, nearly forty musicians showed up, complete with bull fiddles.

Phenomena of this gaudy hue rarely transpired in the more respectable establishments of San Francisco. Visiting the more garish places—with their wonderful clientage of race-tracklings, bail bondsmen, touts and grifters, off-duty cops, career rounders and compulsive spenders, pimps and prostitutes, busman's holidaying out-of-town saloonowners, burlesque queens, decaying demimondaines and brassy lower-level politicians—was always a rewarding combination of business and pleasure to me.

This evening was one that immediately preceded Christmas. The tenderloinings are sentimental and extremely fond of the Yuletide season. It moves them to sincere but impermanent plans to do something for the less fortunate, tender memories of mothers long unvisited, and nostalgia for reform school Santa Claus parties. Many drinks were being bought, many hands shaken, many a nefariously gained buck spent. I was standing at the bar with Eddie Sahati and Bones Remmer, master gamblers both, when I suddenly found myself looking at a man who might have been handsome in an animalistic sort of way, had he not been so repulsive in an animalistic sort of way.

He was large, powerful appearing and well endowed at the

shoulders by both nature and his tailor, who had also provided him with a pin-striped suit that would have offended a zebra. His skin was of freshly powdered corpselike whiteness, and his hair inversely black, worn long and sleekly duck-tailed. The stone that glittered from a bulky setting on his right hand was worn on his little finger, so as to figure effectively in not only the movements of that busy extremity but as an aid to alfresco fisticuffs as well. He was a spectacularly emetic sight and I asked my companions about him.

Sahati narrow-eyed him from over his shoulder and then told me. "That's Tony Barcelona. He's what you might call a pimp's pimp; a dame-peddling creep by inclination, as well as by trade. He's got broads from here to Dixie; some he ain't even gotten around to beating up yet."

At that moment the procurer turned toward me and our stares met. He made a gesture of exaggerated courtesy and nodded grandly.

"Good *even*-ing, Mister Mouthpiece!"

Wordlessly, I looked through and beyond him. He restored his attention to the woman at his side, jerking his head in my direction as he made some comment that I'm certain was no tribute to my substantial gifts. Covertly, she glanced at me. She was attractive in a well-concocted sort of way. I wondered—and not for the first time—what women saw in the human meat-grinder species of male, and then forgot about them both for a few minutes.

My attention was turned in their direction again when another person joined them—a lovely, sweet-faced girl in her middle twenties, who looked as if she might have been more at home behind an office typewriter than in this noisy night spot. Rather hesitatingly, she approached the pimp, and then with a quickly summoned spurt of feminine warmth, put an arm around his shoulders and leaned over as if to kiss him.

The procurer came to his feet with the speed of a disturbed rattlesnake. His self-infatuated leer became a contortion of rage. He crisscrossed her face with blows, and she fell to the floor, bleeding. Before I could clearly understand what was happening, someone had intervened and belted the pimp with a right and a left and another right. I remember coming to the conclusion that a pretty good job of belting had been done, and then I discovered that the someone had been I. Remmer and Sahati and a pair of bartenders had intervened, but Mr. Barcelona had been stopped and didn't seem at all happy with this interference with his inservice job-training program. I asked him why he didn't use male sparring partners.

"Okay, Mister Mouthpiece; I pick *you!*"

There were now more mediators than fighters, and the procurer was borne away and out of the place and into the night, but not until he'd shouted a final word of defiance to me.

"Wait'll the next time we meet, Mister Mouthpiece! I won't be taking anything from you lying down!"

He was wrong. The next time I saw him he was taking *everything* lying down. He had checked in at the coroner's office.

Barcelona's resignation from life took place barely more than two weeks after the Yuletide observances just described. I had returned home with Marjorie after an evening with friends and was preparing for bed when the telephone rang. The voice at the other end was feminine, unknown to me and distraught.

"Mr. Ehrlich, please help me!" it pleaded. "I've just killed a man."

This stark speech was a poignant and drama-filled utterance. *Of course* I was enlisted and without a moment of doubt. I knew nothing beyond the words that I'd heard, and yet I knew that the lady was fair, the killing was merited, and that a tired and sleepy Ehrlich was going to struggle into his armor and climb aboard his white horse.

I questioned her delicately, feeling that she might be getting by for the moment on sheer nerve, with hysteria or worse imminent.

"Your name is . . . ?"

"Jean Collins." It might have been Jane Doe as far as memory served me at the moment.

"And where are you, Jean?"

"I'm in Room 1338 at the Empire Hotel. He was going to throw me out of the window and—"

"*Through* the window, Jean; *through* the window." It would sound better to a squeamish jury later. "And who else knows about this desperate defense of your honor?"

"My honor! It wasn't exactly like that, Mr. Ehrlich. But nobody else knows, yet. I just shot him with his own pistol. Nobody's here and nobody's come. I thought I'd call you . . ."

Snore too loudly in your hotel room and five people will complain to the desk clerk, but this girl had just fired a revolver at her apparently deceased roommate in the middle of the night with less result in neighborhood reaction than if she'd dropped her shoes too loudly. I asked her how she knew the man was dead.

"He's stopped breathing."

He was dead.

"All right, Jean; I want you to do just as I say. As soon as you have hung up, call Sutter 2020. That's the police. When they come, give them only your name and my name. They'll know better than to ask any more questions when you tell them that you've talked to me. I'll be at the Hall of Justice almost as soon as you."

Inspectors Chick Norton and Al Corassa, homicide detectives and old friends of mine, responded to the call. For the most part the girl followed my directives, but she was unable to keep from telling the most unforgettable part of her experience—that the man had clearly expressed his intention of hurling her out into McAllister Street, thirteen stories downward. Inspector Norton looked at the forlorn, pretty young woman as she said this, and felt impelled to help shape up her prospects, I was afterward told.

"Then we better open the window so it'll look logical," he said, and did.

I recognized my distressed new client as soon as I saw her at the Hall. She still had a dark bruise on her right forehead from the pre-Christmas beating I'd interrupted, but she was lovely. I didn't regret my quick decision to help her although

I now understood her slight amazement at my suggestion that she'd killed to preserve her honor. And I now knew the kind of a defense we needed and the kind of an image I would have to build with the press.

I was up to my neck in newspapermen the minute I got out of the City Prison elevator.

"Jake, you've got the baby-faced killer of the century as a client," one of them said gleefully as I headed for the interrogation room. "It's Frankie and Johnny without Nellie Bly and the corn-pone flavoring. *Rooty-toot-toot* went her pistol; *rooty-toot-toot* went her gun! He was her man but he done her . . ."

"Wrong story!" I broke in with a grin I wasn't feeling. "I've known this little girl ever since the day she ran away from the ranch in Chico, seduced by this human scum who tried to kill her tonight. It was providence that put that gun in this poor child's hands in time to save her life . . ."

The newspapermen seemed a little taken aback but they said no more about Frankie and Johnny. I kept talking and walking.

"This girl is one of the few honest-to-God white slaves you'll ever encounter. She's been trying to get out of this bastard's clutches for years. She's run away from him and he's dragged her back. She's tried other employment and he's exerted his malign hold on her and put her back on the street . . ."

"On the street?" stuttered one of the flabbergasted newspapermen. "She ran a swell whorehouse called the Blue Room in an alley up in North Beach!"

"Lies! Police lies," I said, speeding up my pace. "Barcelona kept her penniless and beat her cruelly. Why only lask week I had to step in and rescue her from him in a tenderloin saloon."

Yes, they'd heard of that. My story was now given the appearance of truth. While they were still wondering if this wasn't better than the version they'd had I stepped into the interrogation room and closed the door behind me. Jean, her dark brown eyes moist with emotion, was telling Chick Norton and Al Corassa her story.

"I was at this orphanage in Sacramento. My mother, she left me when I was three and I hated it. I ran away when I was fifteen and Tony was the first man I ever met. I loved him then and I guess I love him now. Even though he turned me out and beat me and never let me quit hustling when I wanted to. Truly, I tried so hard. I ran away from him again and again but he always came and got me. Once I got a job as a cigarette girl at the Silver Slipper, down in North Beach, but like always he came and got me, and nearly beat some guy to death who tried to hide me out . . ."

I listened with amazement. Exchange a ranch for an orphanage and Chico for Sacramento, and we'd been telling the same story without previous collaboration. I decided that either I was psychic or this was a favorable omen, but I broke into her story having no desire to push either omens or coincidence too far.

"That's right, Jean," I said, "and even after you'd saved your life and freed yourself from slavery to this monster, you were sorry. As hard as it was to fire that bullet . . ."

"Those four bullets," muttered Norton.

"One . . . four; an academic subtlety. Even then you were brokenhearted because it's not in you to kill. After you shot him you called me just as I've always advised you to do if the load became too heavy to bear, and you poured out your sorrow and remorse to me on the phone . . ."

She came in like the alto in two-part harmony.

"I *did,* I *did* . . . I didn't mean to kill him. I didn't mean to kill him; it just . . . happened."

I put my arm around her as she sobbed, and for the life of me I couldn't have told you where the deep-felt sorrow left off and the vitally necessary schmaltz began. All I knew was that this bruised and cheated Magdalene had to be saved from the trap she'd stumbled into. If the cold and unfeeling ways of due process weren't enough, I would also employ sophistry, histrionics, artifice, blackmail of the human emotions, and whatever other device it would require to restore her to some measure of happiness and human opportunity.

When I read the newspapers in the morning I knew that I'd made a fair start for my counterhypocritical project. There was no mention of Frankie and Johnny; there was abundant mention of the horrors of perverted love slavery. There was a marvelous front view of the Empire Hotel with a dotted line marking the trip to the street that Jean might have taken. And —*mirabile dictu*—some splendidly enterprising city-desk assistant on the *Call-Bulletin* had resurrected a murky but effective picture of a grim building where the City of Sacramento houses its orphaned young.

As I've indicated, I have no interest in circumventing justice, but I have absolutely no reluctance about circumventing the calloused and impatient misuses of it.

We went to trial rather speedily for a murder case; a little more than a month later on the 17th of February, 1941. The judge was the Honorable Robert McWilliams. McWilliams was not only reputed to be a tough man in the areas of charity and leniency but it was his first murder case and judges new to murder are traditionally inclined toward leaning backward and away from the interests of the defense.

The prosecutor was Joseph Garry. White-haired and stone-faced Joe Garry was an impeccably honest and honorable man, but as a rigorously respectable citizen and civic leader (head of the San Francisco Commandery of the Knights Templar) he could hardly be expected to take a compassionate attitude toward a prostitute who, for whatever reason, had shot her pimp. He would be cold and objective and strongly committed to sticking to his oath and the statutes of the State of California.

The jury was average: 7 men and 5 women. I would have preferred more men, as women rarely go overboard for their own sex, particularly those of the so-called fallen variety. But I had learned that wrangling about the comparative merits of jury talesmen is a self-negating project: the one you finally get is rarely more desirable than the one you have managed to avoid.

During the week before the trial Jean had been very close to coming apart at the seams, both physically and emotionally. I had arranged that she be transferred to the San Francisco City and County Hospital for a short respite before the ordeal. When she sat beside me in court on the first day, she appeared calmer and healthier; however, I've had ample experience with traumatized women and it was clear that my client was in bad shape. I was deeply concerned that she might break down under the pressure ahead.

Her hair was attractively arranged and tied with a blue ribbon, and she wore a simple blue skirt and sweater, but the smile on her lips was frozen and her fingers writhed wretchedly around her handkerchief. She responded to my greeting in a muted tone. Her glance was downward or away. She occasionally shivered as if cold. Inwardly, I shivered too. If ever I'd seen a murdered soul rather than a murderess, I was seeing one now in the girl beside me. I was no longer afraid of the prosecutor or of the jury. I was afraid of Jean Collins.

Joe Garry, an impeccable perfectionist, got underway without vitriol or bombast. With admirable professional skill and objectivity, he stated his case. I'd far rather defend against a vicious and obviously vengeance-centered gallows ghoul than a man of this type. A jury may learn or be taught to hate a ranter, but it is difficult for its members—reasonable, rational human beings, most of them—to resent or reject a prosecutor who does his job well, impersonally and with dignity.

With arithmetical simplicity, he established the facts of the crime, all of which were of but academic significance to the proceedings; they had been clearly acknowledged in my opening statement. Then the prosecutor got around to reading the confession that Jean had so masochistically given him shortly after her arrest, despite my best efforts to the contrary.

" 'I don't know why I loved him so, I can't explain it. I just did. Even though I knew it was wrong, I loved him and stayed with him. Even though he made me a bad girl and often I wanted to die because of it . . .' "

The counsel table was vibrating under my elbows. I looked to my left and found Jean wracked with muffled sobs. Then I glanced at the jury. Number Five, an older woman who had described herself as a librarian, wasn't listening to Garry. She was watching my client intently and with what appeared to be deep concern. Back of her was Number Eleven, a retired foundryman. His face was wreathed with sorrow and sympathy. This wasn't the way jurors should be reacting to the words of the people's prosecutor.

" 'All though the holidays he was unkind to me,' " continued Garry. " 'On Christmas Day he beat me so badly that I couldn't . . . work. He threatened to leave me, and that was somehow even worse, then. I don't know why, because I really wanted to be free of him.' "

Juror Number Eleven knew why—I could see by his face—and he was soul-sick for Jean and all the other lost, confused women who fall victim to the Tonys of the world. The jury's foreman, a phlegmatic type in whom I would have predicted little tendency toward empathy, shook his head slightly, as if in pain over what he heard. Certainly none of these reactions could have been reasonably evoked by the demise of the late Mr. Barcelona. I began to see the mooted confession in a new light now and to wonder if the district attorney might not himself be seeing it in the same way before long. The room began to brighten up a bit for me.

Garry continued in the quiet, cadenced voice that somehow did more for the text than the most impassioned narration might have.

" 'On the night that it happened, Tony said he was moving out. He pulled me out of bed by the hair. Then he beat me with his shoe. I cried and asked him to please stop. He just kept it up. I told him, "Tony, there'll be a bright day for me some day, too." He thought that was funny and laughed at me.' "

Jean was crying pretty hard but she didn't have anything on Number Five. The librarian was pretending to blow her nose with a little blob of handkerchief but she was getting in some fine fringework on her eyes as well. I prayed that Joe would read on to the end. I'd forgotten the end.

" 'Tony said to me, "You bitch, your days are numbered.

You know what I'm going to do with you? I'm going to *cripple* you! I'm going to throw acid in your face; then I'm going to give you a tin cup so you can beg for nickels and dimes . . ." ' "

The foundryman looked as if he'd liked to have had five minutes alone with Tony himself, and the foreman was shaking his head again. The faces on the rest of the jury were still impassive, but I figured that we were at least three-twelfths of the way home. And I knew the direction we were going to take in order to complete the trip.

Gary then described how Jean had stood up to Barcelona, had told him that he'd threatened her for the last time, had declared she was through with him forever no matter what he did to her. At that point he threatened to throw her out the window.

" 'I looked down,' she said 'I told him it wasn't really far. Only thirteen stories. He reached for me but I ran to the bureau where he kept his pistol. I found it and turned on him. He kept coming. I shot him in the arm. He still kept coming. So I shot him three times more . . .' "

I'd have given anything if it could have stopped there but I knew it didn't and so did Joe Garry.

" '. . . I shot him twice in the back and once in the head.' "

The prosecution rested but I didn't; not until about four o'clock in the morning when I finally fell asleep to the slow rhythm of a dirge with lyrics—lyrics that went "I shot him twice in the back, twice in the back, twice in the back . . ."

Bright and early the next morning I put Jean on the stand. Despite certain positive aspects of the previous day's events, I had a lot to counteract and I knew it.

I hadn't planned to have Jean testify because I hadn't been sure that she could stand up under it. I was still unsure of it but I felt that the jurors—at whatever momentary cost—should see something more of what not only Tony Barcelona but life and society had done to an average young woman with less than average protection against a world she never made.

I carefully led her though her entire day-by-day, year-by-year relationship with a creature who played with her in precisely the way that a boa constrictor plays with a captured rabbit. I made her describe her helpless, hopeless addiction to him. I examined her almost clinically about the nature of the brutalities and sadisms imposed upon her. She cried as she answered; not extravagantly and in the manner of a woman who selfishly imposes her misery on others, but with attempted restraint and hard-pressed unwillingness.

At one point she seemed about to faint. I was determined to permit no break in the emotional continuity. Quickly I requested water for her, addressing no one in particular. I knew damned well that the only pitcher of water in the courtroom stood squarely in front of Joe Garry. Unhesitatingly, the prosecutor brought a glassful to the witness stand, obviously intending to pass it to her via me. I stepped aside. There was only one thing he could do and he did it. He courteously handed the glass to Jean. She drank and thanked him and he responded with a courtly bow. The jury loved it and so did I, but Brother Garry didn't and I could hardly blame him.

Now I led my witness through the sordid, inhuman interlude of the final episode. Vividly, poignantly, I let each of them vicariously feel what it was like to be at the complete mercy of a savage, bestial torturer. And when the dilemma of the victim had reached a lonely and apparently God-forsaken extreme of helplessness and frenzied fear, I asked the girl the key question.

"Miss Collins, if you hadn't been wild with fear and desperation, could you possibly have killed this man, Tony Barcelona?"

Her answer came like a shriek from her innermost soul.

"God, no! I *loved* him. I gave everything . . . everything . . . to Tony."

Quickly I turned to Judge McWilliams.

"If Your Honor pleases, I would like to introduce—for purposes of comparison and edification—a life-sized effigy of Tony Barcelona." I knew damned well His Honor wouldn't *please,* so with some prompt and well-planned assistance from members of my staff, I pulled the dummy into the courtroom through a side entrance before anyone really knew what was happening. The entrance was located to the immediate right of the jury box. I'm sure the jurors never forgot my surprise witness.

Boris Karloff would have turned green with envy. My dummy, had it been mobile, would have cleared the courtroom in short order. Poised over frail, forlorn Jean, it clearly told its own story. The gasps from the jury box were audible.

Judge McWilliams was not gasping though. This stern and somewhat humorless jurist was raising judicial hell. Nearly apoplectic with anger, he instructed me to remove "that thing" from the courtroom at once, with collateral remarks about my professional impropriety and lack of respect for proper procedure. I registered bewilderment, chagrin, humility and contrition, in that order, and then removed it. But the point had been made; the point had been very well made. I turned Jean over to Garry for cross-examination.

Judge McWilliams, not fully composed himself, then ordered a recess, "to allow the defendant to compose herself." This enabled the enactment of another little piece of drama. Tony Barcelona's elderly mother was seated among the spectators. I beckoned to her to join us in the well of the court, and she did so, touching Jean's hand sympathetically and speaking to her with obvious kindness and concern.

"We feel bad about Tony but we realize, we realize . . ." she said in her very broken English. The jury, in the process of filing out, realized, too. Another tableau to add to their collection of unforgettable memories.

When the trial recommenced, the prosecutor approached the girl on the witness stand with something almost like diffidence. It was as though he, too, had been touched by what he'd seen and heard. He asked her a number of questions designed—rather perfunctorily, I thought—to reflect upon the sincerity of her anguish and regret, and then he asked what was obviously intended to be his key question.

"Miss Collins, when you did this . . . this thing to the man you say you loved, were you actually in fear for your life?"

Jean's answer was vividly written on her face before the words could tumble from her mouth.

"Oh my God, *yes!*" she said and no one there could have disbelieved her. Garry eyed her intently for a moment, then shrugged and turned back to his seat. I helped Jean to her seat and it was no histrionic gambit. She needed the help.

Now I turned to the jury. I knew exactly what they expected me to say and I was determined to give them something entirely different. There would be no there-but-for-the-grace-of-God-go-you-and-I approach, no sniveling plea for mercy and charity, no compromise with weaseling pseudomoralities. I was out for a guilty verdict against Barcelona and the weakness in our social structure that enables a Barcelona to enslave and exploit a Jean Collins; I was out for an acquittal for the *real* victim of this crime.

I told the jurors about pimps. I told them about the loneliness and rejection and dependency of the women who are the natural prey of pimps. I told them about one particular pimp whose battalion of sex serfs would triply fill this courtroom if they could be dredged from their living graves and assembled here for testimony. I told them of a pimp who would certainly have hurled a girl to her death and then glibly told the police an irrefutable story of suicide, had he not been stopped by lead and that girl's wild desperation.

"I demand that you either send this girl to the gas chamber or release her entirely," I told them. "If you do the first, you will also honor and vindicate Tony Barcelona and all those like him. This miserable pimp deserved to die. San Francisco is a better place because this girl—without meaning or wanting to—put him to death for you. I ask you to enforce this belief by freeing her."

Sweat soaked and not unshaken myself, I sat down. I certainly wasn't prepared for the suddenly quelled outburst of applause from the spectators. Nor was I prepared for Joe Garry's closing statement.

"This was not a murder," he said, "and by no stretch of the imagination should it be regarded as a murder. It can only be called involuntary manslaughter at most." I looked at him with interest as he continued, wondering at the integrity of a prosecuting official who is also a just and scrupulous human being; wondering also at what point in the proceedings he had been so reached by what he'd seen and heard. "Tony Barcelona has been pictured as a panderer, a debaucher of young girls, and an assailant of defenseless women. I have stipulated to this effect. 'He that soweth the flesh shall reap the flesh.' "

The jury took thirteen minutes to come to its decision, or rather to record and transmit that decision, for I believe that it had made up its collective mind to acquit Jean long before leaving the courtroom. The judge promptly issued the usual injunction against the making of a demonstration, but His Honor might as well have been speaking Greek; the spectators cheered as though they were witnessing a home-town victory at the ball park. Even the bailiffs joined in.

One of the many newspaper photographers clustered about us asked Jean to smile for his picture. She was unable to.

"I don't think I'll ever smile again," she told him and it was no mere maudlin sentimentality, as it turned out. She actually never again knew happiness. I received appreciative brief messages from her from time to time for awhile, but I never actually saw her again from the moment she walked from that courtroom.

Today the Federal Government uses the one-time Empire Hotel to house its members of the Bureau of Internal Revenue, and the room in which Jean Collins and her paramour parted company forever now echos to the chatter of business machines. But for me it still has only ghosts for tenants—two of them.

Three years after she was acquitted, almost to the day, Jean fled from life to the cold and cheerless sanctuary of a state hospital for the insane. The venom that was Barcelona's only contribution to the world was of lingering but lethal potency.

Turning away from this melancholy memory, I continued to stroll through the streets of the old Tenderloin, which has turned over quite a number of new leaves and—like many reformed sinners—has become as dull and devitalized as it was once interesting.

Defanged, it hasn't achieved wholesome respectability; it has merely become tiresomely sterile. Laundromats have replaced lottery joints, and the glitter on erstwhile sin centers now peals, flakes and tarnishes. Cabstands are understandably unmanned, and plain-clothes cops hurry through its streets on their way to better prospects elsewhere. The same scarlet women and narrow-eyed males still infest the small-lobby hotels, but the interest they once devoted to suckers, tricks, marks and squares is now allocated to geriatric medicines and the arrival of social security checks. There is even a church or two in the region, and Conrad Hilton has superimposed one of his pseudodeluxe hotels right atop the central block where action and juice were once twin monarchs.

All this is fine for the crime and vice rate but a little tough on folklore, honky-tonk ballad and what slick magazine writers from the East call San Francisco's "cosmopolitanism." Nobody will ever be inspired to write a "Girl With the Blue Velvet Band," or an "Ace in the Hole" by our town today. But we *do* have the freeways. And we *don't* have any lottery or gambling, except of course at our three race tracks, the basements of the churches on benefit nights, and once a year on the 15th of April when we file that list of dubious deductibles. We also have the largest number of homosexual saloons west of Chicago and north of Los Angeles. But otherwise . . . the good old, bad old, days are gone. We are without public sin. Privately, though, we have our problems.

As I've said, this was a beautiful, sparkling, blue-and-gold San Francisco day and when I arrived at Union Square, which is the St. Francis Hotel's own splendid front yard, I knew again for the thousandth or more time why I loved being a part of this wonderful, crazy town. It is the only metropolitan city in the world in which a native scans each passing face in the reasonable assurance that he'll know it, or vice versa. I'd had greetings or smiles from at least twenty persons on the journey from the Federal Building, and had known at least half of them. That doesn't happen to you in New York or Chicago.

13: *Noon*

12 P.M.

Agenda: Testimonial Luncheon, St. Francis Hotel

As in every other community populated with enough people with axes to grind, friends to love, business or political schemes to accomplish and enough dollars to spend, the testimonial luncheon or dinner is a social fixture dear to the heart of the male San Franciscan. Being more realistic or more self-centered —I'm not sure which—the ladies seem to indulge in this gesture less frequently. I have been honored at a number of such premature wakes, and being no more than human, I accept the accolades with enthusiasm and thanks when they are tendered. But between times and especially when in attendance at a testimonial for a citizen whose complete complement of friends could be assembled in a phone booth, I harbor few illusions as to the unanimity or spontaneity of most such clambakes.

The people at the main table and a pallbearer's quorum from out of the body politic may be sincere and even loving in respect to the honoree, but I am convinced that the remainder of those on hand show up because (a) they received free tickets, (b) they honestly wanted to be able to gossip ironically about the speakers-table encomia, (c) they work for the guest of honor or hope to, (d) they are weak-willed persons who weren't able to figure a way out of the situation, or (e) they actually *like* hotel chicken à la king or cold steak. In the main, I am reluctantly forced to conclude that testimonials constitute a snare and a delusion which are hardly worth the money and effort expended, particularily if the guest of honor misuses the occasion to offer "a few remarks" requiring more than four minutes in the offering.

The guest of honor today was an ultrasuccessful businessman and a hydraheaded philanthropist whom I will call the Patriarch, more because of his reproductive talents than for any special patriarchal finesse. I have referred to him as a philanthropist and perhaps I am wrong. His expertise falls more in the category of catalysis: he is a millionaire who has developed a gift for inducing other millionaires to contribute large sums to causes which somehow evoke little or no actual contribution from the Patriarch himself. Still, so subtly devious are the machinations involved and so effective the tub-thumping of his public relations people, that the legend has gone abroad that the Patriarch lives and prospers only to bring millions to the aid of the distressed.

Only the most naive of those at the luncheon today actually believe the carefully foisted legend. The Patriarch is the object of amused or acrid derision and the subject of endless inside stories about his "philanthropies"; his "public services" that so often manage to bring him by-products of private profit; his master strokes of investment so frequently financed by others; his *droit du seigneur* policy in dealing with his feminine employees; and his pathetic compulsion toward gladhanding the famous wherever possible.

Today there would be ardent plaudits, a reluctantly corroborative address by the Patriarch himself, another plaque, and a hurried stampede for the bar as soon as it was politic to get the hell out of the dining room.

Then why was the affair so well attended? For the reasons already advanced and because San Franciscans are habituated to such luncheons, and there's always the chance of running into a lot of people one mightn't have seen for awhile. Why did *I* go? Because I'm a collector; a collector of fatuous social phenomena, of absurd insincerities, of the pompous and the improbable and the ridiculous. I certainly had no more appetite for chicken à la king than I did for the Patriarch.

He hadn't put in an appearance when I entered the room, but a good representation of the town's business, professional and political worlds had arrived and was drawing heavily on the martini supply. In addition to a great number of people of whom I am quite fond and will therefore fail to identify by name, there were present the Patriarch's political protégé of the moment, certain Patriarch-involved members of San Francisco's Board of Supervisors, the honoree's own business hierarchy down to the last genuflecting sycophant, and a full roster of his sons and daughters complete with wives, and husbands. Most of his tame charity contributants were present, looking fearful. And of course the great man's personal secretary was aboard, looking as if scopolamine wouldn't evoke the real truth about the Patriarch and her. During the course of his speech the Patriarch would roguishly refer to "his Girl Friday" as the only one really deserving of credit for whatever little he'd been able to accomplish for the suffering. He would then suggest "a little applause" for her and immediately abort the resultant clapping with a continuation of his "few little remarks." And one of these—but only one—might sourly remember an ugly Sunday afternoon in a shared hotel bedroom. I could foresee every impossible moment of the testimonial affair, as though I'd written the script.

Just as the Patriarch was and is a sardonic caricature of many another whited sepulcher, the luncheon provided other and more acceptable archetypes from the life of a city that goes entertainingly to extremes in all it does, including the production of relatively singular people. Despite the malarkey about our "courageous and questing pioneer spirit" and the truths about the beauty and poetry of our city, San Francisco's best and most interesting product is people. Even the Patriarch was no ordinary pomposity, no mediocre hypocrite. As a spurious humanitarian and a bogus civic leader, he has magnitude; he is a charlatan of stature.

The rest of my gallery of exotic types comprised personalities who are equally unique in their respective ways. I watched with interest the florid discursiveness and manual and facial histrionics of the nationally discussed attorney whose love life is always conducted at school playground levels and for whose wife I had refused to produce a divorce earlier in the day. He was absorbedly dwelling on his favorite subject—himself. Another group included a millionaire liberal who regularly extols the stark austerities of Communism from the unstark opulence of his $100,000 mansion in a racially restricted suburb from which he emerges to make brief forays on racial restrictions. He insists that press photographers snap their shutters at his left profile only.

Seated rather aloofly at another table is a newspaperman for whom I have probably provided more story leads than any other person of his acquaintance, to whom I have extended nothing but cordiality for more than a quarter of a century, and whose first divorce was handled by me without cost to him. Yet he has never been able to restrain himself from applying the editorial shaft to exposed portions of my posterior when clever waspishness was the alternative to reasonable forbearance. Toward him, as the years have passed and the waspishness has broadened to include my family, I have developed an understandable ambivalence. My reaction to him is divided between admiration for his uncompromising relentlessness as a gadfly journalist and distaste for his less uncompromising handling of the role of friend. I am unwilling to believe that even a newspaperman would regard himself as being—like public executioners and tax collectors—above friendship. In a moment or so as our glances meet we will smile and gesture a greeting. After the luncheon we'll probably have a good-humored drink together. Tomorrow I'll warily scan his newspaper.

I've never forgotten what Gavin McNab told me about dealing with newspapermen years ago when I was a young attorney. McNab was a great and colorful San Francisco lawyer. I had just seen a well-known reporter being dismissed from his office under circumstances that amounted to virtual ejection, and I asked the legal giant if his action hadn't been a mite too summary and undiplomatic.

"Son," he said, "two factors govern my relationship with the gentlemen of the press. One is that *I* make the news; *they* have to print it. The other is that when you allow yourself to be put in the position of answering a reporter's questions you are, in gambling terms, playing against the house. For instance, you've been quarreling with City Hall and are asked about it. You have a possible choice of only two headlines, according to your reply and the newspaper's mood of the moment: either 'Ehrlich Admits Breach with Mayor' or 'Ehrlich Denies Breach with Mayor'—both of dubious value to you. Silence, on the other hand, is very difficult to report adversely."

Although I've not always remembered it in time, I've never completely forgotten Mr. McNab's advice.

Another of those present at the luncheon was a man whose particular pleasure is to be within elbow-nuzzling propinquity to the celebrity of the moment—no matter how little reason there may be for such artificial intimacy, no matter how little invitation the celebrity has offered. A number of years ago this addict was eagerly and somewhat incongruously effusive in his overtures (from the standpoint of his own race and patriotism) to a man who moved briefly and noxiously in our midst and toward whom I adopted a somewhat different attitude. I refer to Fritz Wiedemann, Aldolph Hitler's friend and colleague in various ethnic projects.

Herr Wiedemann was popular when he arrived in San Francisco in 1939 to become Consul General for the Third Reich. This despite the fact that there was no lack of information about Brown Shirt activities with the Jews, gas chambers for children, and places like Dachau, Bergen-Belsen and Auschwitz. To some people this was all a lot of propaganda; others thought the Germans knew what they were doing and besides, "it's none of our business"; still others were either open or covert race haters, and the stench from Central Europe was perfume to their nostrils. Even *Life* editorially dismissed Wiedemann as "incapable of subtle intrigue."

He did and said all the "right" things. He "luffed" San Francisco—it was one of his favorite cities in the world. He somehow managed to spread the rumor that he was in Dutch at the Reichschancellory without actually having personally said so. He subtly disassociated himself from his erstwhile collaborator in intrigue, Princess Stephanie Hohenlohe, who had just been scooped up by the Federal Government as a possible subversive alien. He was very smooth indeed and many people regarded him as an utterly delightful gentleman. One society writer described him as "a sweet and bumbling bear of a man who is yet, withal, the living epitome of Old World sophistication." This despite the fact that Herr Fritz had been Hitler's chief personal administrative assistant with rank of *stürmbannführer* at the time of the Seyss-Inquart subversion of Austria; that he was one of the "charming Nazis" who'd been dispatched to London to con Prime Minister Chamberlain into going for the Munich appeasement; that the authoritative *l'Agence Havas* had shortly before described him as "one of the most facile espionage agents in the German diplomatic corps."

All that apparently interested San Francisco's Wiedemann fans was that their new social lion "made" a cocktail party, that he wore his monocle beautifully, and that he told stories well in his charming, bubbling accent. He leased a mansion in socially correct Hillsborough, where he installed his fourteen-year-old son Eduard and his attractive and smartly dressed daughter Anna Marie. Another son, Klaus, unfortunately had been unable to accompany Daddy and siblings to the Far West because he was learning how to mop up on minorities as a storm-trooper pup in the motorized section of the fanatical Hitler Jugend.

Fritz fitted into the San Francisco scene like a knife fits into the wound it makes. He told funny, little whimsical yarns about the British and French, he went to Jack's and Solari's and Vanessi's (the right places, all) for lunch, and he never, *never* let anyone push him into anger with embarrassing questions or remarks. He just laughed and laughed and was so damned lovable that he completely charmed the obtuse and even occasionally disarmed the wary. One set of fans even proposed him for membership in the sacrosanct Burlingame Country Club. Had he made it, he might have felt spiritually at peace during his sojourns there; the Burlingame Club, like Fritz's fatherland of that period, is "racially pure."

He didn't make it with me either. I was neither neutral nor nearsighted about Nazi reality during this prewar period when so many good people found themselves unable to find pigeonholes for the ugly truths provided by their instincts and perceptions. I knew that there were no shades or degrees of badness about Nazis, and I knew that Wiedemann was as large a Nazi as Hitler, and *ergo* a bastard.

I told him as much one noontime at Solari's during this prelude to the ugly reality to come and at the height of the period when he was *persona* fatuously *grata* at many of our best homes and clubs. I had come face to face with the man at the bar of the restaurant and turned away. The Nazi extended his hand as if to stay me. I looked down at it. He withdrew the hand and assumed a tone and manner of eager, boyish friendliness. It was his best tool and weapon.

"You do not like me! Why? I'm a pretty good fellow." He punctuated the remark with his overhearty beer-hall belly laugh. I didn't join in the merriment. I gave him the look that I reserve for the cross-examination of lying witnesses.

"If burning innocent women and children in an oven qualifies you as a pretty good fellow, then you're the best pretty good fellow I've run into. *Auf Wiedersehen,* Wiedemann!" And I started to go around him.

The jovial manner must have been thinly veneered on his face, for it disappeared in a fast second; the appealing pose of "the sweet and bumbling bear of a man" was gone, too. He was just another affronted Nazi storm trooper now.

"This iss an inzult," he muttered, and it looked for a moment as if the panzers were going to roll right there in Fred Solari's grill. But I had to stick with my conviction, blitzkrieg or not.

"If it's an insult why aren't your fists up?"

For a couple of beats of my heart it occurred to me that the first American casualty of World War II might turn out to be I. Apparently the odds were not sufficiently in his favor, or perhaps the High Command had instructed him to by-pass Ehrlich; in any case he suddenly returned to the laughter ploy, and we separated.

I didn't walk away several months later when a Mrs. Alice Crockett came into my office and told me that she wanted to sue the Herr Konsulat General and would I represent her. She couldn't have gotten away from me after a request like that if she'd paid me a retainer. I felt like putting her under contract.

The story I then listened to was pure James Bond. Wiedemann was an extremely busy espionagist but he also liked to mix business with pleasure—amorous pleasure—and this was to be his undoing. He had been buying and stealing and importing secret information; he had been financially seducing government employees; he had been lighting slow-burning fuses to long-range sabotage projects; he had been placing his own men in potential defense industries. That was all. Mrs. Crockett had documents which substantiated most of these charges.

When he first entered the country to "help cement relations between Germany and the United States," his emissary and cat's-paw had been Princess Stephanie Hohenlohe, a latter-day Mata Hari of some skill and eminence who had once comforted Hitler himself during the late nocturnal hours and who was also a very good friend of Lord Rothermere, the British publishing tycoon from whom Mr. Chamberlain derived comfort and encouragement during his soul-searching period prior to Munich. Through Rothermere, the Princess helped the Prime Minister find the answers for which he distractedly frisked his quaking soul.

Then she came to San Francisco as a house guest of Wiedemann, and when not fulfilling his other basic Aryan needs she performed functions which brought her to the attention of the

Federal Bureau of Investigation. Because of our sometimes daffy policy of not prosecuting prominent or well-connected people for the defections of which they are actually culpable, Princess Hohenlohe's case was turned over to the Immigration Service. Immigration immediately captured her, cast her into the bucket, and held her in custody pending deportation.

The intrepid but discreet Wiedemann withdrew from his comforter-collaborator as if she'd become radioactive. He shortly transferred his affections, confidences and subversive assignments to Mrs. Crockett, who had somehow become dedicated to him and to National Socialism and wanted to teach him English. But Mrs. Crockett, who was Swiss and the former wife of an American Army major, was also dedicated to money; a not entirely discreditable loyalty when one considers her alternatives of interest. Fritz later sent Alice to Germany on assignments of a discreet nature, promising her both salary and expenses. She had carried out these assignments, involving auditions with both Himmler and Hitler himself, had delivered the goods in both the literal and figurative senses, and had then returned to San Francisco to find that the fickle Wiedemann had discharged her *in absentia* and without notice. Worse, he evinced no intention of paying for any of her services, diplomatic, linguistic or amorous. She wanted me to sue the many-faceted diplomat for $8,000 for wages and expenses.

The reimbursement and rewarding of my resourceful client interested me not nearly so much as the opportunity to legally light a fire under the charming Herr Wiedemann; an obviously requisite chore than not even the omniscient and omnipotent Federal Bureau of Investigation had been able to accomplish. I told Mrs. Crockett we'd sue.

First we held a press conference.

For this event, I possessed an excellent hole card—Mrs. Crockett herself. Mrs. Crockett, nee Alice Gulden of Zurich, was an extremely attractive woman. I've found that the gentlemen of the press are infrequently disposed to disbelieve the statements of extremely attractive women with clear blue eyes and large bosoms.

The *ci-devant* Mrs. Crockett gave them the facts.

"I first went to him because I admired him . . . he expressed admiration for me . . . and we became very, *very* good friends."

The lady's eyelashes fluttered expressively. "He came to trust me . . . because I was willing to do *anything* for him and because I spoke German, he decided to send me to see Hitler with confidential messages which could not otherwise be dispatched. I was willing. Because I had no other means of support, Fritz insisted on putting me on salary. He gave me a letter to Reichsminister Goebbels."

For the first time, the attention of the newspapermen was almost completely diverted from cleavage. Wiedemann was newsworthy but Goebbels was news vital. Pencils that had been doodling began to scratch out notes.

"When I arrived in Berlin, I took a small apartment in the Grossen Wannseestrasse and sent Wiedemann's letter to Herr Goebbels. Almost immediately I was transferred to a smart and expensive hotel in the Friedrichstrasse and told that I had carte blanche . . . the Ministry of the Interior would pick up the tab. Later I attended a small affair at the Kaiserhof, where I met Hitler and Hermann Goering. Hitler told me that Fritz Wiedemann was the 'best man for the job we have to do in the United States.' "

Naturally we now made Page One with a resounding impact plus repercussions. Wiedemann's pals in the *haut monde* thought the charges were "in extremely bad taste," and tried to bring pressure to stop me in various ways. Members of the German-American Bund telephoned, telegraphed and postcarded their threats. I also heard from the America Firsters and other isolationist groups; it seems that I was dragging the United States into war. I even heard from some members of the Jewish community; I was placing the Jews of the world in jeopardy. The Federal Bureau of Investigation indicated that it was not interested in the charges, and for publication it wasn't, but less publicly I had reason to believe that there was not only ample interest in this quarter but also covert enthusiasm for my project. The State Department took a hands-off attitude of course. But it was looking and listening, too.

Wiedemann was wild. He had also stopped laughing. He immediately retained an attorney, Otto A. Hoecker, and put on his own press conference.

"This voman iss a blackmailer!" he shouted to just about the same group of newspapermen that had interviewed Mrs. Crockett and still remembered her various attributes.

"She came to me to help her find some missing aunts, also because she admired Nazi doctrines, also because she wanted to get into the movies," he said, covering all bases, but evading reference to the passion that had cooled. "I gave her a letter to Heinz Paul, a movie producer in Berlin. When she returned to San Francisco, she asked me for five hundred dollars. She wanted to buy a little shop. I didn't send it and this is the answer. I *did* send her one hundred and twenty dollars . . . and twenty dollars more on her birthday. I sent it as a friend."

In other words, if Wiedemann was a philanderer, he was a penny-pinching, cut-rate one. And if he was the utter stranger that he claimed, he was strangely profligate with unobligated gifts, loans and/or donations.

I filed suit in Superior Court for breach of contract, alleging that, "on or about the first day of May, 1939 Fritz Wiedemann engaged the services of the plaintiff [Alice Crockett] . . . [that he did] then and there agree to pay her the sum of $500 per month and all expenses . . . that she did visit Berlin and talk with Adolph Hitler, Joseph Goebbels, Hermann Goering and other high officials . . . and did then and there determine and was informed by the said officials that Fritz Wiedemann was properly carrying out his duties . . . as head of the espionage service of the Government of Germany in the United States."

Now that the matter was of public record, the situation promptly became more dynamic in new and interesting ways. I received death threats, which are always flattering. The pressures upon me to lay off increased in volume and intensity, some of them coming from my colleagues of the bar. Wiedemann, through his embassy, to the Secretary of State asked to get me off his back; the appeal was "accepted for study." Word began to reach me, however, that the Consul General was receiving fewer invitations to cocktails or dinner, that the labor unions were picketing his Pacific Heights consulate, that someone had climbed its walls and performed rude acts on the swastika banner there, and that two members of the British Purchasing Commission had become so exhilarated with the amount of liquor consumed at a consular corps party that they attempted a frontal assault on Hitler's San Francisco representative. Unfortunately these splendid Britons were thwarted and ejected. But my faith in the ultimate right-mindedness of even the socially elite was pleasantly vindicated when the Burlingame Country Club finally decided to blackball Wiedemann's membership bid. I felt that I'd perhaps steadied the hand of the blackballer.

Meanwhile I wasn't doing so well in Superior Court. I was granted an order requiring Wiedemann to give me a deposition, and he screamed diplomatic immunity. I had him subpoenaed, and his attorney, Hoecker, appeared instead with an argument to the effect that, "The proceedings were void because jurisdiction over foreign consuls is vested in the courts of the United States, exclusive of the courts of the several states."

That was all right with me. Three days later, on March 5th, I filed suit in Federal Court and added some new and thornier blossoms to the complaint, all of them plucked from Alice Crockett's garden of memory. During certain downy nocturnal sessions, according to my client's allegation, Wiedemann had pillow-talked about his plans to "render the Panama Canal Zone useless," to "employ ruffians to stir racial hatred and . . . encourage strikes," and to provide the German-American Bund with ammunition. Alice also deposed that her gabby friend claimed to have sent a substantial number of "secret documents" to Germany and had named as other members of the spy ring a Dr. Mathias Schmitz, a Herman Schwim and the Nazi Consul General in New York, Dr. Friedkelm Draeger. And we still wanted the $8,000.

On June 9th, some five months before the United States would declare war on the Third Reich, we had our hearing before Federal Judge A. F. St. Sure—a crusty but legally able old gent with a reputation for adhering ultraclosely to the letter of the law. Hoecker immediately moved to quash the suit because the Treaty of Versailles contained a clause forbidding individuals from suing representatives of the German Government. He was certainly trying. I countered with an argument to the effect that the German Government had obviously violated the Treaty of Versailles in a number of well-publicized places, that this exemptive provision was thus rendered null and void, and let's get on with the suit.

Hoecker fired the other barrel. The oral contract between Fritz and Alice (which had been utterly denied up to that moment) was illegal, he said, because it called upon the lady to perform an illegal act; namely, service "against the public policy of the United States."

His Honor then got into the act. In the manner of a man who has already read the book and is in no doubt about the ending, the white-haired veteran of the judicial arena told us how things were going to be.

"Assuming the allegations contained in the complaint to be true, it appears that the defendant is guilty of violating the Espionage Act of the United States. It further appears that the plaintiff aided and assisted the defendant in his unlawful acts. Thus she is also guilty."

In his first few words I had accomplished the result that I sought, and I was pleased even though I knew we'd lost. I sympathized with my client but I was convinced that exposing an unsuspected national enemy was more important than getting Alice paid for dalliance with a man who'd hired her to help him scuttle her country. I knew just what was coming next and come it did as Judge St. Sure continued.

"If the allegation in her complaint is true, the plaintiff entered into a contract against all morals and decency. The complaint is dismissed." And then he disappeared into his chambers. He had documented Wiedemann's treachery in effect, but in doing so he'd negated my client's right to be compensated for abetting that treachery.

Wiedemann had very little chance to figure out whether or not he'd won or lost. Seven days later, on June 16th, Undersecretary of State Sumner Welles closed all of the Nazi consular agencies in the United States because they had been, "engaged in activities outside the scope of their legitimate duties," and the San Francisco newspapers hurried their photographers out to Pacific Heights to get shots of smoke issuing from the consular chimney as Herr Wiedemann burned his code book, secret documents and—possibly—a picture or two of the curvaceous Mrs. Crockett.

Later it developed that he had been involved in an aborted plot to assassinate the King and Queen of England during their 1939 visit to the United States—incidentally during the precise period when he was so eagerly sought as a guest in the "better" San Francisco homes. After the Japanese had liberated China from the Chinese, he became Consul General at Tientsin, from which he nimbly eloped to Tokyo when the Americans closed in, only to be guzzled there and held for the de-Nazification courts of the new Germany. He was found guilty. His penalty was a fine of 2,000 deutschmarks which proves that almost anything can be reduced to a matter of dollars and cents—or marks and pfennigs—if viewed from the proper commercial perspective.

Far more recently, Fritz Wiedemann was drawn from his "luxurious Bavarian farm home"—according to an Associated Press story—to appear as a witness against a murderous concentration camp *obergruppenführer*. He testified with alacrity, contributing the authoritative information and opinion that really brought his former colleague to the ax. He also had some things to say about another former colleague—a fellow named Hitler. Hitler was a bad man, he opined, retroactively.

Ist das nicht ein grösse bastard?
Yah, das ist ein grösse bastard.

And now the guest of honor had arrived on the dais and now the cold steaks had been distributed and eaten or ignored, and now the curious-eyed testimonialists were listening thoughtfully, almost warily, as the Patriarch was extolled by a speaker who owed him a large sum of money and hoped to owe him more.

"... and it is our good fortune, as San Franciscans with a vital stake in the future of our great metropolis, to benefit from the presence ... *and* the vision ... *and* the dauntless and selfless initiative of this *great* man, who ..."

I looked over at the great man's secretary. Her eyes were narrowed with private thought and there was a small and remembering smile at the corners of her lips. Later, after modestly describing some of his contemplated benefactions, the Patriarch's expression became roguish and he smiled whimsically down into his coffee cup before continuing.

"I'm actually accepting all of this praise and credit under false pretenses, as a matter of fact," he said. "The real honors should be going to my splendid secretary and girl Friday, who happens to be with us today. She is ..."

I was able to make it to an exit without attracting too much attention.

14: *Afternoon*

1 P.M.

ALMOST ANY WALK through San Francisco's streets is a pleasant one. The walk from the St. Francis Hotel to my office is especially delightful. It takes one through the Grant Avenue shopping district where possibly the most attractive and certainly the most attractively dressed women in the world are to be found—in New York they look like mannequins, in Paris they probably *are* mannequins—and finally to Kearny Street, an old and many-vintaged San Francisco thoroughfare which the natives stubbornly defy all known rules of pronunciation by referring to as "Karny" Street.

"Karny" Street has gone full circle as a civic artery in terms of uses, respectability and social significance, and I regard it as one of the most utterly San Franciscan of San Francisco streets. In the shadowy Spanish past of the town it was a trail and the first and only trail by which His Most Catholic Majesty's swaggering dragoons were able to go to their stockade in the presidio from the boatlanding on the bay.

During the days immediately after the "liberating" Americans brought civilization, wooden sidewalks, gas streetlights, commerce, smallpox and the law and their own greed to the community, Kearny Street became the fanciest avenue of the times, with rococo hotels, fine restaurants and crystal-chandeliered saloons. Somewhat later the north end of the thoroughfare lost a good deal of tone when it became both the locale of the City Prison (where the first woman in California was put to death) and of the burgeoning Barbary Coast, while the central portion achieved a different sort of *déclassé* by specializing in the elegant but earthy French whorehouses that eventually aroused the wrath of every parson between the Barrel House and the Cliff House.

Shortly before and after the turn of the century and with the embittered night ladies turfed from their warm boudoirs onto the cold pavements of the south end of Kearny Street (and into the ironically misnamed off-Kearny mews of Maiden Lane), the one-time Spanish trail degenerated into a community of cheap cafés, Chinese herbalists, tattoo parlors, Filipino pool halls and sad, dispirited hotels. Now, in its newest incarnation and in the wake of the wrecker's iron ball, it has become an awesome showcase of skyscraper magic, with gleaming white towers built or building all the way from Market Street, where it comes to life—appropriately enough—in the shadow of Actress Lotta Crabtree's fountain, to the motley, harlequin North Beach quadrant where Lawrence Ferlinghetti has his City Lights

Bookshop. Ferlinghetti was another of my clients and the innocent pawn in a parody of civic righteousness.

The City Lights Bookshop is an *avant-garde* establishment where beards and berets are standard equipment, where a request for a copy of Louisa Alcott's *Little Women* would unnerve the proprietor for the rest of the week, and where you can buy a copy of Allen Ginsberg's *Howl*. You can buy a copy of *Howl* there because of J. W. Ehrlich, among others, and here's the way it happened.

On May 21, 1957, Patrolman A. Russell Woods of the San Francisco Police Department walked into the City Lights Bookshop and asked a clerk by the name of Shigeyoshi Murao if he had a volume entitled *Howl and Other Poems*. Murao did. Officer Woods then purchased it with 75¢ of the taxpayers' money and the witch hunt was under way.

Arrests were made and the case was set to be heard before Judge Clayton W. Horn, a close friend of mine and a strangely erudite and literary-minded man in a group that usually confines its reading to the law. Two able attorneys, Lawrence Speiser and Albert Bendich, had already been retained by Lawrence Ferlinghetti, owner of the bookshop and publisher of Ginsberg's book, but it was decided that appropriate reinforcement to the defense should be made in view of the fact that rather important literary censorship precedents might be established, one way or the other. I was asked to defend in association with Speiser and Bendich.

I immediately accepted. This was one I *had* to fight.

I believe there is greater peril to books today than at any other time since Gutenberg made printing a practical reality. The peril doesn't flow from a innate desire on the part of the people to censor or suppress the immoral excursions of the written word; it arises from the expansion of authoritarian power and its attendant regimentation of thought and opinion.

Censorship, in the historic sense, means prelicensing. It means the submission of material to an official person or agency for approval in advance of publication or other forms of exposure to the public. Such a fixed procedure in a free and flexible society has its obvious risks and possibilities of extremes of control and bias. Within our own lifetimes we can recall the treatment given such obviously classic works as Aristophanes' *Lysistrata,* Defoe's *Moll Flanders,* the *Satyricon* of Petronius and other writings of undoubted literary immortality, not to mention the newspaper and courtroom donnybrooks that attended the importation of latter-day works such as Joyce's *Ulysses, Lady Chatterley's Lover* and Paul Gauguin's journals. Even more recently the courts of Marin County, California—which is to San Francisco what Westchester County is to New York City—became involved with a soul-searching courtroom inquiry into the literary, moral and sexual merits of a relatively innocuous and certainly unsexy book by Henry Miller entitled the *Tropic of Cancer.* It was a tiresome exercise in social stupidity.

I am opposed to the motivation and principle behind all such superrighteous and unauthorized, unjustified and unknowledgeable attempts to put blinders on the general public. My opposition is based upon such a multiplicity of grounds that it would take an entire book in which to cover them. Suffice it that I say there exists ample police and legal machinery for the eradication of the only possibly harmful subject matter for publication of which I am aware: the willfully salacious material intended to reach the young or the deviate. The screening of general literature (especially by those whose talents for such screening is questionable) is a lot of hogwash. And to countenance a procedure wherein a high school educated functionary in the postoffice department passes upon the acceptability of Swedenborg's *Amor Conjugalis* (as occurred some few years ago), or the practice where similarly uncultivated customs service morals policemen decide what is good or bad for the minds of 180,000,000 people, is pure uncut malarkey.

This is my attitude toward censorship per se and on its merits or demerits as a social control. Jurisprudentially, I see even less justification for its processes, not only because judges themselves are forever emphatically declaring from the bench that it is not the right or the function of the courts to exercise censorship, but because I believe that most judges and juries are no more qualified to pass upon the lasting literary worth or the inspirational value of a book than are postal clerks or customs officers. In such matters I regard the individual as the best possible guardian of his own intellectual and moral weal. I have infinite faith in the capacity of the average American to accept or reject what is good for him in life.

For this reason and others equally cogent I took the *Howl* case.

On August 22, 1957, we went to trial before Judge Horn. There were two counts to the complaint: the first was that *Howl* was an obscene book; the second was that Ferlinghetti had "willfully and lewdly" made the sale. Opposing me for the People of California was Assistant District Attorney Ralph McIntosh, representing not only the People but his boss, District Attorney Tom Lynch.

Tom Lynch is probably one of the ablest and most honest prosecutors San Francisco has ever had. He is awesomely and unimaginatively honest, which is to say that ways in which he might safely detour from rectitude probably *never occur to him* as they do to more facile men. In addition, he is intellectual, self-effacing, a raconteur and—even rarer—a superb listener. There are few district attorneys so admirably and miscellaneously endowed. The only other D.A. who is class is my old friend J. Frank Coakley of Alameda County; all man.

His deputy, McIntosh, though a bright, alert and energetic prosecutor, was not gifted in the enclave of books, literature and counter-Ehrlichian strategy. And in this instance and in liberal-thinking San Francisco he was additionally handicapped by a dearth of creditably documented expert witnesses. But in terms of personal conviction he was certainly the appropriate man to prosecute a lustily robust *avant-garde* book. Four-letter words really shocked him. I decided to shock my friend Ralph in other ways as well.

The trial moved speedily from its outset. After the basic facts of the affair were established through the testimony of the police officer and the prosecutor's statement, I opened the case for the defendant with a résumé of the historical background on literary censorship. I listed words and subjects (syphilis, et cetera) once regarded as improper for use in polite society and now commonplace. I cited abundant legal precedent to prove that willful intent to publish indecent matter had to be proven, that it could not be "inferred," according to the California Appellate Court. I quoted Chief Justice Warren, who had written an opinion on the subject that invoked extreme circumspection of those who would seek to discern evil where evil was moot, on the *honi-soit-qui-mal-y-pense* principle. I offered the court the brilliant Supreme Court-approved jury instruction that:

> The test is not whether it [the book] would arouse sexual desires or sexual impure thoughts in those comprising a particular segment of the community, the young, the immature or the highly prudish or would leave another segment, the scientific or the highly educated or the so-called worldly wise and sophisticated indifferent and unmoved. The test in each case is the effect of the book . . . not upon any particular class, but upon all of those whom it is likely to reach. The books [considered] . . . must be judged as a whole, in their entire context, and you are not to consider detached and separate portions in reaching a conclusion.

Through these and collateral authority I was able to place my opponent in the vise of utter relevancy to an intellectually fair and rational treatment of the situation. He could not confuse the issue with general and statutorily unrelated products of his inhibitions or the inhibitions in the body politic of those to whom departure from propriety is traumatic. He might not consider a four-letter word out of appropriate context; he could not point with horror to an earthy passage that of itself was abrasive but when read in relation to all that followed might have possessed great cosmic content. He must treat with the book as a whole.

I put on my witnesses. They were impressive. They included Mark Schorer, Professor of English at the University of California, novelist, biographer of Sinclair Lewis, Fulbright Scholar and three times a Guggenheim Fellow. He quickly and firmly labeled *Howl* a "sincere literary work" of considerable merit. Cross-examined by McIntosh, Schorer seemed mildly amazed that the representative of the people stumbled gingerly in describing one passage from the book: "... with dreams, with drugs, with waking nightmares, alcohol and cock and endless balls." He had described this reference as, "the language of the street, which is absolutely essential to the esthetic purpose of the work."

Subsequently Mr. McIntosh was equally disturbed about the use of the word "bullshit," and even more subsequently he expressed concern for the assault on the public morals of one of the words in the following excerpt:

> America I've given you all and now I'm nothing
> America two dollars and twenty-seven cents
> January 17, 1956
> I can't stand on my own mind.
> America when will we end the human war?
> Go fuck yourself with your atom bomb.
> I don't feel good don't bother me.

Aside from the fact that a substitution for the frightening word—fornicate, for instance—might damage the meter of the blank verse, if any, there were precedents for even this extreme of Elizabethanism, as I explained when I got the chance. One of England's greatest poets and a writer from whom Shakespeare is alleged to have occasionally cribbed—Christopher Marlowe—wrote:

> I cannot buss thy fill, play with thy hair,
> Swearing, by Jove, 'Thou art most debonnaire!'
> Not I, by cock! But I shall tell thee roundly,
> Hark in thine ear, zounds, I can fuck thee soundly.

I don't know whether such vulgar (but certainly not erotic) frankness can be regarded as a first step in the decline of an empire that 500 years later lost India and the Suez, but I doubt it. I doubt that anyone who wouldn't have wound up badly anyway was ever more speedily expedited downward by having heard or read a four-letter word, even on a washroom wall. And any person who claims to have been started on the road to Hell by the sight or sound of a word used in useful context in a legitimate literary work has to be either a knowing hypocrite, a prurient secret sinner, or too morally frail for this rugged world.

Judge Horn, now thoroughly enjoying the interplay of argument, wanted to know if I quite literally saw no harm in the use of four-letter words. Diabolically, he made any answer on literal terms as difficult as possible.

"If you were invited to a party, Mr. Ehrlich," he asked, "would you use that word while discussing something with someone there? Some ladies, for example?"

I carefully avoided the ironic glint I knew to be in his eyes.

"Your Honor, I don't think that the mere use of any one word is going to destroy anyone's morals or cause them to embrace that which is base and unworthy of an intellect of decency."

He wasn't going to let me off the thin ice that easily. His revised question was put to me with great reasonableness but it was still clear that he was amused by the possibility of getting Ehrlich farther out on the limb and, if possible, to the point where the branch begins to groan and creak.

"Tell me, Mr. Ehrlich," he said, "are you willing to concede that there are certain words in this book that generally—I don't mean in this courtroom, I mean in the community—may be considered coarse and vulgar?"

I decided that now was the time to take the floor and not only advance some basic truths but also lay down a word screen that would end further discussion of the feasibility of four-letter-word usage in the company of ladies at social events, an obviously highly untenable line of polemics.

"Yes, Your Honor," I replied. "I will concede that they may be so considered. I can't visualize the use of so-called discolored words, whether acceptable or unacceptable, unless they are relevant to the theme. But our problem today is whether these words are relevant to the theme of the book and not where and when we should or might use words of this kind. As has been so aptly said, a word is not crystal, transparent and unchanged. It is the skin of a living thought and may vary greatly in color and content according to the circumstance and the time in which it is used. Is the word relevant to what the author is saying or did he use it just to be dirty and salacious and to pervert the mood, mind and action of his reader? It is thus the writer's intent that gives instant and first-priority definition to the word.

"Therefore, Your Honor, it is relevant to what he is saying and essential to the good and important meaning of his statement when Ginsberg cries out in *Howl:*

> "America I've given you all and now I'm nothing.
> America two dollars and twenty-seven cents
> January 17, 1956
> I can't stand on my own mind
> America when will we end the human war?

"He then answers the threat. He says:

> "Go fuck yourself with your atom bomb
> I don't feel good don't bother me.

"What possibly prurient interest could Ginsberg be attempting to generate with that cry of pain? This man is desperate; he is at the end of the road. He is crying out in the wilderness. Nobody is listening. Your Honor can't feel that anguished cry, nor can I. We can't understand it. We've never lived his life. No man knows the pain of a toothache until he's suffered a toothache. In love with your wife and devoted to her, you still can't share or even feel the pain of her childbirth.

"We don't know what Ginsberg's mind was feeling at the moment he wrote these lines, because we haven't experienced hunger, emotional privation or the despair that is bred of dismal disillusionment with his whole world; we've never reached the bottom of the pit. But we can know something of what it's like, because an articulate and uninhibited soul reaches for every implement in the armory of verbiage—even the shocking and ordinarily unacceptable ones—in order to describe his soul-felt reactions.

"Ginsberg tells us in his howl against life that:

> "I saw the best minds of my generation destroyed
> by madness, starving hysterical naked,
> Dragging themselves through the Negro streets at
> dawn looking for an angry fix.

"And he continues to describe the awful things that are going on. He continues to talk about what he sees. Believe me, his vision is good and what he sees is pretty terrible. He sees subways from the Battery to the Bronx . . . benzedrine and its effects . . . the noise of wheels . . . 'battered bleak of brain all drained of brilliance' . . . 'a lost battalion . . . screaming vomiting whispering facts and memories and anecdotes' . . . 'whole intellects disgorged in total recall,' and I'll lead you through portions of the Holy Writ on the same subject that are less revealing of man's torment. Follow some of his frenetic words, if you can bear the honest brilliance of a verbal nightmare. He was 'seeking, seeking, seeking always, broken down, crying, everything is wrong with him, they do everything Solomon [the central character of his poem] is doing, everything he ought not to do, he associates with millions of girls,' 'red-eyed in the morning but prepared to sweeten the snatch of the sunrise, flashing buttocks in the barn and naked in the lake.' He describes the 'Adonis of Denver' with tribute to the memory of his innumerable conquests, except that instead of mentioning innumerable conquests, which is after all a rather dull way of putting it, he says 'lays of girls in empty lots and diner backyards, movie houses, rickety rows on mountaintops.'

"True, he might have handled all this turmoil and technicolor agony by saying that the secret hero of this poem, this nonpareil cocksman, this Adonis of Denver, enjoyed innumerable conquests at the Waldorf Astoria, with more of them after dinner at Jack and Charlies "21", and even more before late drinks at the Stork Club. And it would have gotten by as modern commercial literature. I presume he could have done that, but that wouldn't have described the type of a man he was talking about: the figurative man who stumbles through this life of turmoil and torment and degradation.

"If the prosecution can say that because Ginsberg's Adonis laid girls in empty lots and in movie houses and on mountaintops and in caves and God only knows where else this book is an obscene book, then the law and the decisions of the past that have been so carefully made are valueless. It is not for us to choose the words of a sincere, perceptive and articulate man's torturing experience with life, to adulterate and emasculate his testimony. Such Lilliputian-minded tampering with artistic honesty would constitute an abomination, an abortion and a defiling usurpation of a writer's function. When Ginsberg told his story, he told it as he saw it, used words as he heard them at the time that he saw it, portrayed the world in language consonant to the mood and purpose that he described.

"I have quoted from this book, Your Honor, and I know that you have read all of it. It could be praised or attacked in many possible ways; of that there is no doubt, for both kinds of criticism are the natural lot of any artistic work. But if the judgment on Ginsberg's work be that it is noble or nonsense, shallow or profound, obscure or crystal clear, one thing it certainly *isn't* and one thing it definitely *doesn't* accomplish: it isn't salacious and it doesn't incite one to even the most fleeting of carnal thoughts. I respectfully submit that the only thing that's been proven this afternoon is that a policeman bought a book."

In addition to Mr. Schorer, my expert witnesses had included Luther Nichols, book reviewer for the San Francisco *Examiner;* Walter Clark, author of *The Ox-Bow Incident* and other novels, and a San Francisco State College professor; Leo Lowenthal, the well-known critic and University of California Sociology Professor; Kenneth Rexroth, author, editor and critic; Mark Linenthal and Arthur Foff of the faculties of San Francisco

State College; and writers Herbert Blau and Vincent McHugh. All of them had unequivocably pronounced *Howl* a fine literary work. Poor McIntosh had been able to scrape up but two literary experts who agreed with the authorities as to the non-merit and the potential risk to the public of Ginsberg's book.

The first of these was Professor David Kirk, who taught English and had taught Engineering English at San Francisco State College. His specialty was the English novel and his opinion of *Howl* was that it was "of negligible literary value." He liked Voltaire and approved of the Bible but not of me. He found my cross-examination "frivolous," but eventually experienced difficulty in answering some of the more loaded questions to which the "frivolous" queries led. It transpired that Kirk's literary education had been highly selective ("My studies covered from 1660 to today") and that he was unable to specifically analogize between Ginsberg's philosophies and those to be found in the works of Erasmus or in the Book of Job, both being literature conceivably within an English professor's span of experience. When Mr. Kirk descended from the stand both he and Mr. McIntosh were annoyed with me.

The prosecution's second and only other witness was a lady from the radio business who promptly testified that she was qualified to pass on *Howl*'s merits because she had "rewritten Faust." "Took three years to do it but I did it."

After Judge Horn threatened to clear the courtroom if there were any more outbursts of unseemly laughter, the lady—whose name was Gail Potter—went on to say that she had written from, "the Forty Fausts, there *are* forty so it isn't so laughable unless you have read only one, which most of you probably have . . . excuse me." She also wrote "Drama In the News" once a week in cooperation with *Time*. "*Life* sent me galley proofs to criticize and also I had the 'Romance and Music Series,' taking the great musicians and writing dramas on their lives, and I wrote *Know Your City* . . . for which I was paid." It looked for a moment as if the court might be cleared after all. I found myself completely unable to exploit such an obviously exploitable witness and immediately after McIntosh led her into a gushing avowal that *Howl* had "no literary merit" because "you feel like you are going through a gutter when you read that stuff," I didn't linger on it, I told her to step down.

"There is something else you want?" the poor lady faltered.

"Step down!"

"Oh thank you . . . thank you, Mr. Ehrlich," she chirped, and I was glad she was glad. So was McIntosh, I'm sure. He finally got around to his summation.

Ignoring the court's well-explained dictum regarding judgment of the book as a whole, he returned to an attack on individual words and had to be straightened out by Judge Horn. He averred that, "such dirty words" were never broadcast over radio or television despite the fact that *Howl* in its entirety had been heard over Station KPFA; that they were tabooed by major publishers despite the fact that the literature of postwar America has been abundantly replete with all and any of the hairier four-letter items. He pointed out that even surrealistic paintings didn't go so far as to portray genitalia or the sexual act, and had to be reminded by the Judge that the principal and distinguishing characteristic of surrealistic art was the unindentifiability of the subject matter. He cited corpus juris as endorsement of his definition of obscenity (a rather feeble and undiplomatic gambit in a juryless trial before an able and experienced judge) and was set back on his heels ("Don't cite corpus juris! That's mere textbook language"). And he daringly but somewhat ineptly wound up by characterizing *Howl* as, "a lot of sensitive bullshit, using the language of Mr. Ginsberg."

I was happy to take a final few swings at vested ignorance and smug narrowmindedness in the name of the defense. I had already said most of the things that I deeply felt about a man's compulsion to interfere with man in the benevolent guise of becoming his brother's keeper, but I wanted to buttress conviction and logic a bit with quotations from minds that were better than any locally available. Besides, I knew there was little that Judge Horn liked better than a free roll in the fragrant hay of the classics, and I enjoyed it too.

After the requisite but more or less routine citation of precedents and opinions apropos of James Joyce's *Ulysses,* I asked the court to consider the cynical truism that most of the great classics of literature had initially been condemned by those who see destruction in all that they cannot understand—by the pygmy mentalities of each respective era who have sought and found pornographic skeletons in every closet.

I pointed out that Voltaire's *Candide,* which even the state's star witness (the learned Dr. Kirk) had hailed as a classic, had been condemned as obscene because it dealt with sex. Thus words dealing with and describing sex do not in any way destroy literary merit.

"Shall we cull the lines from Balzac's stories?" I asked. "Shall we forthwith ban his works, take the volumes from the library shelves and hide behind the barn when we read them? Or burn them in a public pyre as Hitler did the classics that he found dangerous and counter to his mores? Seek filth and you will find it. Seek beauty of narration and you will find that, too. But to find filth you must search for it with a wanton mind and eager application.

"Any book publisher could—by some—be declared unsafe, since a moron could pervert to some devious sexual fancy to which his mind is peculiarly open even the listings in a seed catalogue. Not even the Bible would be exempt; the metaphysician Annie Besant once compiled a list of a hundred and fifty passages in Scripture that might fairly be considered obscene. It is enough to cite the story of Lot and his daughters: Genesis eighteen, thirty to thirty-eight. Portions of Shakespeare would also be offensive, and of Chaucer—the gamiest of them all—to say nothing of Aristophanes, Juvenal, Ovid, Swift, Defoe, Fielding, Smollett, Rousseau, de Maupassant, Voltaire, Balzac, Baudelaire, Rabelais, Swinburne, Shelley, Byron, Boccaccio, Margerite of Navarre, Hardy, Shaw, Whitman and even our own wholesome, homespun Mark Twain, among a regiment of others. When do we start plucking these immortals from their high niches in order to reject them for their honest and often inspired references to the anatomical parts and amorous acts for mention of which we meet today to consider pillorying one not yet installed in his niche?

"There are books that have the power to change men's minds and to call their attention to situations which are visible though unseen. Whether *Howl* is or isn't obscene is of small relative importance in a world that is faced with the problem of actual survival, and I hold that if this writing can advance realistic understanding of any ugly prospect that menaces us by even an iota, that it is absurdly and incongruously academic to examine or condemn the means by which this comprehension is accomplished. Secondarily, I hold that what is legally permissible in the description of sexual acts and feelings in art and literature is of the greatest importance in a free society.

"And as to the yesness or noness of this book's obscenity, there is not now nor has there ever been a workable definition of obscenity, and those that are vapidly concocted from time to time by self-appointed measurers of such swinishness usually find that their definitions have become outmoded and irrelevant almost within the moment of utterance. Every person will react to sexual writings according to his own sexual taste, subject to the continuing variation provided by the living and learning experience.

"Applying the legal yardstick to books for the determination of their degree of obscenity, if any, is like judging the color of a horse by learning how fast he can run. It is impossible of accomplishment. Marginally, it is interesting and significant to note that the desire to censor and suppress is not limited to bigots and crackpots. Most of us have a strong and pernicious desire to believe that what is good for us is good for the next man, and it requires all of the force of our own reasoning plus the power and wisdom of our legal institutions to prevent these tendencies toward the mental molestation of others from getting out of control. For that reason, among the others given, the decision of the court in this matter today is of the highest social importance, not only now but forever. Your Honor bears a crucial responsibility, to my mind.

"I have seen the efforts of the prosecution to build up a

case by counting four-letter words. I have seen the honest confusion of honest men trying to determine what is obscene with no real background of information to help them. I have seen the struggle with the semantic nonsense that is written into the law books as definitions of obscenity.

"Let there be light. Let there be honesty. Let there be no more fleeing from the phantom of nonexistent threat to the morals. But most of all, let there be no further stigmatization of that which isn't conventional or understood simply because it isn't conventional or understood. We've moved too far out of the darkness of the caves for that."

We won of course. In a brilliant and learned decision that graded him highly in literary as well as legal expertise, Judge Horn rocked the bigots a bit, commented eloquently on the need to preserve publishing freedoms, and—when the thing was all over and the less formal social amenities re-established—commented with sardonic humor upon my unfailing tendency to quote or misquote the Bible somewhere in my argument.

"That's all right, Judge," I told him, "you'll be delighted someday that there's still someone around who knows the Bible."

And he was.

Just a few weeks ago, Judge Horn found himself faced with the prospect of addressing a few apt and admonitory words to seven clergymen who had been found guilty of trespassing on private premises in the company of several hundred other civil rights sit-in pickets. He reached for Ehrlich's *The Holy Bible and the Law* and found just the quotation. When the smugly errant divines were lined up before him, he gave them his text for the day. It was from Proverbs 25:17.

"Gentlemen . . . Withdraw thy foot from thy neighbor's house lest he be weary of thee . . ."

Which he punctuated with 30-day suspended sentence and a $50 fine to each of the Lord's servants.

Kearny Street also contains a building to which I've alluded before with some degree of nostalgia and perhaps too much sentiment, and in which I've spent many hours of my life and career. This is of course the old, grimy, memory-filled Hall of Justice.

With the glittering new, sugar-white police and law building across town on Byrant Street open and operating for nearly two years now, I rarely get down to my former arena across from Portsmouth Square, so I decided to drop by and see if any memories still clung to the dun-gray ramparts of the old fortress.

At first appearance it didn't seem to have changed at all. And then I saw that it had suddenly and unexpectedly become tired looking and slightly defeated and out of it, the way a human being so often does during the first few years after retirement. But an old building can't move to the country and take up cribbage or raise petunias. It can only sit there on its site, untended and ignored, and gather dust and cracks for its windowpanes. This was no fate for a proud edifice that had for so many years symbolized justice to so many generations of San Franciscans. I felt oddly and ridiculously depressed.

Drawing near the stairwayed main entrance, I found that it was boarded up, with entry now provided through a small padlocked doorway in the hoarding. On the doorway was fastened, with rusty thumbtacks, an extemporaneously concocted sign. The words were chalked on by someone not too heavily endowed with pride of craftsmanship. They read: CLOSED—MOVED AWAY.

They didn't even say where. I felt sadder than ever, and then I noticed a neatly dressed elderly gentleman at my side. He had the well-worn tidiness and constitutionally patient expression of a civil service watchman or caretaker, which he turned out to be.

"You're Jake Ehrlich, aint'cha?" he asked, eyeing me quizzically.

I pled guilty.

"I thought you was, only I couldn't figure what a busy guy like you was doing just rubbernecking on Kearny Street, this time a day especially."

I told him about the sentimental journey and of my disgust with the sign on the doorway, hoping—too late—that he hadn't written it. He chuckled.

"I wrote it," he admitted. "I'm the custodian here and I ain't no signwriter, that's for sure, but it's better than nothin' and nothin' was what the city did about it." He went on to explain that he had once been a fireman but too many hernias had taken him off the trucks. A long career of the right kind of voting had provided this on-the-shelf job for him. I told him that a sound knowledge of how to most profitably make use of the ballot was a career all by itself—it used to be called vocational voting in New York—and we laughed over that. Suddenly he offered me the only hospitality at his command.

"Would you like to come in and look the old joint over?" he asked. "You might run into some ghost you ain't seen for awhile." He laughed heartily to show that it was a joke. Albert Johnson, vice-president of the bank for which I am general counsel, would be at my office at two but I knew he would wait a few minutes if the cause were right. I accepted.

My new friend's duties were obviously limited to maintaining custody; this was clear at first sight of the dusty and moldering lobby that once rang to the brisk foot-clatter of cops, lawyers, witnesses, bondsmen and the other dramatis personnae of the justice drama. As our steps echoed dismally along the shadowed corridor that led past the chief's office and my companion chattered cheerfully away about the growing insolence of the building's rats I peopled the scene from memories of the past.

I saw Charley Dullea, my law partner's father, the way I first saw him many years ago in round-topped billycock hat and a knee-length uniform coat with handcuffs and blackjack stowed niftily in the tails. In my mind's eye I saw Roscoe Fatty Arbuckle, the movie comedian who literally loved Actress Virginia Rappe to death in a St. Francis Hotel room so many years ago, being led toward the old detective bureau squad room (they weren't inspectors then) in a raincoat over pajamas by Homicide Chief Louis de Mattei. I peeped into the old squad room, half expecting to see the rows of old-fashioned schoolroom desks at which the sleuths used to sit to write their reports, but absolutely nothing was there, not even the newer desks that succeeded the incongruous old inkwell-imbedded kid furniture. I glanced in at the chief's office. It was bare now. No sign of the wiring supposed to have been used by one chief to bug the next-door office of his deputy chief. But I looked.

My guide led me around to the southern side of the Hall, past the labyrinthine rabbit warren to which the vice-squadders nightly led their captured Magdalenes for questioning, registration and other dark rites. And lounging in the doorways as we sauntered along I could almost see the faces from the past that belonged so familiarly in this setting: crusty, Scotch-Presbyterian Captain Duncan Matheson who later became city treasurer, Gerald Kenny, the cherubic public defender who could almost absorb the contents of a martini glass at fifty paces; poor Frank Egan—his predecessor—who tried murder when he might have one day been mayor, and spent the next quarter century in Quentin; Judge Sylvain Lazarus, an authentic judicial philosopher; colorful cops like Al Corrasa, Tim Kelleher, Julie Zimmerlin, Frank Lucey, Chinatown Jack Manion and so many others; newspapermen Opie Warner, Neil Hitt, Red Gillen, Hank Peters, Frank O'Mea, Stu McClure. The list is long. As I walked the dusty corridors I found myself thinking of people and cases and clients and heartaches and high moments of victory that had somehow completely fled my memory years before.

On the second floor we found the pressroom still redolant of its own peculiar reek—an aroma composed of tinctures of free spiritus frumenti, the miscellaneous perfumes of stray dames, the slightly defunct odor that is all that's left of a half century of black coffee from the Chinaman's next door, and the scent of perhaps fifty million crushed-out cigarette butts. I thought of the many times I'd been an honored guest here, with inside *eefus* to tell after a spectacular courtroom victory. And I thought of a night, many years ago, when I'd talked late here with novelist Jim Tully about honesty and dishonesty and riding the rods and the kindness of whores and the ofttimes meanness and soul poverty of the righteous. And at four in the morning I'd gone off to catch the first streetcar to my flat in the Richmond and he'd rolled over on the leather divan in the corner —it was still there—for a few hours' sleep before returning to his Hollywood studio for the filming of his book *Beggars of Life.* On the wall, along with other bawdy, irreverent and occasionally near-witty scrawlings, was a large, succinct terminal message in a bold and unsentimental hand. It read: *GOOD-BYE, HALL! IT'S BEEN NICE... ON PAYDAYS.*

Across the corridor from the pressroom is a courtroom that is loaded with memory for me. It is the room in which I was all that stood between an unfortunate woman and the gas chamber. Twice over.

The first woman who faced a homicide charge with me beside her in this courtroom was Laverne Borelli. The second was Gertrude Morris. In addition to a sometime rendezous with death's wayward brother murder, these two women shared another complication: they both possessed problem husbands. Both men were matrimonial embezzlers, but Borelli merely beat his wife to a pulp when she complained of his nuptial defalcations; Morris virtuously threatened to walk out forever on his graying, plain Jane companion of more than twenty-one years.

As I stood there with the custodian at the dark and dusty scene of justice's inscrutable machinations I thought for a moment that I could almost see Gertrude Morris or some ghostly evanescence of this sad, self-doomed woman on that day in January of 1952 when I denied her the fate that she herself devoutly sought... execution by cyanide inhalation at San Quentin.

Gertrude was one of the few people I've ever defended who did not personally retain me, who wanted no attorney at all, whose full and complete wish was that the district attorney would do a good job on her and thus pave the way to another full and complete job by the executioner. No would-be rescuer who ever jumped in the bay to pull out a determined suicide ever had a tougher battle than I did with this poor life-beaten, luck-forsaken, hope-divested, self-hating woman whom one newspaper, in its headline, tastefully dubbed the LOST-LOVE KILLER.

It was her uncle, her only living relative, who hired me. A kind and reasonable man, he was flabbergasted by his gentle and womanly niece's crime.

"I can't figure it out, Mr. Ehrlich," he said tremblingly. "She refuses to talk to me. She won't even see me!"

Gentle and womanly as she was, Gertrude was no swinger in the realm of feminine pulchritude; mousy is more the word. I think perhaps she had always been mousy, even at the time and age when almost all females are reasonably pretty merely because of youth.

All Gertrude had when she arrived at the age where her contemporaries express false indignation at leering glances from disgusting males were bitter memories of twelve years in a Santa Clara County orphanage, one vague and nonresident relative, and the absolute certainty that no one on earth would love her, ever, anywhere, no matter what. So she got a job as a teller in a bank and prepared for a sterile life of trial balances, sardine sandwich dinners and quiet desperation.

Then she met Milton Morris.

Milton was on the mousy side, too, but he was an ambitious mouse, and with a lot of help from Gertrude (she'd worked nine years as a secretary to put him through law school), he became a more outgoing mouse; eventually a successful and reasonably prominent mouse; and ultimately a philandering and fornicating mouse.

When success finally touched Milton, many changes had taken place in his and Gertrude's lives. From a dismal little walk-one-flight-up collection agency on O'Farrell Street, Milton had ascended to a relatively plush office at the Associated Home Builders in the Hearst Building. From a definitely nonplush flat on Duboce Street, they had moved to a nine-room home in the substantial Lakeside District (golf clubs, pavement-to-pavement lawns, etc.). There was a good car (not two, because Gertrude could never quite summon up the self-assurance to drive). There was golf for Milton. There were trips to Hawaii and Miami and even a contemplated journey to Europe if things continued to prosper. There were good clothes for Gertrude and some fair jewelry. There was money to spare. In fact there was everything but children, friends and love.

Milton, in his exclusive downtown identity (Gertrude had long given up the typewriter for radio, crossword puzzles and her own thoughts), was moving along at a pretty fast clip. He was regarded as a comer by his firm, and on several occasions had been nominated to testify before Congressional committees regarding the problems of small business. He was becoming more and more in demand as an after-dinner speaker and was also acquiring some small success as a *before*-dinner and cocktail-hour speaker. And he had a secretary, a young, pretty and blond nymph somewhat incredibly named Miss Sand. I will return to Miss Sand shortly.

Meanwhile Gertrude had undergone changes of another kind; downward changes, alas. Two decades of marriage, Herculean budgetary scheming, and worry had wrought physical and mental deterioration. The few people who knew her even slightly regarded her as odd, which is to say that her actions and reactions were different from theirs and the difference made them uncomfortable. One neighbor labeled her, "a neurotic . . . subject to fits of self-pity . . . a real brooder." A laundress who worked for her claimed she was, "kind but very insecure," which is a hell of a thing to have your laundress thinking about you. Another neighbor with whom she had gossiped about the planting of gladiola bulbs mornings over the back fence said that she always "seemed to be on the border of hysteria."

This was Gertrude on the eve of her big decision.

Naturally the decision concerned Milton and Miss Sand. Mrs. Morris was quite sure that when their business day lapped over into evening and the scene changed from the office to Solari's bar across the street, the topic of their discussions concerned not home building but home breaking. In respect to these mental allegations, Miss Sand later told the press she "could think of no reason . . . why Mrs. Morris should think Mr. Morris and I were involved. He would occasionally give me a ride home, dropping me at the door. He seemed like a solid family man."

Webster agrees with Miss Sand. One of his definitions of the word solid is "capable of resisting challenge," and Milton was all of that on the afternoon of April 10, 1951 when Gertrude dropped in for the big confrontation scene.

She got right to the point when she arrived. She told Milton and Miss Sand that she knew just what they had been doing together, specifying nothing but—with wifely wile—implying anything and everything. She wanted it to stop at once. Flabbergasted, or pretending to be, Milton angrily but coldly denied everything, sent his frightened secretary out on an emergency coffee break, and then had a short, terse, sledge-hammer-frank discussion with Gertrude. When he had finished stating the facts as he saw and felt them, a badly stricken woman fumbled and stumbled her way to the Hearst Building's elevators. Outside in the street, the pulse of traffic was quickening to the evening onrush of happier homegoers. Downstairs as she waited for the elevator to come for her and devoutly prayed that it wouldn't bring Miss Sand with it, the presses of the San Francisco *Examiner* were beginning to rumble with the issue of the first edition. The final run of that same day's paper would headline Mrs. Morris' name and the night's solution of her problem.

She made the long journey to the big, empty Lakeside residence by streetcar, huddled in with homecoming shoppers, workers, and perhaps a handful of other wives equally desperate and distrustful of their husbands. The fog comes into Lakeside from the Pacific far earlier and far more abundantly than it does to other sections of San Francisco, and the Morris home was well shrouded by it when Gertrude arrived there. The Lord only knows what torments that sad, unwanted woman's brain and soul suffered in that dark, empty house during the hours before Milton finally came home. She knew that her once-incredible experience with love and security was at an end. She knew that she was now forever alone with her doubts and fears. She knew that she loved this man with whom she had shared her life. She knew she had to do something final and irrevocable.

Climbing to the attic, she unearthed the garrison bag that had belonged to her long-dead brother, a Navy pilot in World War II. In it was a pistol—a long-barreled pistol. The pistol was still loaded.

Sitting down among the broken furniture, suitcases and the rejected knicknacks with the pistol in her hand, she thought of other times and wept. She thought of the young, eager days when she and Milton had been equally in love, and this reminded her that some of their wartime letters were stored here. She found them and read them through again and wept more abundantly. Then there was the sound of the family car being parked; not in the garage as usual but on the street in front of the house. She heard the front door open.

Milton headed directly and wordlessly for his room. He was a completely determined man and he knew what he was going to do and where he was going. He ignored Gertrude as she pleaded with him from the doorway of his room, and went on implacably filling his suitcases with clothing he would never wear again. The bullet which entered his back ended this activity. Mrs. Morris, frustrated in all other recourses, had shot him. He stumbled toward her, holding his agonized body, then fell.

"Get a doctor . . . for God's sake, get a doctor!" he begged.

But Gertrude, who had listened intently for twenty-one years, was beyond either listening or heeding. She was busy being sick. Very sick indeed. Then she passed out. By the time she recovered consciousness and her wits Milton was beyond help. Wretchedly and only half aware of reality, she crawled to the home of a neighbor and asked that the police be called. Wretchedly and now only too aware of reality, she was hauled off to the women's section of the City Prison where she immediately confessed in full detail and asked to be executed at once. Before breakfast the next morning, if possible.

It was then that I came into the case. I immediately visited my client. I wasn't too impressed by her current self-flagellation; self-recrimination isn't uncommon as a first reaction among sensitive people who have inflicted grievous injury upon those they love. I was a little shaken, however, as the weeks went by, to find that Gertrude Morris was calmly, rationally and unshakably determined to die for the pathologically emotional act of a miserably crucial moment in her life. She was no longer content to await the moment; she was fretfully impatient. She attempted to starve herself to death; they fed her intravenously. She tried to stab herself with the metal knitting needles provided on the women's side of the City Prison. She cut her wrists with pieces of broken glass. She told the press that she was guilty of murder and that she was determined to die for her crime. The press came to me for an explanation. I could only tell them what I thought and how I felt.

"I'm her lawyer. It is my job to defend her against all threats to her life, her liberty, and her constitutional right to happiness. If I must protect her from herself, I will do that, too."

They couldn't square that philosophy with the expressed attitude of a woman who just wanted to die. I told them how I felt about that.

"The woman who killed Milton Morris was a mental invalid who was just as much a menace to herself as she was to society. The woman who is saying these obviously sick things about quick death in the gas chamber is equally ill and equally a menace to herself. I am determined that she will not kill Gertrude Morris as she did Milton Morris."

But the press was more impressed with my client's statements than it was with my interpretation of them. It continued to publish her reiterations that she had known right from wrong when she killed her husband; and thus substantially loused up my chance of saving the woman by proving her not guilty by reason of insanity. Under the universally respected McNaghten Rule, a defendant is not considered insane if he or she is able to tell right from wrong. Murder is clearly wrong. Mrs. Morris was volubly proving that she *had* committed murder, that she *had* known it was wrong, and that—per se—she was no nut.

But I knew better.

My last chance at literal use of the medical defense evaporated when a sanity hearing that I was able to accomplish drew a blank. But it was not a complete blank; I was able to get important information and opinions into the record. In addition, Gertrude's conduct at the hearing was not such as to convince anyone that she was aware of the gravity of the proceedings. She obviously couldn't have cared less if they'd ordered her beheaded on the spot.

One psychiatrist found that she had, "suffered extreme trauma during childhood," an understatement that included physical abuse at the orphanage, deprival of normal affection during the period prior to the deaths of her Italian father and Jewish mother, and "more than the usual amount of economic privation when trying to establish herself" after leaving the orphanage. Another psychiatrist, apparently gifted in female motivation, asserted that Gertrude was "determined that no other woman should have [Milton] and that she would kill him rather than see him devote himself to another. Now she wants to die because the only person who made her life worthwhile is dead."

I was impressed with the testimony of Dr. Walter Rapaport, the state's star witness and the Director of California's Department of Mental Health and all of its many institutions. Long experience with headshrinkers and counselors of all kinds and prices has left me a little dubious of their status as actual scientists (one famed San Franciscan whose specialty is marriage counseling has himself had six wives and six divorces, while another brilliant and expensive therapist flies into a tantrum when waiters fail to warm his rolls), but Dr. Rapaport is a worldly and pragmatic practitioner who somehow succeeds in getting theory and fact to come out, even under judicial cross-examination.

Rapaport opined that Mrs. Morris killed for love, not because of hate or spite or jealousy or because she, "didn't want to see

Milton devote himself to another." He felt that her desire to die was a rational choice by her standards, that she had the mental and emotional capacity—at the moment—to cooperate in her defense, and that she was competent to stand trial. That did it as far as the sanity hearing was concerned: the jury voted 9 to 3 in favor of this opinion, and we were on our way to the murder trial and the moment of truth. But Rapaport's words had given me an idea and considerable hope.

We went to trial ten months and two weeks after Milton Morris was interrupted while packing his suitcases on January 24, 1952. The case was heard before Judge Neubarth (mentioned previously) and the prosecutor was Norman Elkington, now a judge and then one of the toughest operators in District Attorney Lynch's office. He knew that I was a pretty fair pitcher but he regarded himself as a pretty fair catcher. This was no tyro.

The jury was composed of 9 men and 3 woman, and the spectators were composed of Morris sympathizers, to judge from the heartiness of their applause when the judge announced that the state would not seek the death penalty. I could well understand this move. Elkington wanted to make sure that this exemption from death would be the full extent of any leniency my client might receive, to counteract any other move I might make in this direction. Gertrude couldn't have been more bored; maybe disappointed was the word.

She looked like hell. If she'd been an unattractive woman throughout the course of her ordinary lifetime, now she seemed like a downright drab. She wore no makeup and her hair was loosely and untidily drawn into an unkempt bun at the nape of her neck. Her voice had become toneless, and her glances were directed at the floor or the ceiling.

People questioned my putting her on the witness stand; a move that was not legally required of me. I knew that I could not control her. I had no way of knowing what she might or might not say. I was sure that she would neither try to help herself nor help me to help her. Yet I felt that the only way in which to transmit the true pathos and basic innocence and helplessness of Gertrude Morris to the jury was through Gertrude Morris herself. So I called upon her to testify, in full awareness of the risk I was running and with devout hope that the cumulative wisdom of twelve people would somehow reach through the tangles of her mental illness to comprehend the heartbreaking problem of the lost creature we had before us.

It was a difficult and tenuous chore because of the emotional inertia of the defendant, but I finally got her to tell her story. Then Elkington cross-examined. He hadn't made my job with Gertrude any easier, and on one occasion I'd had to straighten him out with a word that usually isn't heard except immediately prior to blows; on another occasion I'd been forced to refer to the actual possibility of blows. He let me alone, but now the gloves were definitely off and his cross-examination reflected both his new mood and his determination to accomplish a quick kill.

"Mrs. Morris, did you shoot and kill your husband?"

"Yes, I did."

"Did you kill with malice aforethought?"

"Yes."

"Did you kill with premeditated thought?"

"Yes."

"You *did* go home with the intent to kill him, didn't you?"

"Yes."

This was suicide, of course. Loudly and with all the fervor at my command, I called upon the judge to take note of the real import of the proceedings; of the unprecedented nature of a situation wherein a defendant's own defense is negated by the defendant's unqualified confession while under oath; of the totally irrational and abnormal . . . *and then, as I spoke,* I began to realize that my *real* defense of Gertrude Morris was just gathering form and substance. I let Elkington proceed.

"Mrs. Morris, you pointed the gun at your husband and shot him at the first opportunity that you got, when his back was turned to you, didn't you?"

"Yes."

"And you fully intended to do that, didn't you?"

"Yes."

"And the fact is that you didn't call the doctor because you intended that your husband die and you intended to kill yourself? That's right, isn't it?"

"Yes."

It was clear that the poor woman thought she had somehow circumvented the state's disinclination to send her to the gas chamber and also labored under the misapprehension that she was talking herself squarely into her grave. And—under different circumstances—it might have happened. But I knew better now. I knew how we were going to use Gertrude Morris' testimony to help Gertrude Morris.

My first move was to ask and obtain the court's permission to cross-examine my own witness. Gertrude was unhappy to find herself answering my questions.

"Mrs. Morris," I asked, "didn't you tell me you never intended to kill your husband when you left his office and went home?"

She stared at me like a woman in a trance.

"Yes."

"Didn't you tell me that you fired that fatal shot on pure impulse?"

"Yes."

Elkington was loudly but vainly interposing objections. Quickly and with machine-gun reiteration—so that the jury would be sure to capture the entire picture of a distraught and mentally capsized woman who would do or say anything that would turn them into accomplices in her own suicide—I asked all of the questions whose answers negated those she gave Elkington. Too late she perceived how she had thwarted her own purpose; too late she attempted to give the answers that would again fix unequivocal guilt upon herself. Now the very ambiguity of these replies told a significant and revealing story to the jurors; I could see understanding and sympathy replacing puzzlement in their eyes.

My next witness was the state's ace of the sanity hearing, Dr. Rapaport. Elkington looked licked. Rapaport testified to a short but impressive slice of scientific opinion that hadn't quite gotten into the record in my previous questioning of him.

"Dr. Rapaport, I'd like your opinion as to Mrs. Morris' mental ability at the time of the shooting. Was she mentally capable of forming the intent to commit murder at the moment?"

"No, sir!"

"*Thank* you, Doctor!"

This time I thought Elkington would flip. This was *his* witness. Now the prosecution was beginning to realize that the tide had turned, and with the unwisdom so often bred of panic they made a mistake. Throughout the trial I had dropped occasional casual remarks regarding my intention of proving that Milton Morris and his secretary Miss Sand enjoyed more than a employer-employee relationship. Now they decided to produce a well-rehearsed and abundantly sterilized Miss Sand, who would prove that Milton Morris had never looked lustfully upon her or vice versa. I was delighted despite the fact that her appearance in the courtroom worked upon Gertrude the first profound emotional response that I'd seen since the grim period immediately following the death of her husband. When her erstwhile rival entered the room, Mrs. Morris drew in her breath sharply, grasped her chair rigidly, and attempted to leave. Restrained, she slumped in a heap and had to be revived.

Miss Sand was small, demure and no longer blond. She wore no makeup or costume jewelry, and a severely conventional pair of glasses sat upon her nose. She had the right answers—from Elkington's point of view—for every question I asked her, but this I expected. After a brief examination I asked her to sit close to the well of the court; I might need to recall her.

Then I called Ralph Isaacs. Ralph, a good attorney, had and has offices in the Hearst Building. He knew Milton Morris very well, he said.

"Did you know his secretary, Miss Sand?" I asked.

"Oh yes. She was a very cute girl. Dressed beautifully; always loaded down with orchids or other expensive flowers. A real slick little chick."

"Did you ever see her with Morris?"

"With Morris? Oh my, yes. Scores of times. He took her out, here and there; lunch, dinner, drinks. I used to see them often."

"Did they appear to be very friendly toward each other?"

Isaacs laughed.

"Friendly? How friendly can you get! He seemed to be pretty well hooked on her, and she on him."

I pointed to the newly fumigated Miss Sand.

"Is that the lady we're speaking of?"

Isaacs scrutinized her for several moments.

"Oh no... Miss Sand is more... *well, I'll be darned!* It *is* Miss Sand! I just never saw her in glasses before. And wearing that..."

That was exactly what I wanted. It wasn't exactly what Elkington wanted however.

"Thank you, Mr. Isaacs! Miss Sand will you please return to the stand!"

She did, but not with enthusiasm. I questioned her at some length about dates, places and her reciprocal relations, if any, with the late Mr. Morris. When she stepped down and away from my questions she was sobbing. I felt no regret. I can offer little mercy or charity to a witness who tampers with the information that will help a defendant on trial for his or her life. But for a woman to let another woman go down the drain in order to protect herself from gossip...

Elkington's summation was not very masterly. He allowed that I was, "a fine lawyer, a very resourceful lawyer," and opined that I could always be counted on to, "come up with an unexpected defense." In this case, however, he hadn't been fooled. My whole defense was a snare and a delusion, a fabrication and a fraud. He was sure that the jurors were clever enough to see through it. My claim that my client and I weren't seeing eye to eye was quite untrue; we were both playing clever roles. My allegation that my client had been mentally ill when she shot her husband and was ill still was another deceit; "She's as sane as you or I." There was really only one thing for them to remember and that was the Elkington version of what had taken place at the Lakeside house. "She shot him... she saw him fall to the floor . . . she heard him say 'Get a doctor!' . . . she walked away and let him bleed to death."

My own closing argument took a little more time and heart. I told the jurors the story of Gertrude Morris' life. I tried to explain to them how important and incredibly valuable the rare and elusive thing called love can be to a Gertrude Morris. I made clear what the loss of this thing did to the delicate human organism called Gertrude Morris, because I had made a searching effort to evaluate the damage inflicted on my client. Then I told them about the puny husband who'd been sent through law school on the hoarded dimes and dollars of a woman whom he wanted no longer after he'd arrived at the point where he could lunch at the Palace Hotel. I discussed the late Mr. Morris pretty thoroughly and without lamentation.

That was enough for one day. Enough for them to think about overnight. The next morning I spoke of the future—of Gertrude's future that was in their hands. I told them again of the little that she'd had from anyone and of the much that they—and they alone—could give her.

I asked them to think of the woman whose entire being they now held in their collective hands as some broken-winged, frightened bird.

"Look at this woman! Look at this poor, confused, unloved, unwanted woman whose one attempt to thrust back at the life that has whipped her unmercifully since birth resulted in this terrible experience. Look at her, sitting here through the terrible weeks, listening to me and the district attorney and the psychiatrists and her husband's matinee wife and all the rest of these people talk about her, turn her life inside out, deprive her of her last privacy, tear her to shreds in the name of justice. . . . I ask you to *look* at her, ladies and gentlemen! Is she here because she committed a crime? You *know* better than that! You know that she is here because she lost at love . . . because she lost the only thing on earth she really loved and hoped loved her. You *cannot* compound the crime that society has committed against this woman; you *cannot* convict her!"

My listeners in the jury box were obviously having trouble

with their emotions. From the spectators back of the rails came sobs. As I looked around me I realized that I was seeing my surroundings through tears. I couldn't believe it. I'd even brought *myself* to the point of tears. I decided I'd better bring the proceedings to a close while I was still ahead.

"In conscience, you cannot convict this woman, my friends! Set her free! Say that she is not guilty! Tell her to go her way, to build a new life and to find a little happiness . . . and perhaps a little understanding from some man who will sense her fineness . . . and at least a little compassion from all men and women of goodwill."

Nothing that Elkington could have said in his final argument would have helped him now. When the jury came back they brought a verdict of Guilty of Manslaughter with them. In California, manslaughter draws a penalty of 1 to 10 years. One to ten years, under the state's indeterminate sentence procedures, is usually served in from 15 to 18 months. A first offender such as Gertrude might make it in 10 months.

But Gertrude was neither grateful nor happy.She merely eyed me dispassionately and—for the first time—somewhat curiously.

"You missed your calling, Master," she said, somewhat wryly. "You should have been an actor. Your oration was a classic."

The reporters asked her for a statement, in full anticipation of headline copy. She didn't disappoint them. Not that she really cared what they asked or what they published about her in tomorrow's paper or whether there would be another tomorrow, now that Milton was gone.

"It was a miscarriage of justice," she told them tonelessly. "I am guilty of murder. I believe in a life for a life. I have taken a life and mine should be taken from me."

"What are your plans for the future, Mrs. Morris?" shouted one of her interviewers.

"I have no future," she replied, and turned toward the matron to be taken back to the solitude of her cell.

She was right; she had no future. She was quickly released from prison but just as quickly she was committed to a hospital for the insane. I never saw her again . . . until today, among the dark and dusty shade of this forgotten temple of justice on lower Kearny Street. She still seemed to be eyeing me ruefully, as if still asking plaintively:

"Tell me, Master . . . why couldn't you have let me *really* die?"

My other lady shade from the past of this long-abandoned courtroom was a far happier memory. As she lingered in the shadow of the bench in my groping memory I seemed to see her smiling, as if in fond appreciation. Laverne Borelli hadn't wanted to die as Gertrude Morris did, and it was a rewarding experience to justify the faith she had that she wouldn't die because Jake Ehrlich was her lawyer.

The defense of Mrs. Borelli's "husbandcide" had its advantages over the Morris case—Borelli beat her brutally and his adulteries were more documentable, plus the fact that she was an appealingly pretty woman—but there were disadvantages too, weighty ones.

Laverne Borelli had killed her husband while he slept. The prosecution possessed substantial tangible evidence of premeditation. And most disadvantageous of all from a psychological standpoint, an attractive physician's wife named Irene Mansfield had just literally gotten away with the businesslike and well-planned assassination of her husband's office nurse. Mrs. Mansfield had escaped with a merely admonitory sentence (she actually served 3 years and 4 months), and ordinarily unrighteous San Francisco was still muttering and mumbling about this tilting of the scales of justice.

I had returned home from the fights on the evening of May 8th in 1947 when the telephone rang. In my hands as I went to answer it was a crisp copy of the morning *Examiner,* the banner headline of which read: WIFE SLAYS SLEEPING AUTO DEALER.

Below it were pictures of a handsome, self-assured man in his early thirties and a slim, lovely, blond woman who, to the practiced eye, might have been rated a few years older. The text of the story was in the familiar, straightaway Hearstian style:

> Eugene "Gene" Borelli, popular young sportsman and Auto Row figure, last night dozed off into a sleep from which he never awoke. While asleep in the spare room of his own home he was immediately killed by four shots from his own thirty-eight calibre revolver. Homicide Inspector Thomas Cahill said that he found Mrs. Borelli in the custody of Borelli's brother, Joseph, and . . .

I picked up the phone.

It was a friend of Laverne Borelli, speaking for himself and others who were concerned about her plight. She was wounded and under guard at the City and County Hospital. Would I take the case? I would. Would I go and see her at once? I would also do that.

It's a dreary journey out Potrero Avenue to The County in the postmidnight hours, especially when misery and desperation wait at one's destination, but the ride gave me a chance to figure out percentages and strategies. With the Mansfield case just off Page One and Mrs. Mansfield still the subject of editorial invective, we could expect a poor press. That meant we'd say nothing for publication until we were sure of firm ground beneath us.

There'd been mention of Borelli's brother Joe taking "custody" of Laverne. That probably meant a highly hostile and perhaps voluble spokesman for the deceased. We'd let him talk his head off to the reporters if he would; people tend to get tired of animose yapping and sometimes reverse early impressions. And Tom Cahill had the case. I knew Tom Cahill well and was to know him for the next twenty years, up to and including the time that he became chief of police. He was a good cop and a thorough investigator. Cahill would never add to or subtract from the facts as he found them. He was always an honest witness. It would be a tough case. It would require care and finesse. But somewhere, somehow, a loophole would finally wink at me. I'd get my break.

At the hospital I found a pale, haggard, almost comatose woman. She was barely conscious of reality and she couldn't talk, thank God, but she knew who I was the minute I stood beside her bed; I knew that from her eyes. I bent close above her face and spoke very clearly, saying the words slowly and emphatically.

"Mrs. Borelli, I am not only your lawyer, I am your friend. Speak to no one else about anything. I am *with* you and I am *for* you. Don't be afraid!"

She nodded her head in an almost imperceptible message of understanding and appreciation and I departed. The woman was clearly in a pitiable condition. She had wounded herself in the breast with the revolver used on her husband and had also taken poison. Fortunately they'd gotten to the poison in time with a stomach pump. But the wounds to her heart and mind were more grievous. The police might as well have applied their tired alphabetical letters—D.O.A.—to her. In this case instead of meaning Dead on Arrival they would have signified Damned On Arrival, for from the very first, authorities, the press, the public and even Laverne herself were in complete agreement that the lady was fit only for burning. What else . . . for a woman who would kill a man while he slept!

By the time dawn began to make pale streaks over the Contra Costa County hills I had pieced together most of the facts of her life and of her husband's death.

Gene Borelli had been a handsome sales dynamiter in the automobile field; superficially dynamic, amiably glib, full of deals. Not all his deals had paid off. For instance, he'd paid $10,000 for the San Francisco franchise for the ill-fated Tucker automobile. When things went wrong he had become less amiable. Once he'd been trapped by an OPA investigator in an illegal ceiling-price-ignoring deal and had attempted to blast himself out of the predicament with a right to the jaw at the cost of a $100 fine plus maximum penalty on the Federal charge. On another occasion he'd become involved in a barroom brawl with a customer who'd naively sought conventional redress of a car sale wherein the satisfaction was unilateral. Nor were Gene's hooks and jabs reserved exclusively for men. Laverne had lost many a fistic decision to her scrappy husband, which was understandable because weight and age were in his favor.

If Borelli was a wild, unstable and improvident sort, Laverne was the opposite. She had brought a kind of dowry to Borelli: prior to their marriage she had run a successful beauty shop in Southern California and sold it in order to accept his proposal. Moreover, she'd saved and carefully budgeted their income to offset her husband's profligacy, and on more than one occasion had come to his assistance when one of his sure things flopped.

Borelli lied to her, cheated on her, beat her, and—for small talk when things were dull—offered to give her a one-way trip to Reno.

True to form and folklore, Laverne adored the man despite or because of her immolation at his hands. This is what plunged her into torment on the evening of May 8, 1947 when she inadvertently happened upon two people in the act of love. The man and woman involved were not merely kissing, nor was Mrs. Borelli naively traumatized at the experience of stumbling upon them. Her shock derived from the fact that the party of the first part was Mr. Borelli and the party of the second part was an erstwhile house guest in her home—a woman who was technically a friend of hers. In our culture, adultery for some reason becomes *adultery ne plus ultra* when committed with a "friend of the family."

This was not the first time that Laverne Borelli had been shamed and hurt by her husband's infidelity but it was the first time she had been literally faced with it. In the words of a close friend who was with her at the time, Mrs. Sidney Halliday, she was "completely stricken." Like many a woman before her (and after) she went with Mrs. Halliday to a cocktail lounge and had herself a few drinks. Unlike most women, she didn't have a lot to say. She was beyond self-pity, and idle recrimination to a receptive woman friend did not seem to make much sense in the light of Borelli's pattern of fornication.

Mrs. Halliday went home to her own husband and that left Laverne to her Manhattans, some pills her physician had given her for her nerves, and her own reflection in the back-bar mirror. What she saw wasn't too bad, she told herself, determinedly composing her wobbling mouth line and trying to look as cheerfully appealing as possible. True, her chin and neckline weren't quite as smooth and clean cut as they once had been, and there were those tiny lines at the edge of the eyes, but her figure was still good and her legs. . . . She wanted to cry—she wanted to have a good bawl—but the liquor and the pills had done something to her and she couldn't do anything but *think.* She was *numb* with thinking. She had another Manhattan. Then another pill.

By ten thirty she had gotten as far as the little neighborhood bar several blocks from where she and Gene *existed.* We don't *live* anywhere, she told herself bitterly, we just exist. She'd reached the point of desperate and dismal philosophical truth, as seen from the wrong end of her psychological binoculars. Her only supper had been pills and Manhattans. Her only companion had been her own reflection in the bottle-framed mirror. The starting and ending point of her thought journeys had been a man and a woman sordidly engaged in the back seat of an automobile. By one o'clock, and with the proprietor pointedly putting out lights, she'd paid her tab, made it to her car, sat there behind the wheel in the darkness for awhile and then driven home.

She wasn't drunk in the usual sense, for not only liquor but pills and the emotional impact of the evening's earlier incident contributed to her strange and peculiar intoxication. Mrs. Halliday was later to testify that Laverne had said she felt as if she were, "up in the air and flying." Her actions and attitude were described as those of an automaton. It is probably closest to truth to surmise that her primitive instincts were probably in complete control for the moment; that her intellect was totally disengaged; that even her conditioned emotional reflexes were temporarily nonfunctioning. She had been, to my mind, as insensate and as unresponsibly lethal as a guided missile.

Home she went—to home and hell, as it was so often for her when Gene was drunk or in a bad mood. Garaging her car, she climbed the inside stairs and went directly to her bedroom. It was unoccupied, the bed untouched, but she could hear the sound of snoring from the guest bedroom and she knew her husband was spending the night there. It was one of his subtle ways of showing his disdain for her when he wished to hurt her. She went to his bureau drawer and, buried beneath his shirts, her hand found what it sought. Holding the pistol before her, she almost somnambulistically walked toward the spare room. I doubt that her face bore any expression. I am sure that her mind held no thought, no pattern of rationale.

Gene Borelli lay on the bed in his underwear, shirt and socks. His tie was thrown across the floor and his suit was crumpled over a sewing hassock. He lay open-mouthed, sweat-shiny and reeking of the evening's pleasures, the picture of sated male lust.

But to Laverne Borelli, standing over him with her pistol, her life in shambles about her, he presented other pictures, too, as he lay there, snoring and sweating and—even in sleep—shutting her out of his life. There were pictures of past beatings, pictures of a thousand wisecracked insults, of untold humiliations and slights. She fired four times into the middle of his body, as fast as the mechanism of the gun would operate.

Borelli, awakened more by the roar of the weapon than the pain, shouted hoarsely, then writhed to the floor beside the bed, clutching himself. He completely disregarded the woman who stood above him in abject amazement at what she had done; her eyes opened wide, as if she had just recovered consciousness. Borelli was fully awake now and very aware of the holes in his body and of the blood gushing from them. He screamed for his brother Joe, who lived in the house. Laverne just stared.

Wild-eyed and uncomprehending, Joe Borelli appeared within seconds. He took the weapon from Laverne, placed it on the bureau, then tried to raise his brother to the bed to stanch the blood that was flowing from him everywhere. Suddenly he heard two more revolver shots, not in the room but somewhere upstairs in the house.

Rushing toward the sound of the shots, he found his sister-in-law leaning weakly against her bedroom door, the pistol hanging slackly from her fingers. She was bleeding from two bullet holes in her chest, the bullets having passed both through her and the door behind her. A bottle lay on its side at her feet. Joe Borelli disarmed her for the second time in five minutes, assisted her to her bed, and got on the phone to the police.

This was the sad, ugly, doom-filled picture that I entered when I took Laverne Borelli's case. And these were the not very encouraging facts with which I found myself faced when I left my office shortly before dawn the morning after the murder, after having spent the night in study of them.

I was keenly aware of the Mansfield case verdict as I climbed into a cab and gave the Nob Hill address; aware of the unlikelihood of legal generosity toward a gun-wielding housewife. I was certain that Mrs. Borelli had been intellectually unconscious of the nature of her acts the night before, but proving such a contention to the degree that her conduct might be mitigated under Section 26 of the Penal Code ("a person who commits an act without being conscious thereof") was going to be difficult in a city that is extremely blasé about drinking. If every woman who allowed herself to become stoned of an evening were *ipso facto* to regard herself and be regarded as "without being conscious of her acts" and thus licensed to shoot at will, all other erring husbands might find themselves in chronic danger. Some variable other than liquor would be required to qualify Laverne as having been as "unconscious" of her acts as Section 26 specified.

As soon as I arrived home I took a hot shower, a sleeping pill, and left word to be called at ten o'clock. Four hours' sleep was little enough but it was better than none.

When I awoke at noon I asked Marjorie why I'd not been called earlier. She told me that I'd been called at ten o'clock and again at ten thirty but that I'd responded so groggily on both occasions that she'd decided to let me sleep until I awakened a little more coherently. This gave me something to think about.

Suppose I had taken the sleeping pill knowing full well that it would leave me too groggy to respond to a summons after only four hours of sleep, then I certainly would have been guilty of ulterior *intent*. But suppose I honestly believed it would bring me just four hours of sleep—from which I would rise refreshed and ready to work—how would the consciousness of my act be defined under Section 26? I remember my satisfaction at my reasoning at this point in its development; I felt that I had the beginnings of a defense for Mrs. Borelli—*if* we were fortunate enough to get a reasonably understanding and compassionate group of jurors. I overlooked another *if* to my problem.

On May 9, 1947 we went to trial before Judge Alfred C. Wollenberg. It was to be Judge Wollenberg's first murder case (he'd only come to the bench in March, sixty days before) and this was not at all good. Not that the jurist wasn't a fine and able lawyer with a distinguished career, but a new judge is like a new broom—he sweeps clean. I had no particular wish to see any of my deviously conceived defensive arguments swept away by rigid, letter-of-the-law judicial Gilbert and Sullivanisms. However, I now had Wollenberg for better or for worse and it would be both before the end of the trial, but not in that order.

Opposing me for the state would be Alvin Weinberger. Al is presently a Superior Court judge himself. He was a very competent lawyer and a tough man to beat; in this situation he had a prosecutor's dream case. He also had a made-to-order star witness, the dead man's loyal and loving kid brother Joe Borelli. I had already checked young Borelli out. He was thirsty for punishment for Laverne.

I was pleading Laverne Not Guilty and Not Guilty by Reason of Insanity. California offers the murder defendant this dual recourse, which means that persons who so plead are tried twice if found guilty on the initial charge of homicide. The second proceeding, obviously, is to determine whether or not they were capable of knowing the difference betwen right and wrong at the moment they committed the crime. It is a rather stupid and ineffectual procedure, on the whole, and I can't remember too many cases where a jury has convicted a person of murder and then reversed its own action by its finding in the second trial. Usually the so-called sanity trial is only the emptiest of formalities and a mere anticlimatic extension of Trial One. In the Borelli case, the second plea was an escape hatch for me. I was hoping for a manslaughter verdict my first time at bat.

In the jury box we had 6 men and 6 women. I had worked very hard to make sure that none of them was a fool, a frivolous time-killer, without reasonable compassion or impelled by any of the wrong obsessions or compulsions from the point of view of my client. One juror with "a thing" about booze, for instance, can ride roughshod over all of the fine points of logic, argument, evidence and testimony in order to render a verdict that supports his or her attitude about liquor. And similarly in respect to religion or politics or sexual habits or a score of other matters. I thought I had a fair jury.

Weinberger led off with a straight, frontal attack. A woman had taken the law into her own hands. Her husband had asked for a divorce—clearly his right. His wife had thereupon shot and killed him, making the act worse by committing it while he was asleep and defenseless. The prosecutor put the younger Borelli on the stand and the latter did everything short of administering the cyanide himself. He not only related the facts of the killing with great and obviously assisted eloquence, but he reached back into his memory and came up with a piece of drama straight out of *Macbeth*. He had been eavesdropping, it appeared, and had heard Laverne openly speak of a plan to kill her husband.

When young Joe was mine for cross-examination, I asked him about this statement, which Laverne described to me as a complete lie.

"Did you ever tell anyone else before that you'd heard such a threat, Mr. Borelli?"

He squirmed and glowered and shot sidelong glances at Weinberger in the hope of being taken off the hook.

"Well, not exactly."

"What do you mean, 'not exactly'? You have or you haven't. Answer the question!"

"I don't remember."

"Yeah! I'm sure of it," I snarled sarcastically. "I somehow didn't think you'd be able to remember mentioning this alleged event to anyone but the district attorney, and somewhat retroactively . . ."

Weinberger attempted to rescue his star performer. He addressed the court.

"I ask that counsel be confined to cross-examining the witness, and not making comments."

"The witness!" I expostulated. "This man is a *false* witness. The Bible says, 'The wicked fleeth when no man pursueth' and this man is running and lying as if he—instead of Laverne Borelli—had something to gain or lose in this courtroom. And perhaps he has, now that we consider it; perhaps he has!"

I abruptly turned to Borelli. I had to annihilate him as a a creditable witness and I had to do it here and now.

"Perhaps you have indeed, sir! Isn't it true that if you can help prove that Gene Borelli was murdered that you—instead of his wife—will inherit his property under the law of the State of California? And isn't it true that if this jury sees this tragedy in its true light and convicts Laverne Borelli of only manslaughter, you will inherit absolutely nothing? And isn't it equally true that for these reasons—which a certain type of man would regard as sufficient to justify ample effort—you have every reason for testifying generously for the prosecution . . . and *remembering* all manner of strange things, right?"

Borelli and Weinberger were loud in vociferation but I'd put into words the thought I wanted to present to the jury. I sat down well satisfied.

Unfortunately Mrs. Borelli had written a three-page letter at some time prior to the night of May 8th. In it, with some obvious premonition of dire developments to come, she had methodically disposed of the property she and her husband owned communally. Weinberger made excellent use of this document. In conjunction with later events, it made a rather substantial case for the state's contention of premeditation.

When I began to advance my theory of Laverne's descent into unconsciousness via alcohol *cum* medicine, I first began to encounter the unexpected *if* in my prospects. This *if* was Judge Wollenberg's adamant unwillingness to entertain any consideration of the possibility that such a psychic condition could have occurred. His ruling on the matter was a little on the arbitrary side, I thought, for it was based on the assumption that the defendant had taken the medicine and liquor of her own accord and volition. This premise seemed to make a great difference to Wollenberg; it suggested that henceforward anyone could take pills and justify a killing if my rationale of Mrs. Borelli's conduct were to be admitted to evidence in this courtroom. At my every attempt to introduce this essential and vital factor of my defense, I would be stemmed from the bench. This was all I had. This was all there was to offer in Laverne Borelli's defense. I knew that whatever hope for her that now remained must derive from the compassion of the jury—the subject of my other if. Here I again drew a blank. The jury found Mrs. Borelli Guilty in the First Degree. I caught her in my arms and she slumped to the floor upon hearing the pronouncement.

Well, the wise guys and the corridor soothsayers had themselves a field day. Ehrlich had at last lost one. The magic record had been broken. What was the cocky little bastard going to say now in explanation of a client turned over to the executioner?

After I had seen Laverne in the lawyer's room at the County Jail and told her things I knew would comfort her, I dropped in on the wake that was going on at Cookie Picetti's saloon, next door to the Hall of Justice. I bought drinks, listened to the condolences—false and sincere—and then made a short statement before picking up the tab and departing. I suggested that nothing reflects more absurdly upon the mourners and pallbearers at a funeral than the presence of an undead corpse. I suggested that they suspend their lamentations until the death certificate of my record and career was actually signed.

When we returned to court on the sanity hearing, I was ready.

I was far readier than anyone thought. The testimony and procedures were routine in nature but now I was more interested in reaching Judge Wollenberg than the jury, whom I knew to be a cold, uncompassionate dozen of humans. Wollenberg was not only a just man and a scholar, he was also a devoutly ethical man and "good" in the Old Testament sense. I knew that the humanities would have real meaning to him.

We got a hung jury (8 to 4) and Weinberger promptly moved for the impaneling of a new jury and the fixing of a new trial. But I had other plans.

"At this time, if Your Honor please, we will withdraw the plea of Not Guilty by Reason of Insanity. We hereby stand upon the conviction in the first phase of my client's trial."

You could have heard a mote drop in the silent courtroom. Wollenberg looked at me as though I were speaking in tongues. Al Weinberger gave me the askant look which said he knew that more was happening than met the eye. My client just stared at me, hurt and unbelieving. I went on.

"Under the dual plea in California, we have excluded the mental processes. Therefore the case is incomplete and a murder conviction cannot stand. My client, Mrs. Borelli, is—in effect—in the same legal position she was in before she was brought before this court."

The expression of dawning admiration on the prosecutor's face was ample reward for the moment. Judge Wollenberg was beginning to smile as he, too, saw the strategy. I continued with my statement.

"I would like to call Your Honor's attention to a valuable addition to the code with which I am sure you are well acquainted. I refer to Section 1181 which empowers a judge, in a case where he feels that a jury verdict is too harsh, to reduce that verdict to one that more appropriately and fairly fits the crime. With all due respect to the present jury, I respectfully suggest that its verdict on the matter at hand has not been exactly tempered with anything that might pass for charity or mercy or even moderation. I therefore move that under Section

1181 the First Degree Murder conviction of Mrs. Borelli be set aside and that a verdict of Manslaughter be substituted."

One week later, on New Year's Eve of 1947, Judge Wollenberg ruled on my motion. He reviewed the two trials at some length and then came up with the statement that sent the reporters racing for their pressroom telephones.

"I have been required to exclude all evidence bearing on the defendant's mental condition and therefore the case before me is incomplete for a murder conviction. The only evidence of deliberation is the note that was left by Mrs. Borelli. . . . This is a suicide note and it does not show intent to take another life. I think that evidence shows the homicide was committed in the heat of passion. It is therefore the judgment of the court that Mrs. Borelli is guilty of manslaughter."

So even with the cards stacked a little against us, Mrs. Borelli and I came out with our respective rewards on that unforgettable New Year's Eve: she with her life; I with my unbroken record for cheating the hangman. I was human enough to find it necessary to drop around at Cookie's to buy drinks and remind the forgetful never to attend a funeral until the corpse is actually lying down.

Laverne Borelli served 5 years, 1 month and 28 days on her manslaughter sentence. Marjorie tells me that she's the best stylist at her favorite beauty shop in San Francisco these days. But as I stood on the threshhold of Judge Wollenberg's erstwhile courtroom today I could recall the way Laverne had looked when I last saw her: her face alive and healthy again with the hope of happiness some day in the future. We'd beaten death together with a second-bounce defense.

My friend the custodian was determined that I should miss nothing. He guided me to the narrow, old-fashioned elevator at the rear of the building—once the only means of transit and entry to the City Prison. Once more and perhaps as the last of a thousand or more journeys that I'd taken to that grim rooftop Bastille, I found myself headed for the eighth floor, the first stop for all persons charged with serious crime in the old days.

"I'll bet *this* place don't have no fond memories for you, Master."

"You lose, pal. *All* the old memories are good—in retrospect—because they're composed of the *real* experience of *real* people, and into them went courage and heart and sacrifice and humor and dreams and hopes. And even in the heartache and the occasional agony there was the drama and the human appeal that make their recollection important and satisfying in retrospect. They're memories I couldn't disown if I would . . . and wouldn't if I could."

We'd stepped out onto the eighth floor. The blotter desk, once the hallowed dais of generations of grimly omnipotent booking sergeants, was now thick with dust; the barred and ponderously locked prison doors of yesterday now stood ajar and revealed rusting cells and tanks in the melancholy half light from the overhead skylights. I walked along a cell tier, observing that from a link of chain which hooked one of the bunks to the wall there still hung a bag of the state-manufactured free cigarette tobacco that prisoners cynically refer to as Duffy's Dust in honor of former Warden Clinton Duffy, who invented this not very smokable would-be facsimile of Bull Durham. On a cell wall some pious soul had carefully etched the words: *Jesus Delivers:* under it some less pious collaborator had penciled: *But When, Man, When?* Over a leprous-looking commode a long-gone talent had been inspired to poesy:

It does no good to stand upon the seat
These jailhouse crabs jump twenty feet.

And at the end of the narrow alley I came upon the high-power tank. This is the prisoners' colloquialism for the special security cell reserved for those for whom the law has special regard; for those whose security, close custody and incommunicado segregation special housing and attention is required; for those who have committed the king-sized crimes. Such a person was Alfred Leonard Cline, the only client I ever had whom I deliberately railroaded into the penitentiary.

Alfred Cline was the sort of an old gent you'd pick to pass up the aisle with the collection plate if you were a naive pastor with a large faith in mild-faced, sedate-necktied, graying-templed oldsters in pepper-and-salt suits. And Mr. Cline would have passed that plate. If it were heavy enough, he might even have passed right on through the vestry foyer with it. But he would have done so in a thoroughly gentlemanly manner, and the pastor and the congregation would never have been quite sure it hadn't really been a misunderstanding of some kind.

The San Francisco Police Department was under no misapprehensions about misunderstandings or other possible rationalizations of Mr. Cline's conduct when they put the gyves on him on December 7, 1945 in connection with fantastically multiple charges that he had been signing other people's names to documents that were bringing him other people's money. Within a mere moment of being captured, he proved that whatever else he was he was a man of keen vision and flawless perceptivity—he hired me.

Our initial interview would have made a convention of deaf-mutes seem like a coffee break at the Tower of Babel. After paying me my retainer (an abundant one and in cash), he succinctly made it clear that the rest was strictly up to me, and from then on clammed up.

I soon found out that the forgery charges upon which he'd been booked were mere technicalities insofar as the authorities were concerned. Alfred Leonard Cline was wanted by more people and was sought in more places than the Holy Grail. The trouble was that they couldn't prove any of the things they were sure were true of him and strangely enough—despite all the grandiose claims made for modern scientific criminological investigative methods—it is very hard to convict criminals, in many instances, unless (a) information can be obtained from an informer or a gabby confederate (the technical term is "fink"); or (b) unless the subject can be induced to fink on himself ("confess" is the term in this usage). Clause A was negated by the fact that Cline was a loner; clause B by the fact that he was an uncommunicative or nonfinking loner. It is a curious but perhaps only coincidental phenomenon that there are practically no deaf-mutes in prison anywhere.

The phase of Cline's vocal reticence that annoyed the police most was the fact that though they had his earthly body they did *not* have his earthly abode. He had been pinched in a hotel room where he had but briefly and transiently resided. The personal effects found there were of nominal significance and threw absolutely no light on his present, past and—unless the forgeries could be proven—his future.

I was as interested as they were in getting the drawings on my nonverbalizing client. If I were defending nothing more than a shady forger and confidence man I wanted to know it at once so that I could protect him from the mass of innuendos, semiofficial inferences and highly damaging rumors that were creeping into even newspaper reporting of the case. If my client was something else, then I wanted to know that, too, and in precise detail and—if possible—before "they" found it out. By "they" I refer to the FBI, the Postal Inspectors, the Canadian Mounties and police chiefs in Illinois, Indiana, Georgia, Florida, Oregon, Nevada and elsewhere—all of whom wanted a piece of my Mr. Cline.

It was as obvious to me as it was to the authorities that the only recourse possibly productive of results would be an examination of his really personal effects. And where were they to be found? There were those among the police who felt that their prisoner had an apartment or a flat or home somewhere under an assumed name, but there were others (and there was I) who believed that Cline was too much of a rover, too suspicious of stability, too wary of neighbors or landlords to let himself become permanently settled anywhere. Besides, there had been a drawing found in his briefcase that seemed to be a diagram of a trailer. I decided that he lived in a trailer, and so did a number of the police investigating the case. All of the trailer camps and parks in northern California were combed for such a vehicle. The result was zero.

Since the principal attribute of a trailer is mobility (our man's trailer might be in any of an endless number of places) and because Cline's principal attribute was unorthodoxy (he would hardly park in any of the conventional places . . . trailer parks, for instance), it occurred to me that the search was being conducted from the wrong end. Instead of trying to find a trailer and then linking it to Cline, I decided that an attempt should be made to link Cline to a specific area of San Francisco, and then the trailer should be sought in that area.

It worked.

My client's little black book contained the names of many ladies who lived or had lived in the cities of twenty states and shared a number of interesting denominators. They were all elderly. They all owned some small competence—a savings account or stocks and bonds or property. They were all unmarried (widowed or maiden ladies) and they were all alone in respect to protective or inheritance-minded relatives. And they were all church centered, since their social lives were strongly interwoven into the activities of the religious congregation to which they belonged.

I obtained a list of the San Franciscans among them and had these devout and impressionable ladies interviewed, finding—as an interesting collateral result—that they shared other common denominators. They all regarded "that poor Mister Cline" as just the finest gentleman ever, and "there simply *had* to be some mistake!" They were convinced that some spiteful woman had placed him in his present predicament. They were each Mr. Cline's sole confidante and best friend; "nothing questionable, you understand!" And they were all communicants of the Hayes Valley Galilee Baptist Church. The last item was the key.

It was the beginning of Christmas week when I received this information. I was in no mood for the gumshoe bit and was half inclined to let the man who'd turned up the gullible old ladies try for the trailer, too. But I was also fascinated with the mystery that lurked behind my client's mute, placid front (he spent his time in the County Jail reading religious books and chewing gum), so the other half of my inclination took over. I climbed into my car one miserable pre-Yuletide evening and headed for the Hayes Valley Galilee Baptist Church.

It was raining very cold and unfriendly rain that night and the downtown sidewalk Santa Clauses were bitterly ringing their bells to nearly empty pavements. The Hayes Valley Church turned out to be a large and ugly bastard-Gothic edifice with a visagelike stained-glass façade that seemed to be glowering enviously at the more recently painted Catholic Church on the corner down the street. The HVGB Church was dark and so was the Catholic Church. I had the clammy, self-disgusted feeling that I was playing a long and forlorn chance.

On the other hand, I was reasonably sure that Cline—if he was all they said he was—would have established himself somewhere close to the scene of his "commercial" operation; that he would want to be able to move promptly and conveniently if the need arose. I rounded the block very slowly, peering carefully into every alley, every mews, every vacant lot, even into such driveways as were open to view from the street. Gradually I widened the orbit of my circling, using the HVGB Church as the axis of this maneuver.

Once I thought I'd dropped my ringer over the stake. I spotted a trailer parked darkly and wetly in a closed gas station and bearing Nevada license plates. Cline had reputedly just departed Nevada. I eagerly pulled up beside it and quickly slid back into gear and away when an angry male Oklahoma voice told a sleepy female Oklahoma voice that he, "reckoned it was them cops again."

Wider grew my circle and fainter grew my hope of success when suddenly I came upon a bright new and rather deluxe house trailer that—at first glimpse—made contact with my ESP equipment. I pulled up and stepped out into the rain which had now found its stride in a strong, stubborn downpour. There wasn't a soul in sight; not even a doorway wino, which is rare for this district, rain or shine. I examined the vehicle I'd found and guessed at its layout; my guess compared favorably with the diagram found in Cline's pocket as I remembered it. The door was locked, of course, but under the latch I found a soggy wad of paper which turned out to be a traffic citation. It was dated December 9th. The trailer had apparently been there, unattended, since at least the second day after Cline had been arrested. I was convinced.

I was convinced, and despite the rain that was beginning to trickle down my sleeves as I raised my arms to work on one of the windows, I was delighted. As a great believer in the infallibility of Ehrlich hunches, I was pleased to have past-posted the master minds at the Hall of Justice. I was also glad to discover that Cline's criminal headquarters had been figuratively under their noses ever since his arrest: it was parked virtually under the shadow of City Hall, in a vacant lot next to the Central Emergency Hospital.

And now an even greater and better piece of luck rewarded my efforts. The window was unlatched on the inside. I tried to reach the inside lock of the door, but couldn't. Though while fumbling about through the window on the inside of the trailer I was able to come upon a shelf, and on the shelf some papers which I withdrew. One of these was a program of divine services for the Hayes Valley Galilee Baptist Church for Sunday, December 4th.

As every customer of any of the large life insurance companies knows, around the first of every year the corporations present each of them with a small calendar printed on heavy celluloid. And as every member of the San Francisco Police Department knows, this calendar's purpose has nothing to do with discovering the day or date. It is used by police and burglars alike for opening spring locks (so-called Yale locks). For this purpose it is superb and possibly superior to even Yale keys.

Within three minutes I was inside Cline's trailer with the rain beating briskly on the roof and my heart pounding. After all, if the suspicions of the police were well grounded, I might conceivably stumble over a defunct old lady or two within the next several minutes. But if I found no old ladies, I did find ample evidence that I was no longer defending a simple forger.

Cline's reasons for concealing the whereabouts of his trailer were now crystal clear. The only mystery remaining about him—as far as I was concerned—was how he expected this mobile treasure chest of evidence and information to remain undiscovered indefinitely.

Cline's carefully filed correspondence with and receipts from undertaking firms and crematoria amply attested to his tendency for tidy terminal disposal of the old ladies who had abundantly enriched his life. And no matter how slow and erring they may be at finding trailers, there's no ground for criticizing the effectiveness of the police at putting records like these together in such a way as to add up to the death sentence. Cline had had it.

Thoughtfully, I let myself out of the trailer and returned to my car. I knew that I still had a client to help and a defense to find. The problem now was to save my man from almost certain death; it was no longer to restore him to freedom. Nothing is gained by the capital punishment of even this kind of man, according to my principles. I was determined that he deserved protection from society as certainly and as importantly as society required protection from him.

On the way home I called a friend in the police department. By the time I'd separated myself from my wet clothes and had a bath, the story was on the radio, and when I sent out for the five-star edition of the *Examiner* I found that the headline was: POLICE FIND CLINE CRIME CENTER. Even the overtime parking ticket was mentioned in the story. I figured that was one rap I might beat for him.

The first voice to which the district attorney listened when he arrived at his office in the morning was mine. Pat Brown, then San Francisco's chief prosecutor (to a very great degree because of the practical and substantial help given him by my friends and me), who later went on to become attorney-general and Governor of California, was a little astounded at my request. I asked him to move to indict Cline on one or more of the forgery charges then pending against him.

"Salt him away on the forgery raps, Pat," I asked. "Later, if these homicide charges prove up and it seems worthwhile, you can bring him back from prison and try him for Murder One. The killings may be hard to prove, as homicide so often is, but the sending him over for forgery will be like convicting Cain of killing Abel."

My job, as I saw it, was to save Cline's life. With all the leads and information that the Federals and the out-of-California jurisdictions now had, plus what they'd previously known and suspected, they could hang him in Montana, electrocute him in Illinois, shoot him in Utah, gas him in Oregon, and then exhume him and give him between 5 and 7 life sentences in several states. But if I could get him sentenced and salted away for a long term in California (consecutive terms on multiple counts would add up to such a term), he would be unavailable for prosecutions elsewhere. As for prosecution for murder in California (as suggested by me in case this seemed a desirable later alternative), I was reasonably sure that this would never happen once my client received a healthy sentence. Pat Brown has long shared my views on capital punishment. He has been the instrument of legally taking life where the occasion and the law demanded it, but he has always devoutly preferred to refrain from doing so where it was possible for him to respect his own instincts and inhibitions.

And so at my instigation my own client was indicted the following January on 9 counts of forgery and 1 count of grand theft. These indictments covered the falsification of the signature of one of his innumerable wives on stock certificates and annuity checks. The evidence against him was ironclad.

Meanwhile the incredible story of Mr. Cline's domestic lethalities began to take form in the reports of the investigators. Mass Murderer Landru—who had more recipes for the charcoal roasting of women than anyone else up to that fatal moment in 1922 when he lost a decision to the guillotine—might have been eaten with envy had he lived to observe Cline. The difference between the two men was solely that of degree of participation. The bearded Landru personally tended the stove at his *charcu-*

terie des dames in Paris. Cline employed the catering principle, preferring to send his late ladies to the local crematoria.

Like Landru though, Cline had spent the forepart of his life in reasonable rectitude. As he approached his forties he had become involved in a slight outbreak of embezzlement, served a year in jail, and turned to the exploitation of gullible and prosperous aging ladies as a vocation, an avocation and a hobby. Shortly thereafter he took up murder as an expedient side line occasioned by an embarrassing tendency toward complaint he encountered among the women he mulcted.

His favorites in dealing with these unfortunate ladies were buttermilk and rat poison. He recommended buttermilk as a specific for all female maladies in the sure knowledge that most women of a certain age are at constant grips with one malady or another and continually seek and eagerly accept remedies. Rat poison was actually his preferred therapy for his patients and the reasons were simple, sensible and expedient. Rat poison is inexpensive, easy to obtain, and not completely unpalatable when served in Cline's other specialty, buttermilk.

My client's other little professional foible was his implicit faith in cremation as the safest means of translating his casualties to the hereafter; safest from the standpoint of his own best interests, that is. His first known experimentation with the reduction of people to cinders appears to have occurred in 1931, although there's no certainty that he didn't warm up with one or more trial annihilations prior to that year. Client Number One was Mrs. Carrie May Porter, an elderly widow who signed some $20,000 worth of assets over to Cline while they were sojourning in Reno and almost immediately suffered what appeared to be a heart attack. The police later became curious and asked to see the body. They were too much later. Mrs. Porter had become a jar of ashes.

Some months afterward Cline was escorting the Reverend Ernest Jones, an elderly British divine, on a tour of California's Spanish Missions. On March 14, 1932, they stayed at the Robles Inn and spent the evening discussing the impermanence of man. So moved by their discourses (and by certain suggestions made to him by his guide) was the Reverend Jones that he felt unable to go to bed that night without first bequeathing his total worldly substance to Cline. The next day he went to a rest that was more eternal; he appeared to have suffered from a massive attack of dyspepsia. The estate turned out to be worth little more than $11,000—hardly worth the trouble.

The following year Cline met and married Mrs. Bessie Van Sickle. Mrs. Van Sickle had a brother named Lucius McCreery and McCreery had peptic ulcers. He also had an apparently unquenchable desire to talk about his experiences during World War I and his admiration for William Jennings Bryan, and on both of these subjects he could be pretty boring. Cline cured him permanently of both his ulcers and garrulity, using his buttermilk plus therapy. Bessie died almost immediately afterward, from what appeared to be an apoplectic seizure, having tried some of the buttermilk as a specific against a kidney disorder. The Los Angeles police, brought into the case a little tardily by the insurance company which had insured them in favor of—naturally—Alfred Leonard Cline, found themselves unable to learn anything useful from either Cline or the ashes. In addition to the double insurance pay-off, the former Mrs. Van Sickle had thoughtfully remembered her bereaved husband with a $20,000 bequest.

Then there was Mrs. Elizabeth Hunt Lewis of Oakland, a California city some 500 miles north of the area where Cline "lost" his wife and brother-in-law. Mrs. Hunt had two supreme desires in life when she met and married Cline. She wanted relief from certain colonic problems from which she suffered and she dearly hoped to see Florida before she died. Her new husband realized both of these ambitions for her, accomplishing the second in what would seem to have been the nick of time. Elizabeth passed away in the bridal suite of their Jacksonville hotel within a day or so of their arrival and shortly after drinking a glass of buttermilk. The rest of the story is the same. Quick cremation, frustrated cops—"I give and bequeath my entire estate to my beloved husband Alfred Leonard Cline."

In 1934, Cline underestimated a would-be legator's capacity to cope with the rat-poison frappés, and his beneficiary-elect—an iron-stomached Los Angeleno named Martin Frame—merely became ill but not too ill to stagger to the authorities with the rest of his buttermilk and all of his suspicions.

Cline spent the next nine years resting and reading up on feminine psychology, little-known poisons and crematorial lore at Represa, California, where the state maintains a penal institution (Folsom), the magnitude of whose rehabilitational program being equaled only by the magnitude of its non-success at rehabilitation.

Emerging from this extended sabbatical, Cline is next heard of in nearby San Francisco where the church bells first chimed merrily and then tolled dolefully for Alma Wilma Carter. Mrs. Alma Wilma Carter Cline apparenty succumbed in Macon, Georgia. Or were the ashes later found there those of Mrs. Alice W. Carpenter of Indianapolis, Indiana, who had also dreamed of visiting Florida before she died? No one will ever really be sure, for despite the fact that Mrs. Carpenter was never seen again after marrying Cline (who "cleared up her estate" shortly after marrying Alma Wilma in San Francisco), she was apparently briefly resurrected seven months later in Dallas, Texas—long enough to be identified by Cline as the name of the woman who lay mortally ill in his Dallas hotel room. So the attending physician said.

On the other hand, there is substantial reason to believe that the unfortunate Dallas lady was really Mrs. Delora Krebs, a wealthy widow from Chicago who had become Mrs. Alfred Cline in the spare moments between her busy husband's dosages of Mrs. Alice Cline in Tampa, Florida, and his cremation of Mrs. Alma Cline in Macon, Georgia.

It was somewhere within this feverish triangle of matrimony, buttermilk therapy and cremation that Brother Cline sowed the seeds of his own undoing. His mistakes were at least two-fold. In Mrs. Krebs he had chosen a wife with too large an estate ($250,000) for her demise to be unnoted or go uninvestigated by her natural legatees. Second, he had somehow fallen behind on his cremation list.

Keeping the score clear on Cline was difficult even for me, as conversant as I became with many of the vital statistics in his life, but as far as I can figure it out, Cline had Mrs. Carpenter cremated as Mrs. Carter and Mrs. Krebs cremated as Mrs. Carpenter. As he now had to have an officially deceased Mrs. Krebs in order to collect her $250,000 estate, he stood sorely in need of someone to cremate.

It was this embarrassing deficit which caused him to perform the only selfless, gratuitous homicide of his career. He journeyed to San Francisco and found Elizabeth Van Natta. Miss Van Natta was a moneyless, propertyless pensioneer living at a senior citizen center on Larkin Street. The poor woman burbled to her friends about autumnal love and marriage and a motel in Corona del Mar, California, which she would assist her new-found husband in operating. Actually she journeyed instead to Portland, Oregon, where she evened up Cline's out-of-balance murder roster by obligingly passing under the name of Mrs. Delora Krebs Cline. Cause of death: cerebral hemorrhage and hypertension.

Actuarially minded readers may wish to hold me accountable for one body that may seem to have been mislaid—that of either Mrs. Carter of San Francisco or of Mrs. Carpenter of Indianapolis, whichever of the two missed the cremator at Macon where Cline first got off on his schedule. As neither women has ever been seen since, I think it may safely be assumed that they both died also.

I have made no mention of those who were *nearly* cremated: of seventy-five-year-old Mrs. Laura Cummings of Boston, for instance, who accepted the offer of a ride home from Mr. Cline at a deep-dish supper at her New England church. The ride eventually extended all the way to Seattle, Washington, where her escort apparently knew of a very dependable crematorium and where Mrs. Cummings fell ill of buttermilk poisoning but possessed the initiative to check in at a hospital. Meanwhile her relatives got word of her condition and prospects, headed for Seattle upon learning that she was under the care of a man to whom she'd just willed $60,000, and had a little talk with their mother at the hospital. Cline arrived while the conference was underway, came to an instantaneous philosophical conclusion, and departed via the speediest transportation. There were to be other troublesome wife patients in the years ahead but none with alert and suspicious relatives.

This, then, was the client whose defense I'd accepted on the assumption that a run-of-the-mill case of forgery was involved. Obtaining for a man of these talents and accomplishments any sort of consideration seemed utterly impossible, and yet—in my personal concept of my professional function and contrary to the contentions of witch-burning public attitudes—it was my duty and obligation to not only make sure that Cline received every protection the law allowed but also to make every effort to save his life and obtain for him as much mercy, charity and consideration as was possible under the circumstance. The only thing I required of the client in order to accomplish this was a reasonable degree of frankness and such information as I needed.

I was not to receive them. Cline had been a loner too long. He had arrived at some weird, terminal point in his solo system of living where confidences with *anyone* were beyond consideration; where he preferred to remain amiably mute with everyone rather than risk inadvertently dropping some minute scrap of information in the course of even the smallest of small talk.

I cajoled, reasoned, threatened. I was unable to break through to him or get him to provide me with one single statement of fact or fancy. I told him that the district attorney had been able to obtain identification of some of the property in his trailer as the effects of Elizabeth Van Natta (namely an umbrella, hats, cosmetics and a cheap oil painting of Yosemite's Bridal Veil Falls) and that the forgery prosecution might suddenly become a murder rap. He hummed and chewed gum. Actually the prospect of any *immediate* prosecution on homicide charges was remote; no sound, fully integrated ground for such prosecution yet existed despite common police knowledge of all of the crimes described. But it was a foregone conclusion that—given time—the authorities would eventually acquire all the evidence and testimony they needed upon which to convict and execute Cline ten times over. For that reason his only hope of survival lay in a quick conviction, a lengthy sentence, and a hasty exit to the sanctuary of prison. I needed full information on his activities as a forger, not in order to defend him better but so that I could be sure the state's forgery case against him would not fail, as well it might in dealing with a man about whom so much fact was only nebulously provable.

On the day the trial opened I attempted to shock him into a change of attitude. I asked Superior Court Judge Herbert C. Kaufman, who would try the case, to call us both before him. Upon his appearance before the judge, Cline was the living prototype of all wholesome, well-intentioned, respectable middle-aged men whom one associates with Rotary luncheons, rose-growing and rubber overshoes. He wore a faintly bemused but completely poised and gentlemanly manner, and the best way I can describe him is to say that he shaped up like the last kind of a citizen I'd have wanted on a jury to judge a man suspected of dosing people with rat poison. I addressed the judge.

"Your Honor, I am at a loss to understand why my client was so anxious to retain me. Everything he's told me since that initial occasion could be written on a grain of rice, with space left over for the Lord's Prayer and the greater part of the Gettysburg Address. Because of this rather vital lack of confidence and rapport between us, I ask to be permitted to withdraw as counsel for his defense."

Judge Kaufman glanced in Cline's direction. The man smiled sweetly at him and then at me.

"I am very much in the dark about all these things that are happening to me," he said. "I couldn't possibly agree to Mr. Ehrlich's withdrawal."

The judge had but one way to go on the basis of such a

response from the inoffensive, appealing little man before him. He denied my request. In his place, I'd have denied it myself. Now I knew why everyone drank his buttermilk.

On April 8, 1946, we went to trial. The prosecutor was Norman Elkington and from the first it was clear that if he wasn't actually charging Cline with multiple murders he was never going to let the jury forget that their forgery defendant was the man who was popularly credited with having fed women to the flames from Maine to Dixie. This was all right with me as long as he continued to buttress a charge of forgery with militating inferences of murder rather than the reverse. I would make the usual objections but not too loudly or passionately.

My client seemed as pleased with the proceedings as if he was the guest of honor at a testimonial dinner. He examined his immaculate nails. Occasionally he benignly gazed at the jury, particularly at one little man who appeared to be participating in his duties with more than the routine amount of civic zeal. And now and then Cline accorded me a formal, friendly and approving smile. He was completely at his ease and with good reason; he was the only person in the place who knew all of the answers to all of the questions about everything.

Close to the end of the first day of the trial he inadvertently created a commotion. Suddenly and as the first overt gesture that he'd made since he retained me, he passed me a note. The prosecutor faltered in midspeech as he tried to continue with his statement and still observe the effect of the note on me. The jurors stared wide eyed. Even Judge Kaufman peered owlishly over the bench toward the defense table. I decided to baffle them all and took the note out to the corridor to read, where I became fairly baffled myself. It read:

> Will you please get me four packages of chewing gum, ten air mail stamps, and a subscription to the *Christian Science Monitor?*

I couldn't have been more flabbergasted if he had asked for a quart of buttermilk and a can of rat poison.

Toward the end of the second week of the trial we had a second diversion. Detective Captain Bernard MacDonald suddenly discovered an ex-convict, a forger and fugitive from justice on the jury. Even worse, the man was a former Folsom colleague of Cline's. And even more fascinating to me, he was the zealous little juror in whom Cline had occasionally taken such a friendly but silent interest.

His name was Thomas Lerrin, and when asked by the outraged judge why he had signed the formal affidavit testifying that he had no criminal record, he had a fairly reasonable reply.

"I signed it without reading it," he said. "I never read the fine print of anything. My eyes are bad and—besides—what does it get you!"

It got him a cell in the County Jail and it got us a new juror.

My client provided the next high point in the proceedings. He asked for a few moments alone with the judge. His request was granted while Elkington stewed feverishly and the police hovered close to the door of the judge's chambers, making ready to rush to the rescue at the first judicial peep. The few moments lengthend to a full hour and ten minutes, and when the two returned to the courtroom their faces were as blank as a pair of poker players with a pair of good poker hands.

Elkington's closing argument was strictly a convincer, and for the first time in my career I was delighted to note that the jury was listening to my adversary as intently as they did to me. As a matter of fact he omitted a few convincing things that I'd have liked him to mention. As for my own remarks, I'll let the quotes from the next morning's *Examiner* describe them.

"Jake soared to oratorical heights [wrote the *Examiner*'s Ernie Lenn]. He exuded histrionics even when disposing of his cleaning tissue in the wastebasket." I was suffering from a bad cold at the time.

The jury took an hour and thirty minutes to bring in a verdict of guilty on all counts, and probably spent the last sixty minutes at pinochle. I leaned over and whispered to Cline, "You lucky bastard!" and he nodded in happy agreement. And suddenly and for the first time Elkington got the complete picture and mouthed a message in my direction that wasn't precisely salutary.

Judge Kaufman's sentencing of Cline was as dynamic in its language as it was in its chronology. First he told the court what had passed between Cline and himself in the privacy of their tête-à-tête.

"Upon coming into my chambers, Cline asked me if I would advise him to plead guilty. I told him that this was a matter that only he and his attorney could decide. I did advise him, however, that every man has to live with himself and that his conscience could and should give him proper advice. He then offered to plead guilty to all counts except one if the court would agree to let the sentences run concurrently rather than consecutively."

Judges never make bargains with defendants, and Kaufman's response to this rather naive offer was a foregone conclusion. But then the judge had something more to say of this ordinarily taciturn man's reaction to what was going on about him.

"Cline indicated to me that he felt that the jury would find him guilty and he expressed surprise over the amount of evidence uncovered against him. He told me that he felt he had wasted his life, that he realized that crime does not pay, and that there is no such thing as a perfect crime because all human beings are imperfect; therefore he must of necessity commit imperfect crimes. He told me he wanted to spend the remaining years of his life in the study of his religion."

In short, Cline devoted his single lapse from his utter silence of the past several months to mouthing all of the banalities of which career criminals usually acquit themselves when they come to the ends of their careers. Outside of information, I realized I hadn't missed much in respect to my client's conversational reluctance.

The sentencing came next. Judge Kaufman looked down at the mild little man as if he'd never heard the virtuous commonplaces uttered in his chambers.

"Alfred Cline," he said, "in my judgment you are a one-man Crime Incorporated. I don't think it's possible that you can ever take your place again as a member of our society. The circumstances surrounding the commission of these crimes indicate a pattern and a course of conduct that is most revolting and which shocks the conscience of all decent people." And then he sentenced my man to 126 years. Cline thanked him politely. He was always a polite man. I made no motion of appeal. I'd won for my client by losing abundantly.

Before the prisoner was taken across the Bridge of Sighs to the county jail, Judge Kaufman again called us both to his chambers.

"You've had excellent legal representation," he said to Cline, "and you've spoken to me about the dawning call of your conscience. I think that such a development should also extend to your just financial obligations such as Mr. Ehrlich's fee. Have you thought of that, Mr. Cline?"

Mr. Cline had. Forthwith he paid me $35,000 for having helped him get 126 years in prison, which saved him from a very much shorter term in Death Row. And he still had ample funds left when he departed for Folsom to take up his study of religion.

There have been those who've criticized me for cheating the gas chamber of this obviously unforgivable and unreformable parasite on the body politic. I respect the intolerance of even the intolerant, as long as they express their views with respect and civility for my own strong and sometimes unorthodox opinions, but I offer no apologies and only the simplest explanation for having snatched Cline from the executioner. I am a defender of those who stand before the bar of justice charged with crime, and I don't believe that any trial lawyer has the professional or human right to reject his responsibility or lessen the full measure of his service to his client because of the heinousness of the client's offense. I am also deeply opposed to the death sentence, and I will fight with all legal skill and personal resourcefulness at my command every attempt by the state to commit murder upon any client that I defend. One more thing. I am addicted to accepting cases where the odds are strongly against any kind of success. And the odds were a 1,000 to 1 against Alfred Leonard Cline.

Mr. Cline, incidentally, eventually defrauded even the State of California. On August 4, 1948, he passed peacefully away in his cell at Folsom, thus cheating society and the state of 123 of the 126 years of penal servitude that he owed them.

My friend and escort, the custodian, remembered Cline quite well. Cline was the kind of a criminal whom a misogynistic middle-aged bachelor with multiple hernias would remember pleasurably.

"I dunno," he said, as we headed for the Hall's dusty entrance foyer again. "I figure he earned whatever he got from those old stoves. A guy has to be able to take a lot of punishment to put up with a dame when she gets to the point where she's more concerned about the fit of her dentures than the fit of her girdle. Of course that rat poison makes a rough diet but . . ."

"You wouldn't have liked him. He was a complete teetotaler."

His eyes narrowed.

"*Agh,* so that's the way he was! Them are the disgusting things you never hear about in the papers."

One more look around the shadowy but still impressive entrance foyer. One more round of memories from the robust, pungent, gone-forever past. Here is where I'd come as a young lawyer, with pockets empty but with head crammed with plans and with heart virile with certainty. Here I'd smoothly phrased many a glib statement of assurance while secretly hoping to come up with at least 50 percent of what my assurance promised, and often—by the grace of God, luck and some personal contributions—accomplishing twice my brash commitment. And here I'd had the occasional momentous setbacks that seemed so unmomentous to me now in mellow retrospect. Here I'd lived most of my life, I realized.

On these same stairs I'd been solicited for advice on a case by another fledgling lawyer, given him the counsel, and been compensated on the spot by a payment of 50 dimes, one half of his fee—and in the same coinage in which he'd received it—from a client accused of robbing telephone coin boxes.

Here in this hallway I'd been accosted by bearded and wonderfully dignified old Judge Tom Graham, now long dead, and seriously requested to give up my avocation of boxing. I'd argued a matter before him that morning with a black eye; His Honor regarded a black eye as unbecoming to a member of the bar. As an inducement to quit the ring, he offered to assign me one case a month—no small subsidy for a struggling young lawyer. I accepted and never put on the gloves for money again.

And here in this foyer and after a morning of outraged feeling at the spectacle of prisoners caged and displayed in municipal courtrooms while awaiting their appearances before the bar, I had gathered a group of my colleagues and initiated the campaign that was eventually to remove forever these vile human sties from the judicial chambers they tainted and degraded.

The custodian let me out of the building through the little door in the hoarding and I was once again on Kearny Street. I'd passed more than the actual hour spent visiting the moldering old building on Portsmouth Square. In some mystic fashion I'd managed to relive a whole half century of my life.

Strolling southward toward my office, I found myself in front of the Star Bar, where several generations of policemen have taken their off-duty highballs, panned the chief and the commissioners, and lost their pocket change at shuffleboard to the invincible Cookie Picetti, landlord and veteran Kearny Street character. For years my courtroom victories were celebrated at Cookie's. For years Cookie's was the finest place in town in which to pick up a square rumor, eat *cioppino* free on Friday night, and encounter adventure in the john, which is coeducational. I ordered a highball, bought one for Cookie, and asked him about the sad building next door.

"I dunno," he said. "There's talk about turning it into a museum. Some jerk Supervisor wants to sell it to be tore down for a parking lot, motel, something. One thing sure; the cops is gone from it for good."

I asked him if his regulars still dropped around for their toddies.

"Yeah," he replied, rather doubtfully, "those that are still in the business. But most of them are retiring or the doctor give 'em the message about no booze; you know how it is. I see 'em less and less."

"You could always put in a combo and hire some waitresses in stretch pants; go after the new business."

He snorted in disdain at this incredible suggestion.

"Not me, Jake! When the last of the old customers from the Hall kicks off or forgets the address, I'll close up along with the others and let them turn the joint into a museum or a parking lot, too. There's some kinds of progress that just don't reach me at all, Master."

I agreed with him, thinking of the crudely lettered sign on the building next door—the one that disposed of a wonderful old landmark with the words MOVED AWAY.

15: *Afternoon*

2:00 P.M.

Agenda: Sally Stanford

The lady swept in—a *mélange* of mink, complicated coiffure and glittering gems. No one could ever accuse Sally Stanford, proprietor of the Valhalla Restaurant and former hostess of a famed love emporium, of being unspectacular.

Sally came up the hard way. Born on a meagerly productive Oregon farm where circumstances limited her education to not quite graduating from the third grade, she found her way to San Francisco and to the management of a bordello at an age when most young ladies of her era were putting up their hair for the first time.

She was a tough, indomitable female operating in a tough, predatory arena at a time and in a psychological atmosphere when and in which most young women merely knuckled down to some knowledgeable male to whom they paid over their earnings without even unfolding the bills. But Sally paid no man for services so ephemeral. No one has dipped into the capacious brassiere in which she then and now stowed her assets.

Sally and I first met as adversaries. As special prosecutor in a vice wrangle of the early thirties, I found myself required to charge a Mrs. Spagnioli with operating a bagnio in a small hotel she owned at the edge of the Tenderloin. In court, Sally expressed herself as being utterly flabbergasted to learn that her tenants (all ladies) were consorting with strange gentlemen in return for financial consideration. In the idiom of the trade, she beat the rap. This was one of the very few occasions in her career when the police were able to entertain her—even fleetingly—at their Kearny Street hostel. Fed up with the seamier aspects of prostitution at the grass roots level, Sally decided for the carriage trade, larger profits, and establishments into which the peasant police might hesitate to intrude.

She opened one of rare and exotic quality on the crest of de luxe Russian Hill, another on the southern slope of Nob Hill. She entertained bankers, Senators, playboy clubmen and even an eminent divine or two, and became wealthy and modestly illustrious. She collected *objets d'art,* stray animals and husbands—one a scion of the famous San Francisco mercantile Gump family. Because of her gift for witty repartee and gifts of whisky which they received, the town's newspapermen esteemed her highly and dealt with her lightly in their accounts of her activities. Her benefactions were many and famous people were pleased to be her friends. I became her attorney.

In November of 1949, as the result of certain civic trends I've mentioned, Sally's halcyon days came to an end. Ironically enough, her career was aborted as the result of the entirely false boast of a young tart. This irresponsible nymphet, anxious to achieve prestige in the eyes of the officers who arrested her for bag-swinging on Eddy Street, claimed that she had worked in Sally's place.

"I wouldn't have let that little bitch walk my dog," snorted Sally when—months later—she saw the girl in court. "She wouldn't have made a decent patch on one of my girls' . . . posteriors." (On another occasion Sally described one of her colleagues, the late Polly Adler, as, "no credit to prostitution.")

But the scrawny little tart's story ended Sally's triple-decade career. I defended her against the state's flimsy charge that she had contributed to the girl's delinquency, which—had she really done it—would have constituted a flagrant case of carrying coals to Newcastle. Sally was vindicated. But the notoriety had been damaging, and I had the feeling that with the changing mood of the people toward commercial fun there would be other attempts to get to her. Besides, the same changing mood extended toward people's own morals, and Sally and her sisters-in-trade were getting a lot of cruelly unfair competition from respectable amateurs. "Scabs," Sally called them. I suggested that she retire and she did.

However, her frenetic energies were not to be merely channeled into gardening, auction sale attendance and senescent bitterness about society's ingratitude. The indomitable Stanford (her surname had been taken in honor of the university of the same name) acquired an ancient rathskeller in Sausalito, transformed it into one of the finest restaurants in California, and made another fortune.

I was pleased to see her and said so. And what could I do for her?

"This is a *social* visit," she growled, "so don't turn the meter on!"

"You'll manage to get some free advice out of it. So—again—what can I do for you?"

Sally wanted to go into politics.

"I don't see why the hell I shouldn't," she said. "When I look around me and see the number of crooks and swindlers who are transformed into statesmen and selfless servants of the public by ballot-box magic, I've come to the conclusion that what the electorate needs is an honest, forthright, clear-thinking ex-madam in a spot where she can keep her eye on all these shifty fakers. After all, I *know* them. I know *all* their tricks. And nobody ever accused me of not being honest and truthful. I'm thinking of running for Councilman of Sausalito, maybe for mayor, if I get lucky. What do you think, Jake? Can I make it? Should I try?"

I thought of the little girl hoeing the corn patch in a dreary Oregon farm, of the world-wary young demimondaine coping with the vice-squadders in a Tenderloin bagnio, of the diamond-studded hostess of the nation's most famous parlorhouse. And then I thought of the smug and pompously respectable exurbanite residents of the little community across the Golden Gate and what might lay ahead for them in terms of shock and trauma if Sally should drop her campaign on them. I was delighted with the prospect.

"Try? I can't think of anyone better qualified. Graft you'll recognize like a good carpenter knows dry rot, and—as for knowing whether the police department is goldbricking or not—you're a qualified expert. I heartily advise you to run. Between your old customers and the new ones you should be a shoo-in."

Sally shook her head dolefully.

"I don't know, Jake. A lot of the squares are apt to be pretty narrow-minded about my past, no matter how far back it all was. The worst kind of a thief they can love—look at that guy in Boston who was elected mayor twice after having stolen them blind and got sent to the pen for it—but a so-called fallen woman's supposed to stay fallen, I guess. I figure the holier-than-thous will scream like banshees. Not that I mind a little legitimate screaming, but I'm worried that they might stampede the voters away from me. What do you think?"

"Sally, the kind of voters who'll put you in office are the lusty, live-and-let-live characters who favor an interestingly tarnished former sinner over a sterile plaster saint, especially if the ex-sinner is a lady. I promise you you'll win, Sal, if you'll just lay it on the line and not hide a single scarlet thing about your past. Run on your record. They'll love it."

She appeared doubtful.

"What about my new image? I've got a pretty classy new image as a restaurateur, Vice-President of the Chamber of Commerce, Little League baseball sponsor, and so forth. Why not bear down on *that* for openers?"

This is the trouble with most reformed characters. Blind to where their real charm and appeal lie, they want to be regarded as pillars of society, even when the base of the pillar is still tinted in strange colors.

"Don't kid yourself, Sally. The success of your new image is largely based upon the exciting quality of your old image. If you think that your restaurant is continually full merely because the steak is tasty, you are conning yourself. People enjoy eating your food because they can stare at you over every forkful. Similarly, you'll be a more interesting candidate because—plus your other statesmanlike qualifications—you are Sally Stanford. So give the full story. That will turn every political brickbat into a bouquet. And it'll turn you into a fascinating and appealing underdog. You know what happens to underdogs who are fascinating and appealing enough."

I could see that she wasn't quite convinced when she left my office.*

I believe that I understand the philosophy of "the public image" about as well as anyone; I've had enough of them. A trial lawyer has no trouble at all acquiring a public image: his daily chores are good copy to all news media at all times. The *kind* of image is to a large degree good or bad or helpful or hurtful to him according to his own handling of his only commodity—himself. I know what my own image is today in San Francisco, the West, and as far abroad as my reputation has drifted, because I've had a large and calculated hand in creating it. I am popularly depicted as a somewhat fantastic character. The mosaic of the Ehrlich image is composed of facets of arrogance, consummate craftiness, amorality, discreet unscrupulousness, vast self-esteem, go-for-broke resourcefulness, relentless reprisalism and so on. I am flamboyant in some concepts of me; mordantly withdrawn in others. I pick the brains of others, according to some stories; I am a respository of profound native lore in others. I am cynical, corrupt and corruptive of others, or I am an integrity-laden Galahad of jurisprudence. Variously and in various interpretations, I am all of these things and more—some true, some untrue, many of them contributed directly to the image by me for reasons mischievous, humorous or expedient to the moment. But nowhere in these categories are the words dull, mediocre or inferior. So I am content to let the public images, like changing wraiths in a spectral fantasy, assume whatever form they will. As long

* Sally did run for councilman and was defeated by the narrowest of margins, obtaining a far greater plurality than a number of other candidates. However, her campaign pitch—contrary to my thinking—gracefully overlooked any reference to her own interesting background. She promises to continue to run for this office at each election for as long as she lives. I earnestly hope she does; there is only one Sally Stanford; there will never be another more honest, nor better friend.

as there *is* an image I know that I am alive and effective and a part of this town and the life I love. The first time that I hear someone say, "Jake Ehrlich! Who is Jake Ehrlich?" I'll consider checking on a reservation at Cypress Lawn. Meanwhile I'll assist my friends and detractors in the building of any kind of an image of me that pleases them.

I am, for instance, just as interested in a certain newspaper writer's recent impression of me as: "The vain, cocky, glory-minded legal Napoleon of Montgomery Street" as in *Examiner* Rick Setlowe's description of me as being: "As scrappy, profane, prideful and philosophic as a Barbary Coast bartender." And when my friend Bob Patterson donned his psychoanalyst's mantle and wrote in an article in *San Francisco Magazine* that I was: "A character who wasted no time on effete scruples when more important happinesses were at stake," I took no exception to this and some of his other rather abrasive comments, except to remind him that the box score of 68 acquittals for Murder One which he gives me is less than the full truth. As for the "flamboyancy" which he attributes to me, I have to wonder how a taste for fastidious dress, frank expression of uninhibited opinion, and beautiful women as luncheon guests add up to flamboyancy. But no matter . . . he spelled my name correctly.

As for the public image of Sally Stanford, I am convinced that she would appeal more compellingly to the interest and admiration of her public in her real role of lusty, worldly sophisticate of the night-life world than as a quasi-repentant and newly pious convert to dull wholesomeness. Madams and gamblers, in American folklore, are the demigods of melodrama; they should make the most of it.

I'll never forget one madam from the earlier days of my career. Her name was Mary O'Brien and she operated an extremely popular establishment at 148 Sixth Street. Captured in full effort by the gendarmes, she seemed certain of a year's sentence at grim Ingleside Jail until I took her case.

I was able to make some change in the conditions of her incarceration by convincing the court that Mary suffered from a dread malady—a "little-known disease that had been discovered in this region only three times in the past half century." My client was permitted to serve out her time in the private hospital of her choice on the condition that she defray the cost of the salaries of a series of matron nurses. She was happy to assume this expense.

The lady was very grateful to me. After she'd paid her fee she made me a generous and unusual offer. Her bankbook showed a current balance of $30,000. Half of it was mine if I would allow myself to be indefinitely retained as general counsel and boy friend. I was deeply touched. I figured that greater love hath no madam.

16: *Afternoon*

2:30 P.M.

Agenda: Albert L. Johnson

One of my alternate roles, as of the year 1964, is that of banker, and my next postmeridian visitor of the day was Al Johnson, Vice-President of the San Francisco National Bank which I helped organize and of which I am general counsel. Any person who might have predicted my participation in banking as a banker a quarter of a century ago would have wound up in the psychopathic ward with my name first on his commitment papers. There were times when I might have qualified as a *broker,* as I was broker than any other lawyer in San Francisco of my age and size during my tenderfoot years, and in fact I can remember an occasion when this sad and painful condition became pretty much a matter of public record.

I was being sued by Ernest Spagnioli, Sally Stanford's third and nearly antepenultimate husband, The amount that Ernest was seeking from my coffers was $575,000. I was truly grateful to Ernest at the moment for, compared to my safe, safety deposit box and savings account, Mother Hubbard's famed cupboard was pretty well stocked. I frankly regarded the Spagnioli suit and the half million plus involved as quite an assist to my credit rating.

His attorney had put me on the witness stand and was attempting to interrogate me into some sort of an admission of cash stashed craftily out of reach of such hunting expeditions as the one upon which he was embarked.

One of my replies was to this effect: "I do a strictly cash business. People who hire me don't leave my office until they pay me. Then I spend the money. I don't have a bank account and I don't keep books. Those are the conditions that prevail. There simply *are* no assets."

That fried the man to a crisp and he immediately asked Judge Frank Dunn to find me in contempt and penalize me accordingly. Judge Dunn shook his head wearily.

"I can't do that, Counselor. You put me in the guise of a mental telepathist, and you ask me to believe that you have occult powers of your own, with both of us capable of presuming to a certainty the extent of Mr. Ehrlich's riches, if any."

The attorney continued to harry and hound me in his pursuit of my obviously nonexistent millions, and when the proceedings were over and both of us just as poor as we'd been at the outset, I spoke to him with extralegal vehemence on the subject of the extraction of blood from turnips.

"Tom," I said, "I'm on my uppers now and money is the thing that I haven't got most of. This is a fact that with reiteration becomes no less true or more pleasant for me to admit. I suggest to you that someday I may be on top—I may even *own* a damn bank—and *you* may be on your uppers. So I give you the hep advice that came from the potter's clay in the *Rubáiyát*... 'gently, brother, gently.' "

I don't exactly own a bank, but Al Johnson and I made dispositions of many of its millions, and some of the other things of my forecast have come to pass. I see Tom now and again these days. Despite my somewhat bitter prophecies of that day, more than a quarter of a century ago, I wish that life had been more generous to him.

Johnson's visit had to do with the current civil liberties turmoil in San Francisco. The pirate pressure group known as CORE (Congress of Racial Equality)—which has but quasi-representational standing as a bargaining and white-baiting organization in the frictions, negotiations and business-blackmailing operations current to the moment—had just threatened the august Bank of America with mass picketing, sit-ins and other troublesome demonstrations. Johnson, an extremely able and tough administrator and an alumnus of the famed Trans-America Corporation, wanted an opinion as to the humanities as well as to the legalities involved.

They were and are clear to me.

Chief Justice Warren and his colleagues of the Supreme Court have wisely and with beautiful clarity and simplicity preanswered all of the questions. The Constitution and the various statutes involved have been so defined and activated by them that in no community where due process pertains in its fullest significance can any person, black, white or yellow, be lengthily deprived of his rights, benefits, protections and recourses. This is all that decent persons—black, white or yellow—seek from the body politic; more they would neither expect nor receive. And one of the chief values of the same codes and Constitution that endow these protections is that they offer equal assurance against those who would exploit the Constitutional guarantees—against those minorities *of* minorities who would use democracy as a club against democracy, who would prostitute mankind's own groping instinct and effort to play the game of life fairly and by the rules.

It is a refreshing truism that the greater majority of those members of minority movements who merit and seek redress of their conditions rarely ask of society more than it can give, more than is needed, more than is fair. It is a less refreshing truism that those few who ask and would take more are disproportionately volatile, articulate and troublesome. For these reasons and with the same promptness and fullness of spirit with which we rushed to implement the rulings handed down by Warren and his Court, I believe that we must invoke the Constitution and the statutes to make certain that the fanatic, self-serving and lunatic fringes of the unjustly underprivileged minority groups shall not be permitted to debase and stigmatize the total cause of their less belligerent brethren.

I am therefore in favor of dealing with authorized and clearly representative organizations—and these do *not* include CORE, the Black Muslims and other splinter-group societies or anonymously membered associations. I am in favor of vigorously repelling any and all attempts by such and other groups and persons to frighten and extort from business and from the community undue privileges in the name of the civil rights movement. And I am unalterably in favor of prosecuting each and every infringement of the law and of the rights of others that are committed in the name of this or any other movement. The end no more justifies the means in this specific frame of reference than it does in any of lesser or greater human importance; not in a social system which refuses with immaculate legal morality to permit wire tapping in the apprehension of national enemies and unwarranted search and seizure in even the arrest of known criminals.

These are the views I gave Johnson, whose observance of and personal respect for Fair Employment Practice laws are second to none in the region, and whose two banks in San Francisco have employed Negroes from the day they were opened. And these are my views in respect to the business and morale-shattering demonstrations that continue and will continue to occur in San Francisco (and elsewhere) as long as fuzzy-minded do-gooders and self-seeking politicians continue to confuse the right to demonstrate with the right to destroy.

My banking friend appeared rather dismayed by what was going on about him in the city which he'd helped put together.

"Do you think we've gotten to the turning point yet, Jake?"

he asked. "Are we headed toward better relations with the recent passage of Federal civil rights legislation?"

"We've reached the turning point but I'm afraid that we've turned in the direction of more darkness and even greater unrest. Unless we can learn to combine hard-boiled, working wisdom with a practical and conscientious application of what the law requires of us in human equities, I am afraid that we may even have turned in the direction—within the next five years—of mass violence and major bloodshed. This isn't a very popular viewpoint and it's one which few men are willing to put into words, but there it is . . . that's the way I see it as of the summer of 1964."

Whenever I observe a claque of hairy and probably unwashed beatniks fouling up some innocent person's property in a demonstration for Negro rights that's rarely also attended by any reasonable number of decent, substantial-looking Negroes, I'm reminded of a fund-raising hootenanny recently held in San Francisco's North Beach by a number of such characters.

The benefit was for the freedom riders, who were then very much in the news. The sponsors of the benefit described themselves in their mimeographed handbills as, "Veterans of the Abraham Lincoln Brigade of the Spanish Civil War," but their project wound up in a sort of a private civil war right here on upper Grant Avenue. It seems that various bona fide Negro groups questioned both the lack of actual Negro participation in the event as well as the unscheduled directions in which the collections were being diverted. As the result of this internecine strife between the skeptical Negroes and the Negro benefactors of upper Grant Avenue, the latter labeled the former "scabs," warfare broke out, and the benefit was canceled. But not before a thirty-six-year-old "veteran" of the Spanish Civil War (circa 1936) named Ron Dillard had struck off another handbill announcing that the fixture had been sabotaged by *"agents-provacateurs* of the forces of reaction," whoever they might be.

I am forever amused at the use of Abraham Lincoln's name in connection with movements to assist the colored race toward the acquisition of its rights and equities. I've made quite a study of the Great Emancipator. Whatever he was to this country's development and history and despite the myth about his deep concern for the Negro that has become part of our folklore and history, I know that Brother Lincoln actually didn't personally give a damn about the disenfranchised dark people whose cause he politically espoused.

This vastly overtouted President never actually freed the slaves nor did he favor Emancipation. Quite the opposite, he opposed it. On one occasion (at Ottawa, Illinois) he publicly stated that Negroes were of an inferior race, adding that, "We cannot, then, make them equals." On numerous other occasions he spoke slightingly of the race which has so apotheosized him in the decades since. Verbatim quotations in support of the above statement are numerous to the point of redundancy.

As far as my contention that Lincoln did not free the slaves is concerned, I refer to the text of *A Reasonable Doubt* written by J. W. Erlich. Without hesitation, I accept these words as final and authoritative:

"Lincoln . . . opposed Emancipation, save on condition that there be organized a gradual emancipation based upon the voluntary action of the states, but with federal compensation to the slaveholders. Needless to say, Congress would not enact Lincoln's concept into law . . . [however] in 1862 abolition first came about when Congress passed a bill emancipating the slaves and prohibiting slavery in the territories and in the District of Columbia. On September 22, 1862, Lincoln proclaimed the slaves in the areas of rebellion against the United States free on and after January 1, 1863. Then, in a second proclamation, on July 8, 1864, Lincoln said he would not admit the right of Congress to abolish slavery in the states. I leave it to you to make of this what you will. As far as I'm concerned Lincoln was always apologetic for an act that many historians would have us believe was the most important thing he did in his entire life. [However] . . . the Proclamation, the history books and Hollywood to the contrary, Lincoln freed no slaves. His proclamation only duplicated what Congress had already done and it applied *only* to areas over which the Federal Government had no control."

That's what I said *then* and I say it again *now*. If that be treason, Veterans of the Abraham Lincoln Brigade, make the most of it! I also say that this unsavory and possibly deranged man was, at best, the phoniest politician to mount the central rostrum of the American Presidency and, at worst, a devious wheeler-and-dealer without whom endless numbers of Americans might never have died "to keep a nation undivided."

17: *Afternoon*

3:00 P.M.

Agenda: George Jue

As I have indicated the Chinese of San Francisco play an important and fascinating part in the life of the town, as they do in the life of this deponent.

George Jue, merchant, restaurateur, occasional movie star and elder statesman to "Gold Hill" (which is the literal translation of the Oriental emigrant's phrase for San Francisco) is one of my oldest friends from the Chinese community. Friend and client, too, for like all Chinese, starting with the first to come here during the gold-rush days, George has had his troubles with the foreign devils' law.

Many of the older Chinese of San Francisco and the other cities of the Pacific Coast came to the United States under circumstances that were less than orthodox, as the immigration laws offered many of them real barriers and problems which they felt unable to handle except in nefarious ways. Later in life and with successful careers behind them and property and families acquired, they were often racked up by authority and

—in many instances—deported to China. For those who have spent all of their adult lives in the United States, such treatment amounts to virtual exile in an alien land. George Jue, whose hope of avoiding such a penalty I am abetting, is excellent proof that the weakness of our immigration laws most often lies in their almost unalterable rigidity. The letter of the code rather than the nature of the case determines the judgment. It is true of course that injustices may eventually be corrected, but in matters of immigration adjudication, due process is characterized by a glacial kind of swiftness, with the victims living beneath the suspended ax of impending deportation for seemingly interminable periods of time.

George Jue is one of these. It is true that his basis for citizenship is technically flawed, but it is equally true that his basis for qualification as a resident and citizen is—to my mind—flawless. His restaurant, the Lamps of China is one of the finest of its kind. His work as a Chinatown civic leader and pillar of the community could serve as an example for some of my paler-skinned brethren. His family is a credit to any community. And so dignified and admirable is his bearing that he was chosen recently to play the King in the cinema version of *The Ugly American.*

For years now George has faced exclusion from all of these activities and from the rewards of a lifetime in the community that he loves, and I have done all that I could to help remove the trap door from under his feet. From time to time he drops in to chat with me and to receive whatever reassurance I can give at the moment. This was one of these calls.

I asked him, as a member of one of San Francisco's earliest minority groups, what he thought of the current hassle for extension of rights and considerations. He gave me a typically Confucianistic reply.

"The cry for civil rights covers a multiplicity of other items which are being arbitrarily blanketed in with the original demand; things like social acceptance, personal respect, unwarranted privilege and the like. Man needs these benefits just as strongly as he needs the right to work, to vote, to have equal economic opportunity, but the Constitution does not guarantee them. The Chinese suffered from these lacks when they first came to this country, and they felt the deprival just as strongly as do the Negroes today, but they didn't go about trying to get them in an aggressive way. They earned them. They worked and prospered and contributed and did everything possible to invoke respect and to inspire trust. They did not demand the rewards before they earned them. Today they are liked, respected, accepted; not because of the law, because of threats or because of the blackmail of implied reprisal. These are the best kind of civil rights to have; the best kind of fringe benefits. We have them."

I asked him about the survival of Chinese customs in his community. When I first became unofficial general counsel to the sons of the Middle Kingdom residenced in San Francisco, it was not easy to get them to put in an appearance in the white man's courts or even to talk nonmonosyllabically to the authorities on matters of moment. This inhibition applied to the utterly innocent as well as to the guilty, to witnesses as well as to plaintiffs, even to the victims of attacks and the bereaved of instances of murder. Complaints, if any, were furtively taken to the tongs, which were primarily family societies having their roots in the homeland provinces in China. Tong leaders would then confer with the elders of the other tongs concerned; judgments would be made, fines or other penalties exacted—the ancient Chinese moralities existing as the only code of reference for such proceedings. The wisdom of the elders evoking more respect among the Oriental populations than the justice to be obtained in the white man's court, breaches of the peace or equity rarely came to light in those days except in such ways as they impinged upon the white man's world. But when they did the Oriental was really in trouble. He didn't know the language. He didn't know the odds against him. Worse, he didn't know the ropes. If attempted bribery failed, he was apt to go down the drain unless he came to the few of us with a taste for underdog representation. I had asked Jue if procedures were materially different now.

"As night is different from day," he replied. "Today's Chinese American has learned that family society jurisprudence and Oriental herbalistic medicine are about on a similar level of effectiveness; they are both useful . . . as far as they go. But we are very much a part of today's complex Occidental society and we can no longer take large-figure litigation to be decided by well-meaning old gentlemen with a lifetime of experience at selling noodles and fish than we can continue to depend on dried lizard to cure leukemia or bronchial pneumonia."

He smiled whimsically at me.

"Besides," he continued, "we and the white man have come to learn the same truth about each other. To him, we were, 'the inscrutable Oriental'; to us he was, 'the inscrutable white man.' Neither of us was inscrutable, actually, especially after we'd gone through a few wars and depressions together. We communicate these days. That easy, trusting communication marked the beginning of the end of the old ways. The tongs are only sociable organizations and burying societies in 1964: a place to play mah-jongg on a dull evening; a hangout for our fathers and grandfathers."

He's right. Chinatown of San Francisco, circa 1964, is a high-powered jet community largely characterized by Ivy League tailoring, Lions Club luncheons, well-patronized stock brokerages, polyunsaturated chow mein, and dynamic Democratic politics (and the last is a little hard to understand, as the Chinese rarely vote). George Jue is right. It's a new and very Yankee Chinatown . . . except for the occasional exception to the rule. The exception of whom I'm thinking at the moment is a wonderful Fu Manchurian character, only one of whose two names I'll give in this chronicle.

I first met Mr. Look Sam Wong at an invitational black-tie exhibit of Chow Dynasty art at the De Young Museum. Under quite another and well-respected name, he was one of the principal sponsors of the show, and his socially and culturally important cosponsors were very grateful to him for the priceless terra-cotta, jade and stone statuettes from his private collection that he'd made available for the evening. They felt honored because the gentleman ordinarily made such concessions to only such big-league institutions as the Metropolitan Museum in New York, the Art Institute in Chicago and other art showcases of similar standing.

Mr. Look was well known in such quarters, I was told by my newspaper critic friends, and he certainly looked the part when I met him: slim, ascetic, ungabby and wearing about $300 worth of dinner coat. This wasn't the sort of a man with whom you traded recipes for egg foo yung, I told myself, so I refrained from discussing possible mutual acquaintances in fan-tan or lottery circles with him. He'd heard of me though, he said with a thin, aloof smile that suggested that he hadn't heard it at a garden party at the Chinese Embassy and that he could get along without my autograph.

Six or seven weeks later I received a late night call from Chin Bok Hing, the notorious gambler who then owned the massive, assembly-line gambling house across the San Mateo County line which was so innocently called the Cabbage Patch. Chin Bok has since either joined his ancestors or some equally remote friends, for several high-powered Federal indictments bearing his name remain unserved. His baggy suit and oversized and ear-supported hat have not been seen in Chinatown for many a moon.

On this occasion he sought my legal assistance in behalf of his gambling partner, the equally notorious Joe Toy. Joe was head of a tong that specialized in *pai giu* (Chinese craps), ladies that were available on the lay-away plan, and Manchurian mud pies, better known as opium. He was also a partner in the Cabbage Patch. Earlier that evening he had been perforated in several places by an irate patron who had rashly invested his life's savings on one of its baize-topped tables and with the usual result. The San Mateo County police, whose hearing wasn't very good where the rattle of dice was concerned during that administration, could hear very well indeed when pistols were fired, and arrived on the run. Handicapped by the holes in his torso, Joe Toy was unable to depart as speedily as other members of his faculty. He was scooped up by the police, which must have been an embarrassment to one and all. He made the prison ward at the County Hospital as a material witness, and his assailant, naturally, was accommodated at the jail.

Not at all surprised at Chin Bok's reasons for wanting to retain me will be all those who understand the labyrinthine deviousness of underworld Chinatown. I was not being asked to invoke justice for Partner Toy nor to provide him with legal advice. I was being sought as counsel for the would-be killer in the hope that my counsel would include sage advice to dummy up and say or do nothing that would keep the shooting on Page One of the newspapers.

Naturally such a caper wasn't my cup of tea, but while I was still in the process of getting the picture and before I finally bowed out in favor of a night's sleep I decided to do a little checking on the unfortunate Mr. Toy. Pictures of the raid and of the principals in the shooting were on *Examiner* Managing Editor Bill Wren's desk, still wet from the darkroom bath, when I got there. They showed a familiar face, its ascetic, art-loving features transcending all pain with a thin, aloof smile. Bill asked me if the picture looked familiar. I looked at it carefully and from all angles—the way you're supposed to case an interesting Chow Dynasty exhibit.

"Possibly," I told him. "But you know these Orientals! They all look alike to me."

As George Jue said, Chinatown has become very modern and American. But now and then there comes the exception to the generality; the throwback to the ways that are dark and mysterious who—thank God and Confucius—suggests that behind all that hygienic, air-conditioned, neon-lighted modernism on Grant Avenue there may still be a colorful, old-fashioned, slant-eyed sinner or two.

18: *Afternoon*

3:30 P.M.

Agenda: Stanton Delaplane

My next visitor was an old newspaper friend.

There are all kinds of newspapermen, but most of them are pretty great people. They are extremely knowledgeable and those I've been privileged to know in the past almost half century have one thing in common with me: they recognize and are captured by the ridiculous aspects of so-called matters of moment. No other class of men does this quite so innately.

I think that Stanton Delaplane, my three-o'clock visitor, heads the list in this category. Delaplane is both a San Francisco *Chronicle* staff writer and a McNaught Syndicate columnist ("Postcard From Stan"). He is also my client (one divorce), my occasional Boswell, and my cosharer of many a pleasant brace of highballs. Futhermore, he inspired and assisted me in my many-splendored relationship with the Ding Dong Daddy of the D Car Line.

Had there been neither an Ehrlich nor a Delaplane—had there been no capacity to recognize the ridiculous aspects of so-called matters of moment—the Ding Dong Daddy of the D Car Line would merely have gone grubbily to oblivion (and to prison) as Francis Van Wie, bigamist.

Francis was fat, bespectacled, no taller than a short Christmas tree, and cantaloupe bald, but none of this hindered him in respect to the stacking-up of twelve wives with no divorces in between. He just loved women, but not permanently. This is understandable but illegal in California. He had a vocation for matrimony; avocationally he was a traveling man. He collected fares (and occasionally wives) on the trolley cars of Los Angeles and San Francisco, and would probably still be traveling and collecting and proposing and marrying had not Wife Number Six and Wife Number Nine decided to attend a department store white sale on the same day and trolley car. This catastrophe brought on a somewhat confusing scene, with Van Wie trying to persuade both women to "Move forward to the front of the car, please," and the Mesdames Van Wie noisily attempting to ascertain which of them had priority. All this occurred in Los Angeles.

The police were called and Van Wie was conducted to the bucket where he demanded to be released at once, as he had to leave for San Francisco on the evening plane in pursuance of the courtship of his latest intended, who was to become Wife Number Thirteen.

The Romeo of the traction system promptly claimed that he was a nut. "I'm nutty, all right," he said. "My head was split open with an ax when I was a child. I was also kicked by a mule, and I have fallen from the tops of a two-story building and a sixty-five foot smokestack—at different times, of course. I'm plenty touched, all right."

It was at this point that Delaplane and Ehrlich got into the picture and in that order. With others, we were guests at a luncheon given by my friend and landlord, Lou Lurie, the amazing millionaire. Delaplane, who'd spent the morning writing up Van Wie's San Francisco love life, gave us the details. Lurie was fascinated with Van Wie's romantic agility and offered me a sizable fee (a deductible tax item under public service, I believe) to defend the man. I was fascinated with both fee and client and accepted without hesitation.

The City and County of San Francisco having had prior claim to the custody of the Ding Dong Daddy, he was to be brought north to us on the morning train, Police Inspector Jerry Desmond having been assigned as escort.

Delaplane and I planned to meet the multiple bridegroom at San Jose, the last stop before San Francisco on the Southern Pacific, but we weren't prepared for what we found there. The

San Francisco *Examiner* had preceded us with two reporters, a cameraman, Mrs. Van Wie Seven, Mrs. Van Wie Nine, and an attorney named Jim Toner whom they'd retained for Van Wie even prior to the altruistic conference at Lurie's luncheon table. Delaplane and I had had our man, our story and even our splendid soubriquet—the Ding Dong Daddy, etcetera—purloined from us without warning or premonition. And Van Wie had abandoned his earlier and better basis for defense. He no longer regarded himself as nutty. He was now a man of deep moral conviction; he abhorred divorce on principle and had not been able to bring himself to divorce any of his brides. His ethical compunction didn't extend to polygamy, adultery or wife abandonment.

I believe that he'd have been better off continuing to claim nuttiness, for moral conviction got him nowhere unless San Quentin can be called somewhere. He wrote me from there later, expressing regret. Not regret that he'd committed a silly crime twelve times over, or regret that he'd not been able to make use of my services; just regret that, "People had no sense of humor." After he was released from Q, he made professional appearances in burlesque houses for awhile and then married four more women and was returned to prison and enforced celibacy.

This was the case into which Delaplane and I had hoped to get our respective teeth. Had I handled it to termination, I would have presented it for what it really was: no grim and sordid instance of man's infamy, but an absurd travesty on one of the more pompous of human phenomena, as it really was. I hoped that Delaplane's current visit meant that he brought me another silly carbuncle which we would lance together, via law and journalism, and I told him so.

This time however Delaplane was seeking the story from me.

"What about the Johnson story, Jake? What really happened there?"

I felt fine about this one. I was glad to give a good reporter the facts on a good job. And for the benefit of those who believe that money is the root of all Ehrlich, this good job was one on the house.

Samuel Johnson was a typical school teacher. His life and character were impeccable. He decided to enjoy a vacation in Las Vegas, packed a bag, and got himself ticketed via airline, with a stopover in Los Angeles. When he arrived in Vegas, he discovered that his modest piece of luggage hadn't been brought along on the same plane.

He made the usual inquiries and the airline people promised him action. They kept the promise. They provided far more action than they'd promised. The bag was located at the Long Beach Airport. It appeared to have undergone molestation and —not being locked—was opened by the baggagemaster. Inside, this worthy found what he thought was marijuana and when he called the police they agreed with him. They notified the Las Vegas authorities and were instructed to send the bag along in the usual fashion; in other words they set the school teacher up for a pinch on possession of narcotics.

When Johnson presented himself with his claim check, he was politely given his property and then promptly arrested. He expressed amazement, claimed to know nothing about the "muggles" they'd found, and then committed a cardinal sin against police officialdom. He refused to cooperate. This is to say that he would not immediately confess to possessing the little batch of dried weed, he did not provide information as to where he had obtained it, he did not offer to testify against his source. The stupid man just continued to protest that he hadn't the faintest idea what the whole thing was about.

Cynicism is a necessary component of the police attitude, and if the baffled pedagogue whom they had in their clutches had possessed a previous criminal record and some minimal appearance of evil, it might have been justified in this case— even with the evidence against him so utterly circumstantial. But Johnson not only *was* a typical school teacher; he looked and acted and told his story like one. He was immediately convicted and sentenced to 10 years in the Nevada State Prison.

Honest citizens, unacquainted with some of the more insensate processes (and defections) of justice, find it difficult to believe that other honest citizens can be and are convicted of crimes they have not committed. However, it happens. It happens so often that I sometimes wish that every case of such bitter, wretched injustice that is uncovered and proven would result in drastic penalties for all those—up to and particularly including the judge who presided—whose lack of professional skill could have let such malpractice occur. There are penalties these days for doctors and lawyers who permit their patients and clients to suffer through ineptness in their professional skills. Why not penalties for judges and officials who are equally remiss in their functions?

In England, just a few years back, a man named Timothy John Evans was hanged for a number of murders that were subsequently found to have been committed by a police constable named John Reginald Halliday Christie. Several years later and after Halliday had committed a number of other murders, he was arrested and convicted and also hanged, and the most august and respected of London newspapers commented that: "It was surprising that the true aspects of the case could not have been comprehended in the beginning, on the basis of what was known then." Those who murdered Evans with briefs and a hangman's rope also had something to say. They were sorry. They were relieved that the right man had finally been found.

In my book, *A Reasonable Doubt,* I relate the true case of a man whom I called Willis Jewel. Jewel was an ignorant and probably feeble-minded Negro who was done to death in the gas chamber by the State of California following conviction for murder on what actually amounted to one man's statement. That man was not an eyewitness. He was what can only be described as an earwitness. A man of documented viciousness with a long police record, this witness spent several hours with Jewel in an Oakland, California, jail cell and later told the police the story of Jewel's "confession" to him. For this service he was given his freedom. There was ample evidence to the contrary of Jewel's alleged guilt and no other real evidence in support of it. But he *was* clearly guilty of several other crimes: he was poor, he was friendless, he was stupid. To quote from *A Reasonable Doubt,* he, "died, as he had lived, in a mute and terrified kind of silence."

Meanwhile, back in the jungle of the Nevada State Penitentiary (where the principal rehabilitative activities provided for the inmates are poker, blackjack, faro and *panguingui*), a crushed and flabbergasted school teacher stared at the gaming convicts around him and wondered what the hell had happened to his world. And in San Francisco I stared at my morning paper and wondered what would be the best way in which to attack this monstrous instance of injustice. I had been convinced that something was terribly wrong with the conviction from the moment I raised my eyes from the newspaper account.

I decided to get in touch with Colonel George White.

Colonel White, head of the Federal narcotic forces in the Pacific area, is an anomaly. As a manhunter and scientific cop, he is a veritable dragon, a relentless, no-holds-barred narcotics bull who would make Victor Hugo's Javert seem like an absent-minded truant officer. He has ferreted out and convicted the biggest of the big game of the narcotic underworlds of this country, Europe, the Middle East, the Orient and South America. On the other hand, George White has and will work just as relentlessly to make sure that no innocent man falls into one of his horrendous bear traps. For this reason and others he is my valued friend. When he is charged with strangling some odious pusher who has been turned loose because the arrest warrant was misdated, I will defend him free.

Colonel White and I collaborated in one little adventure that will win neither of us any kudos, except from our own consciences. This featured a client of mine, a big-time mobster named John the Bug Stoppelli.

Stoppelli was one of the worst I've ever had anything to do with. I've known honest hoodlums and lusty crooks by the bagful, and a great number of them I've liked and even admired for qualities (not professional ones) which I found colorful or uncommon to more respectable ranks. But Stoppelli was a Mafia thug, a lethal and predatory underworld bully, and an active narcotics man.

He had been arrested because a fingerprint from *one* of the fingers of his right hand was found on an envelope containing heroin that turned up in one of White's raids. On this evidence he was convicted by a jury and sentenced to 6 years at Leavenworth.

I was amazed. All of the others concerned in the crime (there were four of them) swore that Stoppelli was no partner of theirs. He had an excellent alibi for the period involved in the actual occurrence of the crime. And it was my informed belief that a single fingerprint was insufficient basis for specifically determining the identity of a person. A single print might *support* an identification otherwise determined, but it had no greater legal weight. I went to White, who had been the motive power behind Stoppelli's conviction.

I didn't convince him that a man had been wrongly convicted. After lengthy interviews with many persons including Stoppelli, and after an exhaustive investigation of the fingerprint evidence, he finally convinced himself. And then he left no means untried which would undo the wrong. There were many setbacks. We finally had to go to the President of the United States for a pardon, which was granted, and largely through the efforts of the toughest narcotics agent in the business.

So I called Colonel White and asked him if he felt like tilting at another windmill with me. He did. I caught a plane to Reno and a taxi to Carson City, some thirty miles away, where the big old penitentiary roosts forlornly on the edge of the broad prairie. After ten minutes with my client I knew my interest and preliminary efforts were justified. This man knew less about marijuana than the Pope knows about tap-dancing.

When I returned to San Francisco I found that White had learned a few things too. He'd checked the airlines baggage records, among other things. The bag that Johnson had checked in at the San Francisco Airport had weighed 18 pounds. The bag that had been checked through to the teacher weighed 11 pounds. There was now no question but what the baggagemaster's first suspicion (that the bag had been tampered with during a period when Johnson couldn't get to it) was justified. And there were other more technical disprovers of the man's guilt.

I went to Nevada's parole board with White's findings and my arguments. Courtroom procedures were open to me, of course, but the board could free the man far more quickly if they could be convinced of our beliefs. They were convinced, and we had our teacher back before the week was out. But not in his classroom. The school authorities had believed the newspaper publicity and fired him. However, this wrong was eventually righted, too, and Johnson returned to teaching. Delaplane thought it was a hell of a story.

"But tell me, Master," he asked, "has the teacher ever been back to thank you for giving him back his life? Was there any pay-off in gratitude?"

We laughed together at this very good joke.

"Senator," I said "ninety-nine and ninety-nine-hundredths percent of the population couldn't produce anything like gratitude except from the pages of Webster's dictionary. Nor do I expect it, except from the one one-hundredth who constitutes the exception and who justifies the help to all the others. The lawyer who contributes without fee to the defeat of what the underworld refers to as a bum rap does so to win the plaudits and respect of the most important spectator of all—himself. He does it because it's fine to prove that the shyster that's in every last one of us in this profession is at an irreducible minimum in *him*. And he does it because it's as wonderful to beat the sick, cynical system as it is to beat the house at Reno or Las Vegas, playing by their rules. But *gratitude* . . ."

He gave me the wolfish leer so characteristic of his more ribald moments.

"I know that you personally pack about a hundred baskets of food every Christmas and take them around to certain addresses. And I know you're the head and principal mover of an organization which provides free milk for school kids. And I—"

"Right facts; wrong interpretation. I do the Santa Claus bit because I can't stand Christmas Eve cocktail parties and because it's a nice excuse for seeing old friends at least once a year. As for the milk, all I'm really doing there is building a little goodwill with the next generation of possible clients. And that reminds me . . . how does Pat Brown's garden grow these days?"

Stan and I both knew that it was the famed Mr. Brown, Governor of California and so-called Presidential timber in at least two elections, who very nearly turned our milk fund quite sour.

The Saints and Sinners Milk Fund has been my baby for a long time. The Saints and Sinners—no relation to the New York organization of the same name—is a group of San Francisco personalities of the kind who couldn't possibly be inveigled into wearing little nameplates on their lapels so they won't forget their own identities.

The initial purpose of the group was to enjoy luncheon without inhibition or formality. Our secondary intent was possibly to parody and caricature the stilted midday meetings of the business and professional men whom we joined at more conventional gatherings. Shortly after our club got under way, however, I became involved in litigation which led to the information that a very considerable number of San Francisco school children went without milk with their lunches simply because milk was beyond the means of their parents and none was available without cost. This condition struck me as a sad lack in a city whose slogan is: The city that knows how. I was able to convince the Saints and Sinners that we should provide milk for *all* children in San Francisco schools under conditions that would remove all stigma of charity or handout from the gesture.

So the Saints and Sinners Milk Fund was created. During the first five years of its existence we raised $1,500,000, mostly through large-scale raffles in which the prizes were homes, automobiles, annuities, etc. I was well aware that we were transgressing some pretty generally transgressed statutes about lottery operation, but I also knew that these codes were regularly transgressed by virtually every church, lodge and service club in the state and—on occasion—by law-enforcement organizations themselves when the cause was right. Certainly no cause could be more right than that of providing milk for children.

In 1951, with some of the leading judges, attorneys, city officials and businessmen of the town freely giving their time and talents toward the gathering, recording and administering of the fund, we raised $107,662.29. In newspaper advertisements that were *not* paid for by milk-fund donations, I reported full receipts and their allocation of disbursals to the various schools. In 1952 we raised $106,802.92; in 1953 the amount was $139,216.55. In 1954 what we raised was an irate outcry from Mr. Brown, who was then Attorney General of California and looking for some way in which to bring his new and somewhat confused image as a statesman before the people.

As I have said, I have known Pat Brown for many years and helped him to become district attorney, and I don't regret it. He is the finest man I can think of to be a district attorney anywhere and at any time. If I could again help him to that spot, I would do so happily.

As a statesman of larger scope, I regard Pat's potentialities as somewhat impaired by his immense gift for instantaneous reaction to the last advice he has received—good, bad or indifferent. A governor and student statesman gets a lot of advice; the impact of this on Brown has been to turn a well-intentioned, guileless but overtractable man into a well-intentioned, people-liking weathercock. He is also an addict for headline-winning gestures, which is why he decided to take on the Saints and Sinners Milk Fund, his old friend and benefactor Jake Ehrlich, and the traditional American institution of the benefit raffle.

I first heard about his decision when the press came to me for a statement on the matter. I decided to give my former protégé a chance to pull in his neck.

"The attorney general can't mean us. We operate a legitimate charity. Our methods are clearly aboveboard. Besides, he is himself a member of Saints and Sinners and has—for years—been a collaborator in our activities. I can't believe that he would have been had he thought them illegitimate."

The reporters went back to see Brown. He squirmed a bit and then provided a brief quasi reply.

"The cause is legitimate," he said, "but the fund-raising methods are illegitimate." There was further hemming and hawing and a not very firm suggestion that there might be prosecution if "lottery tickets" were sold in 1954.

Now I fired both barrels.

"Mr. Brown hasn't thought the matter over very clearly," I said. "The state would have to arrest virtually every civic leader in San Francisco including all of the judges, the superintendent of schools, every bank president in town, the publishers of all of the newspapers, the mayor of San Francisco, a Senator and a Congressman or two, and Earl Warren, Governor of California. All of these persons are members of the Saints and Sinners."

I went to see Brown at the State Building with my rather eminent board of directors and asked for a showdown. He was pleasant and conciliatory.

"There is absolutely no implication of anything being wrong," he told us. "We are making spot checks of all charities in the state. The only thing we can do is see that money given for charitable purposes is used for that purpose. The Saints and Sinners certainly disburses all money received, less prizes." We left his offices feeling that the matter was closed.

It wasn't. Someone apparently got Brown's ear between our departure and his next intake of breath and he made a new statement to the press to the effect that the Saints and Sinners —"in my opinion"—violate the law because they sell tickets that lead to prizes and an element of chance is involved.

Now I really got sore. A brief play for the grandstand was one thing; shutting off the supply of milk for the children was another. I appeared on television with the attorney general and challenged him to prove that his righteous objection to our charity made sense. He didn't perform too well and relied upon virtuous references to "keeping his oath of office" as the best defense of his standpoint. I asked him why it is "not a sin to go to a race track in California and bet money on the outcome of races, but it is a sin—*you* say—to buy tickets that provide children with free milk?" I asked "if it was the board wall that we build around race tracks that shuts out the sin?"

The attorney general allowed that he didn't want "to moralize on this issue" and went on to repeat that, "the law says that I am sworn to enforce what it states," which was as flatulent a slice of dialogue as I'd heard since Calvin Coolidge. Brown wound up with the affirmation of his devout belief that, "No one gets something for nothing." I needed that line. I looked directly into the television camera and hooked my pay-off line onto this corny banality.

"And I say that someone *does* get something for nothing in the Saints and Sinners program." The cameraman, a career horse-player and good Ehrlich constituent, winked at me pleasurably from over the focusing lens. "I say that all the little kids who haven't the money to buy a bottle of milk at lunch get one for nothing and wind up a little stronger because of it—and a little better equipped to meet the challenges of today's tough existence.

"And another thing. If a raffle in a good cause is such a bad thing, then I know of twelve gentlemen who must have been all wrong despite history's opinion to the contrary for the past two thousand years. You can read about them in the Bible in Acts 1:26. They were the gambling and therefore immoral twelve Apostles and they drew lots to pick Matthias to fill Judas' place in their group. As far as I've been able to find out, no one pinched them for it."

We put on our 1954 drive as usual except that I had the tickets printed as "receipts" for contributions to the Milk Fund. There was also a line or so on them suggesting that contributors be careful to hold the serially numbered slips "for tax purposes." Incidentally, of course, the numbers were helpful in identifying the winners of prizes. We sold the usual amount of tickets. No one was arrested.

In fact I sold a few myself to guests at the wedding of the attorney general's beautiful daughter. It was a delightful affair, both for the young couple and for me. Much of my pleasure was derived from the fact that—at a buck a copy for my milk fund ducats—business was quite brisk.

Before the party was over, I found myself addressing a prospect who seemed unlikely to stand still for either the soft or the hard sell. But I wasn't too dismayed. I merely sold two tickets to the man next to him and suggested that he give the extra one to, "your companion, the district attorney of San Francisco." Tom Lynch has official integrity by the bale, but he also has a sense of humor. I was not arrested.

Delaplane, whose widely read column is characterized by a refreshingly different species of genuine humor, interestingly recalled that the governor was a man with no small acquaintance with the principles and practices of gambling basics. While attending law school he often helped out in his dad's cigar shop where as much revenue was obtained from Klondike and bull dice games as from the sale of cigars. Furthermore, as a young attorney he had put together the chartered club bill which, when enacted into law, permitted draw poker to milk the economy of many a California county. And it wasn't children who got the cream from *this* little milk fund.

"But don't be too hard on Pat," continued my columnist friend. "I understand that he's never let himself be photographed in an Indian war bonnet. A politician who can pass up being photographed in an Indian war bonnet can't be all bad."

I told him that I wasn't in the least badly disposed toward Governor Brown.

"How could I be?" I asked. "He saved us from Nixon, water shortage and the Oriental fruit fly. And I believe he's sincerely opposed to sin, Communism and the Bad Guys. Where are you off to?"

"To Chinatown. I've got some visitors coming in from the East and I usually take such people up to Ross Alley—which I call Blood Alley at such times—to show them the bullet holes in the wall from the last hassle between the On Leon Tong and the Hip Sings. But I aways have to go up the day before and dig out the holes. The natives keep puttying them up. It's very annoying."

Another columnist of whom I was very fond was the late Art Cohn, who was killed in the tragic plane crash with Mike Todd, another friend of mine. Cohn wrote of me as follows:

The Master

Two boys wrote a so-called biography of Jake Ehrlich a couple years ago. It turned out to be an inventory of his cases more than a portrait of the man. It was not the truth, the whole truth and nothing but the truth, so help me.

Jake has never pulled any punches and any writer who does must miss him by six furlongs

"I didn't exactly idolize my father," he told me in a typical moment of candor a few years ago when I was toying with the idea of doing a book on him. "Lifting a mint julep was the only work I ever saw him do."

"How about your mother?"

"She wanted me to go into medicine. It is just as well I didn't. I would want to dramatize surgery. Like throwing a scalpel fifty yards."

After several months of research I decided not to write the book. I would rather remain his friend than be his biographer.

You may assume nothing from that last line. In my opinion, and I have studied them all, Jake Ehrlich is one of the three greatest trial lawyers this country has ever known. I rank him above William J. Fallon, Earl Rogers, Sam Leibowitz and Jerry Giesler. Only Moman Pruiett and Clarence Darrow were in his class. And they're dead.

When people who presume to know Ehrlich talk or write about him they speak of his hippodroming and haberdashery, his bluster and bombast; stage business, his sleight of hand with starched cuffs, deceives his friends as facilely as it does judges and juries.

What of the man behind the mask? At fifty-seven what does he really think?

"No man thinks 100 per cent honestly because his own desires add or subtract."

Jake said that the first night I met him back in the mid-thirties. It remains one of his favorite precepts.

"Love has no basis in logic. You can't feel it or see it walk in, only when it walks out."

That was his sole comment after listening to a two-hour lament of unrequited love.

"Man is basically prejudiced against everything except his own image. How can you teach a white man to understand the equal rights of a Negro if he only understands his own?"

He said that 20 years before the Supreme Court of the United States unanimously decreed that all men are equal before the law be they black or white.

He has no illusions about women and has been married to the same one for 37 years.

"People are 100 percent mentally unfaithful but are stopped by cowardice or lack of opportunity. Marriage vows are evidence of possession, not affection.

"Ninety-nine percent of all divorces—I have handled hundreds—can be traced to the boudoir."

"Jake, you take clients obviously guilty of the crimes with which they are charged. Why?"

"Every poor devil I defend in court came before the bar of justice because of the unevenness, unfairness and downright stupidity of society."

"Are you suggesting that all laws be repealed, all prisons emptied, all halls of justice converted into bowling alleys?"

"I am stating there is less justice in the Hall of Justice than any other building in town. I am stating that legalized civilization destroys justice with its respectability masking hypocrisy."

"Spell that out."

"First a man steals to exist. Then he gets everything he wants. Then he becomes holier than thou."

"Cynicism is unworthy of you, Jake."

"I'm not cynical. It says that if a man is aware of his crime he is subject to punishment. What of the mentally distraught? They are aware. Too many practitioners of the Law forget, or never knew, they are dealing with the frailties of men, not the tensile weaknesses of steel."

Jake Ehrlich knows the Law as few men do but believes that law is law and justice is justice, and never the twain shall meet. His definition of justice is a kind of agreement not to hurt or be hurt.

"If I had it to do over again," he told me the other day, "I would not be a lawyer. I would not deal in personal services. I could have been just as successful with less effort in other occupations."

"Name one."

"Show business for one. I would have done all right."

What self-delusion! Jake has been in show business since he came to San Francisco almost 40 years ago. He is the best actor who never won an Academy Award.

The Master is the last of his breed. May he get the Hebraic limit and no time off for good behavior.

And none added for bad behavior, I sincerely hope.

A columnist for whom I have an abiding affection is Herb Caen of the San Francisco *Chronicle*. Of the numerous references he has made to me over the years, the following appeals to me particularly, a story from his April 7, 1961 column:

FRIDAY FISH-FRY

—AND STILL CHAMP: It was like old times on Kearny St. Wednesday. Mouthpiece Jake (The Master) Ehrlich, who has been strangely out of the headlines lately, won a big fraud case in the Hall of Justice, scene of so many of his ancient triumphs, and he had been in vintage form throughout the trial, running his full gamut from George Raft to Edward G. Robinson.

There was even the fight that always marked an Ehrlich trial —at one point he and Asst. D. A. John Dean came to blows, and Judge Harry Neubarth had to step down from the bench to separate them—and there was the usual scenario-type finale: a "Not guilty" verdict for The Master's client. True to form,

Jake kissed the four women jurors and then presided at the bar in Cookie Picetti's, buying drinks for the newspaper guys and coppers.

And late in the afternoon he strolled cockily down Kearny St. toward his offices, the sun glinting off his gray hair, his figure still dapper and insolent—an authentic slice of Old San Francisco on the loose.

19: *Afternoon*

4 P.M.

Agenda: Representatives of Downtown Business Groups

The variety of my practice provides it with an exotic seasoning that makes every hour of every day a constant, changing delight to a gourmet of the living experience, which I am.

The policemen were gone, my session with the alleged murderer was but a half hour away, and now my visitors were a group of men about as far removed from those principals as is conceivable. As counsel for and legislative representative of the groups who own and operate the major part of the office buildings in San Francisco's financial district and adjacent areas, I find myself deeply involved in the shaping and reshaping of what has been described as one of the most colorful skylines in the world.

My clients are the Chamber of Commerce, the Downtown Association, the Real Estate Board, The Building Owners' and Managers' Association and various allied groups. Their opponents are several bleeding-heart organizations, civic dilettantes and alleged public servants who have decided to preserve San

Francisco's topography at all costs on the fatuous premises that the quaint is sacred, the ancient is holy, and esthetics are at least as important as good human living values, better housing for the many, and more abundant prosperity for all.

In other manifestations of their attempt to preserve every last piece of near debris in a town that needs updating, these would-be reformers have fought every attempt to bring San Francisco out of the gaslit era. No one loves the wonderfully rococo vestiges of the old San Francisco more than I, but I refuse to fall victim to blind nostalgia for the stupidities of the past. Spinning wheels are all very well for museums but I get my cloth from Scotland these days.

My function for those who are painfully aware that San Francisco has to grow upward (the encirclement of the bay's waters having made impossible any other recourse) is to fight those who would limit by law "the height, bulk and density of building," and I'm finding it as absorbing a battle as any I have ever fought.

With these men, I worked out a strategy that would enable us to cut loose from the web of restraints employed by the yesterday-admirers. This would mean radio, television and press appeals to logic and reason. It would also mean my personal appearance before the Board of Supervisors. It would mean pressure and manipulation and subtle coaxing and convincing of those in places of influence, so that they—in turn—would bring pressure, manipulate and coax. "Human chess playing," a writer recently called it in a magazine article about me. I plead guilty. This is a pursuit and a contest worthy only of the most facile-minded of men; I love it.

As I watched the men around me today—all of them highly placed and highly capable individuals who represented the best and most dynamic phases of our community life—I thought again of the past. I thought that quite possibly the qualities and strengths they sought in me were those which sprang directly and exclusively from that past: gifts and skills and instincts born in desperate moments in the prize ring, in the scrambling of the early day police court rat race, even in the dilemma of a nineteen-year-old in the Oakland freightyards who was without ferry fare to San Francisco and who had a pair of feral-hearted railway detectives to dodge in the bargain. Many of my courtroom and boardroom victories might actually have been accomplished years before in the squared ring, in grim, grimy police court encounters, even in the cindery labyrinths of the freightyard in Oakland.

"Highly placed and highly capable," are apt as applied to this elite of the business world who chose me to do their fighting for them. It is only for such men that I compromise my credo that few are as splendid as their reputations in this era of purchased, inherited or spuriously conferred prominence. The business aces—the everyday doers of the impossible in big business—are our really strong men today. The Communists can stop worrying about the military generals; our first line of defense is actually composed of tough, hard-boiled, informed business leaders. For them I have a watchful respect and an uneasy but firm admiration.

As for the so-called "socially prominent," the scions of "old families," the self-touted philanthropists and humanitarians, many of the eminent divines and saintly professional men of God, and most of the great and people-loving statesmen of our time . . . they sicken me. At best they are amusing, but their alleged special qualities too often include built-in tendencies toward smugness, self-delight and snobbishness.

Some years ago I had an interesting experience with snobbishness. I had been retained to handle the divorce of a woman who is a well-documented member of San Francisco society. She was beautiful, rich and—in a technical sense—cultured. When sober, she is charming.

This glittering lady had come to me for a divorce—by no means her first—and after I obtained it and lucrative incidentals for her, she celebrated the event with a party. I had refused the invitation pressed on me, but I was urged to attend and finally accepted, planning to put in the briefest of appearances.

Her guests were mostly members of what she would have

described as her own set, which means that they were wealthy, pedigreed or otherwise acceptable wastrels. By otherwise acceptable I mean that they had married eligibles or were in a position to blackmail one or more of them or were capable of performing some unusual cultural, athletic or sexual feat. One thing they shared in common: they were all hundred-proof, road-tested, card-carrying snobs.

After a drink and some meaningless small talk, I was prepared to leave. My hostess had been enjoying a substantial amount of her own refreshments, and in a louder and more leaden tone than usual, she straightened me out about myself.

"You've only just arrived, Jake. Do we bore you, we social butterflies?"

"Not at all," I replied, half tempted to skip the proprieties and cop out. "I have an appointment at the office and I must go. I'm sorry, my dear."

"You *should* be sorry. I don't imagine you often receive invitations of this kind or get to know many people like my friends. Actually you must have met more nice people this afternoon than ever before in your life."

There was a well-bred titter from around the room and now I was more than half tempted; I was fully tempted and I responded.

"Client," I said, "I've been meeting your friends or their prototypes all my life. I am more used to making their acquaintance in the privacy of some miserable jackpot into which they have gotten themselves, and from which I am privileged to extricate them, but I also mingle with them socially now and then. As for those here today, it happens that I know several on a very intimate basis. Those whom I don't know, I know *about.* In some cases I know *all* about them.

"For instance, there is a gentleman present who remembers me well and whom I remember equally well although we don't mention the reason in the presence of other nice people. Nor have his gentlemanly instincts yet prompted him to pay the balance of the fee he owes. I know that it will soothe his fatherly instincts to learn that the issue involved in that case is now seven years old and had very little trouble getting through the first grade last year, as our schools are now integrated.

"The young lady he's paired off with should be one to sympathize with his problems. Her own father divorced her mother on testimony that had to be heard in the privacy of the judge's chambers and that involved the possibility that her elder brother was also her cousin.

"I am looking at a young man [and I did] who spends thousands of dollars annually to play polo in such faraway places as Bermuda, São Paulo and the South of France. Yet his wife, whom I represent, has difficulty in extricating enough money from him to get his children's teeth fixed. His neighbor, who is now making a big thing of lighting a cigarette and looking casual, was a witness against an unfortunate lady client of mine in another divorce suit. He kissed and told from the witness stand. Other ladies present might beware.

"I'll not actually put my finger on the nice person present who came to me—and was thrown out—following a request that I help him railroad his mother into a nut house so that he might control her estate. Nor will I go into details about why the telephone company once protractedly refused service to still another of the nice, socially prominent people whose company I am about to leave.

"I am aware of the respect accorded those of fine family in San Francisco, and I have decided that the reason must be based upon the rarity of the phenomenon: there are so damned few of them. As you all know, I have just had it explained to me that I am lucky to be mingling with this group; a group that includes those whose parents were bogus bankrupts, embezzlers, suicides, perverts and more wife beaters and wife cheaters than I can total without an adding machine. As for the antecedents of my clever but caustic hostess herself..."

I turned and found her gone. There seemed little else to say and I left.

Perhaps my reaction was gauche. I think not. People too

often reserve for later the things they might have said or done against the insolence and viciousness of the socially smug. I was implying no more immaculate status for myself when I leveled with the elite on this occasion. In my own Confederate lineage there are a couple of strange freebooters and perhaps a lady or so who wasn't always as discreet as she might have been. As for me personally, my qualifications for sainthood are somewhat flawed. My counteracting virtue is that I am well aware of all of the Ehrlichian blemishes; nobody will ever catch me whitening my own sepulcher. I may dress it up a bit with an impressive canopy and a red carpet, but I'll never fail my sense of humor and proportion so unforgivably as to claim that the occupant is or was a completely virtuous man.

Another relevant incident comes back to me.

I had gone to Amelio's Restaurant for dinner. Amelio's is to San Francisco what the Tour d'Argent might be to Paris if it had better food and Inez as its *patronne*. It is small, intimate, completely indifferent to the patronage of unknowns, and almost hostile to the average tourist. The food and liquor are superb and the service is comforting, but the bar is tiny.

Which is why, on this occasion, I found it difficult to disregard the unpleasant attentions of an Ivy-League-accented patrician I found there—a broad-A type who was an alcoholic monologist. He needed no companion or even the mercenary ear of a bartender in order to hold a conversation. The gentleman just talked: he asserted, replied, interrogated, commented, interjected, disagreed, ejaculated and expressed shocked amazement, ironic disgust or profane agreement—all in a rumbling sort of mumble.

There was that damned Jake Ehrlich over there at the other end of the bar. He knew him well. And others of his stripe. A blight to an honorable profession! A goddam blight to a goddam honorable profession! There was no longer any place left a gentleman could go for a quiet drink without being affronted by the presence of millionaire ruffians. A man who defends gangstahs and mobstahs and loose women. Gad!

Short of decking him, there was only one thing for me to do. I downed and paid for my Scotch and left.

Down Powell Street a few doors is a pleasant but plebeian little joint called Jake's. The company is robust and Jake himself is fine and hearty in the expansive manner of old-time North Beach sawdust-floor restaurateurs. I had a good dinner and went home to Marjorie, my books and San Francisco's best nighttime view of San Francisco. At eleven I retired.

It was after one in the morning when I was awakened by my telephone answering service. Someone had called me from the eighth floor of the Hall of Justice. As is not uncommon with those who call from this level of the Hall, which houses the jail, this someone was in deep trouble. Sighing unhappily because the night was cold and the pillow soft, I ordered the connection put through.

The party was indeed in deep trouble. He had contrived to get himself arrested in an upstairs room of the Dolphin, a cheap skid-row hotel on Howard Street. He had been with a young man who holds a long record of moral perversion, and the latter had also been arrested. My party went on to say, in a broad-A-toned, somehow familiar, voice that he had accompanied this fellah to his quartahs to see his collection of Indian flintheads, that the fellah had attempted to rob and attack him, that the fellah was now making the foulest kind of charges against *him* to the police! All untrue, of course. Gad!

Wearily but with a certain sense of grim curiosity, I dressed and went down to the City Prison. The dinner coat and starched shirt were no longer in mint condition, but the manner of the man from Amelio's was just as starchy as it had been at 8:30. I explained to him that obtaining the services of a lawyer of the stripe who would defend gangsters and loose women would come pretty high. I told him that this little cellside call would cost him $1,000. I told him that the further chore of restoring him to that world where a gentleman might obtain a quiet drink with or without being affronted by millionaire ruffians would be even more costly.

"Gad!" he said.

But he paid in full; he paid indeed. Not enough though, not nearly enough.

My final story here is somewhat less acrid.

A good friend of mine, a banker who couldn't care less about the loftiness of his high social position, invited me to his club one day. This is an exclusive establishment which the members hope to keep free from taint by excluding Jews —and registered Democrats.

The lunch was long and the drinks were good. The members seated at nearby tables appeared to be eating with good appetite, despite my alien presence. No casualties were reported then or later. My host, liberalized by several drinks, suggested that I allow him to put me up for membership. I replied that I belonged to no clubs or lodges, and that we ought to gradually work up to such a tour de force by first getting me admitted to the Roman Catholic College of Cardinals.

"What do you mean, Master?" he asked, a little baffled and probably wondering why the hell I would want to wear a scarlet hat.

"I just mean it's slightly impossible."

He squared his jaw with relentless Haig & Haig-powered determination and then indicated how far he was willing to go in the interest of tolerance.

"We'll just fight the bigots down," he said. "We'll . . . we'll just . . . *hard-ass* them, the bastards!"

I shook my head.

"Can't do it, pal."

"Why?"

"Why? Good reason why. You'll get me tolerated here, you'll make me a full member, and then what'll happen? You'll want *me* to get *you* into B'nai Brith and *I'll* be embarrassed."

Actually the word tolerance and all that it stands for affects me in the general direction of nausea. Tolerance implies a condescending, patronizing attitude somewhere between charity and forgiveness. This is not what I expect of my fellow man. The intolerant I can tolerate; the tolerant always remind me of Tibetan monks with their prayer wheels revolving at full twirl. They persist in assuming moral merit for an active but empty gesture.

20: *Afternoon*

4:30 P.M.

Agenda: Television Station: The Taping of a Program

Now with the canyons of the financial district blue with afternoon shadows, I climbed into a cab and had myself taxied to the television station. My old friend Roy Meredith was planning to tape an interview with me. It would be broadcast at a later hour that evening.

There have been many of these public tête-à-têtes in my life of recent years, and I take a frank and perhaps immodest enjoyment in them. I know precisely why I am so often picked as the subject (and sometimes the object). I'm well aware that I'm not chosen because of the superlative quality of my wisdom or even because of my charming profile and irresistible cowlick. I know that I often face a camera and a craftily urbane interrogator because I'd far rather commit an indiscretion than a banality, because it is my great pleasure to take on the flatulent idiots of the community and the whited sepulchers who are usually spared by kinder critics, and also because I tend to call a spade a spade if that's what it happens to be. My allergy is for the mealy mouthed.

Tonight Meredith's topics for discussion were strictly miscellaneous, but there was a certain mischievous evasiveness in his manner and I sensed that the verbal dice might be loaded, as they so often were. I didn't particularly care. There's no real advantage to knowing just what's going to happen next except in Russian roulette.

With the tape rolling, we discussed the current civil liberties problem, on which I have already given my views. Roy then switched to the bar association, a topic upon which he knows I harbor inflammatory opinions.

"I understand the bar association's been grumbling a bit about what it refers to as 'flamboyant lawyers,' Jake," he said with a broad smile. "Would you have any views on this subject?"

I had views.

"Roy, this group was once a useful and rather admirable organization. Its original function was the creation of a community of cultured and dedicated men for the advancement of the practice of law on a high and dedicated plane and as a buttress to the art and science of administering justice. It is no longer any of these things. It has been taken over by a small bunch of self-interested, petty-minded personalities whose prime concern is to keep themselves and their kind in perpetual power. It now has all of the high purpose and lofty ideals of a tightly controlled company union. Its relationship to the working careers of its subjects—pardon me, its membership—is largely limited to harassment, censorship and attempted reduction of their abilities and attainments to a common denominator of mediocrity. To paraphrase Mr. Churchill, never have so few done so much harm to so many as has the organized bar against its membership. Does that answer your question?"

"It certainly does," he replied, pleased that he'd gotten just what he expected. "Tell me, Jake, if you had bowed to their policies throughout your career, would you have accomplished all of the things in behalf of your clients for which the record gives you credit?"

"Are you kidding? I'd have long ago wound up in the Home for Defunct, Decrepit and Disgusted Pettifoggers and my clients would have been distributed throughout the poorhouses, nuthouses and jailhouses of this great state. But I've known these gentry for what they are from the first and avoided their influence. As a lawyer, I don't need them. As an individual, I could derive more stimulus from a membership in a good bird-watching society."

"What about the claims of flamboyancy, Master? Do you feel that your career would have sparkled more brilliantly had you been a little less spectacular?"

"I have dressed well as part of my way of life back into the days when my pockets were as empty as my opportunities. As for my exterior conduct, I don't live to produce a picturesque public image. If it is different than the dour concepts of some of my colleagues, it is different because my tastes and interests are robust and uninhibited and uncalculated to compete for the esteem and plaudits of the Audubon Society *or* the bar association. I admire beautiful women, so I regularly escort beautiful women to lunch. I am amused by monstrous gags and practical jokes, and I participate in them and sometimes the newspapers report them. I know many famous and a few notorious people; I am occasionally pictured with them without regret or sheepish excuses. I go to parties; good ones, bad ones, occasionally to wild ones. Being contentious, I become involved in contention, and this again puts me on Page One from time to time. These people and things and events are the breath of life to me. They prove to me that I am very much alive, very much a part of the life of my community. If this be flamboyance, let the bar association make the most of it. I certainly intend to."

Meredith then turned to legal techniques.

"Your defenses haven't always been strictly according to Hoyle, or rather according to Blackstone, have they, Jake? I heard you described as a master of the unorthodox and of the unconventional. Is this true?"

"Roy, a legal defense is no more a matter of mere law than medical care is a matter of mere pills. I and every other resourceful lawyer resort not only to the books but also to applied psychology, Scriptural analogy, humor, satire and even burlesque, induced empathy, political persuasion, blandishment of susceptible lady jurors and even to jiu jitsu, if it will do any good. We're not above skillful use of the dynamics of even personal trauma, as in a case I had a few years back before a federal judge in Reno.

"My client Larry Brady had lost his shirt at Bill Graham's gambling tables and then won back all his money plus a few souvenir greenbacks with the help of a thirty-eight revolver. I slanted my defense so that it became a sort of memorial to all exploited, luck-deserted gamblers, knowing full well that the judge himself had dropped a few bundles at the same tables only a few weeks before. Together His Honor and I sort of sentenced my client into a long term in the Merchant Marine, on probation. He never again sought to balance his losses the arbitrary way. My client, I mean. I don't know about the judge."

Meredith's course of interview now took a different tack.

"Master, you're well known as a tough-on-the-bankroll divorce lawyer—I believe you charged a half-million-dollar fee to one of your more heavily loaded clients—but you also have quite a reputation for wheedling or bullying would-be divorce customers into shaking hands and getting acquainted again. How do you explain this paradox?"

"There are two things wrong with many marriages and they inevitably lead to divorce. The first is woman. The second is man. Many women have sat in my office and told me that their husbands are cruel to them. Hardly any of them has ever described any acts on the part of her husband that add up to the legal definition of cruelty. All that the complaining lady really wants is to be rid of the party of the second part. She is usually encouraged by her certainty that innumerable men are hungering for her, impatiently waiting for her to emerge, single, from the divorce courtroom. She is also not disinterested in her portion of the community property and in the alimony.

"Men, on the other hand, convert a former sweetheart, sentimental companion or red-hot mistress into household vassal, cold-war enemy and second-class citizen the minute the wedding presents begin to tarnish. They've got the same woman that sent them into emotional orbit that year, but they've lost the rose-colored glasses. They see something else.

"Most marriage dissension is merely a matter of the points of view of the yelping parties being out of alignment. As a great admirer of women, I regret having to record myself as convinced that it is the ladies who are most often in the wrong. A woman is a strange form of life. From the moment she is able to think, she anticipates every step necessary to get what she wants. A Napoleon drafting strategy between armies of great magnitude is no match for the sweet but silently fierce female plotting the tactics of attack on the resistance of the man she wants, or when younger, the toy or doll or lollipop she wants. Try as a man will, he cannot beat her at her game. She is forever too far ahead and too sure of herself. When the man discovers what is happening, it is too late for retreat. He surrenders and groggily calls it love at first sight.

"When she starts to *un*want him, it's the same thing all over again but in reverse. By that time his erstwhile dream girl has retained a lawyer, court-ordered him to his club or a hotel room, and prespent the settlement she knows she'll get.

"Nowadays most divorces start in a bedroom. It doesn't make much difference whose bedroom. The lawyers and the perjured testimony come later but the birthplace is the bedroom.

"But it is our archaic divorce law that lays the real basis for the prevalence of divorce, and the California divorce law is the worst. Marriage is essentially a civil contract. Imagine entering into any contract with a second party and not providing that such contract may be terminated by giving notice to each other; and instead stipulating that the parties must call each other vile names under oath, in a court of law, in order to terminate the relationship. I think any law that requires people to lie or vilify or become adulterous or even technically adulterous is a law that's for the birds, and I try to outwit its malevolence whenever I can by counseling its victims to back off and try again.

"The law and the bureaucratic red tape of our time, however, are full of these traps to human happiness. In San Francisco County, for instance, the Public Health Department is forbidden to offer contraceptive treatment to a woman who's been raped. The Public Health Department, whose ambulances are dispatched to all rape scenes, operates the city's emergency hospitals. The contraceptive-*verboten* policy is dictated by no logical reasoning. Recently a young Australian woman, raped in a doorway by a syphilitic Negro thug, had to bear his baby. Not very blessed was the fruit of her womb.

"More recently and with the help of a wonderful old soul, I was able to witness a refreshing victory over the insensate rigidities of record and official pronunciamento. A young couple had come to me with their problems—a very old human problem which concerns impatience, biology, nonappearance at the marriage license bureau and the calendar. I knew them to be good people and I decided to help them but was somewhat handicapped by a certain reluctance to cooperate on the part of some of the town's tonier rabbis. The reluctance in each case seemed to derive from a first glance at the waistline of the bride-to-be, which was not willowy.

"Finally I located a wonderful Old World rabbi in McAllister Street, took my overripe love birds to him, and he married them instanter. When the ceremony was over and the newlyweds were safely outside the *schule,* I offered my bearded friend in the long, black overcoat an appropriately substantial fee. I called it a present.

" '*What* present!' he snorted, looking up from his execution of the marriage document. 'God didn't charge me for charity; what kind of a schnook would I be to charge them! And by the way . . . my eyes are not so good, and my writing hand is poor, too. You got one of those writing machines in your office, *nu?* Just fill in the date for me . . . you understand? A *good* date!'

"I understood. I had the writing machine. I had a *good* date."

Meredith thought that this was amusing, and so I hoped would all our viewers including the Registrar of Vital Statistics. Now he glanced at the studio clock and then dealt me the special question I'd been anticipating.

"Jake, it's common knowledge that you were the first trial lawyer to be asked to represent Jack Ruby, the man who killed

President Kennedy's assassin. You turned it down and your friend Mel Belli then accepted the case and lost it. I'd like to know, in behalf of our viewers, how you'd have defended Jack Ruby had you decided otherwise and gone to Dallas instead."

I'd have preferred to have stuck to divorce cases and the bar association, but I wasn't going to dodge.

"Ruby would probably not have been convicted, in my opinion, had the jury merely been asked to accept the hypothesis that his act was one that was perfectly natural to an emotionally impulsive, completely uninhibited man to whom the sophisticated restraints that apply to the rest of us malfunction at moments of stress. Jack Ruby is a well-meaning and wholesomely stimulated type to whom the sudden destruction of his cherished idol was too much to bear; he reacted in much the way that survivors to fatal automobile accidents do quite regularly to the causers of the accidents; he attacked, he killed. This is regrettable, but also understandable, even forgivable.

"I believe that the scientific or psychiatric approach was both unrealistic in fact and indiscreet as an approach to Texas thinking, although I also believe that Mr. Belli fought a valorous and sincere fight for his client. I believe that the jury would have wanted to be shown a way to be charitable to Ruby, had it been offered them. I believe they could have understood a Jack Ruby with whom, under easy, informal interpretation, and without the obfuscation of scientific jargon, some level of their emotional responses could have been caused to empathize. I am convinced that they would not have decreed death for a childishly impulsive fool who was so completely enraptured with his maudlin fantasy of the Kennedy family that he reacted with wild and broken-hearted rage to a tragedy that struck most of the rest of us in a like but diminished manner.

"On the basis of my own reaction to the tragic killing in Dallas, I'm sure there are many decent, intelligent, totally harmless people throughout the nation whose first, fleetingly-transient but none-the-less heart-felt response to what they saw and heard on the television screen when Oswald was captured, smug and grinning, was 'kill the beast!' I am sure that among the members of that jury were those who, for a rippling half-moment, murmured 'kill the beast!' and thus for that half-moment shared brotherhood of reaction with a man they were later to try and condemn. And I am *completely* certain—after having dealt with juries of all kinds and colors and backgrounds during the past forty years—that this jury would have dealt gently with Ruby. Perhaps they might even have freed him had they been permitted to see him, not as a creature from out of a psychiatrist's gallery of exhibits, but as one of themselves—a life-harassed human being suddenly face-to-face with a situation too massive for his mental and emotional faculties of the moment—everyman's potential dilemma in this unpredictable world."

My interviewer smiled, glanced at the homing large hand on the clock again, then asked one more question.

"Master, why did you refuse to take the case?"

Why not be frank about it! Confession might not augment my public image, but it's fine for the soul.

"Why did I refuse to defend Jack Ruby? Because *my* reaction as I watched the grinning Oswald brought in fresh from his insensate crime, was, 'Kill the beast!' I wasn't at all sure I could go into that courtroom with the pure objectivity and cool detachment required of a legal defender. I was afraid I'd empathize too much."

When I left the television station at 5:30 P.M., I noticed that the last edition of the afternoon *News-Call-Bulletin* was headlining a murder: HOUSEWIFE KILLS 'OTHER WOMAN'; FLEES, PROMISING BRIDGE SUICIDE.

Grim news, but in this strange and sometimes ugly world of ours these words would bring the sparkle of eager interest to hundreds of thousands of eyes, special significances to policemen, bondsmen, lawyers and undertakers, and perhaps a hundred newly thoughtful women might reconsider that evening date with the married man in their lives.

21: *Late Afternoon*

6:00 P.M.

Agenda: Lou Lurie (at his office)

AT THE END of almost every day I ascend from my sixteenth-floor aerie to the eighteenth-floor penthouse office of my landlord, mentor, severest critic and lifelong friend Louis Lurie. There with a highly limited number of kindred souls, a certain amount of tests are run on Lurie's whisky and the day's affairs are post-mortemized. The penthouse lair of the ancient fox of Montgomery Street is a pleasant place from which to review the sunset.

Lou Lurie, as far as San Francisco and I are concerned, isn't merely a person—he's a modern myth. Both Mohammed *and* the mountains come to him. Politicians have become statesmen under his aegis, and accountants magnates merely because they knew him. He owns almost as much real estate as the Department of the Interior, performs more philanthropies than the first fifty millionaires on any charity sucker list, and knows the truth about more notables than anyone west of J. Edgar Hoover. He converts smudged and hitherto overlooked playscripts into Broadway hits with a phone call. He consummates titanic mergers and business deals with a nod. And despite all this Homeric, legend-making grandeur of accomplishment, my friend the billionaire is still just the same plain, unspoiled little pixie he was when he peddled newspapers on the streets of Chicago seventy years ago, marked only by a rare talent for making twenty-three cents seem to be the change from a half-dollar purchase of a penny Chicago American.

Actually Lou Lurie's feats of nimbleness and agility in the

departments of political and financial machination are among his lesser attributes. I admire him because of several rather unusual things which he represents to me. Lurie has helped me to see myself objectively. In addition, he possesses a sardonic brand of humor that is both refreshing and strengthening. Finally, he is mentally tough in a society where toughness is largely verbal. After such qualities, the mere possession of power and money are incidental.

I found out how incidental they were to him recently when I had a sign placed in the lobby of our building. It directed all tenants and other clients of Lurie to pay all monies for rentals, tithes, mortgage payments, interest and otherwise into *my* office on the sixteenth floor. He screamed like a banshee until his sense of humor and a hastily summoned sign repainter took over.

Shortly afterward he attempted reprisal. He demanded his rent in cash, "promptly at 10 o'clock on the first day of the month; not at one minute past ten, but right on the nose at the hour."

At 9:50 on rent day an armored car rolled up in front of 333 Montgomery Street. Armed guards hopped out and took up point duty along the route to Lurie's office. Other guards trucked sacks of coin into the great financier's inner sanctum, upturned them on the floor, 550 pounds of copper coins. For nearly a week he had to climb over, through and around these incredible mounds of pennies before he finally gave up and pleaded for mercy. I sent a man up to his office with a shovel and some sacks.

Lurie himself is not above an elaborate practical joke. Recently at his daily luncheon party at Jack's Restaurant, he presented to us the Director of Public Health of Her Britannic Majesty's Crown Colony at Hongkong. This sharp-tongued gentleman proceeded to excoriate several prominent physicians who were present for the laxity of American medical standards. Professionally aroused, the doctors suggested that the guest give the same criticisms at the next day's luncheon of the county medical society. This he did. So inspired by his high standards were some of the young physicians who listened to his abrasive denunciation of the American way that after the luncheon they consulted him privately about entering his service in faraway Hongkong. About then Lurie felt that it was time to explain that his visiting scientist was actually a contract actor from Metro-Goldwyn-Mayer. Personally I thought the revelation was ill advised. San Francisco has too many brash young doctors. Besides, travel is broadening.

When I arrived in Lurie's office this evening at 5:30, I found that George Killion, President of the American President Lines, Chief Federal Judge George B. Harris and Bob Lurie—my friend's only son—were already there. Killion is a patrician and an unabashed capitalist these days, but he started out as a one-suit-of-clothes reporter for the San Diego *Union & Tribune,* and he hasn't forgotten that currency is also minted in small denominations. My friends had heard of my earlier exposure to television and were characteristically disposed to kid me about it.

"I suppose you gave them the usual pap about corruption in high places and the fundamental honesty of the fundamentally honest, meaning yourself," said Killion, laying some Scotch across some ice for me.

"No," I replied, settling myself across from Lurie's money tree, which burgeons with United States currency. As I've said, he has a green thumb. "When I get around to exposing the corrupt, I'll give everybody enough advance notice to buy airline tickets and throw a few negotiable securities into a suitcase. Today I merely discussed noncontroversial subjects like the hypocrisy of the bar association, the duplicity of women who seek divorces, the virtues of personal profit, and how the Jack Ruby case might have been won."

The others laughed but Lou received the statement with unctuous irony.

"That's fine and will go far to advance the image we're trying to build of you as a sedate lawyer-banker and reformed firebrand."

I reminded them that it was high time for someone—probably

me—to strike a blow against the mouthing of twaddle inhabiting the air waves.

"In the name of truth or information or even cultural edification, the American public regularly permits its ears and brains to be filled with more meaningless pap than has ever been transmitted to any body of people at any period of time within the history of the world. Poor, captive millions are lectured on how to organize their lives by psychological experts who can't keep their own marriages together, can't amicably adjudicate a rear-end street collision, and can't keep their checking accounts straight. Ersatz television messiahs and radio divines thunder at untold millions about how to save their souls and receive preferential treatment from the wrath to come. Panel groups composed of fuzzy wordmongers and pedantic egotists nightly inflict their verbal pomposities on the unwary, and almost any idiot with a paying sponsor can assault the public intelligence with empty conjectures and daffy hyperbole at election times, because there's *no* yardstick of fact in *that* direction. So why shouldn't someone create some precedents and perhaps even standards by laying down some straight, black-and-white truths? Why shouldn't people now and then hear that dirt is black, that manure is odorous, that the Good are not always Right and vice versa, and that even God Himself may make mistakes and become angry with them? The *facts,* gentlemen; what's wrong with giving people the cold and often clammy *facts!*"

They applauded me with appreciation but with absolutely no sincerity.

"You should have been a politician, Jake," commented young Lurie.

"He *was* a politician," his father interjected. "A bad one. Tell them about it, Master!"

I eyed him balefully.

"Bob, your father seeks to expose old wounds. Yes I was a politician, briefly and unsalubriously. I ran for Attorney General of California."

"Ye-e-e-s?" prodded Lurie, with unkind insistence.

"I did not become Attorney General of California."

"The facts, Master," said Judge Harris. "You were just referring to our right to the cold and clammy facts."

"About thirty-five years ago I was the executive secretary of the Democratic party in California. At the time there were less than thirty thousand registered Democrats in the length and breadth of California. Now they outnumber the oranges, not to speak of the Republicans.

"We were few and brash and I was perhaps the brashest, because I allowed Justus Wardell, head of the Democratic party in the state, to talk me into running against the long-time Republican incumbent, a wonderful old party named U. S. Webb, who was sure of re-election. However, Wardell and Henry McPike, later the United States Attorney in San Francisco, and Gavin McNabb and others convinced me that Tom Jefferson would writhe in his grave if I didn't make myself available, so I did and I was nominated at the party's 1930 state convention at Fresno. I stumped the state. I also apparently stumped most of my more realistic friends about why I was wasting the effort and expense and time from my practice, as practically everyone but us few hard-core Democratic campaigners knew that I had a far greater chance of becoming Miss America than I had of beating U. S. Webb for the Attorney-Generalship.

"I kissed every croupy baby available; I addressed every luncheon club, wake, *bar mitzvah,* clambake, barbecue, prayer meeting and dog show I could crash, and I shook every hand in sight, including a number that were only outstretched to find out if it was raining. U. S. Webb nevertheless squeaked in a half-million votes ahead of me, and I don't think he kissed a single damn baby. I *know* he never ate one hundredth of the half-fried chicken that was thrust on me at the sparsely attended Democratic rallies. That was our trouble in California in those days—more chicken than Democrats.

"After the thing was over and my fifty-four thousand, four hundred and forty-two votes were counted (we could almost add *them* up in our heads), my wonderful Marjorie drove me home to our little flat in San Francisco's good, gray, middle-class Richmond District. Most of the way my pretty and practical little wife was silent. Finally she spoke.

" 'You wouldn't have liked being Attorney General. Living in Sacramento would have driven you crazy,' she said.

"I told her she was probably right.

" 'And you'd have been on the wrong side of the fence. Prosecuting people was never your cup of tea,' she went on.

"I told her a man had to do what he had to do.

" 'Yes, but sooner or later you'd have to do something unpleasant to some old friend or drinking colleague,' she continued. 'And that would make you pretty unhappy.' She was right. 'And the next step would be the governorship and more babies to kiss. And more cold chicken to eat.' She was righter than Solomon. I began to feel a lot better.

" 'On the other hand,' she said, 'you're a pretty good lawyer. You're probably the best trial lawyer in the world.'

" 'You're absolutely right,' I told her, 'and what this lucky defeat has saved me from is complete, black and unbearable disaster. Turn the car around and head downtown. What we must do now is celebrate.' Together we jubilantly made for the Morrison's, next door to the Old Orpheum Theatre, and there we dined on cracked crab, pepper steak and hot garlic sourdough Italian bread. Shamefully enough, considering that Prohibition was still in effect, we fractured the law a bit by enjoying some fine Scotch whisky. Perhaps I *wasn't* just the right man for the Attorney General's office.

"U. S. Webb apparently didn't think so. Within the next few days he asked me to become a deputy attorney general. And my Democratic sponsors were still full of glorious plans for my future as a baby-kisser, hand-shaker, chicken-muncher and statesman. I fended them all off. I was no longer a candidate for anything but the high office of—as I see it—being Jake Ehrlich, lawyer."

"A very touching story, indeed," said Killion, who is as deeply interested in politics as he is in steamships. "Are we to conclude by these revelations of your failures and defections—the news that you've violated the Volstead Act shocks me especially—that you now take a dim view of all politics and all politicians?"

I denied this. "Indeed, some of my best friends are politicians, though I can't say I'd want my daughter to marry one. And, in the words of Gelett Burgess in respect to The Purple Cow, I'd rather see than be one. But I think this is as good a cue as I'll ever get for a few sober remarks on the greatest politician of our century, of perhaps any century, and of how I met and knew him. The occasion was the Democratic Convention of 1920, the place was an alcove of San Francisco's Exposition Auditorium, and the day was June 28th.

"Prohibition was rigorously in force and all of the best whisky in San Francisco had been interred in bonded warehouses. From these invulnerable quarters some thirty barrels of the precious fluid had been exhumed and delivered to the aforementioned alcove in Larkin Hall, a division of the auditorium, for those Democratic workers who had been officially cleared with the sergeant-at-arms for the induction of high-proof potables. I of course was among this group.

"I found myself pleasurably drinking with a handsome, cultured and extremely knowledgeable young man with a high forehead, a protruding but not unpleasant Back Bay Boston accent and pince-nez glasses. We discussed the booze, the convention and the favored candidates being considered for nomination by the delegates in the auditorium next to us. In the manner of men at barside, he became 'Frank,' and I was 'Jake.' Soon a delegation arrived to take Frank to the rostrum inside to accept the nomination for Vice-President of the United States. They hoped he'd hurry because the entire convention was waiting for him. Franklin Delano Roosevelt was pleasantly firm.

" 'Hell, I'm not going anywhere until I finish my drink with this gentleman,' was the way he put it.

"Twelve years later, when he was President, I saw him again at the Palace Hotel in San Francisco. He knew me at once. 'Jake,' he said, 'that was a fine drink we shared at the auditorium.' Of all the people I've met in my life I think this man impressed me most lastingly. He was a *true* politician; he didn't have to be reminded who and what people were. He knew and remembered them because he understood and liked them. I saw him again at the White House in 1940, with thousands of days and faces in between our previous meetings. 'Hello, Jake!', at first glance. I asked him why he hadn't declared war against the Nazis. 'I have sons, Jake; I suppose that's one of the biggest reasons.' A year later even his sons were no longer a barrier to his inevitable decision. He was the great one. Perhaps the greatest man I'll ever know."

We gave the memory a moment of silent consideration, and then Lurie brought the conversation back to the subject of the Jack Ruby defense, a topic I'd prefer to by-pass both in public and private inasmuch as Melvin Belli is a lawyer whom I very much admire. But my friend and landlord is a willful and curious cuss.

"You've apparently pretty completely discredited the psychiatric defense in the Ruby case," he said. "Does that mean that you take a dim view of mental illness as a rationale of crime? Are you belittling the role of the psychiatrist in the courtroom?"

"Hell, no!" I replied. "The psychiatrist knows damn well what he's doing; it's the law that fails to understand him and his unfortunate subjects and even his definitions and his idiom; it is the law and the community that fail to understand or to make proper use of his functions, or misuses them as was done in the Ruby case.

"We know that the nature of mental illness is still poorly understood and defined. Individuals may become ill from disturbed human relations as well as from physical causes. Mental disorders are not so much disease as they are disturbances within the person.

"The adjectives *mental* and *emotional* and *neurotic* are simply easy labels with which to codify and at times obscure the difference between two kinds of disfunction. One category consists of bodily diseases—say, leprosy, tuberculosis or cancer—which by rendering a malfunction of the human body as a machine, produce difficulties in social adaptation. The second category is characterized by difficulties in social adaptation caused by the purposes the machine was made to serve by those who built it—by this I mean the subject's parents or society—or by those who use it, namely, individuals.

"Physicians and psychiatrists refer to anything and everything in which they detect any sign of malfunctioning as *mental illness,* without real precision of definition and based on no matter what norm. Hence, agoraphobia is illness because one should not be afraid of open spaces, and homosexuality is illness because heterosexuality is the social norm, and divorce is illness because it indicates that the aberrant partner was unable to conform to marital domesticity. Crime, artistic virtuosity, undesired political leadership, participation in social activities or withdrawal from such participation—all of these and many other types of activities that stand out from the norm in any way may be described as signs of mental illness.

"The field of the psychiatrist is comparatively new in the medical sphere and even newer in relation to the law, but he does give us some knowledge of man's mind, his thinking processes, his compulsions, his pressures and illnesses, and a pretty good idea of what makes him tick. The psychiatrist should not be exploited or used to improper advantage, but he should be introduced into machinery of due process wherever applicable and even in situations not heretofore considered. For instance, the law, in its moldy and decaying progress, has not yet realized that even a judge, with his power of life and death, should be examined regularly by a psychiatrist to see what makes him tick or to find out if he *is* ticking.

"I'm reminded of a man in whose defense Lou here enlisted me a number of years ago. A young army captain named Hyman Cohen left his quarters at the Presidio one night, took his service revolver with him, and in a somewhat stupid and confused fashion proceeded to hold up a tenderloin drugstore. When Lou drafted me for the defense, the police and the prosecution were prepared to send this man to prison as a run-of-the-mill holdup man. No one had taken time out to find why an army officer with a good, wholesome background and no previous record of antisocial activity should be impelled to rob a corner druggist of a few dollars and some morphine tablets. I found that Cohen had been administered a narcotic painkiller in large quantities by his dentist just before the holdup, that he was in the midst of serious personal pressures, and that the combination had rendered him temporarily semipsychotic. I presented these truths to the jury with documentation and expert testimony, and he was acquitted. Without proper consideration of the psychiatric factor in this case, a good man's life would undoubtedly have been ruined, and if any of you gentlemen wishes to be further counseled or enlightened on this or other subjects you'll have to either tune in on Channel Four tonight or see me during my regular office hours, retainer fee in hand."

I was told what I could do with both my counsel and enlightenment, plied with further alcohol, offered the brief for defense in a case of overtime parking, declined the honor and the drink and departed, quite pleased with myself at having held the floor for the better part of an hour in the presence of such irreverent company. As I left, Tevis Jacobs, one of the country's great real-estate lawyers and my friend walked in with more questions but I was in a hurry.

My dinner engagement was with Jerd Sullivan, at Amelio's Restaurant where Powell Street divides North Beach in two. It was a splendid evening and I would walk. The Columbus-Broadway quadrant of the section was beginning to burgeon with neon as night turned this phoenixlike resurrection of the old Barbary Coast into a gaudy, scintillating scene.

I stopped for a drink at Ernie's Restaurant and another at Doros from which landmark much liquor and good conversation have flowed throughout the years. Stopping at Vanessi's, Joe Vanessi was elsewhere; I moved to the bar and drank an utterly sincere and satisfying toast to the bartender.

I noticed that the television set—usually dedicated to the San Francisco Giants—was tuned in on the broadcast of Ehrlich being interviewed by Meredith. I made a very good impression on myself as I watched. Down the bar a bit I could hear the conversation of two other customers, both of whom had apparently spent a large part of their afternoon at Vanessi's bar.

"He's got it made," said the man with too much abdomen.

"Yeah, that's why they call him the Master. Words are his business," the other man said.

"He's got it made," repeated the belly man.

It's pleasant to find that one is a prophet not without honor in his own community, and I idly considered buying these two gentlemen a round of drinks.

One of them had taken his eyes from the television screen and was looking me over in the back-bar mirror.

"I think that's him down the bar a-ways," he said.

"Are you cracked?" the belly man asked. "Ehrlich don't drink in ordinary saloons any more. In fact he don't even show up at his office; just lays around his swimming pool schmoosing with good-looking dolls. Why, he ain't practiced law in years. He's got a stable full of hot-shot young attorneys who win the cases for him while he gets all the glue and the credit. He's got it made!"

"I guess you're right," said the other man. I left full of wonder at the wonderful world of public images. At the corner I noticed another headline: FLEEING FEMALE SLAYER HUNTED BY POLICE. Why do headline-writers prefer "slayer" to "killer"? There are the same number of letters in each word.

I strolled up Broadway and turned northward into shadowy lower Powell Street. Outside the Trei Compari Café, on whose walls hang the portraits of Pope John, former King Umberto of Italy, George Washington and the incumbent chairman of the Alcoholic Beverage Control Board, in positions of equal honor, I came to an abrupt halt. A raffish-looking gentleman with his lapels safety-pinned together at the neck and the look of summary larceny in his eyes, had placed himself in my path. We examined each other solemnly for a moment, and it occurred to me that I was about to be robbed. Then the other man murmured a hurried "Scusi!" and took off. I was relieved and suddenly amused because I remembered that it had been almost on this identical spot, years ago, that I had run into another would-be holdup man.

Several hours before, on that occasion, I'd walked a client out of the Hall of Justice after having had him acquitted on a robbery rap. The fee had been $5,000, but Rudy had only $2,500 to give me. However, on parting from me on the pavement in front of the Hall, he had—being a man of honor—solemnly promised to come up with the rest within the next twenty-four hours.

"Mr. Ehrlich, you can count on me," he said. "You'll be seeing me again before you expect it."

He never spoke a truer word. That night when I was on my way to dinner at the Blue Fox and had just crossed the shadowy stretch of Powell Street below the Trei Compari Café, I heard a muffled sound behind me and felt a highly suggestive nudge just above the belt line.

"Freeze, mister!"

I turned around and found myself eye to eye with Rudy, my superhonorable client. I was furious.

"You son of a bitch!" I said, "don't tell me you're going to take *my* money to pay *my* fee!"

He immediately put the revolver away and started patting me on the shoulder, embarrassed and humiliated.

"It's my goddam eyes," he said, pointing to them ruefully. "I shoulda gone to the oculist long ago. Ain't it the limit . . . hoisting *you,* of all people!"

We smoothed it over with a pair of drinks at the nearest saloon. That's how I know that the owners of the Trei Compari Café think just as highly of the local liquor commissioner as they do of Washington, King Umberto and even the Pope.

22: *Night*

6:30 P.M.

AMELIO'S IS ONE of the principal reasons why San Francisco is so famous for fine food.

It isn't a large place. In fact, it is probably the smallest fine eating place in the world, and yet it encompasses exquisite food, polished service and *gemütlich* atmosphere. Created during Prohibition as a refuge from the surrounding arid wastelands by Amelio Pacetti, an amiable Apennine with a distaste for Mussolini's crude correction of his motherland, the restaurant prospered, acquired a patina of easy elegance, and in time became *The Place* in San Francisco. It is clearly well above the need of publicity or advertising, far beyond the threat of competition, and well exempt from the ebb and flow of business prosperity. Amelio has died and his wife Inez has succeeded him as *padrona.* She led me to a seat opposite the waiting Sullivan.

My regular dining companion, Jerd Sullivan, is a rather special item of humanity as well as my friend and a colorful facet of the San Francisco mosaic. A large, raw and rugged man who looks as if he had spent his life bossing longshore shape-ups along the Embarcadero instead of being president of the Crocker First National Bank, he is a financial Brahmin of consequential caste, a permanent fixture of the *Social Register,* and a particularly tough and admired former president of the police commission. What he and I have in common, aside from our long-time mutual participation in some of the stormier aspects of the life of our town, is an immense curiosity for each other's opinions, particularly on subjects about which we are in congenital disagreement.

"I hear you're writing your autobiography, Jake," he said as soon as I'd firmed myself into my seat.

"I'm writing a *kind* of an autobiography. I've taken stock of some of the supersententious, untrue-to-life samples turned out by some of my colleagues, and I've decided that whatever else I do I'm not going to impose any similar literary deformity upon posterity."

"It's true that a lot of nonsense is created in the name of autobiography. Are you going to defy tradition by revealing your sins as well as your virtues?" He offered me a twisted, sardonic grin with the question. "If so, this should become a work of Homeric proportion."

"As with right and wrong, just where does sin leave off and virtue begin? Our motivations are pretty mixed at all times, and I'd be the last to try to define mine with any real objectivity. I am frankly reporting what I've done and thought and said—letting the reader make his own judgment. That's the way I'm writing it, and if I'm revealing too much, so be it; let the psychoanalytical chips fall where they may."

He offered mock applause with the tips of his fingers.

"Bravo! If you're writing it the way it really is, you should be busy for the next decade or so explaining and defending those chips. Perhaps you'd better reconsider and publish a routine job."

My predinner cocktail had been served. I was ready for not only Crocker First National *and* the Police Commissioner but the *Social Register,* too.

"There's been nothing routine about my life, *Mr.* Sullivan; there'll be nothing routine about my book. Short of libel, I've tried to label and measure things honestly and realistically, even at the expense of perhaps losing a quasi friend or two. With due regard for the statute of limitations and the possibility of reopening old wounds, I've told the truth as I know it. I've pictured exactly what it's been like to spend a lifetime at successful nonconformity with the commonplace; to win by ignoring rules I couldn't honor, taboos only vindicated by tradition, and barriers dictated by the self-interest of others. I've described swimming upstream against the tide, with every silly son of a bitch in sight signaling a return to the safe, slack waters of easy passage. I can't remember anything routine about my life; my autobiography must reflect that. Does that answer your question, Mr. Sullivan?"

It did and he was sufficiently amused and we ordered the *vol-au-vent* and *broccoli à la maison,* and then my friend check-listed some of the items of my career which he considered integral to the book. I had covered them all until he came to one I'd wondered about including.

"You mean you don't intend to give them the Bellamy case?" he asked. "Why?"

"I don't know. Too often a lawyer's biography is just a scrapbook of the trials in which he has appeared . . . the Case of the Woman In Red . . . the Enigma of the Limping Man, etcetera. In time, they all merge in the reader's mind and become fictionlike carbon copies of each other. In the Bellamy case the principals are long gone from the public scene—one through death and the other through public forgetfulness. I wasn't sure its inclusion wouldn't be redundant."

"Redundant, hell!" said Sullivan. "Since when is a story about a beautiful woman, a fickle millionaire and gunfire on Nob Hill a redundancy! Tell it, tell it!"

San Francisco's Nob Hill is neatly planed off at the crest like high-budget theatre-in-the-round for Olympian drama. For a large block square it is flat and level and surrounded by high-toned commerce—the Mark Hopkins, Fairmont, Park Lane, Huntington, Brocklebank and others—that provides an effective backdrop for the center setting of the diminutive but deluxe building called the Pacific Union Club. The stairway of this club is the setting for Act One of our drama.

For the benefit of strangers to the Bay Area, the Pacific Union Club is where God stays when he is in San Francisco. Or where He is *eligible* to stay from the standpoint of the House Committee. This of course depends on whether or not He is Jewish, a contingency that would indeed present a problem. The Pacific Union Club houses only simon-pure, card-carrying, fully checked-out patricians, only a limited number of these, and all of them must be rich. But *gentlemen,* too.

On the day I have in mind, all was serene within and without the exclusive multiple gates. Outside, the California Street cable cars floated decorously by toward bay or ocean at the soporific rate of eleven miles an hour, gold-braided hotel doormen inertly tootled at unresponsive taxicabs in behalf of lethargic dowagers, and massive but comatose squadrons of pigeons frittered the afternoon away in the eaves of the elegant monoliths that fence in this rectangle of elegance.

Inside the club it was equally inactive. Brokers and bankers and bishops, plus a graying sprinkle of those who had accomplished too many luncheons with too little exercise to be further active in anything were lolling in the deep card-room upholstery, picking their teeth just as they do down on Howard Street, and wondering if their coronaries would stand still for another brandy over the rocks. The servants were picking up coffee cups and ashtrays but no tips (gentlemen tip only at Christmas); the bar steward was considering running dead-or-alive tests on one member on a library sofa, and A. Stanwood Murphy, fifty-four-year-old millionaire lumberman, was getting his hat and top-coat from the front-door porter.

Two minutes later the entire scene had turned into the equal of a Wagnerian Valkyrie debacle.

As A. Stanwood Murphy emerged from the Pacific Union Club, one hand under his coattails, pulling at his suit jacket from the bottom, and the other doing the opposite from the top, a woman jumped from a parked car and began to zero in on his derby with a thirty-eight revolver. Those who were fortunate to have witnessed this epochal exhibition of freehand shooting and broken-field running claim that it was very much like a speeded-up motion picture.

The pigeons began to whirl about in frenzied circles, the cable car passengers found themselves dissatisfied with their rate of speed and hastily disembarked without requesting transfers, and most of the doormen, passersby and bystanders became highly mobile in the direction of the lobby of the Mark Hopkins

Hotel, which has a heavy, bronze door. Inside the Pacific Union Club, utter consternation gripped the membership and many thought that the proletariat had arisen at last and was storming the gates.

Meanwhile the lady who had started all this was still trying to pick Murphy off, and Murphy was doing his best to find cover. He tried the underside of a Buick parked at the curb but found it too underslung. A Chevrolet pickup proved more helpful, but the lady marksman changed her vantage and was soon pinging them in midway between Murphy's cranium and the oil pan, and he had to evacuate this position for a hydrant. Fortunately the police arrived and ended the activity.

The lady was taken off to the Hall of Justice in tears; Murphy, though unwounded, was ambulanced to Central Emergency Hospital; and shortly afterward my telephone rang.

It rang twice. The first call was from Jerry Geisler's office in Los Angeles. It asked me to take care of an old friend and client, Madge Bellamy, who was in trouble in San Francisco. The second was from Madge herself, who was being booked at the City Prison. I left for the Hall of Justice.

If you are mature enough to remember that automobiles once had running boards and rumble seats, you will remember Madge Bellamy. She was one of several movie stars who were declared the Most Beautiful Woman in America, and her first starring role was in a Broadway production of *Pollyanna.* She followed the natural gravitation to Hollywood and starred in *Lorna Doone, The Playgirl, Ankles Preferred, Hail The Women, Summer Bachelors, Soft Living, Silk Legs,* and *The Iron Horse.* She was not precisely the kind of an actress you'd find playing in *Anna Christie* or *The Merchant of Venice,* but she had her moments and many of them were fairly golden.

I'd met her at Hollywood parties and had always been impressed by the fact that though she was beautiful she was neither dumb, egocentric, wanton nor transparently money-minded. She seemed reasonably smart, direct and a good deal nicer than most of the dolls I'd met on the moving picture assembly line. I attributed this to her origins: she'd been reared in a wholesome Southwestern home by a pleasantly normal, nonmovie-struck mother and a father who taught at the University of Texas.

Madge Bellamy was no multiple marrier. When she was first successful and might have gone to the altar with any of a number of glittering imbeciles, she fell for and married a not particularly loaded young San Francisco broker by the name of Logan Metcalf. They'd met on the set of one of her cinema epics, a saga of deathless romance entitled *Mother Knows Best,* but apparently Madge hadn't known best, because her real-life romance was ready for the lawyers in four days flat.

She then established some kind of a precedent by neither giving harrowing reports of her treatment at Metcalf's hands nor accepting alimony or other financial gratuities from the court. Her reasons were sound if slightly incredible.

"I'm a firm believer in the principle that payment should never be exacted in cases of no value received," she told goggle-eyed Los Angeles reporters, "provided the goods aren't damaged. Mr. Metcalf didn't get his money's worth. He shouldn't get the tab." That's the kind of class Madge had.

From then on Madge avoided marriage but not men. Several years later and at a point where her career had begun to lose momentum, she met a big, handsome lumberman from San Francisco named A. Stanwood Murphy. Not only the pines, firs and cedars fell to A. Stanwood's action—so did the ladies. Including Madge, despite the fact that he was married and hardly the type to abandon his comfortable social San Francisco life, his lumber company, his millions, and the Pacific Union Club to fly with her to Pago Pago or Port Said.

But Murphy had convinced Madge that if he ever *did* happen to dissolve his marriage, she would be the second Mrs. Murphy. Immediately before the noisy ambuscade on Nob Hill, A. Stanwood suddenly, unexpectedly and rather convulsively divorced his wife and married a glamorous ex-mannequin named June Dibble-Almy. Madge Bellamy knew the difference between a kick in the pants and a slight oversight, and she oiled up her Smith & Wesson.

At the City Prison I found that the arrival of even a somewhat dated movie star had worked a certain magic on even this fortress of law and order. The reporters were waiting for me with unusual eagerness, and the photographers accompanied their pleas for "the right kinda picture, Jake" with certain lewd eye closures that boded ill for any immediate hope of a sob-story approach to the situation. I knew precisely what the first edition headlines would say.

I shed my newspaper friends as quickly as possible and made for the rear elevator of the Hall. The operator's eyes were aglow. "She may have been around awhile but she's still a honey," he said, motioning in the direction of the eighth floor.

The booking office was full of a daffy excitement. I must admit that Madge looked pretty glamorous, considering her vintage and the day's activities. She was prettily perched on a table, her long, lithe legs crossed in the way a hundred press agents had taught her, and she wore a tailored fur jacket over a rightly tight cashmere sweater and a snug beige skirt. Her hair was beauty-shop perfect. I had to admire her poise but my forehead moistened when I listened to her dialogue. She was telling *all* to some of the most irresponsible lurid-story specialists in the San Francisco press, two dozen beaming cops (including the full membership of the Homicide Squad) and some equally delighted representatives of the District Attorney's office.

"I told him I'd kill him," she said, looking quickly around for sympathy and approbation and getting it. "I told him if he ever married anyone else I'd kill him. And I very nearly did. If I'd only—"

I hurriedly eased myself into the happy little group.

"Stop kidding them, Madge! You know you're a dead shot—reared as you were on a Texas ranch where you learned marksmanship before you were out of rompers. Why, one shot was all they'd allow you for a rattler... you could have plugged Murphy this afternoon the minute he came out the door, if you'd wanted to."

She gave me a full, open-eyed look and then nodded. She was a quick study.

"Why of course, Jake!" she said. "I don't know how anyone could have gotten any other idea. I didn't intend to shoot Stan. I just wanted to *scare* him—to make him *think* a bit. I'm a marvelous shot. I could have killed him left-handed."

Easy! Don't overdo it, I thought, but I was relieved. Madge went on to tell what a hell of a shot she was, how she had only wanted to injure poor Stanny's pride, that she really loved him with all her heart. The boys ate it up and soon forgot her self-proclaimed vendetta; at least I saw no mention of it in the first editions and this was a further relief.

Despite the Mack Sennett aspects of the shooting and the fact that my client presently enjoyed the momentary sympathetic press which any charming female can command when the breaks go well, I was under no illusion as to the lack of prospects ahead. I knew that Murphy drew a lot of water in San Francisco, both in the newspaper world and in the murkier political depths where the big sharks lurk. I knew that when his shock and alarm abated he would become humiliated and then angry and then vicious. I felt sure he would try to strike back at this impulsive little woman. I was also sure he would attempt to have her put some place where she could less freely discuss things that embarrassed him. The most logical place was jail. I didn't want this poor, silly, fading woman to wind up in a cell merely because she'd dusted her jilter with a few soft-nosed slugs. I decided not to let it happen.

The first thing was to attempt to get her out of sight, out of mind, out of jail. Judge Clarence Morris, a wonderful man where the more appealing human frailties are concerned, helped with this project. The bail for Madge's charge (Assault With a Deadly Weapon) was $5,000. Judge Morris shrank this amount a bit for me and I met it, much to the distress of the press. When they discovered that I'd also sent Madge to her mother in Los Angeles, they acted as though I'd poisoned the reservoirs. Traitorously and with utter lack of civic spirit, I'd smuggled their best Page One fixture and favorite interviewee to the feudal enemy, Los Angeles. But the move served excellent purposes. It closed my talkative client's mouth and it gave us a little time in which to find out a few things.

I found out two things. And they made it possible for me to prevent an ugly mismanagement of justice and permitted a gift of charity and forbearance to Madge Bellamy.

On January 29, 1943 we went before Judge Morris to find out if there were grounds enough to remand Madge to Superior Court for felony prosecution. Despite the fact that my client was no longer very big box office, the press and wire services were well represented. It turned out to be strictly a feature writer's story, however, with tear-jerking adjectives and well-vantaged photographs carrying most of the load. Madge, starring in what was to be her last major production, was effective in dramatic black, a flattering hat and a silver-fox cape.

After the usual establishing testimony by the state, all of which we were willing to stipulate, the district attorney put Murphy on the stand. The lumberman hadn't looked at Madge or me since entering the courtroom. He certainly didn't stare at the newspapermen or at the crowd, but after watching him throughout the first part of the hearing I became convinced that he was taking a keen professional interest in the beams of the floor and the ceiling; he never let them out of his sight. I could hardly wait to question him, and a long-standing curiosity on my part was satisfied when Judge Morris asked what the A in A. Stanwood Murphy stood for. "Albert," was the reply. Now I was *really* baffled. Why keep "Albert" a secret?

The prosecution questioned Murphy, or perhaps it would be more appropriate to say that they *interviewed* him, so respectful and solicitous was their wording. The millionaire responded with all the directness and spontaneity of a Viet Cong prisoner at a U.S. Marine command post. I felt good about that. Dawn was beginning to break. The corn was beginning to pop. Madge could read travel folders.

As soon as Murphy was turned over to me for cross-examination, I asked him one question—if it were not true that he had

had "a relationship of several years standing that culminated in the incident at the club." I had no remotest idea that he would answer the question or that the court would permit him to answer it. I'd have been furious if I'd received an answer.

Pandemonium broke loose. The prosecution objected uproariously; the judge sustained the objections. I yammered away about precedents and fumbled about on the defense table for God only knows what. Madge looked crushed. The newspapermen added to the turmoil, and the spectators, like well-rehearsed extras in a mob scene, whispered noisily among themselves. When I looked back at the witness stand, Judge Morris was earnestly advising the confused lumberman of his legal rights in this and perhaps in other matters. At least when I peeked again, Murphy had edged from the witness stand and was apparently trying to extend the maneuver into a discreet departure from the court itself. With all the confusion he was doing a pretty fair job. I hastily went back to searching the counsel table for missing evidence and doing my best to ignore my newspaper friends, who were noisily trying to put me wise to Albert's tiptoe toward the exit.

When I was damned good and sure that the man had made his escape and was at least half way to a limousine parked in the nearest red zone, I returned to the witness stand. To my utter amazement I found that it was *empty,* completely and absolutely *empty!* I demanded to know what had happened to the witness. I was told that the prosecution had no further need of him and that he had been excused. Through an unfortunate oversight, my agreement to his dismissal had not been obtained. It was regrettable. I was obviously aggrieved but sat down.

The judge then announced that if all the testimony were in, the hearing was concluded and he had no alternative but to remand Madge Bellamy to the Superior Court for trial.

I couldn't permit that. It was illegal.

"You can't try my client on the felony charge, Your Honor. There *is* no charge. And from all I can see, there's no complainant."

This brings me back to the two things I'd found out some

weeks before. They were that the humiliated and socially devaluated Mr. Murphy had absolutely refused to sign a complaint, and that he had determinedly planned to get out of the courtroom, out of the city and out of the state just as soon as he'd answered the subpoena the District Attorney had pressed on him.

Now the courtroom was again in a hassle—a happy hassle, for no one really wanted to see the tired, once-beautiful woman thrown into prison. The judge ended the matter by asking Murphy's attorney, Harold Faulkner, if the lumberman would sign a complaint. Faulkner made it extremely clear that he would not.

We weren't out of the woods yet.

Chief of Police Charles Dullea, whose son I've already mentioned as my close friend and law partner, was the sort of a cop who would never condone the kind of thing that had inspired Miss Bellamy.

"No one can come to San Francisco and shoot up the town and not be prosecuted!" was the way he put it. He required a police inspector named Frank Lucey (better known as Buffalo Head) to sign a complaint against Miss Bellamy alleging that, "to the best of his information and belief" the lady had committed the act that Mr. Murphy wanted to forget about.

Shortly thereafter, in court, I had a question for Frank Lucey, whom I knew very well indeed.

"Inspector Lucey," I asked, looking deeply into his eyes, "did you witness the actual shooting? Are you in a position to conscientiously prosecute this case from the sound position of being able to tell exactly what happened?"

"No I didn't and I'm not," Lucey said miserably. "I wasn't there and all I'm doing is what I'm told to do."

The next day the District Attorney's office announced that, "having reviewed the legal aspects of the case," it was of the opinion that "a conviction of the defendant on an assault charge was very unlikely" and that "a Superior Court trial would only put the city to unnecessary and futile expense." The felony charge was dismissed and Madge—to satisfy the chief and whatever minority resentment might exist against her—was given a six-months suspended sentence for possessing a pistol. She dissolved in a flood of happy tears.

I put her on the plane to Los Angeles with a kiss and a real feeling of fondness and admiration. As outdoorsman, Murphy very well knew that the lady was a sportsman. She had carefully waited until he was flushed from cover before firing, and she had only shot him when he was on the rise. Real class, under all circumstances.

Now we'd finished our excellent dinner and were winding up on the Ehrlich epic over coffee. Sullivan wanted to know about the frustrations involved in attempting to write modestly but with reasonable thoroughness about significant acts of one's own. This was a problem for masochists, I felt.

"Modesty carried to excess inverts to immodesty, in my belief. Where else but in one's autobiography can such matters be treated more expertly? And how more surely can one prove being pathologically obsessed with one's magnificence than by ignoring obvious personal skills and attainments? It's actually a device to gain undue attention for an accomplishment when you downgrade or ignore it. I regard it as just as honest for a man to exercise his ego in the right place as it is for him to state his full cash position upon demand. There will be no modest reticences in my book. What I've done that I've liked or found interesting I've told. To hell with backing into the limelight. We're all actors, as Shakespeare said, and actors subsist on deserved applause."

"I wasn't particularly concerned about your reluctance to do justice to your accomplishments, Jake," said my dinner partner. "I'm just wondering how you can refer to some of the honors that have been conferred upon you and which you've every reasonable right to want to see mentioned in your book, if only for the purpose of showing appreciation of them. I mean —for instance—your lectures at Yale University, your—"

I snapped my finger.

"I've got it! I'll put the words in *your* mouth. Just as you are saying them now." We both laughed. After a moment I told him what really troubled me about the book.

"The story is *me,* Jerd, and I'm trying to tell it honestly and with complete frankness because I want every reader who might someday have to call in a lawyer in defense of his life to know what he has a right to expect—to know what one lawyer was able to come up with when the chips were down and the odor of death was seeping in through the courtroom doors. I want them to know that these are the self-same extremes that any man—in his moment of desperation—can demand of any really good lawyer.

"I want them to know that the law is not just a fancy chess game to be folded up and put back on the library shelf when the last pawns are lost; or a genteel, stylized contest played by soft-spoken, rule-strangled members of a holy priesthood called the Bar—no matter *what* the Bar Association says; or red tape or law books or words on paper with seals attached. The average man should know that the law courts are not only his protection against trouble, but that they might also become the arena in which his liberty or life are forfeited and that he has every right to expect an unlimited defense that will include trick, device, savage belligerence when it is called for, eloquence when it will work, the cunning of a Machiavelli, the denunciation of authority where it applies, and the most brain-exhausting effort humanly available. This is what he has a right to expect and demand and obtain from his legal defender if he is to survive. That is what I've given to those who have brought their private hells to me and said, 'Save me, Jake!' And that, Jerd, is why I'm writing this book. I want people to know what it takes to defend the innocent, the unfortunate and the unlucky from that cold, unfeeling and utterly fallible thing called justice. I want them to know that such defenses are available. I like to feel that I've established standards for the bar by my story—some of them high, some high and wide, a few of them maybe not according to Hoyle, but *all* of them effective at plucking some unhappy person from out of the arena."

It was past ten when I left Amelio's, saw Sullivan to his car, then started up Powell Street to my Nob Hill home. It was still clear and beautiful but the first phalanxes of the fog army were moving toward the Bay from the Marin hills, and the Belvedere and Angel Island horns were beginning to low like unmilked cattle.

Out on the dark waters beyond the glittering profile of Fisherman's Wharf, grim, deserted Alcatraz lay like a shoal-bound sea monster deprived of both its fangs and its prey. As I watched the white finger of searchlight at its crest moved swiftly on its perimeter and lingered for a fraction of a moment on the building I was passing. I thought of a man I had interviewed there; a man who wanted me to try and have his sentence reduced from life to fifty years. I thought of another prison a few miles father north in the fog where I'd gone on a night such as this with bad news for a man who couldn't have cared less. I brought him word of the denial on his appeal for a commutation of a life sentence for murder, but when I got to San Quentin I found that he'd commuted his own sentence with a Gillette blade. Now as I climbed Powell Street in the gathering fog I shivered as I remembered the raspberry hue of Allan Bogg's prison sheets, and I hurried on my way.

At the intersection of Powell and Clay, where householders tell when it's two o'clock in the morning by putting their heads out their windows and listening for the stilling of the cable car line's cable, the yellow beam of two bright headlights swept up beside me and I was greeted by Jack Cruikshank, a police inspector of the Robbery Detail, on patrol with his partner Al Podesta.

"Good evening, Master! This is a good spot for a friendly stick-up."

I admitted it and reminded them that it wouldn't be so if our police department spent less time "checking out leads" in friendly saloons and more of it harassing the underworld. This brought the accusation that I was illicitly suggesting that they drum up customers for me. And so on. I found myself liking another facet of my town—policemen who prefer humor to pomposity or snarling grimness. They went on and so did I.

I made a mental note to call my brother Jack about his new apartment and arriving at the Powell-Sacramento corner, I entered the Francesca. I ascended to the completely unique Nirvana which is magically available to me every time I put my key in the lock, turn, push and say "Marjorie?" For forty-four years she has been waiting on the other side of the door.

My grandsons David and Joseph are also waiting, having been allowed to stay up to greet me. They are the sons of my daughter Dora Jane, who is as stubborn and contentious as I ever was about things in which she believes. There are some who claim that I get my good looks from her. Perhaps they're right.

My remaining grandchild Cindy, the daughter of my only son Jake Ehrlich, Junior, was in school in Switzerland, a matter of some satisfaction to me as proof that the Ehrlich banner has a foothold in both the New and the Old Worlds. Young Jake also brings considerable satisfaction to me and is the object of my great admiration as a man who has countered the bitterest of unearned adversity with courage, grace and charm.

The grandchildren now gathered with me in my library and I prepared to end the day in the way all good days should end—in my home, with my wife and a few slices of personal posterity at my feet, a little Scotch in hand, at ease with the world. Or most of it.

As I've said, it wasn't always easy. Quite clearly tonight I remembered a certain Christmas Eve some forty years ago when the cast of characters also included me, a wife and two children, but there was no money, little food, and absolutely no gifts to go under the tiny Christmas tree that Marjorie had contrived in some difficult and possibly nefarious fashion. I was ending the day in my mop-closet office in the De Young building when I suddenly added up all this deficiency and misery and—to the tune of the merry Christmas bells clanging tinnily from the hands of tired Salvation Army Santa Clauses in the streets below—realized that it was time to do my Christmas shopping.

I left the grim little office and headed for a toy store several blocks down Market Street. Pushing a relentless way through the package-bearing crowd, I reached the store only a few short minutes before it closed. Shirt-sleeved employees were closing some of the doors. Removing my coat, I quickly grabbed a large carton and filled it with toys, obviously one of my functions as a shirt-sleeved employee. Minutes later I had recovered my coat and was on my way to the saddest little apartment in the Richmond District, which was promptly transformed into the gladdest of scenes.

For those who hold out for a just and moral ending, let it be known that years later the owner of this store sat reverent and spellbound at a luncheon and listened to me praised and applauded and then heard me tell the story of the Stolen Christmas. As a pay-off, I had the waiters take him a substantial check.

I told this story to David and Joseph as they sat with me in the library on Nob Hill, and they also stared at me narrowly. I'm sure they believe I made it all up, and this grieves me. In today's cool world I'd much rather they regarded me as sharp as a carp than square as a bear. To bed with them!

I sit here, close to midnight of another full San Francisco day, and wonder what it would have been like had I never gone to "court day" in the little Maryland county seat or so greatly admired the lawyers in their long coats and tall hats and vowed to study law. Would I instead have sold locomotives or been killed in a gang war or administered meaningless medicines to fat old dowagers from a Park Avenue consulting room?

No, I think I'd have become a lawyer just the same.

And what would have happened had I gotten along with my father and never quarreled with him or left home for the cavalry? Would I now be a tobacco-chewing, cockfight-watching burly planter, running the old plantation and getting up to New York twice a year for new clothes and a night on the town?

I think I'd have still become a lawyer, a San Francisco lawyer, a damned good San Francisco lawyer whom the bar association worries about and calls flamboyant.

I thought then of what my life, my practice, my beloved city had done for me. I thought of the kaleidoscope of experiences, material rewards, honors, kindnesses and expressions of appreciation; of the opportunities to serve my community, my kind, my friends, my country and my ideals; and of the rich drama that has unfolded for me since that first exciting day when I set eager, fearful, hopeful foot on Market Street. These are the rewards of the strange, good kind of life I've been privileged to know.

But the greatest gift of my times has been people—all kinds of wonderful people. I see and feel and hear them about me now as I take accounting of these years, and this is the most stimulating phase of the reckoning. Fine old Jerry Geisler, who helped me up the ladder; Greg Bautzer, Robert Eaton and Bentley Ryan who are now *the* lawyers in Jerry's Southland; Senator Warren G. Magnuson and Bill O'Dwyer and Walter Winchell; the Cancer Fund's John Teeter; Joe Benjamin, Dempsey, Lucius Beebe, Joe Bernstein, Charles H. Mayer and so many others whom I see less often than I'd like these days.

Some are gone: Sunny Jim Rolph, who wore cattlemen's boots just like mine, Tyrone Power, and Clarence Darrow, who invited me to join him in Hawaii on the Massie case. The wonderful newspaper people: Winchell, who once told 130,000,000 people that I'd married Gambler Arnold Rothstein's girl friend; and Sheila Graham, Hedda Hoppa, Randy Hearst, Leonard Lyons, Joan Woods, Frances Moffett, Charles Gould, Ed Dooley, Louella Parsons . . . so many others. From New York, Pete, Mac and Jack Kriendler; from Chicago, Irving Kupcinet; from Washington, Lyndon B. Johnson; from Honolulu—

The telephone shrilled an interruption to my reverie. My answering service wanted to know whether I'd speak to a woman "with a very troubled voice." She wouldn't give her name. I would. I *always* would.

There was the usual clatter of connections being made, then a silence that was not a silence, for behind it was the sound of breathing—quick, shallow breathing, the kind that often comes after tears. I waited.

"Mr. Ehrlich?"

The operator had been right about the very troubled voice. As gently as possible I admitted my identity.

More silence, with breath, then . . .

"I'm in trouble. Terrible trouble. I'm lost and frightened . . ."

"Tell me about it. Take your time."

"I'm the woman in the headlines. I just killed . . ."

A few minutes later I stepped out onto Powell Street and inhaled a full, fragrant lungful of the ocean-fresh fog. I felt good, useful, important. It's great to have been around a long time and not be old. It's great to be a part of this fantastic experience called San Francisco. It's fine to be a lawyer, a lawyer who's wanted and needed, to be the only one that's wanted for the job. It's fine to be Jake Ehrlich.

Now for that very troubled voice . . .

To be continued.

Index

Index

''The Lady in Red'' in court

My associate Gerry Giesler during Pantages trial

My grandsons David and Joseph, with Rex Bell, then Lt. Gov. of Nevada

My granddaughter ''Cindy with friend

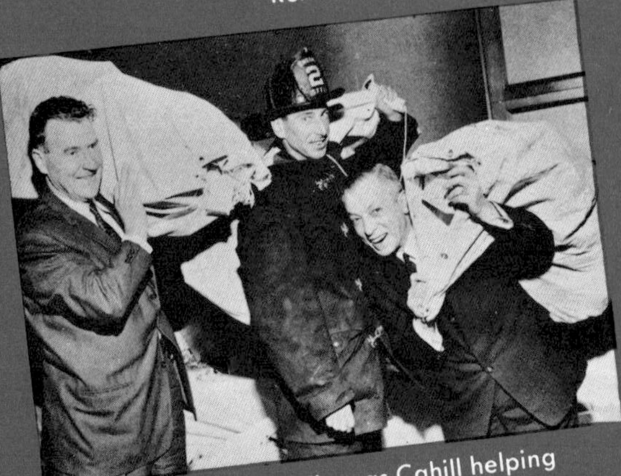

Chief of Police Thomas Cahill helping with Xmas toys at Saints and Sinners

Al Malnick of Miami and George Raft